Public Choice and the Challenges of Democracy

NEW THINKING IN POLITICAL ECONOMY

Series Editor: Peter J. Boettke
George Mason University, USA

New Thinking in Political Economy aims to encourage scholarship in the intersection of the disciplines of politics, philosophy and economics. It has the ambitious purpose of reinvigorating political economy as a progressive force for understanding social and economic change.

The series is an important forum for the publication of new work analysing the social world from a multidisciplinary perspective. With increased specialization (and professionalization) within universities, interdisciplinary work has become increasingly uncommon. Indeed, during the 20th century, the process of disciplinary specialization reduced the intersection between economics, philosophy and politics and impoverished our understanding of society. Modern economics in particular has become increasingly mathematical and largely ignores the role of institutions and the contribution of moral philosophy and politics.

New Thinking in Political Economy will stimulate new work that combines technical knowledge provided by the 'dismal science' and the wisdom gleaned from the serious study of the 'worldly philosophy'. The series will reinvigorate our understanding of the social world by encouraging a multidisciplinary approach to the challenges confronting society in the new century.

Recent titles in the series include:

Governance and Economic Development
A Comparative Institutional Approach
Joachim Ahrens

Constitutions, Markets and Law
Recent Experiences in Transition Economies
Edited by Stefan Voigt and Hans-Jürgen Wagener

Austrian Economics and the Political Economy of Freedom
Richard M. Ebeling

Anarchy, State and Public Choice
Edited by Edward Stringham

Humane Economics
Essays in Honor of Don Lavoie
Edited by Jack High

Public Choice and the Challenges of Democracy
Edited by José Casas Pardo and Pedro Schwartz

Fiscal Sociology and the Theory of Public Finance
An Exploratory Essay
Richard E. Wagner

Public Choice and the Challenges of Democracy

Edited by

José Casas Pardo

Professor of Applied Economics, University of Valencia, Spain

Pedro Schwartz

Professor of Economics, Universidad CEU San Pablo, Spain

NEW THINKING IN POLITICAL ECONOMY

Edward Elgar

Cheltenham, UK • Northampton, MA, USA

Published by
Edward Elgar Publishing Limited
Glensanda House
Montpellier Parade
Cheltenham
Glos GL50 1UA
UK

Edward Elgar Publishing, Inc.
William Pratt House
9 Dewey Court
Northampton
Massachusetts 01060
USA

A catalogue record for this book
is available from the British Library

Library of Congress Control Number: 2006037996

ISBN 978 1 84720 064 8

Printed and bound in Great Britain by MPG Books Ltd, Bodmin, Cornwall

Contents

Figures

Tables

Contributors

Charles B. Blankart   Humboldt University, Berlin, Germany.

Vani K. Borooah   University of Ulster, Northern Ireland, UK.

Núria Bosch Roca   University of Barcelona, Spain.

Giorgio Brosio   University of Turin, Italy.

Francisco Cabrillo   Universidad Complutense de Madrid, Spain.

José Casas Pardo   University of Valencia, Spain.

Roger D. Congleton   George Mason University, Fairfax, VA, USA.

Domenico D'Amico   University of Rome La Sapienza, Italy.

Anthony de Jasay   Retired and not affiliated to any institution, France.

Francesco Forte   University of Rome La Sapienza, Italy.

Bruno S. Frey   University of Zurich, Switzerland.

Arye L. Hillman   Bar-Ilan University, Tel Aviv, Israel.

Manfred J. Holler   University of Hamburg, Germany.

Peter Sandholt Jensen   University of Aarhus, Denmark.

Dennis C. Mueller   University of Vienna, Austria.

Stefan Napel   University of Hamburg, Germany.

William A. Niskanen   Cato Institute, Washington, DC, USA.

Martin Paldam   University of Aarhus, Denmark.

Pascal Salin Université Paris IX Dauphine, France.

Pedro Schwartz Universidad San Pablo-CEU, Madrid, Spain.

Albert Solé-Ollé University of Barcelona, Spain.

Alois Stutzer University of Basel, Switzerland.

Gordon Tullock George Mason University, Fairfax, VA, USA

Viktor J. Vanberg University of Freiburg, Germany.

Frans van Winden University of Amsterdam, The Netherlands.

Acknowledgements

This project was financed with the help of IMADE (Instituto Madrileño de Desarrollo) and grants from Fundación ENDESA and Unión Fenosa.

The editors also wish to thank Universidad San Pablo CEU, María Blanco and José María Rotellar for their help in organizing the conference where the papers in this book were presented.

Introduction

José Casas Pardo and Pedro Schwartz

This volume contains the papers presented at the international conference on 'Public Choice and the Problems of Democracy', organized by the Centre for Political Economy and Regulation, which took place in Madrid from 1–3 December 2005 at the University San Pablo CEU.

At this conference, some of the most prestigious public choice scholars presented their analyses of the main threats faced by democracy at the beginning of the twenty-first century and put forward some possible remedies, using the instruments and history of their lore. The 19 major chapters in this book cover issues ranging from general threats to a democratic way of life, to faulty institutional arrangements and defective voting rules that plague the political system, down to fiscal issues that affect the governability of democratic nations.

Public choice theory finds itself at present in a professional limbo. The *Journal of Economic Literature* subsumes it in microeconomics, or includes it in the theory of the firm, or notices it in regulation studies. The young see it as a mongrel of public choice theory and welfare economics and give it a wide berth. Others lump it with Austrian economics, implying an uncalled for disregard of both. It is too practical for today's model mongers or too humdrum for refined political philosophers. This is one reason why public choice scholars increasingly need to meet and publish the papers regularly presented at such venues as the annual meetings of the European Public Choice Society. This is what led us to convene this conference to see whether public choice scholars still had something useful to say about a real problem affecting us all: we chose democracy and its dangers.

We usually take it for granted that democracy is solidly established in the advanced developed countries and is here to stay. But history tells us that successful political regimes are not everlasting. True, never before in history have so many countries in the world (perhaps 86 out of the 192 independent countries in the world today) enjoyed a more or less stable democratic system. But even within old democracies, and indeed in the world at large, social, cultural and political divides have appeared that threaten democracy with strife and chaos.

Part I of this collection includes four chapters dealing with general problems of democracy. Chapter 1, 'Threats democracy faces: an overview', by one of the two editors of this book, José Casas Pardo, offers a general view of the problems of democracy in developed countries. He distinguishes between the endogenous and exogenous factors that are causing these problems. Among the endogenous factors is the generalized and deep uneasiness of citizens about the performance of political institutions. He argues that citizens ideally would want an improvement in the quality of performance, conduct and behaviour of politicians, an improvement that can only come about with drastic changes in institutions and behaviour. He also analyses the fact that voters have become unpredictable (so-called vote 'zapping'); that politics has become a self-regarding profession; that political parties, obeying Mosca's iron law, seem to have given up any pretence of internal democracy; that Friedrich von Hayek's remark that 'the worst come to the top' in centrally planned societies now seems more and more frequently applicable to democracies; that economic and social changes have blurred the dividing line between the old middle classes and the new working classes, leading to the 'rebellion of the masses' and the hectic and superficial lifestyles traduced by Ortega y Gasset in the 1930s; that voters are even less properly informed about issues than 'rational ignorance' would lead one to expect; and that the younger generations exemplify with a vengeance the lack of social values induced throughout society by the game of free riding on the welfare state. Among exogenous factors, Casas Pardo analyses the financial crisis of the welfare state and the refusal to reduce it in size; mass migration, multiculturalism and terrorism as a result of globalization, leading to a willingness of citizens to give up civil liberties in exchange for security and even to social conflicts and xenophobia; the short-term effects of globalization on labour markets and local firms; and relationships among individuals becoming ever more a zero-sum game.

In Chapter 2, 'Social justice examined: with a little help from Adam Smith', Anthony de Jasay, ever the unforgiving logician, shows that, despite its name, social justice is not a part of justice. The correct application of justice relies on previous rules. Social justice or taking from the rich to give to the poor can never be subject to rules since such redistribution must be unceasing and capable of continuously correcting its own consequences. However, *ad hoc* majorities will always be ready to coalesce with the aim of taking from the few to redistribute among themselves. Since these redistributive coalitions are of the essence of majority rule, de Jasay comes to the dismal conclusion that democracy as we know it will never be just and therefore never be stable. He then proceeds to examine whether democratic redistribution through forcible taxation can be justified in terms of a virtual social contract. He finds two widely canvassed solutions wanting: that of an agreement to redistribute, made by the fearful rich behind a veil of uncertainty as to their future position, which, in his view, was proposed by James Buchanan and Gordon Tullock; and that of a compact reached behind a veil of ignorance by people wanting to have a minimum of 'primary goods' guaranteed, as put forward by John Rawls. He ends by examining neo-socialist justifications of 'social justice', based on the idea that what a person sells to others cannot be conceived to have been produced only by that person. But de Jasay counters by pointing out that all previous or concurrent producers have been paid for their contribution to the social product. Whether liberals in the American sense will be convinced is doubtful. The problems posed for our democracies by a proper understanding of justice seem to be insoluble.

In Chapter 3, 'Affective public choice', Frans van Winden argues that, due to the neglect of the role of the affective side of human nature in decision making, public choice scholars find it hard to explain some political and economic phenomena, for example: tax revolts such as the Boston Tea Party; casting votes that count for almost nothing at national elections; expensive and powerless monarchy in democratic countries; suicide bombings; and the preference for welfare entitlements compared to pure transfers. Taking into account the effects of emotions such as resentment, hatred, shame, fear and hope on action and choices will make those phenomena more understandable. Frans van Winden recalls that Adam Smith in the *Theory of Moral Sentiments* and indeed Benedict de Spinoza in his *Tractatus Politicus* present a more complete picture of humanity than some of the more orthodox economists of today. To these classics he adds evidence from laboratory games showing the importance of anger, shame and friendship to explain the evidence of what one might otherwise be tempted to dub irrational. Thus he recalls research suggesting that the eradication of poverty and illiteracy may not reduce the incidence of terrorism, since well-off educated youngsters may feel the emotions of resentment of oppression and involvement in a lost cause more keenly than needy and ignorant people. And he adds that it is not for nothing that Franklin Delano Roosevelt called welfare benefits and payroll taxes 'social insurance' and 'payroll contributions' – names that conjure up positive emotions and make it difficult to abolish them. One should not assume then that *homo sapiens* is purely *oeconomicus*. Emotions (such as enthusiasm, anger and fanaticism) must be taken into account when analysing behaviour in social and political contexts. His chapter is a useful addition to Jon Elster's 'Emotions in economy theory' (*Economic Journal*, March 1998) and he amusingly summarizes it by saying that 'those who cannot stand the heat should stay out of politics and public choice'.

In Chapter 4, Pedro Schwartz presents Jeremy Bentham as a very early forerunner of public choice. There was a deep inconsistency in his theory of utility, namely that individuals, though in fact driven by self-interest, have the obligation to work for the general good. But this inconsistency paradoxically helped him formulate the 'agency problem', a central topic in our field, and propose some remedies for ever-present power abuse. For Bentham, men and women were governed by two sovereign masters, pleasure and pain: their actions driven by an unceasing need to increase their personal happiness. However, enlightened self-interest should also lead them to work for the good of humanity, to be more precise, for the maximization of net social happiness summed over individuals. But even so, why should anyone not free ride on the cooperative behaviour of others? Hence the need for institutional arrangements to contain 'sinister interests' that Bentham explained in painstaking detail in the *Constitutional Code* (1830). The trouble is that he conceived the law as the changing expression of mere political will, and social life as an unremitting clash of opposed interests. As he did not understand the possibility of self-denying ordinances and overlooked the importance of mutually profitable exchanges, the mechanisms he proposed to harmonize individual aspirations had therefore to be all-embracing and infinitely particular. The resulting utilitarian commonwealth would be what Schwartz calls a 'glasshouse democracy', where nothing can be hidden from the penetrating vigilance of public opinion.

In Part II, six chapters deal with various institutional aspects of democracy. In Chapter 5, 'Towards a more consistent design of parliamentary democracy and its consequences in the European Union', Charles B. Blankart and Dennis C. Mueller argue that in most parliamentary democracies, parliament is elected to represent the opinions of the population, whereas the government is elected by parliament to carry out a particular political programme, which leads to inconsistencies. The combination of the two procedures often results in political outcomes deviating more from voters' preferences than if only one of the two procedures is applied, since the preferences generated collectively in parliament often conflict with the programme pursued by the government. Unaccountable governments, voter alienation, strategic voting and governmental instability are shown to be consequences of this institutional mix. The authors propose reforms to produce two logically consistent alternative models of parliamentary democracy: either a pure form of representative democracy, where collective opinion is formed in parliament, or a pure two-party form of representative democracy where the government programme is chosen directly by the voters. Either system reduces the cost of the democratic process. This chapter is especially interesting when we examine the possible application of one of these two forms of governance in the European Union, though the authors incline towards a pure form of representative democracy as the most suitable for Europe.

In Chapter 6, 'Democracy, citizen sovereignty and constitutional economics', Viktor J. Vanberg has undertaken a major exercise in conceptual clarification, as he himself explains. He explores the contributions that constitutional economics can make to the theory of democracy and how it supersedes welfare economics and the more invasive of the contractarian theories. Constitutional economics is the study of how the choice of rules affects social, economic and political interaction. As the applied science that it is, constitutional economics inquires into how people may realize mutual gains from joint commitments, or, in other words, how they can play 'better games' among themselves by exchanging commitments to common rules. Democratic polities are 'cooperative ventures for mutual advantage'; hence their citizens are the natural addressees for the kind of advice that such an applied science as constitutional economics may be able to provide. Vanberg draws a distinction between two different levels at which constitutional economics may provide advice to citizens: the first is that of operating rules; and the second is that of constitutional rules, that is, rules for choosing rules. The constitutional economist may proffer advice if he or she feels able to show that the changes proposed will allow citizens to reap mutual benefits. Such advice has two kinds of components, namely hypotheses about the factual working properties of rules on the one hand, and, on the other, assumptions about what, in terms of final outcomes, the citizen concerned will find preferable. The citizens are the ultimate judges. Vanberg concludes that the validity of such conjectures is to be judged in terms of empirical and theoretical arguments, not by second-guessing citizens' preferences under the assumption that they choose behind a veil of ignorance, as some contractarians are inclined to do.

In Chapter 7, 'Diffuse and popular interests versus concentrated interests: the fate of environmental policies in divided government', Giorgio Brosio refutes two connected ideas: that a Montesquieu arrangement of divided powers always favours the status quo; and that special interests always prove a match for more general interests prevalent in public opinion. Environmental policies could in principle be a case where concentrated interests should prevail over diffused interests. Brosio, however brings to bear numerous cases of countries where legislation for environmental protection is passed despite the contrary interests of industry, even where constitutional arrangements make change more difficult. Most of the countries he analyses (France, Germany, Italy, the Netherlands and the USA), where stringent environmental protection has been passed and is in fact applied, have bicameral non-congruent systems. The USA and Germany in particular, which both have non-congruent and asymmetric federal systems, should fulfil the conditions in favour of the preservation of the status quo; and the veto power of the US president adds another feature to the divided governance, which could further delay environmental legislation. How, then, is one to explain changes in favour of environment protection and charging industrial groups accordingly? He conjectures that voters judge politicians, not on the basis of a detailed knowledge of their programmes but by a personal feeling as to how their past performance has affected their personal lives. Elections can be lost if voters have strong feelings of having been let down, which reduces the sway that special interests may have on legislators and governments. It seems clear that for some large issues people believe that important democratic decisions seep through the cracks of defective institutions.

In Chapter 8, Pascal Salin asks 'Should the democratic model be applied to non-governmental organizations and firms?' Democracy is the dogma of our time, as it is assumed that being democratic is good and not being democratic is bad, full stop. This has led to demands that a wide range of institutions be organized according to democratic rules. There are many institutions, both public and private (the army, the bureaucracy, churches, clubs, corporations, the family), to which democratic decision making cannot strictly be applied. However, the general feeling is otherwise. Why, people ask, should wage earners not participate in the strategic decisions of the firm? Should the family not be organized under the majority principle? Or perhaps the student body and the administrative staff of a university ought to take part in the selection of teaching staff. The pervasive demand for democratic solutions forgets that collective decision making is only to be resorted to when purely individual solutions cannot be used. Private property is not democratic; nor are human rights, to use the expression of the first liberal revolution in France: property excludes everyone but the owner and human rights permit us to resist the will of all other members of society. For large swathes of social life the application of democratic decisions is unacceptable. Instead of trying to extend the scope of democratic decisions, one ought to consider whether a better definition of property rights would not rather rid us of many collective decisions and, as a consequence, of democratic processes. Also democracy, whenever it exists, ought to be the result of free choices and not imposed by the state. That is, instead of wondering to what extent non-governmental organizations ought to imitate the decision-making processes taken from the political domain, one ought to consider to what extent the tasks actually performed by a democratic state could not be fulfilled by private contracts, and therefore according to non-democratic processes.

In Chapter 9, 'Citizenship and democracy in international organizations', Bruno S. Frey and Alois Stutzer start by quoting Robert A. Dahl, who categorically asserted that it is difficult if not impossible for citizens to exercise any effective control over most decisions on foreign affairs and that popular control over international organizations is practically impossible. Frey and Stutzer take the view that one should not only subject their undemocratic aspects to scrutiny and criticisms, but also make proposals for greater democratization. Today's international organizations perform an important and indispensable role in our world by carrying out allocative, redistributive and stabilizing functions, but they suffer from a lack of democratic legitimacy and participation. They take a leaf from the Athenian Constitution and later experiences, ranging from medieval city-states to the institution of the jury, and propose a novel idea for increasing the direct involvement of citizens in the governance of international organizations. A number of citizen trustees from each of the member countries of an organization, say 10,000 for the larger ones such as the United Nations, would be selected by lot at perhaps five-year intervals. They would have the power of initiative to propose policies and of recall to dismiss officials. Their decisions would be taken by mandatory referendum, on the basis of simple double majorities of trustees and countries. In sum, randomly selected trustees would have the final say. There is no doubt that choosing trustees by lot would result in a much fairer representation of people's preferences than parliamentary elections or winner-take-all presidential elections. The experience of Switzerland in semi-direct democracy, where citizen initiative and recall powers through referenda complements representation in parliament and indirect political participation via elections, should not be overlooked lightly. In any case, it is clear that many international organizations, not least the European Union, need to redress their democratic deficit.

In Chapter 10, 'Law and economic development: common law versus civil law', Francisco Cabrillo criticizes the generally accepted view that common law is a better framework than civil law for economies based on the principle of free exchange, and hence it is more conducive to growth. His evidence suggests that both civil law and common systems have followed a parallel evolution, leading to similar situations and adapting to the ideas and dominant values across societies in each historical period. To this end he compares the evolution of the major branches of private law, namely contract law and tort law, in Spain and the United States, one belonging to the civil law tradition and the other to common law. As regards contract law, he shows that, during the twentieth century, there has been a whittling down of freedom of contract in both systems: in Spain, through changes in the opinion of jurists and through law reforms; in the US, through judicial sentences. Again, in the matter of tort, during the nineteenth century there was in both countries a bias in favour of industrialization: in Spain through pro-industrial administrative law; in the US, by judges moving away from the principle of strict liability to that of negligence. Then the twentieth century saw a marked increase in administrative regulation in civil law countries and in tort adjudication in favour of workers and consumers in US common law. The word *Zeitgeist*, Cabrillo argues, has influenced legal evolution to a larger extent than the differing structures of civil and common law legal systems.

In Part III, on voting issues, we include four chapters. In Chapter 11, 'A reformulation of voting theory', William A. Niskanen argues convincingly that our existing theory of voting behaviour (which is the core of public choice theory) is in total confusion because the theory of voter behaviour is asymmetric with the theory of candidate behaviour. The root of the problem is that the median voter theorem does not separate decisions *whether* to vote and decisions *for whom* to vote. In that model, voters are assumed to decide whether and for whom to vote at the same time, based on their understanding of the issue positions of alternative candidates. By contrast, the candidates are assumed to know the preference distribution of those who vote before they themselves choose and announce their issue positions. But the possibility that the party faithful may abstain changes the picture. Niskanen produces empirical evidence that incumbents courting the median vote in congressional elections are in greater danger of losing the vote of the faithful and therefore their seat. This leads him to conclude that American politics is becoming more polarized than can be predicted with the median voter theorem. He then comes to the rather dismal conclusion that 'Congress is becoming more like the Italian parliament – more partisan, a reduced ability to address major reforms, and an increased centralization of political power in the executive'.

In Chapter 12, 'Informational limits to public policy: ignorance and the jury theorem', Roger D. Congleton applies Condorcet's jury theorem to explain the success of democracies relative to other forms of governance since the industrial revolution. In its modern form, the jury theorem predicts that despite voters' rational ignorance, majority outcomes will be extremely accurate. Congleton uses simulations to explore the power and limitations of the jury theorem. The extent to which the mathematical results require very large electorates and independent datasets is not obvious in the jury theorem literature. The simulations that Congleton presents make some of the properties of the jury theorem less abstract and prove that many of the desirable properties of majority rule apply to relatively small electorates of poorly informed voters. This statistical property of democratic decision making has been well known among the broader range of scholars who study political economy or public policy in general. On the other hand, it is evident that democratic politicians and politics are not always as good as the jury theorem implies they should be. If voter ignorance is deeper than usually assumed and some voters do not inform themselves at all about some relevant parameters, results may be biased.

In Chapter 13, 'Democratic decision, stability of outcome and agent power, with special reference to the European Union', Manfred J. Holler and Stefan Napel show that in order to understand policy making in a democratic setting characterized by voting, one has to take into consideration both the preferences of the decision makers *and* the procedural rules. Three prominent procedural rules are selected from the infinite set of alternatives – proposal-veto rule, gate-keeping and a simple sequential incumbent-opposition game – and analysed with respect to their implications for decision making, stability of outcome and discretionary power of the agent (that is, the policy maker). Analysis of the incumbent-opposition game shows that there is a chance for a rather stable policy arrangement, despite the fact that voter preferences are non-single peaked and incumbency may change over time, if the candidates are interested in both the policy outcomes *and* winning a majority in the 'voting game'. The most fascinating part of the chapter is the application of its conclusions to decision making in the European Union. No doubt the Versailles Convention, which prepared the draft of the ill-fated European Constitution, could have usefully consulted with Holler and Napel.

In Chapter 14, 'The unequal treatment of voters under a single transferable vote: implications for electoral welfare with an application to the 2003 Northern Ireland Assembly elections', Vani K. Borooah analyses the 2003 Northern Ireland Assembly elections. Here again we have an illuminating application of public choice analysis to real situations. Borooah points out that the method of single transferable voting (STV) shows a disquieting feature, that has hardly been commented upon. This feature is that the second property of the STV (that it takes into account each voter's range of preferences in determining the electoral outcome) does not work as it is meant to. Some voters have more than just their first preference taken into account, others only their first. This creates two categories of voters: favoured 'further-preference' voters and discriminated against 'first-preference only' voters. Applying these concepts to the STV-based 2003 Northern Ireland Assembly elections, this chapter shows that half of the voters were 'further-preference' voters. Also, the different parties had different endowments of voters from these groups. In particular, the Unionist parties had a disproportionately larger share of 'further-preference' voters compared to the Nationalist parties. According to Borooah, this could help explain why, even though the vote share of the

Democratic Unionist Party was only slightly higher, and the vote share of the Ulster Unionist Party was actually lower, than that of Sinn Féin, those two parties had disproportionately more seats in the Assembly than Sinn Féin. The chapter proceeds to argue that, if society is averse to inter-voter inequality, it might prefer a voting method that treated all voters equally rather than the STV method, even though the new method allowed a more limited expression of preferences for candidates.

Part IV, dealing with democracy across the world, includes two chapters. In Chapter 15, 'The pattern of democracy in the twentieth century: a study of the Polity index', Peter Sandholt Jensen and Martin Paldam apply the Polity index to measuring the evolution of the degree of democracy during the twentieth century for most countries. Starting with 52, the number of countries gradually increases to 160. The Polity index is a long-running project at the Center for International Development and Conflict Management, University of Maryland. Most economists usually rely on the Freedom House Gastil index and the chapter includes a useful appendix comparing both and explaining the authors' preference for the Polity index. Through their sophisticated statistical analysis, Jensen and Paldam measure the relative importance of the forces that make for democratization. They show that the effect of income on the political system is substantial, but that it takes some time for the full effect to seep through. Although it appears that democracy is path dependent and that therefore the Polity index contains strong inertia, economic growth at a certain point coincides with what they call the 'Grand Transition', when many parameters of society change together, giving increases of 30 to 40 times in income. Another result is the consistently negative sign to the Oil variable, especially clear if combined with the effect of Islam: it seems that a country getting rich on rents from natural resources does not democratize so readily and this observation is stronger when 'oil rich' means 'Muslim'. However, the authors note that, given the instability of the 'Muslim' coefficient, there is some hope that political divergence with the West may be transitory.

In Chapter 16, 'Democracy and low-income countries', Ayre L. Hillman explains why low-income countries, where economic development has failed, are in general autocracies rather than democracies. This goes contrary to the principle of encompassing interests, which predicts that autocratic rulers have personal incentives to seek economic efficiency and high economic growth, since they are residual claimants to take a share of national income or wealth for themselves. Consequently, it is necessary to identify why the personal interests of the autocratic rulers do not correspond to the encompassing interests of economic growth and efficiency. In his analysis, Hillman goes back to Nietzschean hierarchies, where the 'strong' in autocratic regimes exercise their will over the 'weak' without ethical restraints, that the poor are held as hostages for foreign aid, and autocratic rulers fear that economic progress will create a middle class who will seek political participation through democracy. Consequently, Hillman has sought an explanation for regime change or transition from a Nietzschean hierarchy to the rule of law and an ethical society.

Part V, on fiscal issues and democracy, includes another two chapters. In Chapter 17, 'A theory of the democratic fiscal constitution', Franceso Forte and Domenico D'Amico start by pointing out that the four maxims on taxation laid down by Adam Smith in *The Wealth of Nations* in fact make up a fiscal constitution. They proceed to present an overview of the linkages between the neoclassical theory of fiscal economics, public choice and constitutional economics, and to outline constitutional fiscal rules based on the individual choice principle. They contrast this set of rules with the more generally accepted notion of a social welfare function in fiscal matters and what may be called the 'deceptive individualism' of social choice theory with its neglect of institution building. One of the defects of this latter view is that it focuses on *ordinary* political decision making, thus lacking the rudder of constitutional fiscal rules to guide the ship of state. Those basic rules should not be viewed as mere textbook benchmarks but as practical guidelines capable of application – rules of a fiscal constitution, both inside and outside the constitution itself.

In Chapter 18, '(When) do tax increases cause electoral damage? The case of local property taxes in Spain', Núria Bosch and Albert Solé-Ollé start by stating that it is often assumed that voters are aware of the money they pay in taxes, and that when they vote they make politicians accountable for tax increases. But the empirical analyses show only mild effects of taxation on voting. The authors set out to investigate two different answers to this contradictory phenomenon. One is that the voter decision is complex, and that voters take into account other issues when they go to the polls. The second answer is suggested by the fact that only governments who *raise* taxes suffer vote losses, and that those losses depend on the specific type and timing of the tax increases. To check these hypotheses they use an enormous database with nearly 3000 Spanish municipalities, and analyse three local election (1995, 1999 and 2003). In order to obtain unbiased estimates of the effects of taxes on voting, they control for other variables, such as national political shocks, ideological preferences of the citizens, the political hue of the government, and others. The results suggest that although non-tax issues to a large extent determine voting decisions, property tax increases have a non-negligible effect on the return of incumbents, especially when the government is a right-wing one, when it is a coalition and it is not in its first term, and when the tax increase is approved by the municipal legislative chamber and it is enacted in the second half of the mandate.

The final part contains the keynote address. The conference was honoured by the attendance of Gordon Tullock, one of the founders of public choice and an honorary doctor of San Pablo University. When addressing 'The mystery of Brazil', Tullock pointed out the geographical similarities of Brazil and the United States and the differences in exploitation of the hinterland and in general economic development. US citizens have a high standard of living, and their country is the major power in the world at this moment; Brazil on the other hand is still a developing country, albeit one of the important emerging countries. Tullock then started to look for possible explanations. He contrasted population size and demographic distribution, and differences in climate and food production. He also mentioned that in the United States, until recently, most of the immigrants were of European stock, while in Brazil immigration has been smaller and of more varied traditions. So the culture of the different population mixture has also played an important role. But on the whole, Tullock tended to think that the crucial differences lay in vastly different cultural and political traditions. He pointed out that the Portuguese and Spanish cultures are quite similar, and they both were different from the Anglo-Saxon one. English colonists had originally shown a tendency to engage in aggressive wars. US citizens (originally of British stock and mindful of the political system of their countries of origin) have shown much greater readiness to develop their natural resources, including those in the Mississippi basin, while Brazil has not yet fully developed theirs round the Amazon. Also the United States and Brazil have quite different legal and administrative systems. Finally, he underlined that the United States has enjoyed a democratic system from its birth, while Brazil is still handicapped by deficient popular representation and corruption.

PART I

General Problems of Democracy

1. Threats democracy faces: an overview

José Casas Pardo

1 INTRODUCTION

We have reached a point in history when serious threats hang over democracy, even in those countries in which it has been established for centuries, to say nothing of the developing and the underdeveloped countries. It is true that never before in history have so many countries in the world enjoyed a more or less democratic political system, something that has taken place mainly in the twentieth century.

In 1900, out of the 49 existing independent countries, only six were democratic according to the standards of that time. By the end of the twentieth century, out of the 192 existing independent states, 86 could reasonably be called democratic, according to present-day requirements. Those 86 states represent approximately half of the world population, and in 22, among which are the richest countries in the world, democracy has had a continuity of at least 50 years. It would seem that after so many centuries of having organized undemocratic states, in the twentieth century the democratic ideas, beliefs and types of government conquered the globe.

But it is also true that new and powerful developments are seriously threatening democracy all over the world. Terrorism, the immediate consequences of globalization, the financial problems of the welfare state and the need to cut down its size, the very powerful pressure groups of all kinds, the large-scale migration and immigration movements (which are producing enormous immigration waves into the developed countries), multiculturalism and the problems it raises in the advanced countries, the possibility of a deep worldwide economic depression, plus the not too positive developments which are taking place in the workings and performance of democracies, and the taking for granted of the most advanced democracies, are only some of the threats which can jeopardize democracy around the world. Also, we are used to thinking that in the Western developed countries, plus Australia, New Zealand, Japan, South Korea and Singapore, democracy is firmly established and that it is here to stay. But history tells us that is not so.

In order to deal with the topic of this chapter, I shall distinguish between two kinds of problems that democracy faces: those coming from its own political structure or endogenous factors; and threats arising from external or exogenous phenomena, such as terrorism, globalization and so on.

It is fair to say that my analysis of the threats that democracy faces is very much influenced by my observations of how Spanish democracy performs. As a young democracy, it is therefore bound to have more shortcomings than the older democracies.

In addition, in this analysis, I shall largely address the subject of democracy in the developed countries. Of the 86 countries which at the end of the twentieth century had a more or less democratic political system, only 22 fulfilled the requirements of a real democracy. My purpose is to try to analyse the problems that democracy faces in those 22 countries; the others, mainly in Latin American and Asian countries, tend to be 'formal' democracies, and do not fulfil the standards of a true democracy.

2   ENDOGENOUS THREATS: THE SHORTCOMINGS OF THE WORKINGS OF DEMOCRACY

Among the endogenous problems that democracy faces is the deep uneasiness felt by citizens about how political institutions work and perform in those countries with the oldest democratic tradition, and which have been the main protagonists in their long march towards a fully political democratic system. The signals about their future seem to be so ambiguous that we cannot be sure whether they will prevail or even whether they will be positive for democracy. What is at stake at this historical moment is not democracy itself. The citizens of the countries which base their political institutions on the democratic creed feel uneasy not so much about their democratic political system itself, but about its daily practices and workings. By observing this phenomenon, it would seem that what citizens really want is a higher level of the global quality in the performance, conduct and behaviour of political professionals. But this is not the only issue that concerns them. There is also a demand for a much wider and deeper transformation of democracy, which implies deep institutional changes and other important changes in the daily practices of democratic life (Dahl, 1989).

The critical scenery of present democracy begins with the public themselves. Not only have they a rather pessimistic and negative view of the fundamental political institutions and agents of the democratic system, they themselves have also become unpredictable. Sociologists and politologists, who make electoral predictions, describe this situation as a destructuring of the electorate. What the voters are offered is little and even less attractive. Nowadays, at elections, such important issues as opposed conceptions of life and society are not debated; in advanced democracies there is practically no debate about ideologies. The public are more willing to change their vote, and generally they do not conform to predictable patterns of age, religion, class or sex. Voters tend to change their vote quite suddenly. They follow emotions (the physical appeal of the candidates being very important) that are aroused by the candidates, and sometimes they vote for populist candidates. The abruptness of the change of voting allegiance has given rise to the expression 'zapping vote', which is a difficult phenomenon for politicians to control.

2.1 The Professionalization of Politics

On the other hand, a large share of public criticism is addressed to the politicians, who for some time have generally been regarded as belonging to one of the least respected professions existing in a democratic society, something that is poles apart from the conception of political activity prevailing in the Athens of Clisthenes. It has become a common view (not lacking some measure of truth) that many politicians have made a profession out of politics. Many of them spend most of their active life filling one or other political post, which is contrary to what happened in Athens. In Spain, quite a number (of course, not all of them) of politicians have never practised a profession; indeed, it is a popular saying among the sceptical and ironical public that people who are no good at anything, go into politics. This depreciation of politicians and of politics does no favour to democracy. Although it is not good for democracy that politicians make a profession out of politics, there is no reason why able politicians and those whose record is good in their performance in the political institutions, in the defence of the public interest, and even in sometimes disagreeing in public with the policies of their own party and its leaders, should not remain in politics for a long time.

2.2 The Lack of Enough Democracy within Political Parties

Relatively, there is too little democracy within the political parties. To begin with, their members include only a very small fraction of the population. In addition, the means of becoming the leader of a political party (and therefore, a potential ruler) is generally rather undemocratic: manoeuvring, being subservient to the people above, creating power groups within the party, being photogenic and so on. Generally speaking, elected leaders are not necessarily the most able ones.

The system of closed lists of the candidates put forward by the parties for the various elections (national, regional and local) is a serious hindrance to the election by the voters of the most able candidates. The party leader decides who are to be the candidates on various grounds: their role within the party; favours the leader owes to them; loyalty and discipline; and so on. The electorate votes for the leader of the party (or for the party), and not for the ability of the candidates. In fact, the system of closed lists, which is used in several countries, is a serious obstacle to the election of the most able candidates, and it contributes to the impoverishment of the standard of the members of the different parliaments of the countries which use it. It also reduces enormously the freedom and autonomy of the politicians elected to parliament. In fact, people seldom know the names of most of the people who represent them at the various levels of parliament (see Zakaria, 2003).

Another phenomenon that is quite general among the political parties is that there is not enough democracy within their internal structure. Appealing to their supposedly democratic internal structure, the outcome of the struggle among their members to be appointed to the leading posts (and therefore, to be nominated as election candidates and to the possible political appointments in government, parliament and all public institutions) depends very much on their capacity for manoeuvring, their loyalty to the powerful groups and persons within their parties, and to their image fabricated by the image experts and by the mass media. As a result, the most able candidates are often not elected.

A pernicious consequence of not having democracy within the parties is that a very hierarchical structure of power prevails in them. This leads to a high concentration of power within the parties in the hands of a few main leaders, which ensures that the rest of their members have practically no political capital of their own; that is, they have no or little power of their own. In parliament, the main job of the parliamentarians of the various political parties is to vote according to the wishes of their leaders. Most people do not even know who their representatives are in parliament. Those representatives can be dismissed from the lists of candidates at the next elections by the leaders of the party almost at will, regardless of the quality of the job they have done.

2.3   Influence of Opinion Polls on Politicians

In general, rulers govern on a day-to-day basis, according to the latest opinion polls. We know that the difference between an ordinary (not to say mediocre) politician and a statesman lies in the fact that the former rules according to the preferences of the public as expressed in the opinion polls, whether the outcome would be reasonable and good for the community or not; while the latter is a politician who can convince people that some policy, which is not popular but which is good for the community, has to be implemented. A clear case of a statesman was Charles de Gaulle who, when he first came to power in France in 1958, asserted 'Algérie Française', and a little later negotiated Algeria's independence with Ben Bela. Obviously their job is to win elections. As Gordon Tullock has said on many occasions: 'In order to be a good president, first you have to be elected president', and obviously, to be elected president one has to offer the policies preferred by the majority of the public.

2.4   The Political Market

The political market is an oligopolistic one, with a small number of political parties, all of which supposedly have a different ideology and, accordingly, they offer different policies on the various issues and problems faced by society. But this factor ensures that the entrance barriers in the political market are very high, and the products (policies) that various political parties offer to the public are differentiated from those of their competitors largely through their presentation in publicity brochures and the mass media. Ideology plays an ever-decreasing role. The best theoretical instruments to analyse the political markets are modelling the latter as an oligopolistic market, strategic behaviour and games theory. The political market is imperfect because:

1.   The large majority of voters have incomplete information, preventing them from understanding the complex issues on which they have to decide. But often politicians are also hampered by a lack of information in an uncertain world.
2.   Mass media, particularly TV and other factors, do not necessarily lead to the election of the best candidates (being photogenic and having a career within the party are important elements in the selection and election of candidates).
3.   Political parties talk less and less in their campaigns about ideological issues, and they compete less and less over ideology and important public issues; indeed, they often trivialize the important issues at stake (see Lindblom, 1988).

2.5   Recent Social and Economic Changes and Their Consequences for Democracy

There is another phenomenon which is also affecting democracy, although I am not a specialist in this field, and therefore I cannot tell whether it will have an effect, either positively or negatively. We know through history that the revolutions which had lasting effects and which have led to democracy in the Western world were conducted by the middle classes, or, in other words, by the bourgeoisie. Let us remember who brought democracy to England, France, Denmark, Holland, Sweden, Norway, Switzerland, and even Germany, Italy, Spain and Portugal. The historical tragedy of Spain not being able to establish a true democratic political system until the 1970s was due to the fact that it had not developed a widespread and strong middle class in the period from the sixteenth century to the middle of the twentieth. In a recent book, Daron Acemoglu and James A. Robinson (2005) conclude that democracy is a solution to the elite's commitment problems.

The point I want to make in this respect is that, although I am no sociologist, the latest rapid economic development, due mainly to the advancements in technology and the enormous increase in productivity and, therefore, in the income of most individuals, has to a large extent blurred the dividing line between the old middle class and the lower class, mainly in terms of an enormous increase in the educational level and, in income and purchasing power. Except for a small economic elite, most people belong at the same time both to the middle and to the lower class. In principle, this is a welcome development, but it is having consequences for democracy, some positive and some negative. The positive effects are that a larger percentage of the people in any community participate in the elections, and, to some extent, the former lower classes do it in a more educated way. The negative aspect is that, in spite of their higher level of education, what we could call the old lower-class people (those doing the traditional jobs and the new jobs that the new services and technology have introduced), generally speaking are not yet in a position to reach a well-informed decision about the complex issues implied in the public policies advocated by the political parties.

I am certainly not questioning the basic principle of democracy of one person, one vote. I agree with James Buchanan when he writes that democracy requires that all individuals be considered as morally equal, even if we know it is not so (Buchanan, 1997). I am merely saying that the present social and economic structure of modern societies is likely to have a negative influence on the quality of public decisions, mainly in the election of their representatives, but also in the decisions taken directly by the people on public issues and policies. And, what seems to be even more important, the traditional middle class has lost its identity and its old public virtues. We know that many of the members of this class used to lead a leisurely and cultural life until the First World War (the end of the *belle époque*). I am not saying that such a society was ideal; I am simply pointing out the fact. Today practically all of us are middle class, and lead a hectic and frantic life in order to earn more money and to consume more. Hedonism is the name of the game. The old upper class has almost entirely disappeared. Its traditional families have withdrawn into their mansions (should they have been able to keep them), and have been joined by a small group of people who have made a lot of money or the '*nouveaux riches*'. I am not talking in moral terms, or asserting which class is in my opinion morally superior to the others. In this sense, I totally believe in Thomas Hobbes's approach. Of course, it is good that the outlook for the lower class has improved, both economically and culturally, although the externalities of this phenomenon are still to be quantified and resolved. Nevertheless, this development has diminished the quality of collective decisions. Most lower-middle-class people do not have the leisure, the interest, the time or even the education to collect the information, and to analyse it in order to participate in a well-founded way in collective and public decisions, and in the *res publica*.

Another consequence of this phenomenon is that, at least in Spain, most citizens are much more conscious of their rights than they are of their obligations. They are always ready to claim and assert their rights as citizens and persons, but they are less ready to accept and fulfil their obligations in order to coexist with other citizens. Their awareness of their democratic and human rights is excessively strong. Life in modern societies is becoming increasingly difficult for all individuals.

2.6 Interdependence of Consumption and Production Functions and Their Externalities

Due to the enormous interdependence of the production and consumption functions of firms and individuals, negative externalities are becoming larger and larger. This implies that living together and coexisting in modern societies is becoming increasingly costly, taxing, time consuming, complicated and difficult for all individuals. Many interrelationships are becoming ever more a zero-sum game. Such a phenomenon is making citizens more selfish and disunited, and less law abiding, something that will affect democracy negatively in the future, as individuals will become more unruly, and, consequently, governments will find it increasingly more difficult to govern, in spite of the great improvements that people have experienced in their living standards and education. Also, politics and the lives of ordinary people are becoming more and more litigious as, instead of negotiating, politicians and political parties, as well as private citizens, tend to resort to court action to resolve any conflict among them. Courts of justice are becoming overwhelmed by the many trivial conflicts.

In a recent book by Theodore Dalrymple, *Our Culture, What's Left of It: The Mandarins and the Masses*, he writes: 'The civic virtues, good manners, ingrained personal habits of self control and moderation, and the natural mistrust of excess have all been jettisoned or destroyed. Violence, hysteria, meanness and vulgarity are surely now among the leading traits of the prevailing English temper' (2005, p. 3). Dalrymple sets out to map 'the moral swamp' that is contemporary Britain, and to study the low-level but endemic evil that he says is an unforced and spontaneous effulgence in the British underclass. He admires that most aristocratic of virtues, fortitude, and he detests the way that the 'hug-and-confess' culture is extirpating emotional hardness and self-reliance from the British national character in favour of a banal, self-pitying, witless and shallow emotional incontinence. Overall, Dalrymple argues strenuously for the reassertion of the traditional English virtues: prudence, thrift, industry, moderation, politeness and self-restraint.

Those traits that he sees in present English society tend to be quite common in most advanced societies. Consequently, democracy has lost in quality, and governments find it more difficult to govern, to reach agreements with the increasing number of the ever-more difficult to govern, to reach agreements with the increasing number of ever-more powerful interest groups, either to avoid or to solve continuous strikes, and, ultimately, to govern in a coherent way for the common well-being and the community as a whole.

This is an important phenomenon. Half a century ago most of the members of the middle class had some sense of the *res publica*. Something similar has happened in some countries to the upper class. Let us remember that, until the middle of the twentieth century, most English upper-class families kept the tradition that at least one member of the family would enter politics. It is logical to think that most of these individuals were educated, and that, generally speaking, they did not need to go into politics in order to make a living out of it. In general, they had the education, the economic means and the leisure to be able to thoroughly analyse the political issues and the policies on which they had to decide. Nowadays, the traditional upper class has practically disappeared. And the very lower-middle class (which comprises the vast majority) lead extremely busy lives, working very hard in order to maintain the ever-higher consumption and hedonistic lifestyle to which they and their families have become accustomed. Leading such a life barely leaves them with enough time or interest to gather the necessary information in order to properly analyse the issues on which they have to vote. We obtain most of our information through the media – TV, radio and newspapers – which generally offer a biased and limited point of view.

If we relate this to the tremendous influence of the mass media, the importance of the attractiveness of political candidates, the ill-informed voters, the actual power that pressure groups exert through the mass media, and the want of internal democracy within the political parties, then my analysis is not totally wrong. The fact that political parties very often choose candidates largely on the grounds of their physical appeal and their faithfulness and submission to the party leaders, and that many voters vote for the most physically attractive candidates is having a pernicious effect on democracy: there is, generally speaking, a lack of enough able politicians and at the same time an impoverishment of politics and democracy. This phenomenon can be observed if we compare the calibre of the majority of the politicians in the twentieth century, with the majority of those we have nowadays; in addition, the advent of closed lists of candidates decided by the party leaders for the various elections makes it impossible for people to vote for the candidates most able to defend their interests.

2.7   Low Participation of Voters at Elections

Another important problem of modern democracies is the relatively small public participation in decisions on the issues that concern them, and which are therefore decided by their governments. Obviously, in the modern nation-state, with its large population, asking the public to vote on every policy issue would be too costly and taxing. Nevertheless, the point is that the electorate vote every few years to elect their parliamentary representatives, that the latter go to the capital and occupy their seat in parliament, and that during those years, they vote according to the wishes of their party leader, and those who voted for them have no power or control over the vote, and do no know what has been voted for or against. Of course, this is well known in political theory as the 'principal–agent' problem. This also seems to be a threat to democracy, as the public tend to lose interest in the *res publica*, unless the issues voted for or against affect their interests directly.

One only has to look at the generally low turnout at the various elections in most developed countries. However, with new technologies, this shortcoming of democracy could be improved. Switzerland is already employing modern methods to conduct referenda at the local level to decide on all relevant public issues. Also, political parties are to some extent discredited in the eyes of the public. Not only do political parties attract only a very small fraction as members; what is even worse is that only a very small percentage of the latter feel identified with their party's ideology. In a recent Spanish survey, only 26.4 per cent identify with the ideology of a political party, while 42.3 per cent say that they do not identify with any political party (see Sartori, 2003).

2.8   New Generations and the Future of Democracy

Another phenomenon that can be observed in modern advanced societies is the following. The latest generations are growing up in an atmosphere in which civic values and virtues are somewhat weaker than in previous times. Values such as responsibility, work and effort, duty, solidarity, thriftiness, family, abiding by the law, respect for the elderly and for other people and their property, and even for their parents, and good manners are not totally accepted and even less practised. School failure is quite a general phenomenon in Western countries. Children obtain almost everything they want from their parents. Their main concerns are consumption and hedonism. How well will society and democracy fare when these generations grow older and obtain positions of responsibility? Also, the younger generations generally show very little interest in public affairs. However, they are already having an impact on social and political life. How they will behave when they grow to adulthood, is impossible to predict, but if they retain their present mentality, concerns, values, attitudes and behaviour, they might become a danger to democracy as we know it.

3   EXOGENOUS THREATS

3.1   Terrorism

Among the exogenous threats to democracy, I shall outline those arising from terrorism, globalization, the financial crisis of the welfare state and its consequences, immigration and multiculturalism. Terrorism is a real threat to democracy. Obviously, this is not a new phenomenon in history: ancient Persia had its assassins; more recently, at the end of the nineteenth and the beginning of the twentieth centuries there was anarchist terrorism in the Western world – but it was short lived. However, not only will fundamentalist Islamic and other, less-ideologically inspired, terrorism continue, but also it is likely that terrorists will extend their global scale, their intensity and their destructive power, as most experts and institutions who study terrorism are concluding. Industrialized countries are very vulnerable to terrorism: although they have the resources to defend themselves, their nerve centres are not too difficult to attack and destroy. Also, modern technology allows terrorists to have at their disposal means of communication, transport and weapons (including nuclear ones) which give them a tremendous power and mobility.

Logically, Islamic terrorism is bound to increase its deadly activities. In addition to all the historical grievances that Muslim countries, and mainly followers of Islam, have against the West, there are profound ideological and religious differences between the Western and the Muslim worlds. For centuries, Western countries have dominated, colonized and exploited most of the Muslim world. Even now, the West is having a profound influence on Muslim countries, both on the economic sphere in their need to secure their supply of oil, and on the way of life of their people (and perhaps on the secularization, mainly of the young and upper classes). Both these factors are very much resented by the religious and nationalist Muslims.

But those two factors are not the most important ones for explaining a possible future escalation of Islamic terrorism. The most important elements that are likely to lead to such an intensification lie in the incompatibility between the philosophical and religious vision of the world and of the life individuals should lead held by Western and Islamic people. We know that the Western world, in the last four centuries, has become a rationalist world. Most individuals have secularized, leaving religion on the sidelines. According to the Egyptian philosopher Qutb (1949, 1954, 1964) Western civilization has evolved to a point at which individuals have completely separated in their mind and life the material, natural world from the spiritual one, the mind from the body. This radical separation, and therefore atheist or, at the least, agnostic attitude of Western people makes it very difficult for them to reach an equilibrium between sensual experience and spiritual elevation; other factors are the depersonalization of the power of the state, modern technological innovation, and social injustice. According to Qutb, this is why most people in the Western world live a kind of schizophrenia, why they experience psychological disorders, and, therefore, why there are so many psychiatrists, and why so many people indulge in excessive drugs and alcohol. They have abandoned the biblical code of conduct in all spheres of life that God handed down to Moses. The separation between state and religion is another very important consequence of this development. By contrast, the Islamists have a code of conduct (the Qur'an) which regulates, in a precise way, all aspects of life – spiritual, political, family, commercial and so on. This code integrates both the spiritual and material aspects, leading to a way of life that is both more harmonious and balanced.

Starting from this simplified explanation of the philosophical and religious foundations of Islam, the Western and the Islamic worlds are totally incompatible, with little possibility of reconciliation. However, the opposed economic and geopolitical interests of the two worlds are not the real cause of the conflict between them. Qutb thinks that for true Islamic believers, the jihad is an imperative obligation, which must be undertaken both against Muslims who have abandoned the sincere practice of the true faith (both the leaders who have sold themselves to the pleasures of the Western world, and the ordinary people who have become westernized in their way of living), and, most important, against Westerners, the infidels, who live their lives in a relentless and damaging way. Suicide in the jihad is both justified and expected from the true believers, who, according to these principles, do not die because their spirit remains alive within the community of believers.

If these philosophical and religious premises are taken seriously by Islamic fundamentalists, it can be expected that Islamic terrorism against the Western world, not only will not abate, but can be expected to increase in the future. There are between 800 and 1000 million Muslims in the world, and therefore it is likely that among them there must be some hundred million fundamentalists.

The financing of terrorism is apparently no problem for terrorists. An article in *El Pais* claims that in Spain alone there is a network of about 10,000 people who collect money from Muslim immigrants to send back to their families. This money, from 100,000 Pakistanis, is not actually sent to Pakistan. An agent in Pakistan receives a fax to pass on the amount deposited in Spain to the families of the senders, but the money remains in Spain, deposited in numerous bank accounts, and is then forwarded to bank accounts in other countries (France, the UK, the US). In this way the money is laundered and some of it is used to finance terrorism (Irujo, 2005).

The efforts of Western countries to encourage democracy in the Islamic world, as well as the recent democratic measures introduced by some Islamic leaders in their countries, will probably not be very successful. Recently *The Economist* carried on its front page a headline that read: 'Democracy stirs in the Middle East' (3 March 2005). However, the future is uncertain. Today the mass media bring to the Islamic world all the attractive features of life in the West, and this might gradually change their attitudes towards their religion and their way of life, and bring them closer to Western values and its hedonistic way of life. However, it is evident that the current policies in Afghanistan and Iraq are meeting with little success.

But assuming that Qutb is right and that Islamic terrorism will increase in the future, this could become a real danger and a challenge to Western democracies. Most probably there will also be other kinds of terrorism in this troubled world we live in, such as trafficking and smuggling of powerful weapons (including chemical, biological and even nuclear ones). In such a situation, people would feel even more insecure than they feel now, and it is likely that they would be willing to exchange civil liberties for security, thus demanding that their governments introduce ever-more restrictive measures curbing civil liberties. We have already seen evidence of that phenomenon: the Patriotic Act passed in the United States; the recent increase from 14 to 28 days for the police to arrest suspects without charge in the

UK; and the decision of Nicolas Sarcozy to expel all immigrants from France, whether they are in the country legally or illegally, who participated in the recent French riots. Sarcozy is the French Minister of the Interior and a serious candidate for the presidency. He was previously instrumental in persuading the French parliament to pass legislation to introduce a generalized video surveillance; to extend the period of the provisional arrest of suspects; to extend phone tapping; to compile annual records of telephone calls and electronic e-mails; to facilitate police access to such data; to control movements of individuals both inside the country and those going abroad; and to increase penalties. An even more important effect of the terrorist attacks in the Western countries is the hypothetical belief of some Spanish people that three days after the terrorist attack in Madrid, the Popular Party, in government at the time, lost the general election to the Socialist Party. Of course, it is risky to make such an assertion, but there is no doubt that the terrorist attack on 11 March 2004 in the Madrid underground, which left 192 dead and hundreds wounded, plus the poor handling of the information on the authors of the attack by the Popular Party, helped to overturn the predictions of the opinion polls.

So far there seems to have been no outcry or even any complaint or any serious criticism of these measures by any organized group of individuals, newspapers, TV channels, human rights organizations, constitutional lawyers, or any prominent individuals. This shows the tremendous importance that people give to their security and to be able to sleep soundly at night, something that Osama Bin Laden has threatened he would not let them do. This being the case, it is likely that, in a more extreme situation of insecurity, the people of democratic countries would be willing to sacrifice many of their civil liberties in exchange for some security, thus eating away at the basic principle of democracy, and potentially opening the way to the rise of populists and eventually of dictators.

3.2 The Financial Crisis of the Welfare State and Its Consequences

We know that the welfare state, particularly the so-called 'Rhenish' type (the German, continental one) is in serious financial trouble. It had already begun to be unsustainable some years ago, but its problems have increased enormously in the last few years due to the ageing of the population and to the rapid increase of globalization. Germany has nearly 5 million unemployed, and the average rate of unemployment within the European Union (EU) countries is 10 per cent (this rate in Spain is 8.6 per cent). Competition from the emerging countries (above all China, India and Russia, but also Brazil, Mexico and others) is becoming fierce. The so-called advanced democratic countries are finding it more and more difficult to compete with the emerging countries, and, what is even more damaging, many manufac-turing firms from the former are moving their factories to countries with lower salaries and where social security contributions are either non-existent or very low (China included). In Spanish this phenomenon is called '*deslocalización*' or relocation. Obviously this contributes greatly to increased unemployment, which means that the ratio of the number of workers employed and contributing to social security to each pensioner is decreasing rapidly in countries where the welfare state is extensive. Since the fiscal burden is already very high in these countries, governments have a tough job making ends meet and maintaining the welfare state on its present scale. The last meeting of heads of state and government, called by UK Prime Minister Tony Blair in his capacity of President of the EU, took place at Hampton Court on 22 October 2005. The meeting was dedicated to two main issues: how to meet the challenge of globalization and, at the same time, how to retain the European social security system. In fact, in the last few years nearly all the EU countries, regardless of their political per-suasion, have been obliged to cut down on welfare services: increasing the number of years of social security contributions in order to enjoy the right to a pension; reducing the number of medicines paid for by social security; increasing university fees; paying to see the health service doctor; reducing the length of time for receiving unemployment benefits; or even obliging the unemployed to take the first job offered by the unemployment office or lose their unemployment subsidy.

These are hard facts. The public debt is high in nearly all EU countries, and the public deficit is generally more than 3 per cent of GDP, thus exceed-ing the limits set by the Stabilization Treaty. This situation represents a threat to democracy. What this threat implies is that politicians find it very difficult to go to the voters with an electoral programme in which they propose to curtail some of the social services that people have become accustomed to and have enjoyed for many years, and which they have come to regard as their right. Politicians are obliged to juggle in order to make ends meet, that is, to maintain the Maastrich requirements – and polit-icians, whose priority is to win elections, naturally do not put forward radical measures to tackle the problems. So these countries continue to lose competitivity, the social services are facing greater financial difficulties, and pensions have become a time-bomb. The public are becoming increasingly uneasy, and they will become more so in the near future, unless either some magic solution is found or people are willing to accept sizeable cuts in social services.

Since neither solution is likely to happen, it can be concluded that there will be some social unrest, and political election outcomes that will make it difficult for political parties to govern. The case of the latest general elections in Germany (18 September 2005) is paradigmatic: when Gerhard Schroeder tried to face the problems of the welfare state with measures included in his Agenda 2010, he was defeated. How politicians will solve the problem of reducing the unwieldy welfare state, whether people will accept it and how they will react to it, is something that cannot be foreseen. There is already some social unrest (witness the 2004 riots in France), which, as more stringent measures are taken by the governments of parties of all shades, is bound to increase, and might even take the shape of various forms of rebellion: social unrest, strikes, disorders, social conflicts, conflicts between immigrants and natives, and ultimately, public disillusionment with politicians and the democratic political system. Such an atmosphere would become a breeding ground for demagogues and populists, none of which would be very favourable for democracy; on the contrary, they could become a real danger for democracy.

3.3   Effects of Globalization

The potential effects of globalization on democracy are also related to the near bankrupt condition of the welfare state. Of course, globalization has been taking place throughout history. From the moment a primitive tribe exchanged some apples for a rabbit with members of a different tribe, economic activity began to expand, both quantitatively and geographically; other examples are the Viking trade trips (and raids), the Silk road, the discovery of America and of the Far East by the Spaniards and Portuguese, the Dutch and the English, and the invention of the steam engine, the telegraph, the telephone and the aeroplane.

What has made the present globalization particularly intense, large scale and rapid are the wireless telephone, the internet, the fax, the speed and the low costs of transportation of goods, the enormous advancement of technology (most of it at the disposal of all countries and firms), the increase in the number and size of multinational firms, the free trade policy rules adopted by the large majority of countries through the World Trade Organization, and the free movement of capital and to some extent of persons on a scale never known before.

Competition among firms of all countries is global and very strong. To these factors we have to add the quite rapid entry of the so-called emerging countries, mainly China with its 1300 million inhabitants, India with 1000 million, Russia and other countries such as Mexico and Brazil. These additions have effectively doubled the global labour force, hugely boosting the world potential output, and hence its future prosperity. The entry of China's massive labour force into the global economy may well be the most profound change for 50 years and perhaps for 100 years. China's growth rate is exceptional compared with previous or current economies in Asia, but China is having a more dramatic effect on the world economy because of two factors: not only does it have a huge, cheap labour force, but also its economy is unusually open to trade. As a result, China's development is not just a powerful engine of global growth, but its impact on other economies is also more pervasive. China's growing influence penetrates much more deeply than its exports of cheap goods. It is revolutionizing the relative prices of labour, capital, goods and assets in a way that has never happened so quickly before. A recognition of China's profound and widespread impact on the world economy explains various current economic puzzles.

Such are the problems that globalization poses to the EU countries that, as mentioned above, Tony Blair called a meeting of the presidents and chiefs of governments of the EU countries which took place at Hampton Court in 2005, dedicated exclusively to a debate on the problems that globalization is creating for EU business interests. The conclusions they reached concerned the measures that should be taken, in particular:

1. an increase in research on technology and innovation, with more money allocated from the EU budget;
2. a common policy on all kinds of energy must be designed and executed;
3. an improvement in the quality of the universities in order to compete with those in America – today 17 of the top world universities are American;
4. the control of immigration in order to employ legal immigrants;
5. the development of a common policy on demography, as the EU population is ageing rapidly; and
6. the creation of a fund to help those firms and workers who are negatively affected by globalization.

This brings us to the potential negative effects of globalization on democracy. Obviously, in the long run, its effects will be positive, as trade has always been. But in the short run, the ferocious competition that firms from the traditionally advanced countries are encountering from firms from the emergent countries, which are paying much lower salaries and social security contributions, is forcing the former either to drastically cut down the number of their employees or to relocate their factories to low-salary countries, China included.

This is exacerbating the unemployment situation in the EU countries, with the possible exception of Spain. Almost every day we read in the newspapers that some big firms are planning to cut down the number of their employees. The rate of unemployment in the whole of the EU is about

10 per cent and in Spain it is 8.6 per cent; Germany has 5 million unemployed. Naturally, this is creating serious problems for the governments of these countries. Such a negative phenomenon is having, among others, two dramatic consequences. On the one hand, there are many strikes and social conflicts, which governments feel helpless to solve and often they are obliged to use force to repress them. This not only makes politicians unpopular, but it also increases the public loss of confidence in government, and, consequently, in the democratic political system. People elect their representatives on the assumption that they will be able to solve their problems. But in this global economy, neither economic nor political power, is in the remit of the nation-state. The real power lies somewhere else – in the offices where the governing board of the big multinational firms meet, in the large financial centres and institutions, in the governments of the big powers and so on. This power is globally pervasive, so governments have little authority to solve their own problems, and, consequently, the electorate become disillusioned and lose confidence both in the government and in democracy *per se*. On the other hand, the high unemployment is taxing the already fragile social security system, putting pressure on politicians and governments to make ever-more cuts in social services, thus further weakening the welfare state. It is becoming a vicious circle that is very difficult to break.

In its issue of 5–11 November 2005, *The Economist* carried the front-page headline: 'Tired of Globalisation. But in Need of Much More of it', which succinctly summarizes the effects of globalization.

3.4   The Effects of Immigration and the Multicultural Society

Finally I shall address the problems that large-scale immigration and multicultural societies represent for democracy in the advanced countries. Since the rich countries have been unable, or unwilling, to help the poorer ones to develop economically, socially and politically, the result has been massive migration from the latter on a scale not known for many centuries. But it is clear that immigration into the rich countries must be regulated and kept under control. This is very difficult to achieve as illegally introducing immigrants into the rich countries has become a very profitable and big business. In Spain there are more illegal than legal immigrants.

Obviously immigration at this time has a positive side for democracies. In all European countries, the population is ageing rapidly. Life expectancy has reached 80 years. Young immigrants supply the labour force that these countries need. Also the legalized immigrants who have a job contribute to the social security system, which, as we have said above, is in a very fragile financial situation. In Spain it has been calculated that the country needs

250,000 new immigrants every year who would make social security contributions, in order to keep the system financially viable. In addition, immigrants will do the jobs that the locals do not want to do.

But this phenomenon, which has become so large in the last few years, also has negative effects for democracy. In the first place, and under the present existing unemployment situation in the receiving countries, people are beginning to see immigrants as unfair competitors for the existing jobs. There are numerous reports in, many European countries of social conflicts that are increasing every day; the dangerous increase in zenophobia, racism and intolerance can lead to populism and ultimately to nationalism, both of which erode the very bases of democracy. Also, immigration has its own particular economic requirements, and governments have to provide housing, schools and hospitals for the immigrants and their families. On the other hand, the mixing and coexistence of cultures, which some years ago seemed to be so easy (the UK and the USA were good examples) is now somewhat more difficult – witness the events in France, Germany, Spain and even the UK. The prognosis is difficult, as we do not really know how tolerant EU citizens will be in the future. But we do know that immigrants tend to be poor and of a low cultural level and that as a result of their difficult economic and social conditions, some of them create drug problems, occupying buildings, stealing and taking part in street fighting.

EU citizens might be inclined to blame all these problems on the immigrants. In the future there may be a total rejection of the latter by the former, who might demand that their governments expel immigrants and who might take the law into their own hands. Such phenomena would destabilize democracy. There might be social disorder, riots and social conflicts, and governments might be obliged to introduce measures that would curtail the civil rights of the indigenous population, and violate the human rights of the immigrants and even of the EU citizens. To integrate immigrants into European societies is turning out to be more difficult than expected. The case of France is a warning of what might happen in other countries in the future. If the governments of the European countries are obliged to introduce measures against the immigrants and terrorism, democracy could be seriously jeopardized. Other evidence to support this hypothesis is that as mentioned above, in 2005, the UK parliament approved a law by which the police can hold suspects for 28 days without charge; and in France, the Minister of the Interior has decreed that all immigrants (be they legally or illegally in the country) who have participated in the recent riots, be expelled. The UK law has raised a debate on what is more important: national security or civil liberties.

4 CONCLUSION

In this chapter I have perhaps drawn a gloomy picture about the future of democracy. However, I am optimistic about the prospects of this political system. On the one hand, the advanced democratic countries have the material, social and cultural means and resources to face and to overcome the threats and dangers which hang over their political system. Also, more and more countries in the world are making progress in establishing a political democratic system. Some theorists assert that the movement towards democracy is both worldwide and unstoppable. But most important is the fact that the values of freedom, liberty, justice, human rights, freedom to make one's own life choices, the desire and the right to participate in decision making on public and private issues which affect lives, interests and communities, are eternal values which human beings worldwide cherish in both mind and heart. These values and ideals will ultimately encourage the spread of democracy throughout the world, and to prevail over both the threats which menace it and all other types of government.

BIBLIOGRAPHY

Acemoglu, K.D. and J.A. Robinson (2005), *Economic Origins of Dictatorship and Democracy*, Cambridge: Cambridge University Press.

Buchanan, James, M. (1997), 'Lectio' Delivered at his Doctor Honoris Causa Degree ceremony at the University of Valencia, 5 December; also in Pardo Casas J. (ed.), *Economía y Política*, Valencia: Servicio de Publicaciones, Universidad de Valencia, 1997, pp. 51–6.

Dahl, Robert A. (1989), *La Democracia y sus Críticos*, Barcelona, Buenos Aires, Mexico: Ediciones Paidos and New Haven, CT: Yale University Press.

Dahl, Robert A. and Charles E. Lindblom (1976), *Politics, Economics and Welfare*, Chicago: University of Chicago Press.

Dalrymple, Theodore (2005), *Our Culture, What's Left of It: The Mandarins and the Masses*, Chicago: Ivan R. Dee, from the review of the book by Richart Davenport-Hines in the *Times Literary Supplement*, 28 October, p. 3.

Irujo, Jose Maria (2005), 'La Ruta Española del Halawa', *El País*, 10 October, pp. 17–18.

Lindblom, Charles, E. (1988), *Democracy and the Market System*, Oslo: Norwegian University Press.

Qutb, Sayyid (1949), *Al-adala al-Ijtima'iyyd fi-l-Islam* (Social Justice and Islam), Wikipedia, the online encyclopaedia.

Qutb, Sayyid (1954), *Fizilal al-Qur'an* (In the Shade of the Qur'an) commentary of the Qur'an, his most important work, Wikipedia, the online encyclopaedia.

Qutb, Sayyid (1964), *Ma'alim fi-Tariq* (Signposts on the Road or Milestones), Wikipedia, the online encyclopaedia.

Sartori, Giovanni (2003), *Qué es la Democracia?*, Madrid: Taurus.

Schumpeter, J. (1974), *Capitalism, Socialism and Democracy*, London: Allen & Unwin.

Vallespin, Fernando, Giovanni Sartori and Robert A. Dahl (2004), 'El Futuro de la Democracia: Problemas, Reglas y Medios de la Nueva Convivencia Politica', eteceter@politica y cultura en lineas.

Zakaria, Fareed (2003), *El Futuro de la Libertad*, Buenos Aires: Taurus.

2. Social justice examined: with a little help from Adam Smith

Anthony de Jasay

1 INTRODUCTION

We shall not go far wrong if we think of justice as a quality that members of groups who habitually congregate together would wish their relations to have – at least most of the time. Justice, then, is intrinsically 'social'. It would have no meaning with respect to an isolated individual. If so, it is hard to see what the word 'social' is doing in the phrase 'social justice'. It looks very much like a harmless pleonasm – though it may be suspected that expressions loaded with superfluous words are seldom quite harmless.

It goes with 'social justice' as with 'distributive justice', and the two are frequently treated as synonymous. All justice is distributive, either because benefits and burdens accruing to persons are generated in obedience to the rules of justice (notably those relating to property and contract), or because they are generated in violation of them and attract redress and retribution. However, while 'distributive' may be a redundant word, it has an empirical content that is not too hard to understand. The 'social' in 'social justice' has no discernible meaning apart from its being a term of approbation; 'social' is something good, and its immense strength comes in large part from its inchoate vagueness.

If social justice is not a harmless pleonasm, what is it? I think we come closest if we treat it as a password that, once uttered, validates claims for altering the distributional status quo.

Its name carries the tacit suggestion that social justice is a branch of justice, by analogy with such branches as civil or criminal justice. It is easy to accept this suggestion by sheer inadvertence. A brief examination, however, reveals that the suggestion is quite false. Justice in all its branches is expressed in the language of rules, moral or institutional, and it is both constrained and guided by these rules. It is at least logically possible to conceive of a state of affairs which is perfectly just, in that all rules of justice are respected and none is breached. Redress is called for only when a rule is breached. In clear contrast to this dependence on rules, social justice

35

simply has no rules that could ever be satisfied. Every state of affairs is in want of redress by social justice. Redress consists in altering the distribution of goods in a more egalitarian direction. It may be thought, therefore, that once successive acts of redress have finally achieved a perfectly equal distribution, social justice would be satisfied, for its implicit guiding rule is 'social justice requires equality of condition'. However, imputing to it this rule, or any rule, would be sheer guesswork, for there is nothing to stop proponents of social justice from claiming that a state of perfect equality is unjust and requires redress by altering the distribution to favour one deserving group of persons after another.

The power of the term is constantly being reinforced by everyday usage in which the tacit identification of egalitarian changes with 'social' justice (presumably a branch of justice) is hardly ever challenged.

The central object of this chapter is to argue that what passes for social justice is intrinsically unjust, though this obviously does not exclude value judgements where the injustice is outweighed by other considerations. It will be suggested that while 'social justice' is alien to the requirements of justice, it is strongly related to the requirements of democracy.

* * *

Adam Smith, in his *Theory of Moral Sentiments*, approved of 'generosity, humanity, kindness, compassion, mutual friendship and . . . all the social and benevolent affections . . . [that] please the indifferent spectator'.[1] In modern language, we could translate this to mean that public opinion, when it does not consciously realize that its interests may be affected by it, is favourably disposed towards manifestations of social justice. It has, to put it crudely, a 'good press', 'it plays well'. Other things being equal, this makes it obviously easier to expand the scope of social justice than to restrict it – as long as it is overlooked that generosity, humanity, kindness and compassion involve benefits to some but costs to others, and the balance between the benefits and the costs is not self-evident. Some, including the present writer, doubt that the idea of such a balance makes any real sense at all.

About the prima facie goodness of social justice (as distinct from its appeal to neutral public opinion), Smith had his doubts. In the *Moral Sentiments*, he quite bluntly declares: 'Every man, as the Stoics used to say, is first and principally recommended to his own care and every man is, certainly in every respect, fitter and abler to take care of himself than of any other person.'[2]

However, Smith's judgement leaves open the possibility that while the needy man is best able to take care of himself, he would take even better care if he were less needy. Transfer of resources from the well-to-do to the needy might still be a good thing, though we may not be able to say that it would be demanded by justice. This, I believe, would sum up in a nut-shell the utilitarian position that held sway for over a century from Jeremy Bentham to Arthur Pigou. For these utilitarians (who, mistakenly, are still regarded as classical liberals), any rich-to-poor transfer must increase total utility in society and hence it must *by definition* be approved. Although the underlying welfare economic argument is no longer accepted, the memory of utilitarianism still lingers on in educated public opinion and lends instinctive, almost knee-jerk support to programmes of social justice.

1.1   Charity versus Obligation

From the fall of the Roman Empire to the early part of the twentieth century, generosity was not a public function. Rich-to-poor transfers, mainly of goods but also of money, were made voluntarily though sometimes under some moral pressure from priest, pastor or rabbi. Donors gave locally to 'their' poor, favouring the 'deserving' and motivating the undeserving, idle and feckless to become deserving. Administration was easy – indeed, non-existent – aid efficient, though coverage was no doubt uneven, partly a matter of luck, and some deserving poor were certainly overlooked. Nevertheless, the system had all the advantages of the decentralized over the centralized arrangement. Above all, it had the great moral merit of not putting donors under compulsion.

Charity was, and remains, a moral duty that is not enforced, except pos-sibly by social disapproval of the uncharitable. The recipient has no claim on the donor, and must depend on his/her good will.

When governments started to install the system of compulsory transfers from rich to poor that led to the welfare state, public opinion welcomed the innovation. It was understood to be doing social justice. The needy no longer had to rely on charity, a reliance that progressive opinion, probably including Adam Smith's 'indifferent spectator' came to find humiliating. Donors were now under an enforceable obligation to pay enough taxes to enable the needy to exercise their newly con-ferred right to be helped. Involuntary transfers amounted to doing social justice.

I believe, and will now argue, that what began as compulsory giving to the needy and ended as the fully fledged welfare state owes little or nothing to the public's sense of social justice, though it is approved as if it were done in deliberate pursuit of that justice. Its motive force, however, comes from a very different source.

2   A DISTRIBUTION GAME

Adam Smith wrote near the middle of a remarkable, nearly unique period in English history – between the Glorious Revolution and the First World War – when property was considered sacrosanct, secure from the power of the Crown, and income taxation was only just beginning on a negligibly small scale. This period was brought to an end by the succession of electoral reforms leading to universal suffrage and the secret ballot.

In the modern age, collective choices can to a large extent override individual ones, and appropriate for public use a share of the property and income of individuals that in earlier times used to be regarded as their own by law. These collective decisions are taken by the counting of anonymous votes for alternatives, nobody having more votes than anybody else. The consequence of this type of decision rule is that majorities can exploit minorities, and the prospective gain to be made in this manner serves as a magnet, inducing voters to enter into a voting coalition just large enough to be decisive. Rival coalitions will each aspire to reach the required size and become the decisive, winning coalition. Prima facie, a coalition that would distribute to itself some of the income of the rich, can offer a bigger gain to its members than a coalition that would distribute to itself some of the income of the poor. Under the assumption that other things being equal, voters cast their votes according to how they expect them to affect their future net income (after taxes and subventions), prospective coalitions that do not propose rich-to-poor redistribution will lose members to ones that do, provided that the number of prospective gainers exceeds the number of prospective losers. (In fact, to have a chance of winning, all rival coalitions must promise to distribute income from the rich to the poor, including any coalition whose membership is rich.)

A general and powerful representation of democratic redistribution is the three-person distribution game. It works by the simple rule that the total property or income of three players shall be distributed among them as any two players jointly decide. The rational solution is that the two poorer players jointly exploit the richer one. Instead of three persons, the game can be played by three groups that together make up a society, namely the rich, the middle and the poor. If majority voting is decisive, the three groups must be formed in such a way that any two is always larger than the third, a grouping that rational voters would evidently adopt. The resulting solution is again that poor and middle exploit rich. In a repeated game, the role of rich rotates because it is always a different player who comes out rich from the previous round of the game. If, however, production takes place and one player (or group) continues to be more productive than the other two, he/she will be the exploited rich in each round.

3   DISGUISING THE INJUSTICE

Two persons robbing a third is unjust. If it is the rule of the game that two persons may rob a third, the rule is unjust. If the sum to be distributed is not owned by any of the players, so that none is deprived of any of his/her property when the distribution is made, the rule that two decide for three is still unjust.

Stripped of its rhetorical embellishments, and allowing for the rule of law and the restraint which must be exercised if the enforcement of rules is to remain peaceful, the practice of democracy at its inner core is no different from the distribution game where two join forces to rob a third. It is easy to overlook that this is so, for the two are not acting out of any wickedness, and the third does not really look like a helpless victim. It is nevertheless the case that forcible redistribution of wealth or income by applying an unjust rule is an injustice. It would be no less so if it could be established beyond dispute that the initial distribution itself was not just and ought to be redressed.

However, establishing that the initial distribution was unjust to start with is problematical, to put it no higher. Justice is a property of acts or of their direct consequences. Injustice is not self-generating, but must be traceable to unjust acts. For the situation of the poor to be unjust, the rich must be found guilty of unjust acts. This can be done in particular cases, but not as a generally valid finding. 'Possession is nine points of the law'. The owners of property and the earners of income enjoy a presumption in favour of their title to their property and income. The very political authority which is redistributing them accepts this presumption and promises to protect the security of property and contract. It cannot very easily argue that protecting a distribution with one hand and redistributing with the other are both justified.

One way out of this conundrum is to say, with the legendary Scottish parson, 'Here is a great difficulty. Let us look it firmly in the face and pass on'. Many democratic governments in fact do this. They do not seek to explain away the contradiction, if only because doing so would be to draw attention to its existence. Instead, they rely on the principle of 'least said, soonest mended'.

The other way out is to dress up the injustice of redistribution as an act of social justice by constructing a doctrine that, if plausible enough, will persuade the 'indifferent spectator' of Adam Smith that the rule of the democratic distribution game is in fact a rule of justice.

In what follows, I shall briefly survey two types of this doctrine. One is contractarian, and its central thesis is that redistribution is agreed by all, including those who are made to bear its cost, and therefore just. The other might be called neo-socialist in that it has nothing to do with the old social-ist labour theory of value. Its central contention is that the creation of wealth and income cannot be imputed to the individuals who hold title to them under the initial distribution, and this for two alternative reasons: either because we do not know how much is imputable to particular indi-viduals, or because we know that nothing is imputable to them.

3.1 Contractarian Social Justice

The essence of contractarianism is a claim that there are certain contract terms to which every rational individual would agree to under suitable assumptions about rationality, expectations and moral sentiments. Two general objections to such theories should be borne in mind before consid-ering the detail of particular versions. One is that a *hypothetical* agreement to given contract terms can never have the same moral weight and binding force as a *real* one. The other is that every rational individual would expect every other to default rather than fulfil the contract, hence he/she would not want to fulfil it all by him/herself – in other words, the contract would be a classic single-round prisoner's dilemma whose solution is that the contract is simply not concluded. The only way out of this dilemma is to assume that the contracting parties are not rational in any accepted sense of the word, but 'moral' in a peculiar way – a gratuitous assumption. Although I regard them as valid and even decisive, I propose to leave these criticisms on one side and look at the detail of two representative contractarian theories. Both employ the device of the 'veil'.

One of these, associated with the names of James Buchanan and Gordon Tullock (1962), assumes that persons look at their own future through a 'veil of uncertainty' which is thick enough to stop them from making educated guesses about their likely future income. The well-to-do fear that in the future they might become the needy. Therefore they agree to a redis-tributive scheme that taxes them and transfers their taxes to the needy, expecting to benefit from this scheme if and when they become needy. The result is that social justice is being done with the agreement of the well-to-do who voluntarily bear its cost.

To assess whether this agreement would be a plausible, let alone a ration-al one, consider the choice the well-to-do (above the median) have between a social contract under which they are taxed but promised to get subventions when they become needy, and paying no such tax but putting the same money instead in their own private piggy bank and taking it out if future need so dictates. Whether the social contract or the piggy bank gives them the better result depends, under the simplest possible assump-tions, on how much of the time they turn out to be well-to-do. If a person is well-to-do more than half the time, he (or she) will have put away more in his own piggy bank than he has taken out, whereas under the social contract he would have paid more taxes than he received in subventions. If he is well-to-do half the time and needy the other half, the piggy bank and the social contract would yield him roughly the same result (the social contract giving him a slightly better deal if he is mostly needy in the near future and well-to-do in the distant one). Finally, if he is needy more than half the time, he gets a better deal under the social contract – but this deal is impossible to realize collectively, for it is impossible to redistribute more to the needy as a whole than the taxes the well-to-do as a whole are paying.

In other words, the well-to-do would be agreeing to an insurance scheme that would generally take from them more premium than it paid in benefits, and in the limiting case it would just repay them their money. Voluntary acceptance of such a scheme is wholly implausible. Therefore voluntariness cannot rescue the redistributive scheme from being unjust, since it takes resources from their recognized owners without their consent.

The other representative theory is John Rawls's (1971) 'justice as fairness'. Here, the contracting parties act as if they were behind a 'veil of ignorance' that hides from their own eyes all their inherited or acquired personal qualities or other advantages that make them different from one another. In this situation of mutual 'fairness', where they are supposed to ignore what their real earning power and real position in life might in fact be, they agree on an income distribution where all get equal shares except if, and to the extent that, an inequality works to the advantage of the worst-off. This kind of qualified egalitarianism would be the rational choice of individuals who 'played maximin', that is, who, in facing uncertain future outcomes, were only interested in making the worst outcome as good as possible; the devil take the better ones, and never mind how much better they may be.

'Maximin', a key building block of the much invoked 'difference principle' proclaimed by this theory, presupposes a strange mentality in that those who adopt it as a guide to their risky choices are simply not interested in any potential outcome except the worst, and in order to maximize the worst, they are quite willing to give up the most tempting odds of even very good outcomes. Such behaviour, described by Rawls as rational, would reflect an almost morbid fear of any risk. For this and a large number of other reasons that space does not permit me to discuss, it is difficult to accept that a hypothetical contract establishing qualified equality of material welfare, could be willingly agreed by all if they were placed in a position of 'fairness'.

3.2   Socialist Social Justice

In orthodox socialist theory, only labour creates value, hence any initial distribution in which capital earns a return is *ipso facto* an injustice to be redressed. Redistributions in favour of the working class qualify as acts of social justice. This doctrine rests on a theory of value that has, at best, only an antiquarian interest and does not warrant being discussed.

Two versions of what might be termed 'neo-socialist' doctrine, however, are worth brief consideration. One of them starts from the indisputable fact that any valuable product, say a pair of shoes, is not produced by a single individual, say the shoemaker. Starting with the farmer who grew the food that fed the shoemaker, the mason who built the house where he lives, the tanner who prepared the leather he uses, the master who taught him to make shoes and the teacher who taught him the three Rs, and ending only with more remote persons on the edge of our horizon, all these countless people past and present have contributed something to the shoe. It would take a Leontiev matrix with many thousands of rows and columns to start giving some idea of how complex a product a simple shoe was, except that we would not have the knowledge to put actual numbers into the matrix.

Since individual contributions cannot be assessed and remain unknown, the distribution of the social product cannot be based on who contributed how much to it. The only solution is for society as a whole, speaking with the voice of its government, to decide what would be a socially just distribution, and proceed to put it into effect.

The common-sense refutation of this argument is simply to point out that while it is obviously true that the farmer, the mason, the tanner and the teacher and everybody else one can think of, had to make contributions to the making of the shoe, all their contributions have been paid for at the time it was made. There is no need for any mind-boggling input–output matrix. Everybody's contribution to every product is duly measured by the price at which each contribution is sold on to the next one in the endless chain that is the production process. All value is contributed by individuals in proportion to factor ownership and marginal factor productivity, and they are rewarded for it in the same proportions. Interference with these equalities in the name of social justice is prima facie unjust.

Another neo-socialist apology for social justice dismisses the very idea of factor productivity and of individuals, as owners of factors, being responsible for producing total output. Nobody is responsible and nobody can take the credit for it. At best, individuals can be assumed to have contributed a tiny fraction of the social product – a fraction no larger than what primitive Polynesian tribesmen or other pre-civilization people are capable of producing. (This point was made by Herbert Simon, but it was not this that earned him his Nobel prize.) All the rest must be ascribed to civilization.

Civilization is a single, indivisible externality. Individuals owe to it all or nearly all their well-being. It is manna, a gift falling from heaven, and individuals cannot claim it as their own, as if they had deserved it. As before, it is society acting through its government that must determine how much each individual should in fact get, and it will make this determination according to its judgement of what is socially just.

To say that civilization is a giant externality responsible for the production of all material wealth, is to forge a metaphor, not to construct a theory.

However, if for argument's sake one took the metaphor as a true reflection of some reality, it would still remain the case that an externality produces no output. Individual action, facilitated by the externality, does. The individual's marginal product will no doubt be higher than it would be without the externality, but to take some of it away from him/her and give it to others is no more a matter of justice than it would be to tax us for the blessings of a temperate climate and give the money to the inhabitants of the North Pole and the tropical jungle.

4 WHERE DOES THE IMPARTIAL SPECTATOR STAND?

The promise of redistribution from the better-off to the worse-off, as we have seen, gathers the votes needed in a vote-counting polity to obtain and hold the power to redistribute. The rule that authorizes this to be done is, to put it crudely, that two can decide for three. Yet a rule that delivers one to the other two very clearly and blatantly violates the precepts of justice. The idea of social justice is a truly audacious device meant to disguise this plain fact by declaring that black is white.

Many intellectual cases can be constructed to support the argument that distributive injustice is, in fact, an act of doing social justice. Each and every such case is as easy to knock down as it was to put up. In the nature of the case, a conclusive, 'value-free' argument to establish social justice as a branch of justice, is an impossible undertaking.

Failing the support of logic, the case for social justice must fall back on judgement. Judgement is intrinsically subjective, and to overcome this intrinsic flaw as far as it can be done, recourse is had to the 'impartial observer' who has no interest of his (or her) own in the matter he must judge.

Nineteenth-century utilitarians had great confidence in the impartial observer and cited his putative testimony to bolster their cause when the utility gains of some and the losses of others had to be compared. He was supposed to rule that a dollar taken from the well-to-do and given to the needy increased total utility because the latter had a greater use for it. His judgement may have been a quite reasonable account of how he would feel in the place of the well-to-do and the needy. Whatever that feeling signified, it had said strictly nothing about justice.

More than a century earlier, Adam Smith called his 'impartial spectator' to bear witness to justice in sharp distinction from utility: 'to take from him what is of real use to him merely because it may be of equal or *of more use to us* . . . is what no impartial spectator can go along with'.[3]

If there were a truly impartial spectator hidden inside each of us, where would he take his stand on this matter? It may well be that he would be less stern than his Smithian counterpart and, like most contemporary opinion, he, too, would like to take from the better-off and give it to the needy. But intellectual honesty could not, and would not, let him 'go along with' the pretence that to take from one and give to the other is doing justice.

NOTES

1. Adam Smith, *The Theory of Moral Sentiments*, 1759, Part I, Section II, Chapter IV.
2. Ibid., Part VI, Section II, Chapter I.
3. Ibid., Part II, Section II, Chapter II, my italics.

REFERENCES

Buchanan, James M. and Gordon Tullock (1962), *The Calculus of Consent*, Ann Arbor, MI: University of Michigan Press.
Rawls, John (1971), *A Theory of Justice*, Cambridge, MA: Belunap Press.

3.   Affective public choice
Frans van Winden

---

1   INTRODUCTION

The economic theory of political decision making, also labeled 'public choice' or 'political economics', has seen an impressive development over recent decades. It is no longer (strongly) contested that the motivations of political agents deciding on government policies are not fundamentally different from those driving economic behavior in the private sector. But, what are these motivations, more precisely? Even allowing for the presence of people that are not only promoting their own narrow selfish interests, the following phenomena are puzzling:

1.   mass protests and mass voting even if those involved run a serious risk of losing their lives (recently in places such as Iraq, Ukraine, Lebanon and Belorussia);
2.   the explosion of riots in the Paris suburbs;
3.   the socio-political impact of terrorism;
4.   suicide bombing;
5.   the maintenance of a costly monarchy with related national rituals in full-blown democracies where the monarch has no formal power; and
6.   Soviet premier Nikita Khrushchev removing his shoe and banging it on the table during a UN conference in 1960, calling Filipino delegate Lorenzo Sumulong 'a jerk, a stooge and lackey of imperialism'.

The first two phenomena are puzzling if one assumes, as in the theory of collective action, that political participation is the outcome of a rational cost–benefit analysis. Why would people risk their lives in that case? And why all of a sudden these French riots, without any clear changes in the individual economic benefits and costs of participation? The third phenomenon is hard to understand in view of the small chance of getting involved in terrorist attacks. The other phenomena are also difficult to explain from a rational point of view, although not always impossible with a stretch of the imagination.[1] In this chapter I shall argue that it is due to our neglect of the affective side of human decision making that we find it difficult to explain these and other political economic issues to be addressed below. For example, taking into account the action tendencies of emotions such as resentment, hatred, shame, fear and hope makes the kind of behavior mentioned under the first four points more understandable and predictable. Similarly, to understand phenomena like those mentioned under points five and six it seems helpful to reckon with the affect component of social identity and the impact of anger, respectively. To phrase the argument of this chapter in a more polemical way: those who cannot stand the heat should stay out of politics and public choice!

The organization of the chapter is as follows. Section 2 starts with some historical notes. Then, Section 3 briefly addresses the nature of emotions. The next three sections are concerned with the significance of affect for some important facets of public finance: taxation and regulation (Section 4), expenditure (Section 5) and collective action (Section 6). Section 7 concludes.

2   BACK TO THE ROOTS

An important decision taken by the pioneers of public choice (Downs, 1957; Buchanan and Tullock, 1962 [1974]) was to equate the behavioral motivation of *homo politicus* with that of *homo economicus*. Whereas the latter model–agent, with its determining characteristic of rational self-interested utility maximization, figured pre-eminently in the way economists studied the behavior of producers and consumers in the private sector, the assumption of a benevolent dictator dominated in public finance. To apply the same fundamental behavioral assumption to politicians and bureaucrats in the public sector was a daring step, with wide-ranging implications. It revolutionized the way economists thought about politics.

From a research-strategic point of view, the consistent claim that these pioneers made was the best they could do, given the reigning paradigm of neoclassical economics. However, they could have taken an even more daring step, challenging simultaneously the maintained view of how people behave in the private as well as the public sector. They could have opted for a 'warmer' model–agent, an agent with a 'heart and a mind'. And they would have been in some very good company, pleading for such a view. It has gradually been realized among economists that the second great book written by founding father Adam Smith – *The Theory of Moral Sentiments* (Smith, 1759/1790 [1982]) – is equally important for understanding economic decision making (Smith, 1998; Ashraf et al., 2005). Especially, if markets are not involved, because for that institution *The Wealth of Nations* (Smith, 1776 [1971]) was written. According to Adam

Smith, morality is rooted in feelings, like shame and guilt, which play an important role in decision making. Perhaps even more appropriate would be to refer to Spinoza. In an appendix to his path-breaking work with Tullock – *The Calculus of Consent* – Buchanan notes: 'Spinoza's work, in many respects therefore, may be taken as the most appropriately chosen classical precursor to that of this book' (Buchanan and Tullock, 1962 [1974], p. 313). Reading Spinoza's *Tractatus Politicus* (1677) makes this perfectly clear, but Spinoza went much further. The next two quotes from the English translation by Elwes (1951) illustrate Spinoza's position:

> For they [philosophers] conceive of men, not as they are, but as they themselves would like them to be. Whence it has come to pass that . . . they have never conceived a theory of politics, which could be turned into use. (p. 287)

> And that I might investigate the subject-matter of this science [politics] with the same freedom of spirit as we generally use in mathematics, I have laboured carefully, not to mock, lament, or execrate, but to understand human actions; *and to this end I have looked upon passions, such as love, hatred, anger, envy, ambition, pity, and the other perturbations of the mind, not in the light of vices of human nature, but as properties.* (p. 288; emphasis added)

Incidentally, according to Schumpeter (1972, pp. 126–7) every economist ought to be able to repeat the last sentence on his deathbed!

Thus, we find two great scholars, who can be regarded as founding fathers of (political) economics, pleading for the incorporation of affect in our conception of what drives human beings. How to deal with this? Of course, one could argue that emotions and the like are just noise or correlates of what economists already take into account. As Buchanan and Tullock rightly emphasized, the crucial insight is that: 'A shift of activity from the market sector [to the political sector] cannot in itself change the nature of man' (1962 [1974], p. 306). But, they also wrote: 'The ultimate defense of the . . . behavioral assumption must be empirical' (p. 28). So, let the data speak. To prepare the discussion, I shall first say something about the nature of emotions in the next section.[2]

3   EMOTIONS

An emotion arises when an individual appraises an event as being relevant to an important concern or interest (for example, Oatley and Jenkins, 1996).[3] If the interest is advanced, a positive emotion arises. If the interest is thwarted, a negative emotion is generated. Emotions have a direct hedonic quality. Although emotions may entail a conscious feeling, the processes underlying them are unconscious and are not cognitively pene-trable. In this sense, they are involuntary or unbidden; one cannot simply choose an emotion. Emotional processes are accompanied by physiological changes (arousal, visceral responses) and may lead to bodily changes, like facial expressions. Central to an emotion is an action tendency, an urge to execute a particular action. According to Frijda (1986), these action ten-dencies – of the approach or avoidance type – can be considered as pro-grams that have a place of precedence in the control of action and of information processing. Whether an action tendency will actually lead to some action depends on the influence of further appraisals regulating the emotional process. It involves a more refined context evaluation, the check-ing of coping possibilities, and the measuring out and trading off of the possible implications for the individual's interests. The impact of these higher-order appraisals depends on the intensity of the emotion, deter-mined by factors like the importance of the interest involved, the reality and proximity of the emotion-eliciting event, the level of arousal, and the degree of unexpectedness (Ortony et al., 1988). If the intensity is strong it may surpass a point of no return or regulation threshold (Frijda, 1986), leading to a mode of operation where we just react rather than think. Goleman (1996) speaks of 'emotional hijacking', in that case.

In the following, I shall investigate the significance of emotions for several important areas of government decision making.

4   TAXATION AND REGULATION

This section is concerned with the most characteristic government func-tion: taxation. Taxation stands for forced transfers, implying the use of coercion. Regulation can be seen as a form of taxation, because, through the constraints that it imposes, it enforces a change in the utility or profits of the regulated ('taxation by regulation'). Classical authors like Thomas Hobbes and Adam Smith had already pointed at the emotional dimension of taxation. According to Hobbes (1651 [1973], p. 53): 'in all places, men that are grieved with payments to the Publique, discharge their anger upon the Publicans, that is to say, Farmers, Collectors, and other Officers of the publique Revenue'. Adam Smith, in his maxims with regard to taxation, even explicitly referred to the excess burden of the 'vexation' caused by tax-ation: 'though vexation is not, strictly speaking, expense, it is certainly equivalent to the expense at which every man would be willing to redeem himself from it' (Smith, 1776 [1971], Book V).

Smith's observation brings me to a novel issue concerning government policies: 'emotional hazard' (Bosman and van Winden, 2002). Emotional hazard refers to welfare losses (excess burdens) due to emotional responses to the decisions of policy makers.[4] I shall illustrate this below with experimental evidence from a decision situation capturing some fundamental aspects of taxation: the power-to-take game. Taxation involves the appropriation of resources. As argued by Hobbes and Smith, psychologically this induces the emotion of anger on the side of the taxpayer, characterized by an action tendency of aggression, which may lead to welfare losses. Manifestations of anger by taxpayers include the well-known phenomena of the destruction of crops by farmers and road blockades by truckers. Tax revolts, with a strong emotional component, are historically a steady companion of taxation. Dramatic cases in point are the levy by the Duke of Alva which sparked the 80-year war between the Dutch and the Spanish, the tax-induced American revolution against England, and (albeit less dramatic) the more recent revolt in the UK against the poll tax that contributed to the fall of prime minister Margaret Thatcher. Welfare losses related to emotional responses to taxation may show up directly – as in the case of the destruction of crops – but also indirectly. The latter happens when the frustration caused by taxation leads to an emotional response to reduce effort (labor supply) which is to be distinguished from the (reasoned) price-distortion-induced substitution effect acknowledged in tax theory. Note, furthermore, that these behavioral responses make lump-sum taxation no longer a guaranteed efficient tax instrument, one of the main tenets of the theory of optimal taxation.

In addition to anger, taxation may also evoke the emotions of shame and guilt, both in the taxpayer and the levier of the tax (the taxman), with an action tendency to make up for one's misbehavior (if this is perceived to be possible). These emotions are triggered if a (social) norm is violated. This may happen to the taxpayer in the case of tax evasion and to the taxman if taxpayers react angrily to a tax. It follows that if shame and guilt are underdeveloped in those involved or if norms related to taxation or tax evasion are weak (or insufficiently internalized) these emotions cannot bite. In those circumstances, less inhibition of tax evasion and excessive (grabbing hand) taxation can be expected.[5]

Note that in making their decisions people may anticipate their emotions. In the case of anticipated emotions like anger and shame, with a negative hedonic value, an additional cost will be perceived, which makes the activity concerned less likely. For example, concerning tax evasion, Erard and Feinstein (1994) incorporate the anticipated moral sentiments of guilt and shame directly into the utility function, hypothesizing that a taxpayer will feel guilty when s/he underreports and escapes detection and will feel ashamed when s/he underreports and gets caught. Their results indicate that accounting for moral sentiments helps explain compliance behavior.

4.1   Evidence from Power-to-take Experiments

I shall now illustrate the importance of anger and shame (guilt) in situations resembling taxation with evidence from experimental studies of the
power-to-take game (introduced by Bosman and van Winden, 2002). The
(basic) power-to-take game is a one-shot, two-person, two-stage game, in
which a proposer and a responder are randomly and anonymously
matched. Both the proposer and the responder are endowed with an equal
amount of money or income. At the first stage of the game, the proposer
can make a proposal of how to divide the responder's [!] income. Then, at
the second stage, the only action the responder can take is to destroy own
income and s/he can do this in any proportion, ranging from 0 to 1. More
formally, let the proposal of the proposer at the first stage of the game be
indicated by the *take rate* $t \in [0,1]$, which is the part of the responder's
income E_{resp} that will be transferred to the proposer after the second stage.
At the second stage, the responder decides on the *destruction rate* $d \in [0,1]$,
the part of E_{resp} that will be destroyed. For the proposer the payoff of the
game thus equals the transfer $t(1-d)E_{resp}$, generating a total earnings of:
$E_{prop} + t(1-d)E_{resp}$ (where E_{prop} denotes the proposer's income at the start of
the game). For the responder, the payoff equals $(1-t)(1-d)E_{resp}$, which also
determines this player's total earnings. Note that the initial income of both
the proposer (E_{prop}) and the responder (E_{resp}) is exactly the same ($E_{prop} =
E_{resp}$) and leaves no doubt about property rights.

The following behavior is typically observed.[6] The mean as well as the
median take rate of the proposer is about 60 percent (which amounts to a
claim of 80 percent on total income). Responders destroy about 8 percent
of their income when the proposer's claim is below 60 percent, whereas
58 percent is destroyed if the claim exceeds 80 percent. Furthermore, in
several experiments concerning this game, emotional arousal was measured
using self-reports and skin-conductance measures.[7] A consistent and
robust observation is that destruction of income is significantly related to
the experience of anger-like emotions (anger, irritation, contempt), as illustrated by Figure 3.1.[8] This relationship bears out the emotional hazard
involved in taking. Moreover, it turns out that responders' destruction and
anger are particularly related to being negatively surprised (the gap
between take rate and expected take rate) and *not* to the perceived unfairness of the take rate; see Figure 3.2.[9] The figure shows that people who did
not destroy were typically 'pessimists', that is, they expected a higher take
rate than the one they were confronted with, while 'optimists' (who
expected a lower take rate) typically destroyed their income.

Whereas anger plays a significant role in the responder's retaliation decision, shame appears to be important in the proposer's (taker's) decision to

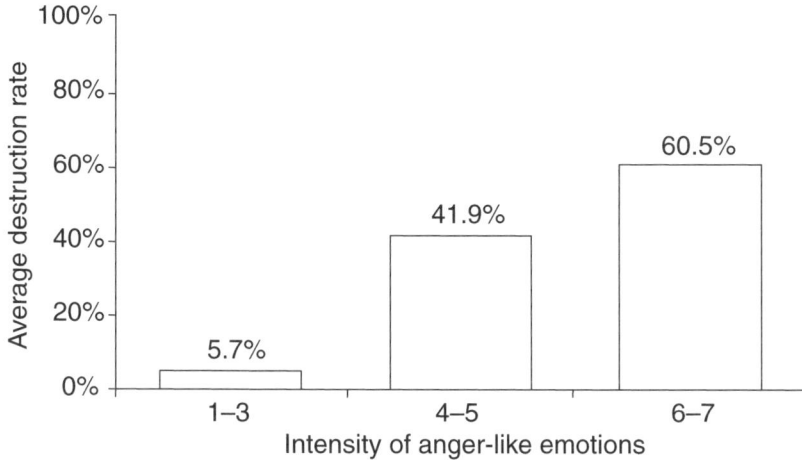

Figure 3.1   Anger and destruction

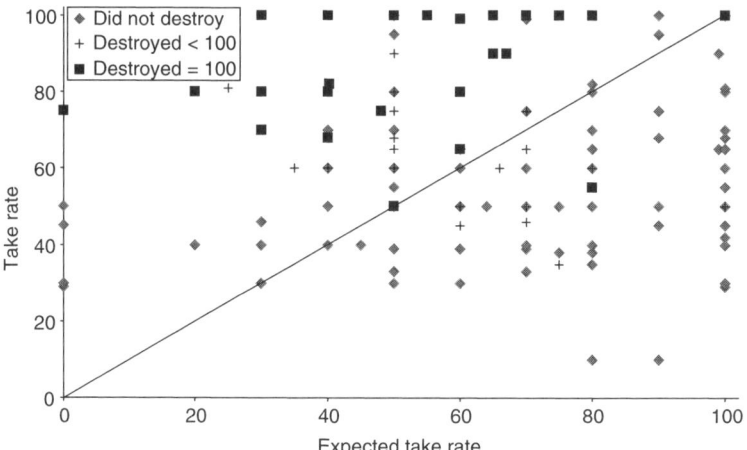

Figure 3.2   Destruction: optimists versus pessimists (similar results for anger)

choose a lower take rate. Its role is linked to the take rate that the proposer perceives as fair. The following results come from a repeated power-to-take game, where participants had to play the game twice (Reuben and van Winden, 2005). Proposers who lowered their take rate in the second game (against a new randomly chosen responder) were in particular those who experienced a high intensity of shame at the end of the first game. Moreover, the experience of shame was particularly strong if the chosen take rate

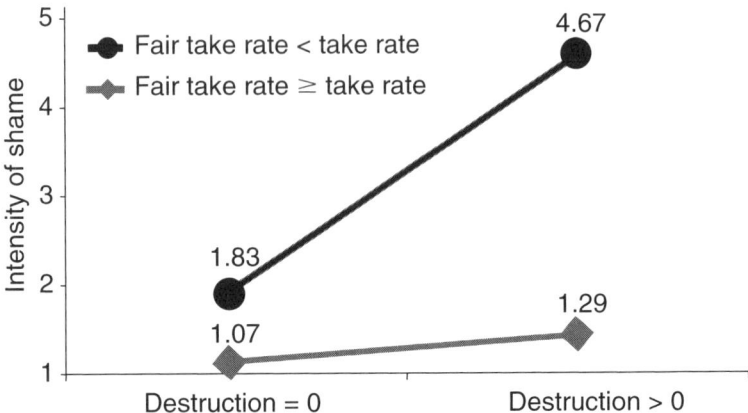

Figure 3.3   Fairness, retaliation and shame

exceeded the perceived fair take rate *and* destruction was observed.[10] Figure 3.3 illustrates.

For taxation these findings suggest, on the one hand, that (the threat of) retaliation by angry taxpayers functions as a means to enforce norms regarding taxation, and on the other, the anticipation of shame or guilt can motivate taxmen to restrain themselves, that is, to comply to an existing norm (see also Hopfensitz and Reuben, 2005).

5   EXPENDITURE

In this section I shall discuss three issues related to government expenditure. The first issue deals with an asymmetry in the emotional responses to taxation and expenditure, the second concerns entitlements, and the third relates to moral hazard.

5.1   Good versus Bad

Whereas taxation – the coerced transfer of resources – in itself is likely to generate negative affect, the benefits that taxpayers derive from government expenditure may induce positive affect (like joy or gratitude). Although for a formal economist expenditure may be like negative taxation, from an affective point of view this symmetry does not hold. Positive emotions are different from negative emotions.[11] Different brain systems appear to be involved. Whereas negative emotions stimulate attention and focusing, positive emotions are more associated with exploring, experimenting and creative problem solving. Also, people's perception, thoughts, memories and judgement tend to be biased toward greater negativity (positivity) in case of a negative (positive) mood, an effect known as mood congruency. Moreover, whereas at low levels of activation positive stimuli appear to have a greater impact, a negativity bias shows up at higher emotional intensity levels (Cacioppo et al., 2004; see also Offerman, 2002). One potentially important consequence of this asymmetry is that it can help explain why incumbents are hurt more by deteriorating economic conditions than they are helped by improving economic conditions, as observed in election studies (see, for example, Bloom and Price, 1975; Kiewiet and Rivers, 1984; Ansolabehere et al., 1999).

5.2 Entitlements

Granted that adverse conditions, for which politicians are held responsible, affect voting by triggering negative emotions (like anger or revenge), this mechanism can be exploited proactively by incumbents in the following way (Romer, 1996). Promises play an important role in politics, for instance, in the form of entitlements. An entitlement can be defined as a transfer bundled with an explicit, credible promise (commitment) from the government about the duration and level. If created for a sufficiently large number of voters, it may significantly shape the subsequent political dynamics. The reason is that if a successor reduces the transfer under the entitlement program, this will induce anger and thereby an action tendency in voters that are hurt to take revenge (retaliate) by voting for the opposition. The standard economic model does not allow for such a distinction between transfers and entitlements. Romer argues that creating a strong sense of entitlement played an important role in the development of the US social security program and the rhetoric in which it was clad, particularly the emphasis on pension *insurance* and payroll *contributions* (instead of welfare benefits and income tax). Voters strongly believed that they had earned their benefits as a matter of right, and showed a tendency to react furiously when these perceived rights were encroached upon (as under the Reagan administration). Franklin Delano Roosevelt seems to have anticipated this correctly. 'We put those payroll contributions there so as to give the contributors a legal, moral, and political right to collect their pensions . . . With those taxes in there, no damn politician can ever scrap my social security program' (ibid., p. 198). Similar reactions by voters have been observed in other countries where this type of state pension system has been implemented.[12] This mechanism whereby preferences are influenced by affective states has two important political economic consequences: on the one hand, it can generate an emotional hazard (potential social welfare losses due to emotional responses) that politicians may want to take into account; on the other, it offers politicians an instrument to change the future political landscape by influencing the values (concerns/interests) of voters, reckoning on the affective responses that this will generate in the future. Note that 'preferences' may still be stable at a higher mental level, due to the non-random way in which emotions are triggered and influence behavior. Furthermore, it is noted that emotions can also work as a commitment technology on the side of the policy makers themselves. For example, the anticipation of guilt or shame may guarantee threats and promises (see Hirshleifer, 1987; Frank, 1988).

5.3   Moral Hazard

Moral hazard refers to the fact that people may change their risk attitude once they are insured (for example, by becoming less careful). Not surprisingly, it is an important concept in insurance theory. Several major public expenditure categories are vulnerable to moral hazard. Think of health care and social insurance (unemployment, disability), for example. In *The Theory of Moral Sentiments*, Smith claimed that feelings are the source of morality. In a neglected part of *A Theory of Justice*, a similar position was taken by the philosopher Rawls (1983) arguing that moral sentiments are crucial for the viability of justice principles. A recent survey of psychological (including neurological) studies concludes that moral action covaries with moral emotion more than with moral reasoning (Haidt, 2001). From this perspective, moral hazard, with its concomitant chance of welfare losses, may be a special case of emotional hazard. In this case, however, it would be a lack of emotional responding – insufficient inhibition by moral emotions (guilt and shame) – causing the change in risk attitude. This is another instance where the political economic importance of values (here, internalized norms) shows up, due to the functioning of emotions.

6   COLLECTIVE ACTION

Why would an individual bother to participate in collective action – like voting in large-scale elections or mass demonstrations with serious risks – if the chance of being decisive is negligible? For *homo economicus* the relevant cost–benefit calculus, based on expected utility theory, is typically predicted to show a negative outcome (Olson, 1965; Mueller, 2003). Prospect theory (Kahneman and Tversky, 1979) offers some help by allowing small probabilities to be overestimated and by assuming that people become risk seeking in bad times (the loss domain). Other instances of bounded rationality, like voters taking their own single vote as diagnostic for millions of votes (Quattrone and Tversky, 1988) may also explain part of this puzzle. Here, however, I want to focus on affect as a neglected driving factor.

Whereas Alexis de Tocqueville and Joseph Schumpeter already pointed to the role played by emotions in political behavior (see the quotes in Mueller, 2003, pp. 303–4), more recently several theoretical and empirical studies have appeared concerning the significance of emotions for collective action. For example, Romer (1996) and Glazer (1998) present formal analyses of how voting behavior can be influenced through the anger and frustration of potential voters concerning broken promises and relative status, respectively. Javeline (2003) argues that how people understand causal relationships and attribute blame for a grievance plays a crucial role in their decision to redress the grievance through protest (see also Chong, 1991). Interestingly, according to Raghunathan and Pham (1999), angry people show higher assessments of blameworthiness and lower assessment of risk, in contrast with fearful people who demonstrate the reverse. Krueger and Malečková (2003) – who find little evidence of a connection between education, poverty, and terrorism – write: 'We suspect their primary motivation results from their passionate support for their movement. Eradication of poverty and universal secondary education are unlikely to change these feelings. Indeed, those who are well-off and well-educated may even perceive such feelings more acutely' (p. 123). Marcus and MacKuen (1993) demonstrate that anxiety (fear) and enthusiasm play an influential role during campaigns. Anxiety stimulates attention, moves people to learn policy-related information about candidates, and discourages reliance on habitual cues for voting, while enthusiasm stimulates interest and involvement without much deliberation in campaigns (see also Marcus, 2000). Abelson et al. (1982) find that affect scores of presidential candidates are highly predictive of political preferences (see also Rahn et al., 1990). A related, and longstanding issue, concerns the importance of emotional arousal in persuasion, providing emotionally intelligent politicians the opportunity to affect opinions and thereby the chances of their policies and their political position (see Glaser and Salovey, 1998). One way in which affect influences beliefs is via mood-congruent biases: we are more likely to notice, encode, remember and make use of information that is congruent with a prevailing mood (Frijda et al., 2000).

When emotions are allowed for in the analysis, collective action becomes easier to explain. As discussed in Section 3, emotions have some direct hedonic value and can be difficult to control. Regarding the former, suppose on election day one feels angry about the government. In that case, turning out to vote gives the opportunity to do something about one's negative emotional state, which may be worth the cost of voting. Moreover, the greater the emotionality the more likely it becomes that one just acts without thinking (emotional hijacking). The anticipation of emotions, like the feeling of guilt or shame if one does not live up to a social expectation or one's identity (Akerlof and Kranton, 2000), may have a similar effect. In a sense, it requires the traditional (monetary) cost–benefit calculus to include affective costs and benefits. For our understanding of how collective action comes about, another important affective mechanism concerns 'emotional contagion', defined as: the tendency to automatically mimic and synchronize expressions, vocalizations, postures and movements with those of another person's and, consequently, to converge emotionally (Hatfield et al., 1993). This mechanism can explain 'ripple effects' in social groups (Barsade, 2002).

An interesting issue in this context is whether people with social ties behave differently from people who are strangers to each other. Are the former better able to overcome the free-rider problem of collective action, because of the influence of affect? To investigate this issue, Reuben and van Winden (2004) ran a three-player power-to-take game experiment, with two responders instead of one randomly matched to (again) a single proposer. Note that in this situation punishment through the destruction of income is like a public good for responders, which may induce free riding and thereby too little destruction (from the responders' perspective). In one of the experimental treatments the responders were strangers to each other, whereas in another treatment they were friends. Emotions concerning the take rate selected by the proposer (which had to be identical for both responders) as well as regarding the destruction of income by the other responder were again measured with self-reports. The main finding is that friends destroy more and are better at coordinating their punishment. Interestingly, it turns out that the emotional response towards the other responder facilitates the coordination among friend-responders but not among stranger-responders. Whereas stranger-responders experience stronger negative emotions if they notice that they destroyed more that the other responder than when they destroyed less, emotions are similar for friend-responders in these cases. In addition, and in contrast to stranger-responders, friend-responders get a positive emotional boost if they succeed in coordinating on the same level of punishment. Because of these emotional mechanisms, the situation resembles a coordination game with punishment being the risk-dominant choice for friend-responders, whereas *no* punishment is the risk-dominant choice for stranger-responders. Thus, it appears that affective ties are important for overcoming the free-riding problem in norm enforcement.

7   CONCLUSION

In this chapter, I have argued that affect (emotion, mood, feeling, senti-ment) plays an important role in politics. I have illustrated this for some broad areas of relevance to public choice: taxation and regulation, govern-ment expenditure and collective action. Because of the space constraint, some other important topics had to be left out, like the role of affect in social welfare and justice (see van Winden, 2006). In his recent book *Politics and Passion*, Walzer (2004, p. 130) writes:

> No political party that sets itself against the established hierarchies of power and wealth, no movement for equality or national liberation, for emancipation or empowerment, will ever succeed unless it arouses the affiliative and combative passions of the people at the lower end of the hierarchies. The passions that it arouses are certain to include envy, resentment, and hatred . . . They are also the emotional demons of political life . . .

This last point about demons resonates in the expressions 'politics of hatred' and 'politics of fear', issues that political economists have recently begun to explore (Glaeser, 2005; Lupia and Menning, 2005).

The evidence presented in this chapter has an important methodological consequence for the theory of public choice. As argued by Buchanan and Tullock (see Section 2), the ultimate defense of the behavioral assumption maintained by public choice must be empirical. In my view, by now sufficient evidence exists to replace *homo economicus* by *homo sapiens*, a boundedly rational and emotional agent, in the private as well as the public sector. This also has implications for the foundation of democracy, for, to cite these pioneers of public choice once more: 'The assessment of the nature of man himself will, or should, determine the respective importance that is placed on institutional-constitutional restraint' (Buchanan and Tullock, 1962 [1974], p. 306).

Finally, I would like to point at some research and policy implications of affective public choice. First, emotional hazard, as defined and illus-trated in the previous sections, becomes a phenomenon to be reckoned with in analyses of policy making. Although more empirical research is needed before we can be more secure about its relevance, it is likely to affect some basic tenets in public economics, like the efficiency of lump-sum taxation, which is no longer guaranteed. Second, granted the significance of affect, the dynamics of emotions becomes an important issue. When do emotions arise and when do they cool off? Which factors determine their intensity? How does our emotional memory of political events work? What is the role played by psychological traits (like a fear or anger trait), habituation and behavioral contagion? Third, given that *homo sapiens* is boundedly rational and is typically confronted with scarce information in matters of politics, the significance of affect in communication requires more attention. How does persuasion work, and what is the role of the various media in this context? What amount and kind of information is optimal, and for whom? Clearly, much work remains to be done, but one conclusion seems safe: those who cannot stand the heat, that is, *homo sapiens* is emotional, should stay out of public choice!

NOTES

1. For example, the belief in an attractive afterlife may explain suicide bombing if the perceived chance of getting there is sufficiently high.
2. 'Affect' is a general term for emotions, moods, feelings, sentiments. Because I do not need a stricter definition in this chapter, I shall use the terms affect and emotion interchangeably.
3. This section borrows from van Winden (2001).
4. More generally, these effects may also be related to a lack of emotional responses (as in the case of the absence of shame or guilt; see Section 5). In principle, emotional responses can also lead to welfare gains (negative losses).
5. Moral hazard in insurance may be a form of emotional hazard, because the change in risk attitude once insured (for example, less careful behavior) can be due to a lack of moral sentiments (see Section 5).
6. See Bosman et al. (2005). The results are taken from the ('no-effort') case where income is not earned but simply given as an endowment.
7. See van Winden (2001); Bosman and van Winden (2002); Ben-Shakhar et al. (2004); Reuben and van Winden (2004, 2005); Bosman et al. (2005). According to Robinson and Clore (2002, p. 934): 'Self-report is the most common and potentially the best . . . way to measure a person's emotional experiences.'
8. Based on data from the experiment of Reuben and van Winden (2004).
9. See Reuben and van Winden (2004). In Reuben and van Winden (2004, 2005) proposers and responders were asked at the end of the experiment what they considered to be the fair take rate.
10. Similar results are obtained for guilt. Proposers who increased their take rate typically did so after facing no destruction and the experience of regret.
11. See, for example, Leith and Baumeister (1996); Ashby et al. (1999); Raghunathan and Pham (1999); Cacioppo et al. (2004).
12. There is substantial evidence showing that people are prepared to make costs to punish those who violate their concerns, even if they cannot profit from an induced change in the behavior of the punished (see, for example, Fehr and Gächter, 2000, 2002).

REFERENCES

Abelson, R.P., D.R. Kinder, M. Peters and S.T. Fiske (1982), 'Affective and semantic components in political person perception', *Journal of Personality and Social Psychology*, **42**, 619–30.

Akerlof, G.A. and R.E. Kranton (2000), 'Economics and identity', *Quarterly Journal of Economics*, **65**, 715–53.

Ansolabehere, S.D., S. Iyengar and A. Simon (1999), 'Replicating experiments using surveys and aggregate data: the case of negative advertising', *American Political Science Review*, **93**, 901–9.

Ashby, F.G., A.M. Isen and U. Turken (1999), 'A neuropsychological theory of positive affect and its influence on cognition', *Psychological Review*, **106**, 529–50.

Ashraf, N., C.F. Camerer and G. Loewenstein (2005), 'Adam Smith, behavioral economist', *Journal of Economic Perspectives*, **19**, 131–45.

Barsade, S. (2002), 'The ripple effect: emotional contagion and its influence on group behaviour', *Administrative Science Quarterly*, **47**, 644–75.

Ben-Shakhar, G., G. Bornstein, A. Hopfensitz and F. van Winden (2004), 'Reciprocity and emotions in bargaining: using physiological and self-report measures', *Journal of Economic Psychology* (forthcoming).

Bloom, H.S. and H.D. Price (1975), 'Voter response to short-run economic conditions: the asymmetric effect of prosperity and recession', *American Political Science Review*, **69**, 1240–55.

Bosman, R., M. Sutter and F. van Winden (2005), 'The impact of real effort and emotions in the power-to-take game', *Journal of Economic Psychology*, **26**, 407–29.

Bosman, R. and F. van Winden (2002), 'Emotional hazard in a power-to-take experiment', *Economic Journal*, **112**, 147–69.

Buchanan, J.M. and G. Tullock (1962 [1974]), *The Calculus of Consent*, University of Michigan Press, Ann Arbor, MT.

Cacioppo, J.T., J.T. Larsen, N.K. Smith and G.G. Berntson (2004), 'The affect system', in A.S.R. Manstead, N. Frijda and A. Fischer (eds), *Feelings and Emotions*, Cambridge University Press, Cambridge, 223–42.

Chong, D. (1991), *Collective Action and the Civil Rights Movement*, University of Chicago Press, Chicago.

Downs, A. (1957), *An Economic Theory of Democracy*, Harper & Row, New York.

Elwes, R.H.M. (1951), *Benedict de Spinoza: A Theologico-Political Treatise* and *A Political Treatise* (translated from the Latin), Dover, New York.

Erard, B. and J.S. Feinstein (1994), 'The role of moral sentiments and audit perceptions in tax compliance', *Public Finance/Finances Publiques*, **49** (Supplement), 70–89.

Fehr, E. and S. Gächter (2000), 'Fairness and retaliation: the economics of reciprocity', *Journal of Economic Perspectives*, **14**, 159–81.

Fehr, E. and S. Gächter (2002), 'Altruistic punishment in humans', *Nature*, **415**, 137–40.

Frank, R.H. (1988), *Passions within Reason*, Norton, New York.

Frijda, N.H. (1986), *The Emotions*, Cambridge University Press, Cambridge.

Frijda, N.H., A.S.R. Manstead and S. Ben (2000), *Emotions and Beliefs*, Cambridge University Press, Cambridge.

Glaeser, E.L. (2005), 'The political economy of hatred', *Quarterly Journal of Economics*, **120**, 45–86.

Glaser, J. and P. Salovey (1998), 'Affect in electoral politics', *Personality and Social Psychology Review*, **2**, 156–72.

Glazer, A. (1998), 'Political equilibrium under group identification', in B. Grofman (ed.), *Information, Participation, and Choice*, University of Michigan Press, Ann Arbor, pp. 81–92.

Goleman, D. (1996), *Emotional Intelligence*, Bantam, New York.

Haidt, J. (2001), 'The emotional dog and its rational tail', *Psychological Review*, **108**, 814–34.

Hatfield, E., J.T. Cacioppo and R.L. Rapson (1993), 'Emotional contagion', *Current Directions in Psychological Science*, **2**, 96–9.

Hirshleifer, J. (1987), 'On the emotions as guarantors of threats and promises', in J. Dupré (ed.), *Latest on the Best: Essays on Evolution and Optimality*, MIT Press, Cambridge, MA, pp. 307–26.

Hobbes, T. (1651 [1973]), *Leviathan*, Dent, London.

Hopfensitz, A. and E. Reuben (2005), 'The importance of emotions for the effectiveness of social punishment', CREED working paper, Centre for Research in Experimental Economics and Political Decision Making, University of Amsterdam.

Javeline, D. (2003), 'The role of blame in collective action: evidence from Russia', *American Political Science Review*, **97**, 107–21.

Kahneman, D. and A. Tversky (1979), 'Prospect theory: an analysis of decision under risk', *Econometrica*, **47**, 263–91.

Kiewiet, D. and D. Rivers (1984), 'A retrospective on retrospective voting', *Political Behavior*, **6**, 369–99.

Krueger, A.B. and J. Malečková (2003), 'Education, poverty, and terrorism: is there a causal connection?', *Journal of Economic Perspectives*, **17**, 119–44.

Leith, K.P. and R.F. Baumeister (1996), 'Why do bad moods increase self-defeating behavior?', *Journal of Personality and Social Psychology*, **71**, 1250–67.

Lupia, A. and J.O. Menning (2005), 'When can politicians scare citizens into supporting bad policies? Emotions and strategies in an equilibrium of fear', mimeo, University of Michigan.

Marcus, G.E. (2000), 'Emotions in politics', *Annual Review of Political Science*, **3**, 221–50.

Marcus, G.E. and M.B. MacKuen (1993), 'Anxiety, enthusiasm, and the vote: the emotional underpinnings of learning and involvement during presidential campaigns', *American Political Science Review*, **87**, 672–85.

Mueller, D.C. (2003), *Public Choice III*, Cambridge University Press, Cambridge.

Oatley, K. and J.M. Jenkins (1996), *Understanding Emotions*, Blackwell, Oxford.

Offerman, T. (2002), 'Hurting hurts more than helping helps', *European Economic Review*, **46**, 1423–37.

Olson, M. (1965), *The Logic of Collective Action*, Harvard University Press, Cambridge, MA.

Ortony, A., G.L. Clore and A. Collins (1988), *The Cognitive Structure of Emotions*, Cambridge University Press, Cambridge.

Quattrone, G.A. and A. Tversky (1988), 'Contrasting rational and psychological analyses of political choice', *American Political Science Review*, **82**, 719–36.

Raghunathan, R. and M.T. Pham (1999), 'All negative moods are not equal', *Organizational Behavior and Human Decision Processes*, **79**, 56–77.

Rahn, W.M., J.H. Aldrich, E. Borgida and J.L. Sullivan (1990), 'A social-cognitive model of candidate appraisal', in J.A. Ferejohn and J.H. Kuklinski (eds), *Information and Democratic Processes*, University of Illinois Press, Urbana, IL, pp. 136–59.

Rawls, J. (1983), *A Theory of Justice*, Oxford University Press, Oxford.

Reuben, E. and F. van Winden (2004), 'Reciprocity and emotions when reciprocators know each other', CREED working paper, Center for Research in

Experimental Economics and Political Decision Making, University of Amsterdam.

Reuben, E. and F. van Winden (2005), 'Negative reciprocity and the interaction of emotions and fairness norms', CREED working paper, Center for Research in Experimental Economics and Political Decision Making, University of Amsterdam.

Robinson, M. and G. Clore (2002), 'Belief and feeling: evidence for an accessibility model of emotional self-report', *Psychological Bulletin*, **128**, 934–60.

Romer, P. (1996), 'Preferences, promises, and the politics of entitlement', in V. Fuchs (ed.), *Individual Social Responsibility*, University of Chicago Press, Chicago, pp. 195–220.

Schumpeter, J.A. (1972), *History of Economic Analysis*, Allen & Unwin, London.

Smith, A. (1759/1790 [1982]), *The Theory of Moral Sentiments*, Liberty Fund, Indianapolis, IN.

Smith, A. (1776 [1971]), *The Wealth of Nations*, Dent, London.

Smith, V.L. (1998), 'The two faces of Adam Smith', *Southern Economic Journal*, **65**, 1–19.

van Winden, F. (2001), 'Emotional hazard exemplified by taxation-induced anger', *Kyklos*, **54**, 491–506.

van Winden, F. (2006), 'Affect and fairness in economics', *Social Justice Research*, **54**, (2–3), 491–506.

Walzer, M. (2004), *Politics and Passion*, Yale University Press, New Haven, CT.

4. Bentham on public choice: utility, interests and the agency problem in democracy

Pedro Schwartz

1 INTRODUCTION

May I be allowed the slight anachronism in the title? The expression 'public choice' had not been coined in the 1820s and early 1830s, when Jeremy Bentham (1748–1832) wrote extensively on constitutions. However, he did apply the analytical method of what we today would call public choice to discuss the proper arrangement of representative democracy, especially as concerns rent seeking, colonies and political economy, bureaucracy, the organization of legislatures, and the 'supreme operative' of a state.

The positive theory of utilitarianism lends itself easily to the study of the actual behaviour of politicians, bureaucrats and citizens in a representative democracy for it posits that individuals are governed by self-interest in all walks of life. But Bentham was not content to determine how and why humans act. He also wanted to say how they should act. However, basing the rules of moral and civic conduct on utility is more difficult than factually discovering the consequences of human self-interest in politics. In Section 2 I shall discuss the shortcomings of utilitarianism as an ethical theory despite its usefulness as an explanation of social behaviour.

In Section 3 I shall address what Bentham had to say on the agency problem in some of his writings on constitutional matters. Especially interesting was a book he published in 1830, the *Constitutional Code, Volume I*, the complete text of a 'Fundamental Law for any nation on Earth', where he set down elaborate precautions against misrule, corruption and overspending. It is at this point that I shall propose that we grant Bentham the honorary paternity of the discipline of public choice – if only for having coined the expression 'sinister interests' to denote pressure groups.

Section 4 may be bleaker. From the *Constitutional Code* and other texts written in the last 10 years of his life one may cull a detailed picture of the kind of commonwealth Bentham wished to see universally established.

Two elements of his political philosophy played a crucial role in his proposals: the concept of law as command backed by punishment, and the representation of society as continuously immersed in conflicts of interest, to be adjudged by mere head-count so as to see which group summed the greatest happiness. The result was a glasshouse democracy that could easily and inadvertently deteriorate into a stifling form of democratic despotism.

2   UTILITARIAN ETHICS

'Nature has placed mankind under the governance of two sovereign masters, *pain* and *pleasure*. It is for them alone . . . to determine what we shall do', said Bentham when defining the principle of utility in one of his earliest works, *An Introduction to the Principles of Morals and Legislation*. He was thus proposing a theory of actual human behaviour, applicable not only to economics but also to sexual conduct, crime and punishment, public administration and politics. But Bentham was much more ambitious than this. When quoting the above passage a few crucial words were left out: 'Nature has placed mankind under the governance of two sovereign masters, *pain* and *pleasure*. It is for them alone to point out what we ought to do, as well as to determine what we shall do'.[1] 'Ought to do': he was after a science of morals.[2]

Now, building a political philosophy on the principle of utility is not as straightforward as analysing and predicting actual group behaviour. Why should men and women suspend their personal search for pleasure, or avoidance of pain, to 'augment the happiness of the community' (Bentham, 1789 [1970], ch. 1, §7, p. 13) What is the community to them if they see a chance to profit at the expense of their fellows? How could one explain feelings of sympathy for fellow human beings so evident in public-spirited utilitarians? Bentham himself, after all, spent his life writing on political philosophy and devising efficient social arrangements, despite repeated disappointments, lack of recognition and pecuniary losses. The utilitarian usually answers these uncomfortable questions by an appeal to enlightened long-term self-interest. But in this case, why should there be any need to guard against people in power overlooking 'the greatest happiness of the greatest number' and shamelessly or surreptitiously seeking rents? Why and when are people unenlightened?

2.1   J.S. Mill and Happiness

After his mental breakdown, the young John Stuart Mill (1806–23) came to doubt that utilitarian morality and regard for the well-being of humankind were a natural derivation of the search for individual happiness that Nature had planted in the breast of man. 'It was the autumn of 1826', Mill recalled in his *Autobiography*. He was in a dull state of nerves, a mood when everything seems insipid or indifferent, when he directly asked himself:

> 'Suppose that all your objects in life were realised: that all the changes in institutions and opinions which you are looking forwards to, could be completely effected at this very instant: would this be a great joy and happiness to you?' And an irrepressible self-consciousness directly answered, 'No!' At this my heart sank within me: the whole foundation on which my life was constructed fell down . . . I seemed to have nothing left to live for. (Mill, 1873 [1981], p. 139)

Paradoxically, a conception of man as a seeker of pleasure had been transformed by Bentham into the foundation stone of what Mill would later call 'the religion of Humanity': individual utilitarians must have as an aim in life the reform of society for the happiness of others, not be on the look-out for personal satisfaction. A creed almost hedonistic in its principles had been changed into a severely altruistic calling.

> I was thus left stranded at the commencement of my voyage, with a well equipped ship and rudder, but no sail; without any real desire for the ends which I had been so carefully fitted out to work for: no delight in virtue or the general good. (Ibid., p. 143)

No doubt there were personal causes for the mental breakdown of the 20-year old Mill, among which the hard labour of his edition of Bentham's five-volume *Rationale of Judicial Evidence* (1827). But there was also a philosophical flaw in his upbringing: his father had not attempted to help him educate his feelings and tastes, and his mother seemed not to have been up to the task of the *éducation sentimentale* or any kind of education of her offspring. As he recalls in his *Autobiography*, 'the description so often given of a Benthamite, as a mere reasoning machine . . . was during two or three years of my life not altogether untrue of me' (1873 [1981], p. 111). Critics of the sect denounced 'utility . . . as cold calculation; political economy as hard-hearted; anti-population doctrines as repulsive to the natural dealings of mankind'. Emotions and feelings, which are part of human nature and play a central role in group preservation during the course of natural selection, were disregarded by utilitarians as mere 'sentimentality' (ibid., pp. 111–13). Bentham even said that 'pushpin is as good as poetry'!

So Mill embarked on life with no ideal of personal relationships, no inkling that one has to plan for them and work constantly to bring them to fruition. His remedy for such barrenness was to turn romantic and to overvalue eccentricity to the point of total tolerance.[3] Thus were the seeds planted of the strange death of classical liberalism in the twentieth century.

2.2 Three Fallacies in Bentham's Utilitarianism

Bentham passed from 'is' to 'ought' in a far from imperceptible manner:[4] he jumped from analysing political life on the assumption of individual self-interest, to demanding that politics be governed by the rule of 'the greatest happiness of the greatest number'. In doing so he committed a number of fallacies that have tainted utilitarian thought ever since.

The first one is a misapplication of a private notion to public action, the idea that happiness should be an aim of public policy – *pace* Bruno Frey. It is doubtful that happiness should even be a direct object of individual endeavour: Mill himself came out of his miserable state of dejection believing that happiness 'was only to be attained by not making it the direct end' of life. 'Those are happy . . . who have their minds fixed on some object other than their own happiness' (ibid., p. 145). Be that as it may, it is presumptuous to try to make people happy by collective action. The US Declaration of Independence speaks of the inalienable right of men to the *pursuit* of happiness, but not of a political right to happiness itself. The belief that humans can claim happiness from the state as of right is the seed of the welfare state and all its corruptions.

The second fallacy consists in the implication that society is all politics. I do not think I am being unfair when I say that Bentham seemed to have no notion of the spontaneous harmony of most social transactions. Bentham portrayed social life as a perpetual conflict of interests, to be adjudicated by authority with a calculation of 'the net amount of happiness', thus:

> the greatest happiness of the greatest number is the only right and proper end of government: of all, in so far as the happiness of all can be encreased without lessening the happiness of any: of the greatest number, in so far as the happiness of some can not be encreased unless by defalcation made from the happiness of others. (Bentham, 1822 [1989], p. 3)

I know that in his peculiar style of prose he is speaking here of public action, in principle leaving aside the sphere of individual action: the sovereign, however constituted, and the laws he made were always needed to impose artificial harmony on a fractious commonwealth. Also, there is no guarantee in his principle of 'the greatest good for the greatest number' that the personal sphere will not be invaded whenever some authority finds it convenient. As we shall see, Bentham understood political economy as the science of administration and presented liberty as merely a subordinate

means to obtain some of the conditions for social happiness. Indeed John
Mill had to graft liberty artificially in the tree of utilitarianism, where it
gave the shoots of hedonistic permissiveness.

The third fallacy is one of not understanding the character and role of
morality in social life. A society with a policeman behind every citizen (and
behind every policeman) could not function. As H.L.A. Hart said in *The
Concept of Law* (1961), coercion must be applied only at the margin where
people are tempted to cheat, a different margin for differently law-abiding
people: but the greater part of social rules must be and will be obeyed spontaneously and willingly. One must distinguish different kinds of human
action framed by three kinds of rules:

1. One kind of action is that of personal intercourse with people one
   knows within one's immediate circle where the rules of personal morality obtain – the world analysed by Adam Smith in *The Theory of Moral
   Sentiments* (1759). Smith's opening words are famous:

   > How selfish soever man may be supposed, there are evidently some princi-
   > ples in his nature, which interest him in the fortune of others, and render
   > their happiness necessary to him, though he derives nothing from it but the
   > pleasure of seeing it.[5]

   These sentiments, which grow into personal morality, conscience and
   a measure of altruism are seen today as the genetically inherited incli-
   nations of man within his family and tribe.[6] If it were not for these sentiments one could not understand why a man should die for Queen and
   Country. Bentham contradicted Smith's view that sympathy was due to
   something different from *personal* self-interest:

   > In self-regard even sympathy has its root: and if in the general tenour of
   > human conduct, self-regard were not prevalent over sympathy – even over
   > sympathy of all others put together – no such species as the human could
   > have existence.[7]

   Smith had gone out of his way to deny that sympathy had its root in
   selfishness. Implicitly rejecting Bernard Mandeville, he wrote:

   > Those who are fond of deducing all our sentiments from certain
   > refinements fo sle-love, think themselves at no loss to account [for feelings
   > of spontaneous sympathy]. Man, say they, conscious of his own weakness,
   > and of the need he has for the assistance of others, rejoices whenever he
   > observes that they adopt his own passions, because he is then assured of
   > that assistance; and grieves whenever he observes the contrary, because he
   > is then assured of their opposition. But both the pleasure and the pain [in
   > feelings of sympathy] are always felt so instantaneously, and often upon

such frivolous occasions, that it seems evident that neither can be derived from any such self-interested consideration.[8]

2. Human action takes another shape in the spontaneous order of the market, where pure self-interest, given 'the stability of possession, its transference by consent, and the performance of promises',[9] permits the division of labour with strangers (Seabright, 2004, part I; see also Vernon Smith, 1998); this is the world of Adam Smith's *The Wealth of Nations* (1776 [1976]), a world where competition controls the X-inefficiency of bureaucratic institutions (Leibenstein, 1966).

3. Most visible in Bentham's philosophy is political action, but he conceived it wrongly as enforced harmony in search of the greatest happiness for the greatest number, imposed on perpetually conflicting interests. If, more realistically, one admits both the need for a modicum of collective action and the insuperable personal differences among individuals, then a constitutional arrangement is called for quite at variance with Bentham's: a unanimous agreement on the rules of the game and free political competition in everyday matters – just as all teams agree on the rules of football before knowing who is the likely winner (Buchanan and Tullock, 1962). Such a constitutional agreement can be explicit in a written fundamental law or can be the result of customary evolution; and even in the case of a written constitution much will be customary and implied, as Hayek explained in his 'Epilogue' to *Law, Legislation and Liberty* (1973–79).

These three fallacies would mark the measures he proposed to correct the agency problem in a democracy, the main foe he wanted to confront when proposing new constitutional arrangements to the countries of the world during the last 10 years of his life.

3 BENTHAM AND THE AGENCY PROBLEM

Bentham's contributions to what we now call 'public choice' are mainly to be found in the only volume of his *Constitutional Code* (1830) published in his lifetime.

The constitutional part of his thought gathered importance with the years. There was a time when Bentham wrote for enlightened despots. After a first flirtation with democratic opinions, when he prepared a book of rules for the French Assembly in 1792, the cruelty of the French Revolution made him a conservative for a time, and a defender of peaceful change for the rest of his life. At the turn of the century, under the effect of his disappointment with parliament for reneging on the agreement to build his *Panoptikon* prison and for balking at Scottish law reform, and under the influence of the arguments of his new friend James Mill, he became a radical democrat and never looked back. In 1810 he adapted that Book of Rules for the Spanish Cortes gathered in Cadiz. In 1811 he drafted the rudiments of a press law for General Miranda on his ill-fated expedition to liberate Venezuela. His studies for the political democratization of Britain he had started in 1809, culminating in his *Plan for Parliamentary Reform* published in 1820. When the Spanish *liberales* rose against Ferdinand in 1821, he published in Spain an attack on the idea of a House of Lords and another one on the prohibition of the importation of textiles. By the time absolutism was re-established in 1823 he had nearly finished a book titled *Rid Yourselves of Ultramaria*, in which he enjoined Spaniards to give up their colonies in America: it remained unpublished but contains many of the ideas for solving the agency problem that were to find a place in the *Constitutional Code*. He also had received a short-lived commission from the Spanish and Portuguese Cortes to write various legal codes for them. Then he turned to Tripoli and Greece, sending them large parts of what was to be his 1830 *opus*. On the way he left a number of manuscripts preparatory to writing the *Constitutional Code*.[10] Finally in 1830 volume 1 of the *Code* was published, edited by his amanuensis Richard Doane, and then republished by Bowring in 1843.

The *Constitutional Code* is an important work, though not many people read it: 13 copies were reported sold in 1830 and 1831 by Bentham's publisher;[11] and not many must have read it in the tiny script and two-columned pages of Bowring's edition. But the work is such a clear exposé of utilitarian democracy that it helps one understand real-life developments better. Great books have a way of working out the logical consequences of diffuse ideologies and helping to point out developments as yet unseen when they were written. His *Code* contains a working model of an economically built and closely controlled welfare state that may help us by contrast to understand why the real thing has turned so profligate and corrupting.

3.1   Reducing Expense and Harmonizing Contrary Political Interests

Before entering the *Code* itself it may repay us to give a quick glance to 'Economy as applied to office' and 'Identification of interests' (Bentham, 1822 [1989]). Both especially interesting as regards the second kind of rules ignored by Bentham due to what I have pointed out as his third fallacy above: his misunderstanding of the spontaneous workings of the competitive market.

Bentham was concerned with the tendency of societies, not least democratic societies, to spend excessively. Some years ago, Fred Rosen noted that 'his belief that the problem of expense is a major constitutional problem is probably unique in the history of democratic thought' (Rosen, 1983, p. 94). The problem of expense Bentham encased in a more general question of 'Securities for good government', the main object of 'Economy as applied to office'. A useful summary of what he had to say in 'Securities . . .' can be found in a manuscript list of 22 July 1822:

1. Minimizing the quantity of power in the hands of the functionaries.
2. Minimizing the quantity of the matter of wealth in the disposal of functionaries.
3. Minimizing the quantity of the matter of wealth employed as pay of functionaries.
4. Applying legal counterforces to the power of functionaries.
5. Applying moral counterforces to the power of functionaries.
6. Exclusion of factitious honor, or say factitious dignity.
7. Exclusion of other factitious instruments of delusive influence. (Schofield, 1989, p. xxxiii)

This indicates how Bentham wanted the powers of the non-sovereign part of the commonwealth to be controlled. The sovereign people itself and the Chamber where its representatives sat must, however, have total power and undivided sovereignty.

By 'identification of interests' Bentham meant not identifying what the interests of the different functionaries were but how to make the interests of the executive identical with that embodied in parliament, and the interest of rulers identical with that of the ruled – a problem he would fully address in the *Code*. He also noted the lack of appropriate attitude on the part of the people to invigilate its representatives and the functionaries, as he called them. He proposed that ordinary voters should solve it by taking advice of qualified critics. 'Aptitude through advice is within the reach of the least instructed: no one but has time for taking the opinion of one whom general estimation points out as the best qualified for giving such advice of all who are within his reach' (Bentham, 1989, § 11, p. 144). This is a part of the wider problem of what we today call 'rational voter ignorance' and Bentham's proposed solution was not up to the task.

3.2 The Institutions of the *Constitutional Code*

It is time to describe Bentham's main contribution to 'public choice' theory and policy, to wit, the agency problem, and the remedies he proposed for it. To that end, I shall summarize the main features of Bentham's commonwealth as explained in endless detail in the *Constitutional Code, Volume I*.

The overall end of political action and institutions, it may be surmised, was to obtain the greatest sum of happiness in the country concerned. This aim was attained by pursuing four subordinate aims, which were, in order of decreasing importance: security, subsistence, abundance and equality. Note that liberty, economic or personal, was not among them, for, in the opinion of Bentham, the goods for which liberty was normally desired were precisely the four mentioned. These four could be attained directly. Security, by guaranteeing the individual the enjoyment of his life and property, allowed him to do as he wished within his own sphere. Without a minimum of subsistence, Bentham alleged, there could be no happiness; hence, the state should guarantee it, but without loosening the springs of activity which brought about abundance. Equality could conflict with security, when ill-distributed private property had to be reformed or taxed to foster this fourth subordinate aim. However, security was to prevail over equality, save in the most extreme cases. Liberty was thus redundant as a goal.

The utilitarian commonwealth was to be a republic, though some of the institutions proposed by Bentham, especially those giving security against misrule, or guaranteeing an economical management of the public administration, could be applicable in a monarchy. Bentham in his later years was as adamant an anti-monarchist as he was a convinced atheist. The sovereign in this sort of commonwealth was the people. When they exercised their vote they became the Constitutive Authority. Hence Bentham wanted to extend the franchise as widely as possible; but he agreed rather unwillingly to exclude females for the sake of feasibility, though they could be a part of the Public Opinion Tribunal. The implication was that the Constitutive Authority could do no wrong, for it could not or would not take any decisions against its own interests.

That Public Opinion Tribunal was a second channel through which the people exercised their sovereignty. They could sanction their representatives either by 'dislocating' them electorally (in Benthamic language, dismissing them) or by criticizing, denouncing and traducing them in front of all the citizens or any assembly of them and through the free press: 'The military functionary is paid for being shot at. The civil functionary is paid for being spoken and written at' said Bentham in a memorable line (1830 [1983] V.6.A2). To the pernicious exercise of the power of government it is the only check; to the beneficial, an indispensable supplement. Able rulers lead it; prudent rulers lead or follow it; foolish rulers disregard it' (V.4.A4).

The people elected the Supreme Legislature. Constituencies were single seated. Parliaments lasted for a year. Deputies had to sit every day except on the seventh day of the week and were paid daily on attendance. Two parliamentary institutions were of special importance: 'The Legislation Inquiry Judicatory', established to gather facts, statistics and information, with judicial powers to obtain it; and the 'Legislation Penal Judicatory' whose function it was to punish the misbehaviour of deputies, of prime ministers and of ministers of justice. The Legislature was not bound by any previous decision and could not thus bind its successors; no act was to be struck down for being unconstitutional; hence the constitution could be amended at any moment by simple majority; but such a parliamentary decision could be punished at the next election by dislocating the peccant deputies. One of the securities for appropriate aptitude of the deputies was the Legislator's 'Inaugural Declaration', the Benthamite blueprint for which ran to 14 pages! The deputy would promise 'economy and honesty' and that the law would be declared to all; and would abjure 'insincerity and arrogance'.

The prime minister was elected by the Legislature for four years and could not be re-elected until there were three or four former prime ministers to choose from. His powers were very wide, but he could be 'dislocated' or displaced by a vote in parliament. He appointed the ministers for life but could just as easily dislocate them. Their departments were as follows: Elections, Legislation, Army, Navy, Preventive Service, Interior Communications, Indigence Relief, Education, Domain, Health, Foreign Relations, Trade and Finance.

The functionaries or civil servants were designated for life. They were chosen among the 'List of Locables', who had passed the course of education, and the examinations which secured their aptitude. (Deputies also had to pass these two hurdles.)

Bentham was obsessed with preventing political agents from exercising oppression: of functionaries over other functionaries, and of functionaries over 'non-functionaries' (which is what ordinary people were called in the *Constitutional Code*!). He was also intent on preventing the undue appropriation of rents in public office. In Chapter VI of the *Code* he inserted a section 31, titled 'Securities for appropriate aptitude', which started thus:

> Art. 1. The assemblage of securities, here proposed with reference to the highest department, the Legislature, forms the commencement of an all-pervading system of like securities, covering the whole field of the Official establishment, and applying to all public functionaries in every department and subdepartment . . . Art. 2. For this purpose . . . confidence (it cannot be denied) may with truth be said to be minimized: *distrust* and *suspicion* maximized. (VI.31.A1–2, pp. 117–18, original emphasis)

The securities against oppression included architectural features, such as carefully designed cubicles in the ministries: they allowed both for secret meetings between the functionary and the non-functionary, and for the public listening in for open meetings as a sort of committee of the Public Opinion Tribunal.

Of great importance for Bentham were the arrangements for combining cheapness with efficiency in government. Thus the arrangements he proposed for bettering the vigilance of contracts and stores, for ensuring the attendance of functionaries, and for collecting usable information for ministerial work, down to multiple copying of documents and speaking tubes – all indicated a man well versed in the science of bureaucracy. He laid great store by competition in pay, whereby the 'locables' aspiring to a post could bid for it by accepting a reduction in their salaries.

Justice was to be prompt, cheap and based on codified and easily comprehensible law – or rather law couched in very precise Benthamese that Bentham thought would be easily comprehensible.

No doubt Bentham was a little batty, but who in the public choice fraternity is not.

4   A GLASSHOUSE DEMOCRACY

Such was the glasshouse society, the efficient, centralized, socially controlled and, above all, happy society that Bentham wanted to build on England's green and pleasant land and also on foreign parts for the lesser breeds without the Law. The question is whether it would have been a despotic society.

It would certainly have been efficient, through the minimization of expense and the speed of decision of a single-seated, centralized authority. There would have been measures in place to ensure the appropriate aptitude in all functionaries, through the strict system of selection and the nicely calculated incentive structure. The office holders would certainly have been responsible for their mistakes, watched over as they were by the Public Opinion Tribunal, and 'dislocable' by their superiors or the voters. But would this commonwealth have been as free as one could wish?

Before answering this question I should like to emphasize two elements in his thought: (a) that the essence of the law is an act of will or command on the part of the sovereign (or his deputies when the sovereign is the people) and the laws of all countries can, and had better, be re-written anew in a series of Codes forming a *Pannomion*; and (b) that political economy was a branch of legislation, a part of government business concerned with abundance (Hume, 1981, pp. 93ff.), not the emerging result of the unregulated activity of self-interested individuals.

4.1   The Law as Will

Bentham's concept of law is not of the essence of utilitarianism but does reinforce the character of a benevolent dictatorship often associated with societies organized under that philosophy – especially in its modern form of the welfare state. Bentham defined the law as the command of the sovereign backed by coercion. This definition of the law, as Hayek rightly noted, goes quite contrary to the tradition of

> the ancient Greeks and Cicero through the Middle Ages to the classical liberals like John Locke, David Hume, Immanuel Kant and the Scottish moral philosophers, down to various American statesmen of the nineteenth and twentieth centuries, for whom law and liberty could not exist apart from each other. (Hayek, 1973 [1982])

Bentham, in following the positivistic tradition of Hobbes and many French thinkers, saw the law as a necessary evil, for it stopped men from indulging their whims and passions to impose an artificial harmony necessary for social peace. On the contrary, said Hayek, well-conceived law is no reduction of individual freedom but the condition and basis of individual liberty.[12] There is no personal autonomy worth mentioning without the law.

The next step logically implied in this concept of law as coercion is that the unlimited will of a properly constituted authority is the law. Bentham says: 'The Supreme Legislature is omnicompetent . . . To its powers there are no limits, it has checks. These checks are applied, by the securities, provided for good conduct on the part of the several members, individually operated upon' (1830 [1983], VI.1. A1, pp. 42–3). The undivided sovereign is the people and the channel for its sovereign will is the legislation passed by parliament.[13]

Another peculiarity that throws light on Bentham's philosophy of law is the subordinate place he gives the civil law in the *Pannomion*. The civil law is the 'right conferring' part of the law while the penal is the 'wrong repressing' part. All is well up to here. But Bentham wants 'from each portion of the *Civil* Code, reference to be made to the correspondent portion of the *Penal* Code' (ibid., Preface, pp. 4, 6). It is true that one of the essential elements of the legal system is the ultimate power of injunction and punishment exercised by the courts and their executive arm, the police. The whole law, however, is much larger than what has to be enforced. In fact, the law is there to *diminish* the total sum of coercion in society. Much of the law simply establishes the way individuals can best reach mutually beneficial agreements. The greater part of Company Law, for example, is there to help individuals agree with each other to attain their ends. The Highway Code does have coercive elements but most of it is about agreeing unanimously about which side of the road to drive on and where and how to stop. By *reductio ad absurdum*, a Benthamite would have to say that the institution of the family would dissolve if adultery were not punished in the penal code. It seems that for Bentham, individuals have to be permanently controlled by penal authorities if they are to respect the rights of others or the full tenor of agreements voluntarily entered into.

Finally on this point of the philosophy of law, one must wonder at the belief that the rules of society can be changed at will and that the whole of the legal system should be totally redone from scratch. Even the ministries should be rebuilt to conform with the optimal architectural rules set down in his *Code*. All this characterizes Bentham as a utopian thinker, with all the dangers implied in social constructivism.

4.2   No Mutually Beneficial Free Bargains

Nor did Bentham gauge the importance of mutually beneficial bargains, as formulated by Adam Smith. In his mind, except in those cases where individual interests coincided perfectly, there has to be collective intervention to maximize the welfare of society. He seemed to have no notion of the fact that beneficial trades were based on differing non-coincidental individual interests. He even lacked the intuition of the role of logrolling in politics.

As Rosen aptly noted, Bentham's argument was in two parts. First, each person desires his (or her) own happiness and endeavours to secure his at the expense of everyone else; as each individual tries to achieve this end, he runs into the opposition of everyone else and often fails. Second, people do perceive that they have common interests; hence, adds Bentham, 'what is by all believed to be the common interest of all, is endeavd. to be promoted by all'.[14]

There is no idea here that the common interest may not need to be promoted by all, but attained through trades among differing individuals in their own interest. It is precisely because people have different utility schedules or different initial resources that they can profit from voluntary bargains. Voluntary trades and agreements, such as clubs, marriages, firms and contracts, form the great majority of common agreements reached in society and they need not be imposed by legislators or government.

In consequence, Bentham was no defender of *laissez-faire*. Despite his more than Smithian stance in his 'Defence of Usury' (1787), his true beliefs were better expressed in some phrases of 'Defence of a Maximum' (1801), where he asked for the imposition of a maximum price for corn in times of dearth. He there likened *laissez-faire* to letting a boat sink when it has sprung a leak:

> The particles of a mass of water have a propensity, when left to themselves, to range themselves upon the same level; human creatures have on their part, a propensity to save their own lives: and when water in search after a level is making its way too fast into a ship, pumps are employed by men to prevail on it to get the better of that propensity, and betake itself to a higher level, and this

may serve as an argument in favour of a maximum to any gentleman who finds himself ready to consider it as such. (1801 [1952–54],Vol. III, p. 258)

One could also recall the pamphlets on paper money written by Bentham at the turn of the eighteenth century and published by Stark in Volume II of *Jeremy Bentham's Economic Writings* (1952–54). All the texts contained in that volume proposed schemes for extending the government monopoly from coinage to notes, thus making the state the sole issuer of paper money; for increasing government revenue with the issue of notes (he did not baulk at the use of inflation as a tax on many by the government); and for displacing private bankers in favour of some government department.

I would like to conclude with a passage of Mill's in his 1838 essay on Bentham.[15]

> We cannot think that Bentham made the most useful employment which might have been made of his great powers, when, not content with enthroning the majority as sovereign, by means of universal suffrage without king or house of lords, he exhausted all the resources of ingenuity in devising means for riveting the yoke of public opinion closer and closer round the necks of all public functionaries, and excluding every possibility of the exercise of the slightest or most temporary influence either by a minority, or by the functionary's own notion of right. ... The power of the majority is salutary so far as it is used defensively, not offensively – as its exertion is tempered by respect for the personality of the individual, and deference to superiority of cultivated intelligence.

Mill's tone may be a little patronizing but the fear of democratic despotism is well taken.

NOTES

1. Bentham (1789 [1970], ch. 1, § 1 and § 2, pp. 11–13), original emphasis.
2. Bentham, it appears, was well aware of Hume's arguments against the general tendency to slip from 'ought' to 'is' and vice versa. Thus he criticized Blackstone 'for talking to us of what *ought* to be' and then insensibly 'finishes by telling us what *is*' (Bentham, 1776 [1977], p. 498), original emphasis.
3. Mill (1859 [1977]), chapter IV, 'Of the limits to the authority of society over the individual'.
4. Hume (1739–40 [1978]), III.i.1, p. 469, says that the change from 'is' and 'is not', to 'ought' and 'ought not' in most authors is 'imperceptible'. The gear was changed by Bentham with an audible clang!
5. Smith (1759 [1976], I.i.1, p. 9).
6. Ridley (1997, ch. 7), Smithian sympathy is not incompatible with Darwinian 'survival of the fittest' if we accept Richard Dawkins's theory of selfish gene: it could be the case that altruistic and sympathetic behaviour on the part of individual human beings (especially mothers) maximized the survival chances of their genes. Dawkins (1976) and Ridley (1997, pp. 17–20).

7. Bentham (1830 [1983]), vol. I, VI.31.A-8, p. 119). However Bentham did not totally deny sympathy as enlightened self-interest a role: though he enjoined that the legislator should not overly rely on it: 'To give increase to the influence of sympathy at the expense of self-regard, and of sympathy is the constant and arduous task, as of every moralist, so of every legislator who deserves to be so. But, in regard to sympathy, the less proportion of it is, the natural and actual existence of which he assumes as and for the basis of his arrangements, the greater will be the success of whatever endeavour he uses to give increase to it' (ibid., VI.31.A-10, p. 119).
8. Smith (1759 [1976]), I.i.2.1). In support of the instinctively social character of sympathetic feelings, Smith went on to say: 'A man is mortified when, after having endeavoured to divert the company, he looks round and sees that nobody laughs at his jests but himself. On the contrary, the mirth of the company is highly agreeable to him.'
9. Hume (1739–40 [1978], III, ii, VI, p. 526).
10. Bentham (1989) 'Economy as applied to office', 'Identification of interests' and 'Supreme operative', see below.
11. Rosen and Burns, 'Editorial Introduction', Bentham (1830 [1983], p. 13).
12. Hayek (1973 [1982], vol. 1, part 2: 'Cosmos and Taxis', esp. p. 52).
13. Further, the unlimited character of the sovereign will leads Bentham to do away with the time-honoured distinction between private and public bills. Bentham (1830 [1983], IX.4.A25-7, p. 191).
14. Rosen (1983, pp. 49–50, quotes from Box xxxviii at University College, folio 217).
15. Mill (1838 [1969]), pp. 108–9. Rosen (1983) drew my attention to this passage, p. 195.

REFERENCES

CW stands for *The Collected Works of Jeremy Bentham*, variously by Athlone Press, London and Oxford University Press, Oxford.

Bentham, Jeremy (1776 [1977]), 'A Fragment on Government', in *CW*, J.H. Burns and H.A.L. Hart (eds), *A Comment on the Commentaries and A Fragment on Government*, Athlone Press, London.

Bentham, Jeremy (1787 [1952–54]), 'Defence of Usury; Shewing the Impolicy of the Present Legal Restraints on the Terms of Pecuniary Bargains in a Series of Letters to a Friend to which is Added a Letter to Adam Smith, Esq. LL.D. on the discouragements opposed by the above Restraint to the Progress of Inventive Industry', in W. Stark (ed.), *Jeremy Bentham's Economic Writings*, Vol. I, London, pp. 121–207.

Bentham Jeremy (1789 [1970]), *An Introduction to the Principles of Morals and Legislation*, in *CW*, J.H. Burns and H.A.L. Hart (eds) Athlone Press, London.

Bentham, Jeremy (1801 [1952–54]), 'Defence of a Maximum containing . . . Hints respecting the Selection of Radical Remedies against Dearth and Scarcity', edited from MS in W. Stark (ed.), *Jeremy Bentham's Economic Writings*, Vol. III, London, pp. 247–302.

Bentham, Jeremy (1822 [1989]), 'Economy as applied to office' and 'Identification of interests', in *CW*, Philip Schofield (ed.), *First Principles Preparatory to Constitutional Code*, Oxford University Press, Oxford.

Bentham, Jeremy (1830 [1983]), *Constitutional Code. Volume I*, in *CW*, F. Rosen and J.H. Burns (eds), Oxford University Press, Oxford.

Bentham, Jeremy (1843), *The Works of Jeremy Bentham*, John Bowring (ed.), 11 vols, William Tait, Edinburgh.

Bentham, Jeremy (1989), *First Principles Preparatory to Constitutional Code*, in *CW*, Philip Schofield (ed.), Oxford University Press, Oxford.

Buchanan, James M. and Tullock, Gordon (1962), *The Calculus of Consent: Logical Foundations of Constitutional Democracy*, Vol. 3 of *The Collected Works of James M. Buchanan*, Liberty Fund, Indianapolis, IN.

Dawkins, Richard (1976),*The Selfish Gene*, Oxford University Press, Oxford.

Hart, H.A.L. (1961), *The Concept of Law*, Oxford University Press, Oxford.

Hayek, Friedrich (1973 [1982]), *Rules and Order*, Vol. 1 of *Law, Legislation and Liberty*, published in a one-volume paperback, Routledge & Kegan Paul, London, pp. 35–54.

Hayek, Friedrich (1979 [1982]), 'The three sources of human values', in Vol. 3 of *Law, Legislation and Liberty*, published in a one-volume paperback, Routledge & Kegan Paul, London.

Hume, David (1739–40 [1978]), *A Treatise of Human Nature*, edited by L.A. Selby-Bigge, 2nd edn revised by P.H. Nidditch, Oxford University Press, Oxford.

Hume, L.J. (1981), *Bentham and Bureaucracy*, Cambridge University Press, Cambridge.

Leibenstein, Harvey (1966), 'Allocative efficiency v. "X-efficiency"', *American Economic Review*, **56**, 392–415.

Mill, John Stuart (1838 [1969]), 'Bentham', in Vol. X of *The Collected Works of John Stuart Mill*, edited by J.M. Robson, F.E.L. Priestley and D.P. Drier, *Essays on Ethics, Religion and Society*, University of Toronto Press and Routledge & Kegan Paul, Toronto, pp. 75–113.

Mill, John Stuart (1859 [1977]), *On Liberty*, in Vol. XVIII of *The Collected Works of John Stuart Mill*, edited by J.M. Robson, *Essays on Politics and Society*, University of Toronto Press and Routledge & Kegan Paul, Toronto, pp. 212–310.

Mill, John Stuart (1873 [1981]), *Autobiography*, in Vol. I of *The Collected Works of John Stuart Mill*, edited by John M. Robson and Jack Stillinger, *Autobiography and Literary Essays*, University of Toronto Press and Routledge & Kegan Paul, Toronto.

Ridley, Matt (1997), *The Origins of Virtue*, Penguin, London.

Rosen, Fred (1983), *Jeremy Bentham and Representative Democracy*, Oxford University Press, Oxford.

Schofield, Philip (1989), 'Editorial Introduction', in Jeremy Bentham, *First Principles Preparatory to Constitutional Code*, in *CW*, Schofield (ed.), Oxford University Press, Oxford.

Seabright, Paul (2001), *The Company of Strangers. A Natural History of Economic Life*, Princeton University Press, Princeton, NJ.

Smith, Adam (1759 [1976]), *The Theory of Moral Sentiments*, Glasgow edn of the Works and Correspondence of Adam Smith, Oxford University Press, Oxford.

Smith, Adam (1776 [1976]), *An Inquiry into the Nature and Causes of the Wealth of Nations*, Glasgow edn of the Works and Correspondence of Adam Smith, Oxford University Press, Oxford.

Smith, Vernon (1998), 'The two faces of Adam Smith', *Southern Economic Journal*, **65**(1), 1–19.

PART II

Institutional Aspects of Democracy

5. Towards a more consistent design of parliamentary democracy and its consequences for the European Union[†]

Charles B. Blankart and Dennis C. Mueller*

1 TWO WAYS TO DEPART FROM DIRECT DEMOCRACY

During the last decade of the twentieth century, a large number of democratic states emerged out of the ashes of the Soviet empire. They all took the form of parliamentary democracies, that is, of governments mostly elected by parliaments re-sorting themselves from elections on a proportional basis, some with an elected president, some with a second chamber. Their relative merits have rarely been questioned. An often-mentioned exception is Barro (1997) who has asked whether more authoritarian or more pluralistic democracies are able to generate higher rates of economic growth. His intention was to find an optimal democracy with regard to growth. In our view, however, democracy is not so much an instrument to generate growth, but rather a mechanism to find out and to execute what voters want. The question we want to ask is: what is the form of democracy that most faithfully transforms the outcome of democratic voting into collective actions? A point of reference to this question is direct democracy of the town-hall type. For in a direct democracy, there is no need of an intermediating agent interpreting and transforming the outcome of voting into political action. Political decisions are rather simultaneously decided and put into action by the citizens themselves.

Direct democracy rests on the following three core principles:

1. sovereignty is exercised directly by the citizens;
2. the condition of one man, one vote applies; and

† Originally published as Charles D. Blankart and Dennis C. Mueller, 'The advantages of pure forms of parliamentary democracy over mixed forms', *Public Choice*, **122**, 2004, pp. 431–53. Reprinted with kind permission of Springer Science and Business Media.

3.   citizens engage directly in the deliberative process of opinion forma-
     tion.[1]

Direct democracy, however, applies only in small communities. In practice, deviations from the pure principles of direct democracy are required.
Principle 1, that of citizens' sovereignty, is obviously unlikely to be given
up, for it would turn democracy into a farce of a dictatorship dressed in the
clothes of a democracy. Therefore either one may prefer to reduce the
number of active participants in the democracy (principle 2) or one may
simplify opinion formation by condensing the number of alternatives (principle 3). In the first case, the 'pure form of representative democracy'
(PRD), citizens vote for persons sharing their views and forming opinions
similar to theirs in the parliament. They economize the time used for
debates by reducing the number of participants. In the second case, the
'pure form of two-party democracy' (TPD) the voters are confronted by
platforms of policy bundles between which they can choose in a similar way
as they choose between single issues in a direct democracy. They decide
themselves, but among a small set of alternatives.

In most parliamentary democracies, however, the second and the third
principles are applied in combination. Citizens are supposed to give their
parliamentary representatives a mandate, to let them speak, discuss and
decide for themselves, and they choose among the party programs in the
election. We shall argue that the mixture of these two procedures leads to
inconsistent results which are farther away from the outcome of direct
democracies than if only one or the other principle is applied.

We proceed as follows. In Sections 2 and 3, the properties of the PRD and
the TPD are presented. Section 4 explains the disadvantages of mixed forms
of the two systems, and yet why they nevertheless are often found to exist.
In Section 5, we evaluate the combination of PRD or TPD with elements of
a direct democracy such as a referendum or a popular initiative. A brief look
at bicameral systems is presented in Section 6, while Section 7 discusses the
proper role of the executive branch in each form of government. Finally the
results of our analysis have implications on the design of a constitution for
the European Union which will be discussed in Section 9.[2]

2   THE PURE FORM OF REPRESENTATIVE DEMOCRACY

PRD rests on the institution of parliament, which has to be elected in a way
that it mirrors as closely as possible the preferences found in the population
at large. It simulates the town hall meeting, but with fewer citizens. Such a

procedure was described several years ago by Gordon Tullock (1967, ch. 10). Citizens are allowed to transfer their vote to another citizen, whom they trust will vote in the assembly in the same way that they would have voted if they had participated. Under this procedure, citizens would be expected to transfer their votes to those representative-citizens whose preferences come closest to matching their own preferences. Each representative-citizen taking a seat in the representative assembly would then possess as many votes as the number of citizens having the same preferences in the community at large. The representative assembly fulfills each of the three characteristics of direct democracy listed above, albeit with each citizen participating only indirectly by proxy through the person to whom the citizen assigned his/her vote (see principle 2, above).[3] Despite these attractive properties of the procedure, it has some potential disadvantages:

1. It is still possible, of course, that the number of individuals needed to represent all citizens' preferences faithfully is too large to allow effective deliberation in the representative assembly. This difficulty can easily be overcome, however, by limiting the number of representatives to some manageable number, say, 100. If the first round of voting produces too many representatives, a second round is held with only the 100 persons participating in it being allowed to run. Votes in the assembly are then assigned to the 100 representatives in proportion to the number of votes that they receive in the *second* round of voting. This amendment to the procedure would continue to ensure that each person would be represented by someone to whom his/her vote was entrusted. Assuming that the number of different sets of preferences in the community is not inordinately large, and 100 seems a much larger number than would be needed, each citizen would be represented by someone whose preference came very close to matching his/her own preferences. Given this property the procedure would again fulfill the property that the assembly constituted an accurate representation of all preferences in the community in terms of both their characteristics and their numbers. Even an assembly of only 100 would allow for the representation of a far wider spectrum of preferences than are represented in the parliamentary systems of the major developed democracies.
2. The voters could be overwhelmed by having to compare too many candidates, and the candidates may be overwhelmed by the challenge of having to make their positions on issues known to all voters. However, in this situation intermediaries have an incentive to intervene to facilitate the dissemination of information on candidate positions. For example, interest groups on both the left and right of the political

spectrum can be expected to make efforts to inform voters of the positions of candidates who favor the interest groups' positions. And, of course, they have an incentive to contribute funds to their favorite candidates, so that the candidates themselves can inform the voters. Alternatively, the distribution of state funds to candidates for the purpose of informing voters can also be justified on the grounds that this sort of information constitutes a pure public good.

3. The citizen-voters are confronted with a principal–agent problem. They deliver their vote to an agent who will, they hope, vote in the way they would have had they been in the assembly, and not merely to serve the agent's own interests. This principal–agent problem is present under all systems of representative democracy, however, and is if anything likely to be a smaller problem with this procedure than it is when citizens are represented by parties. Citizens can observe the voting record of their representative and have a wide spectrum of alternative candidates to choose among should their representative deviate from his/her promised positions. Citizens can also count on both other candidates and interest groups to inform them about any 'shirking' by their representative.

Voters will have the broadest possible spectrum of positions from which to choose, if the polity is treated as a single electoral district with citizens free to choose among all of the candidates rather than having the polity divided into geographic districts. Each set of preferences will then be represented in the assembly in direct proportion to their number across the entire polity, irrespective of the geographic location of the person holding a given set of preferences. Persons representing the preferences of citizens from a particular geographic area might also get elected, of course, but in general one expects representatives of narrow geographic interests to gather fewer votes in a national assembly than those representing positions that appeal to citizens from all parts of the country.

Just as under direct democracy, the proposal, discussion and determination of policies under PRD takes place within the assembly. The only difference is that under PRD, an assembly of faithful representatives of citizen preferences discusses and decides issues, while under direct democracy, the citizens themselves determine 'the general will' of the community. Political theorists from Jean Jacques Rousseau to Knut Wicksell (1896) to James Buchanan and Gordon Tullock (1962) have proposed that this general will should ideally be determined by demanding *unanimous* agreement among the members of the assembly. Although fulfilling such an ideal would be impractical, this does not imply that the best voting rule would be the simple majority rule. This rule is known to be prone to cycles. If one confines one's attention to the family of qualified majority rules (for example, two-thirds or three-quarters), then some higher qualified majority is required.[4] But there is no reason to confine one's choice of a voting rule to this limited set. Public choice has developed several voting rules – such as point voting and voting by veto – which do not produce cycles, and which give every member of parliament an impact on the outcome (see Mueller, 1996, ch. 11).

Once policies have been proposed, discussed, perhaps amended and eventually ratified in the legislative assembly, the only remaining step is to implement the policies. This is the task of the executive branch under the PRD. The implementation of policies is logically a separate function from their determination, and should, therefore, be administratively separate from the legislative process. Such a separation between the legislative and executive functions of government is, of course, not characteristic of the parliamentary forms of government prevalent in Europe and in many other countries. We shall return to this point in Section 7, but we turn now to a discussion of the pure two-party form of representative democracy.

3   THE PURE TWO-PARTY FORM OF REPRESENTATIVE DEMOCRACY

The point of departure of TPD is direct democracy, too. Citizen preferences should determine policy outcomes. But the process by which this determination takes place is quite different. Instead of citizens choosing a person or party to represent their preferences in the legislative assembly where policies are decided, under TPD citizens effectively choose the final set of policies themselves. TPD intends to overcome the large number problem of direct democracy by economizing on the number of alternatives presented to the citizens (principle 3, above). Each of the two parties competing in the election proposes a set of policies, which they promise to implement if they obtain a majority of seats in parliament, and the citizen votes for the party promising the most attractive set of policies. The party receiving the most votes in the election is awarded a majority of the seats in parliament and implements its promised platform. As under PRD, the entire nation should be treated as a single electoral district with seats in parliament awarded in proportion to the votes won across the entire nation. But if parties are free to enter the competition for votes, how can one be sure that the voters have but two parties from which to choose? To ensure that this is the case, or at least that the winning party has obtained a majority of the votes cast and seats in parliament, TPD requires that there be a second, run-off election between the two parties getting the most votes in the first election. Voters would then have to choose between only two parties if a run-off were needed, and in the long run such a system should result in there being only two major parties competing for votes across the country (Cox, 1997).

At first glance the TPD resembles the so-called 'Westminster system' of government. In both systems one cannot presume that there will be only two parties competing for votes, but in the long run one expects this to be the case as the smaller parties drop out or merge with other parties to avoid always being in the opposition. The TPD proposed here has, however, two important advantages over the Westminster model: (i) the convergence process should occur much faster, since in any election with a run-off the parties coming in third or lower in the first round would receive *no seats* in the parliament; (ii) the Westminster system does not ensure either that a single party wins a majority of the seats in the parliament or that a party which does obtain a majority of the seats has won a majority of the votes. We return to this point in the third example in Section 4.1.

Unlike in the PRD, the function of the legislative assembly under TPD is not to formulate, debate and determine policies. This takes place either during the election when the parties formulate their platforms or in caucuses held by the majority party outside of the assembly. To maintain the appearance of deliberative democracy, the opposition may be allowed to express its dissatisfaction with the majority party's program, and the majority party may defend the virtues of its program, but this is mostly show. The real policy choices are made outside of the legislative assembly by the majority party alone and by the voters who elected it.

Another important difference between PRD and TPD is that the logic of TPD demands that the majority party form the government, that is, select the prime minister and cabinet. Under TPD the executive and legislative branches are combined. The election has expressed the 'will of the people' in so far as which party platform is most preferred. The winning party will be in the best position to implement its platform if it controls both the legislative and executive functions of government. Thus, it is possible to characterize PRD as 'parliamentary democracy without a government (cabinet)', and TPD as 'government without a parliament'.

While the simple majority rule is unlikely to be the optimal choice for the legislature under PRD, it is the appropriate voting rule under TPD. The electoral rule ensures that a party wins a majority of the votes and thereby obtains a majority of the seats in parliament. The parliamentary voting rule should ensure that this party can implement its program. The simple majority rule achieves that goal. Unlike with PRD, however, under TPD cycling will not be a problem when the simple majority rule is used, since one party has a majority and it will simply choose its most preferred outcomes. Assuming that elections are fought over a multidimensional issue space, cycling could conceivably be a problem at the electoral stage. The probabilistic voting literature suggests, however, that equilibria in two-party elections will exist, and furthermore that they have the attractive property of maximizing some form of social welfare function. In this sense, the TPD also achieves the goal of matching policy outcomes from the democratic process to the preferences of the citizens.[5] Once one allows for campaign contributions and other interest-group activities, however, the individual utility functions, which appear in the social welfare function that is maximized through the competition for votes by the two parties, receive different weights, and the normative attractiveness of the TPD is somewhat reduced (see Coughlin et al., 1990).

4 PRD AND TPD IN COMBINATION?

We have seen that both PRD and TPD have attractive properties. PRD ensures that *all* citizens' preferences are faithfully represented in the legislative assembly that decides government policies. TPD allows the citizen to choose these policies and the government directly. Neither system in the pure form described here exists anywhere, however. *Mixed* systems are the rule. This fact raises two questions: what produces mixed systems and what are their properties in comparison with the ideal types described here? This section attempts to provide some answers to these questions.

4.1 The Emergence of Systems of Combined Representation?

Combined systems come about through a combination of provisions in the constitution that, for example, specify that the parliament should form the government, that is, the cabinet as under the TPD, and the use of an electoral rule that produces a multiparty parliament in which no party has a majority of the seats. Space precludes an exhaustive discussion of all of the electoral rules in use and their properties, so we shall content ourselves by describing only a few illustrative examples (see Coughlin et al., 1990).

First, the smallest deviation from the PRD comes about when a country elects its parliament using some form of party list system rather than the kind of vote-transfer system described under the PRD. In a national list system as employed in the Netherlands and Israel, voters in all parts of the country are presented with the same lists of candidates. Each citizen votes for one party and the parties are awarded seats in parliament in proportion to the numbers of votes they receive. The seats are filled by the people whose names appeared on the lists. This system resembles PRD except that citizens transfer their vote to a party instead of a person. Instead of a representative who received 10 percent of the votes getting 10 percent of the votes in the assembly as would occur under PRD, each representative gets one vote under a list system, but his/her *party* gets 10 percent of the votes in parliament if it got 10 percent of the votes in the electorate. This system is inferior to PRD in so far as it greatly reduces the range of choice for the voters for any given sized legislative assembly. Voters in Europe, for example, typically choose among five or 10 parties even when there are hundreds of seats in parliament, while under PRD a voter would choose from among 50 positions on issues with a parliament as small as 50. The range of choice facing voters is further restricted in many multiparty systems by denying parties any seats at all in parliament if they fail to reach a minimum threshold of votes that can be as high as 5 percent, as in Germany and Austria. Such a rule guarantees that at most 20 different sets of preferences are represented in parliament, and de facto that far fewer are. Minimum cut-offs such as these are defended on the grounds that reduce the number of parties in parliament and thereby make the task of coalition formation to form a government easier. They are an obvious compromise between trying to represent all citizens' preferences fairly, as PRD would do, and producing responsible government, as TPD would do. Such systems produce large parties and hence make the emergence of fixed coalitions more likely.

Second, most countries are divided into several voting districts and citizens can vote only for candidates or parties with lists in their districts. When the districts are large and many representatives can be selected from each district, the outcomes of these systems approximate those of the national list systems. When only a few persons can be elected from each district, these systems further disadvantage small parties and those voters whose preferences do not appear in greater number across the country. These systems also have the disadvantage of giving representatives elected on a regional basis an incentive to introduce regional/local issues into the national legislative agenda. This tendency is readily apparent in the European Parliament whose members are all elected from electoral districts corresponding to the boundaries of the member countries (see Section 9).

Third, the polar case of a system of geographically defined electoral districts designed to disadvantage minority parties is the system of single-member-district representation practiced in the United Kingdom, the United States and many other Anglo-Saxon countries. The rationale behind these systems is generally not only to disadvantage small parties, but to produce a *two-party* form of government. Within a district they tend to achieve this goal, but there is no guarantee that they will produce two dominant parties across the entire country. Both Canada and India have single-member-district representation systems and neither of them comes close to having two dominant parties today, and even the UK – the archetype of the Westminster system – has had three major parties (and a half dozen or so minor ones) for many years now.

Fourth, perhaps the most mixed of the mixed systems of representation is the increasingly popular tendency to elect some representatives to parliament using single-member-district representation and the rest using some form of multimember-district representation. Germany elects half the Bundestag from single-member-districts and then fills the remaining seats applying a proportional representation formula to the votes across the entire nation. The result is a fairly close approximation to what one would get using a national-list, proportional representation (PR) formula, but with a local flavor. Italy has attempted to introduce a degree of stability into its system by implementing such a mixed system. So far it has produced neither stability nor two-party government.

4.2   How Should Systems of Combined Representation Be Evaluated?

Combined systems have several disadvantages with respect to the pure systems of PRD and TPD.

The confounding of the objectives of representation and responsibility

Although the PR systems of continental Europe come closest to the PRD, they do not achieve its potential as a system for representing the preferences of *all* citizens. In a PRD system not only would all preferences be represented in parliament, they would also have the potential to affect the outcomes. This influence would be felt both through discussion and debate and also through the use of a voting rule that allows all members of parliament the opportunity to affect the outcome. In contrast, by requiring that majority coalitions form to choose a cabinet, European PR systems ensure that the process of discussion and debate is limited to members of the parties forming the majority coalition. The other parties are left to criticize, but not to influence the legislative outcomes. At the same time, European PR systems do not produce the kind of responsible government that would arise under the TPD. None of the parties in a coalition government can claim sole responsibility for the program implemented; nor can they promise with any conviction that they will be in a position to implement a particular program in the future, since under the best of circumstances they will only be in a position to bargain with other coalition partners over the characteristics of the government's program.

Voter alienation

The inability of parties to take responsibility for policies undertaken, and to make and keep credible promises during elections reverberates back onto the attitudes of the voters to the parties. Often during an election, a member of the coalition that formed the government will try to dodge criticism of the government's program by blaming other members of the coalition for some of the outcomes. Voters who are unhappy with a government's achievements often do not know which party to punish, nor can they believe the promises of the parties in opposition, because the latter, too, are going to have to reach compromises with other parties should they be part of the next government. The difficulties voters have under existing PR systems trying to decide whom to punish and whom to trust may help to explain the increasing alienation of voters to electoral politics in Europe in recent years.

Strategic voting

Should citizens vote for the party that comes closest to their favored position on the issues, if they think that this party has a small chance of joining the government, or should they cast their ballot for a party with a better chance of joining the government? Many voters in Europe do not vote for their most preferred parties for this sort of strategic reason and thus an election outcome does not in fact constitute an accurate representation of the preferences of the electorate across the ideological spectrum.[6]

Instability

Any party that deviates from its promised program to become a part of a coalition government stands to lose votes in the next election. Recognizing this, parties in the government often have an incentive to exit the coalition sufficiently far in advance of an election, so that they have time to stake out their position on the issues for the next election and to distance themselves from the programs of the present government. Such exits from the government can lead to its premature downfall and helps to explain why coalition governments tend to be shorter lived than one-party governments. More generally, the multidimensionality of the issue space combined with the lack of a single party with a majority of the seats in the parliament makes PR systems prone to cycles, and thus to unstable governments.

Majority parties with minority support

When single-member-district representation does succeed in producing a single party with a majority of the seats in the parliament, as has generally been the case in Great Britain, the party winning a majority of the seats seldom wins the support of a majority of the voters. The Labour Party's landslide victory in the 2001 election in terms of seats occurred despite its gaining the votes of only slightly more than 44 percent of the electorate – about what the *losing* candidate gets in a landslide presidential election in the United States. Not once during the last century did the party, which 'won' the election in Great Britain, also win a majority of the votes cast.[7]

5   SUPPLEMENTARY REFERENDA IN PRD AND TPD?

The pure systems of PRD and TPD, we have argued, would be superior to the combined forms of proportional representation and two-party systems that are observed in practice. We have also extolled the virtues of direct democracy, however. Are the properties of the PRD and the TPD as mechanisms for representing individuals' preferences so attractive that institutions of direct democracy are not needed? If this is not the case, what role would referenda play in an ideal PRD or TPD system? Should citizens be allowed to supplement the actions of their elected governments with proposals of their own approved in a referendum? Should citizens be free to introduce initiatives in which an action of their government is reversed? As it turns out the answers to these questions differ somewhat depending on whether the PRD or the TPD has been chosen.

Under the PRD, the preferences of all voters should be faithfully represented in the legislative assembly, and thus it might appear that there should be no need for additional referenda. They should simply reproduce what the legislature does or would decide. Further reflection suggests, however, that the option to call referenda might still have a beneficial role to play under PRD. The possibility of citizens calling referenda should increase the incentives that their representatives have to vote in accordance with their campaign promises. In addition, the possibility of calling referenda allows citizens the opportunity to take actions that their representatives have failed to undertake, perhaps out of ignorance of what the citizens' preferences are on a particular issue. Thus, the potential for calling referenda should be an important aid to overcoming the principal–agent problem between citizens and their representatives that would exist even under PRD.[8] In a well-functioning PRD system, one would not expect that citizens would need to resort to referenda very often. In Switzerland, where referenda and citizen initiatives are firmly established, the actual outcomes from referenda and their preventive role of keeping representatives in check have both proven to be of considerable importance (see Blankart, 1992).

The situation is quite different under TPD. In choosing a party to form the government, citizens have effectively endorsed the platform of the party, which consists of positions on several issues. One citizen might vote for Party A despite its position on issue X, because she strongly supports its position on Y. If then A wins the election and implements Y, but Y is reversed in a referendum, the citizen will in some sense have wasted her vote for Party A. More generally the role of elections as mechanisms for picking the best platform (package of issues) will be vitiated, if citizens are able to reverse parts of the platform through referenda. To put it differently, citizens would have to make unduly difficult calculations to anticipate the outcomes of possible referenda before casting their vote.

Against this position there are naturally some counterarguments that can be made. Because two-party elections revolve around a large number of issues, it can happen that some issues receive little attention from either party during an election campaign and thus the winning party does not have a clear picture of the voters' preferences on this issue. New issues can also arise that were not even discussed during the previous election. Despite these possibilities, we find it somewhat problematic to couple the TPD with citizen initiatives that would reverse parts of the winning party's platform, given the normative justification for having the entire winning platform implemented.

An additional danger arises when governments themselves call referenda to induce the citizens to ratify decisions that the government has already made. Such plebiscites are almost always called to manipulate the voters into taking an action that strengthens the existing government. They thus serve no constructive purpose in an ideal form of representative government and should not be allowed. The only forms of referenda whose potential goal is having government policies advance citizens' interests are the ones that they themselves initiate.[9]

Referenda over constitutional questions are a quite different matter, on the other hand. In many countries, parliaments are able to change the constitution. Here the danger of significant principal–agent problems arising is very great, particularly when it comes to changes in electoral rules and the like, which have direct effects on the welfare of the elected representatives. To maintain citizen sovereignty over constitutional matters, we recommend that all changes in the constitution introduced by parliament, however elected, be put before the citizens in a referendum.[10]

6   A SECOND LEGISLATIVE CHAMBER?

A further, possible variant on the PRD and TPD would be to introduce a second legislative chamber. Many countries have a second chamber with a similar or slightly narrower jurisdiction than the first. In the United States,

France and Italy the second house is called the Senate, in Great Britain the House of Lords, in Germany the Bundesrat, and in Switzerland the Council of the States (Ständerat). Historically these second houses came into being to represent the interests of a particular group or class. The Roman Senate was supposed to protect the rights of the patrician families of Rome; the House of Lords was to protect the interests of the British aristocracy. Der Reichsrat, the forerunner to the German Bundesrat, was supposed to protect the rights of the federal states of Germany. The British House of Lords was also the model for the American upper house in the minds of many of the drafters of the US Constitution. The Senate, not being popularly elected, was supposed to protect the interests of America's landed aristocracy. The Senate was seen as both contributing to the overall structure of checks and balances in the constitution, and more specifically to the protection of the privileged classes (see Sundquist, 1986: 22–3; Nedelsky, 1990: ch. 2). Today second chambers are not generally defended on the basis of protecting class interests, but rather that they somehow improve the process of representation of citizen preferences. Such an argument is difficult to sustain, however, if the first chamber has been properly constituted as under our PRD and TPD systems.

Under the PRD *all* citizens' preferences are faithfully represented in parliament. Collective decisions are made following discussions in which the views of all citizens can effectively be heard. The principle of one man, one vote is satisfied and, if a voting rule has been selected that allows all voices represented to influence the outcomes of the collective choice process, all of the goals of PRD are fulfilled (see Section 3). What purpose can a second chamber fulfill? If it is less representative of all citizens' preferences than the first, the legitimacy of the collective decisions will be reduced to the extent that they are influenced by the second chamber. If the second chamber is equally representative, it will merely reproduce the outcomes of the first. The latter outcome seems highly inefficient, and the former implies that for some reason the preferences represented in the second chamber should get more weight than those in the first. Given that the first chamber has been fairly constituted, it is not clear how such a reweighting can be defended. Alternatively, one might ask why, if a second chamber improves the outcomes of the collective choice process, would a third not improve the outcomes still more, or even a fourth? Nor is it easy to defend the existence of a second chamber under the TPD. Each citizen votes for the party promising him/her the best platform of policies and the winning party's platform maximizes the welfare of the community. Why place a second chamber against the first and risk delaying or distorting 'the will of the people' as expressed in the election? How can the party ruling the lower house be held fully responsible for the government's policies, if it shares authority with members of an upper house chosen under some other principle? The entire *raison d'être* of two-party government – that it produces responsible and accountable governments – gets called into question, once responsibility for the outcomes of the governmental process is shared between two or more seats of authority. If the goal of representative government is to bring about a correspondence between these outcomes and the preferences of the citizens, then there is no place for a second chamber in a system of government in which the first chamber has been properly constituted under either the PRD or the TPD.

Anyone who shares this view regarding the merits of a second chamber must view with considerable skepticism the proposals of several authors to have two chambers in the European Union, one in which the *citizens* are directly represented, and a second in which EU *states* are represented. It would be much better to set aside the current practice of electing representatives to the European Parliament from the individual member states with a system in which voters from across the entire EU can transfer their votes to individuals, or choose parties under a party-list system. Either proposal would result in a representation of citizens' views on EU matters that was proportional to their appearance in the EU at large. The wrestling over the distribution of representatives across national parties would disappear, and along with it the struggle among the delegates from each country over the geographic distribution of the EU budget. At the same time, responsibility for the budget could be shifted from the Council to the parliament. With representation according to geography eliminated in the parliament, and with it in charge of the budget, perhaps it would come to pass that less money gets allocated to geographically defined redistribution programs than the 80 percent that is now so allocated.

7   DESIGNING THE EXECUTIVE UNDER TPD AND PRD

In a TPD, the two parties present platforms to the voters, the voters choose the party/platform they prefer, and the party delivers the promised set of policies to the people. Combining the executive and legislative functions of government should facilitate this delivery. The logic of the TPD demands that the executive and legislative functions of government be combined. The leader of the party winning the election becomes the chief executive, the winning party chooses the cabinet and forms the government.

What should the relationship between the legislative and executive functions of government be under the PRD? In Section 2 we described the PRD as a parliament without a government. The logic underlying the PRD demands that the parliament, in which the preferences of all citizens are represented, *not* choose the cabinet to avoid the parliament's having to form a stable coalition in which some representatives are excluded, and to avoid the possible instabilities that often accompany coalition governments. The logic underlying the PRD demands that the legislative and executive functions of government be separated. We describe two alternative models for accomplishing this goal.

7.1 An Executive Committee

At a minimum the PRD requires that there be some sort of executive committee separate from the parliament to propose issues and set the parliamentary agenda. This committee might be elected by the citizens or appointed by parliament. The Swiss Federal Council (Bundesrat) is an example of such a committee.

7.2 A President

Under the American-style presidential system there is a complete separation of the executive and legislative branches of government. The president is directly elected by the people, and appoints the cabinet ministers who are in charge of carrying out the programs passed in the legislature. Although the president might be assigned certain proposal and agenda-setting powers, it is important to avoid the kinds of political stalemates that have plagued Latin American countries and have become common in the US, that the president *not* be given veto power over the decisions of the legislature. His duties should be confined to literally that of the chief executive of the government bureaucracy.[11]

In both of these models, the executive is separated from the legislature. The Swiss Federal Council is dependent on parliament in the sense that it appoints each of them, but the appointments are for fixed terms and thus the Council can carry out their tasks without fear of parliamentary interference. The American president's selection is totally independent from that of the legislature. Combining either variant of these two models with the PRD would leave the legislative assembly free to carry out its function of debating and deciding the legislative program of the country. This process would not be constrained by the need to form a stable majority coalition. All representatives could be expected to participate in the collective decision-making process. If some sort of qualified majority rule was the parliamentary voting rule, then one would expect shifting coalitions to form to pass different pieces of legislation as occurs today in the Swiss Parliament and the US Congress under the simple majority rule.

8   SUFFICIENT CHECKS AND BALANCES?

Checks and balances are a central characteristic of the American Constitution. The Founding Fathers of the United States were greatly concerned about the possibility of one branch of government overstepping its authority and undertaking actions that harmed the citizenry. This fear led them to introduce an elaborate set of checks and balances into the US system. Our proposals in contrast focus upon the design of institutions that would better align the outcomes of the political process with citizen preferences. Many will object that our proposals contain *insufficient* checks against possible misuses of power by one or the other branch. It is impossible to design a political system, which provides the state sufficient authority and legitimacy to carry out 'the will of the people', without at the same time granting it sufficient discretion to implement policies that harm the people. And it must also be recognized that failing to introduce good policies can harm citizens just as much as the introduction of bad policies. It would be wrong to conclude, however, that our proposals contain no effective checks on the state. Under both PRD and TPD the parties in parliament have an incentive to adopt policies that advance citizen interests, if they hope to win seats in the next election. This constraint is particularly salient under TPD, since a party can only fulfill the wishes of its supporters if it wins an absolute majority of the votes cast. Under PRD there is the additional constraint of the parliamentary voting rule which should, as we have stressed, ensure that a mere majority of the members of the parliament cannot continuously impose their preferences on the remainder. To these constraints we would add referenda called by the citizens, and a judiciary sufficiently powerful to block the implementation of policies that violate citizen rights as defined in the constitution. An additional possible constraint on the state, which we do not have space to elaborate upon, would be a strong federalist system.

9   CONCLUSIONS FOR A CONSTITUTION OF THE EUROPEAN UNION

In this chapter we have evaluated two forms of parliamentary democracy. Both have their merits. But we do not want to reconsider them in this conclusion. We rather want to apply our findings to the questions: which of the two systems is more appropriate for the European Union and what does that imply for the executive branch of the government and for citizens' participation in referenda?

We have seen that both systems reduce the costs of the democratic process compared to direct democracy. PRD economizes on the number of people participating in the political discussion and in opinion formation. TPD, in contrast, reduces the discussion, but allows all citizens to express their views directly by choosing a particular party program. Concerning the EU we have to ask: what is more important – political discussion and opinion formation or direct voting on particular programs? We believe that, for the European Union, it is the former. The EU consists of a large number of rather different member states forming a confederation rather than a federation. Discussion is needed among the elected representatives in the European Parliament to detect their citizens' preferences in the different member states. Therefore we would propose an election system for the European Parliament similar to that proposed by Tullock (see Section 2) or alternatively a list system (see Section 3). We recommend that the European Parliament be voted in one electoral district. For it grants minorities a higher chance of being represented in the parliament than in the present system of multimember districts.[12] In the case of the list system, the persons to be sent to the parliament may be chosen by the parties according to the number of votes they received or they may be selected by the voters under the single-transferable-vote (STV) system[13] in which they designate not only the party they prefer but also their ranking of candidates within the party. The restriction to one electoral district moreover avoids quarrels about which member state should receive how many seats in the European Parliament (see Section 6). The only way national government can influence the number of their own representatives is by promoting a high voter turnout. But even then, it is not evident that the representatives will support the goals of the particular member state government. For voters may prefer to vote for cross-country candidates promising to promote Europe-wide instead of domestic public goods.

Hence, the ever-returning question of whether Europe already has its own demos and could therefore be regarded as a federation or whether it is a confederation because it consists of several peoples with different views and attitudes has not to be resolved by introspection and collective decision; it results from the voting behavior, that is, from the extent to which citizens prefer cross-country candidates over own-country candidates under STV.

A European government that is formed according to the logic of PRD does not need a powerful government. It would suffice to have an executive board (see Section 7), say the Commission, whose members may be elected for a fixed period of time by the European Parliament. Overlapping of the terms of office of the commissioners may be desirable in order to suppress any tendency to establish a mixed system of PRD and TPD.

The Council actually has no role in our design of the European Union. Indeed, it lacks democratic legitimacy and could only be considered as a form of a second chamber. But we have shown above that a second chamber cannot improve democratic decision making in the Union when the first chamber is representative in the sense defined. It would be superior and indeed to be recommended to require the European Parliament to decide by qualified majority rule or by an inclusive voting procedure such as voting by veto or point voting (see Section 2). These voting rules would also set a brake to the actual tendencies to centralize national competences on the Union level.[14]

Collective decision making has to be checked by referenda and by the European Court of Justice. Optional referenda are designed for acts of legislation. They have to be held at the request of say 5 percent of the citizens or of 10 percent of the member state governments. For changes in the constitution, however, a mandatory referendum is required; political agents must not be able to set their own rules.[15]

We believe that our institutional design could serve as a starting point for a new constitution of the European Union, an alternative to that discussed by the European Convention. There is not enough space to elaborate further issues such as the assignment of power, taxation, rights and citizenship and the subsidiarity principle. But our approach is enough to emphasize the need to start from citizens and their preferences and to postpone other issues such as supreme values which are thought to be common (or imposed as common) for all citizens of Europe. We propose a bottom-up approach, whereas the ongoing constitutional process in the European Convention is rather one of top down. It risks adding to alienation instead of consensus.

NOTES

* The authors wish to thank Kirchberger Rencontres, the discussants and participants at the Public Choice Conference in Rome and the Belgirate Meeting of the European Public Choice Society and their colleagues Dr Pio Baake and Dr Rainald Borck for valuable discussions of the topics in this chapter.

1. An often-mentioned fourth principle, simple majority rule, is, however, deliberately excluded. For direct democracy can be practised with different less-than-unanimity rules and obviously also with unanimity rule. We shall show below that more inclusive rules generate political outcomes which are more faithful to individual preferences.

2. The material in Sections 2–7 is partially taken from Blankart and Mueller (2004) and Mueller (1996).

3. For further discussion of this procedure, see Mueller et al. (1975).

4. Caplin und Nalebuff (1988) have demonstrated that the probability of a cycle declines as the required majority is increased, when voting is restricted to issues having the characteristics of pure public goods, and that this probability reaches zero at a majority of 64.

5. Kirchgässner (2000) has questioned the plausibility of the assumptions under which these results follow, and shown that cycles may appear when these assumptions are changed. Unfortunately, since no TPD systems exist, Kirchgässner's hypothesis cannot be tested. Mueller (2003, ch. 12) defends the plausibility of equilibria existing in an electoral competition involving only two parties.
6. In Germany the Free Democratic Party has often been the beneficiary and victim of this sort of strategic voting, see Cox (1997: 197–8).
7. Although the British-style Westminster system can be said to result in stable government, it cannot be claimed that it results in some form of social welfare maximum as can be demonstrated for the TPD. Because there are generally at least three parties winning votes in the UK, it can happen that a majority of the voters would actually have preferred one or both of the other parties to the one that wins a majority of the seats in parliament. To avoid this sort of outcome and achieve the other possible advantages from two-party government, the winning party should be selected using the kind of two-stage procedure described above as part of the TPD.
8. For a closer examination of the organization of referenda, see Blankart (2000).
9. See the examples and discussion in Butler and Austin (1978: 5–16 and 221–37), and Mueller (1996: 182–5).
10. From time to time questions arise that are of a quasi-constitutional nature, but do not technically require a constitutional amendment, as for example whether a country should adopt the euro or not. These sorts of issues are quasi-constitutional in the sense that once made they need to be taken off the normal political agenda, since a continual shifting back and forth of policy would have high costs. Allowing the citizens to decide these quasi-constitutional issues via referenda is an attractive option.
11. Although deadlocks in the United States to date have merely meant that neither the program of the president nor that of the Congress gets implemented, in Latin America political impasses have often been followed by military coups and dictatorship. For more on Latin America and references to the literature, see Mueller (1999).
12. A minimal number of some seats may be granted to the very small member states.
13. As used in Ireland and Northern Ireland.
14. The European Constitutional Group (1993) proposes a second chamber consisting of members of the national parliaments in order to safeguard the subsidiarity principle and to prevent centralization. We believe that inclusive voting rules represent a more efficient way to achieve this goal.
15. As far as rights and citizenship are concerned, see European Constitutional Group (1993, 2006) and Mueller (2004).

REFERENCES

Barro, R.J. (1997), *Determinants of Economic Growth: A Cross-Country Empirical Study*, Cambridge, MA: MIT Press.
Blankart, Ch. B. (1992), 'Bewirken Referendum und Volksinitiative einen Unterschied in der Politik?', *Staatswissenschaften und Staatspraxis*, **3**, 509–23.
Blankart, Ch. B. (2000), 'Wie sollen Abstimmungen auf Bundesebene organisiert werden? Lehren aus der Weimarer Verfassung', *Wirtschaftsdienst*, **80**, 607–10.
Blankart, Ch. B. and D.C. Mueller (2004), 'The advantages of pure forms of parliamentary democracy over mixed forms', *Public Choice*, **122**, 431–53.
Buchanan, J.M. and G. Tullock (1962), The Calculus of Consent, Ann Arbor: University of Michigan Press.
Butler, D. and R. Austin (1978), *Referendums*, Washington, DC: American Enterprise Institute.

Caplin, A. and B. Nalebuff (1988), 'On 64%-majority rule', *Econometrica*, **56**: 787–814.

Coughlin, P., D.C. Mueller and P. Murrell (1990), 'Electoral politics, interest groups, and the size of government', *Economic Inquiry*, **28**, 682–705.

Cox, G.W. (1997), *Making Votes Count*, Cambridge: Cambridge University Press.

European Constitutional Group (1993), *The Constitution of the European Constitution*, London: European Policy Forum, www.fnst.org.

European Constitutional Group (2006), *A Proposal for a Revised Constitutional Treaty*, www.fnst.org.

Kirchgässner, G. (2000), 'Probabilistic voting and equilibrium: an impossibility result', *Public Choice*, **103** (1–2), 35–48.

Mueller, D.C. (1996), *Constitutional Democracy*, Oxford and New York: Oxford University Press.

Mueller, D.C. (1999), 'Fundamental issues in constitutional reform: with special reference to Latin America and the United States', *Constitutional Political Economy*, **10** (June), 119–48.

Mueller, D.C. (2003), *Public Choice III*, Cambridge: Cambridge University Press.

Mueller, D.C. (2004), 'Rights and citizenship in the European Union', in D.C. Mueller and Ch. B. Blankart (eds), *A Constitution for the European Union*, Cambridge, MA: MIT Press, pp. 61–84.

Mueller, D.C., R.D. Tollison and Th. D. Willett (1975), 'Solving the intensity problem in a representative democracy', in R.D. Leiter and K. Sirkin (eds), *Economics of Public Choice*, New York: Cyro Press; repr. in R. Amacher, R. Tollison and T. Willett (eds), *Political Economy and Public Choice*, Ithaca, NY: Cornell University Press, 1976, 444–73.

Nedelsky, J.L. (1990), *Private Property and the Limits of American Constitutionalism*, Chicago: University of Chicago Press.

Sundquist, J.L. (1986), *Constitutional Reform and Effective Government*, Washington, DC: Brookings Institution.

Tullock, G. (1967), *Toward a Mathematics of Politics*, Ann Arbor, MI: University of Michigan Press.

Wicksell, K. (1896), *Finanztheoretische Untersuchungen nebst Darstellung und Kritik des Steuerwesens Schwedens*, Jena: Gustav Fischer.

6. Democracy, citizen sovereignty and constitutional economics

Viktor J. Vanberg

1 INTRODUCTION

This chapter is an exercise in conceptual clarification. Its purpose is to explore the contribution that constitutional economics can make to the theory of democracy. Constitutional economics as the *economics of rules* is concerned with the study of how the choice of rules in the social, economic and political realm affects the nature of the processes of human interaction that evolve within these rules. The theory of democracy is concerned with institutional-organizational problems of self-governing polities. The purpose of the chapter is to examine some of the fundamental issues that are brought into focus by applying the perspective of constitutional economics to the rules and institutions of a democratic polity. Sections 2 and 3 discuss general characteristics of the constitutional economics paradigm that are of particular significance to the study of democratic institutions. Sections 4 and 5 explore the contribution that a constitutional economics perspective can make in diagnosing organizational problems of democratic polities. Section 6 concludes.

2 CONSTITUTIONAL ECONOMICS AS APPLIED SCIENCE

Constitutional economics in the Buchanan tradition is based on a methodological as well as a normative individualism. It starts from the presumptions that, first, social aggregate phenomena should be explained in terms of the behavior of individual human beings plus the combined effects of their interaction, and that, second, the values of the individuals involved should be regarded as the normative measuring rod against which the legitimacy of social institutions and collective arrangements is to be judged. Because of its normative individualism, constitutional economics is often considered a 'normative' branch of economics. If this is meant to imply that, by contrast to 'positive' economics, constitutional economics issues *value judgments* rather than refutable statements about matters of fact, it is a misleading description. It is misleading because it tends to blur the important distinction between what one might call 'genuine' value judgments and the kind of 'conditional' normative statements that applied sciences typically make. Or, in technical philosophical terms, it tends to blur the distinction between categorical and hypothetical imperatives.

Theoretical sciences provide insights into how the world works, and applied sciences make use of such theoretical insights in order to propose potential solutions to practical problems. As a *theoretical* science constitutional economics seeks to provide insights into how the framework of rules and institutions conditions the ways in which individuals interact with one another, and the social outcomes that result from their interaction. As an *applied* science, it seeks to provide knowledge for how the choice of suitable rules – or, respectively, suitable changes in the existing institutional framework – can help to solve problems in human interaction. All applied sciences, including applied constitutional economics, make statements about what one 'should' do or 'ought' to do, if one wants to solve certain problems. In contrast to 'genuine' value judgments or categorical imperatives, such 'should' or 'ought' statements are hypothetical imperatives that can be rationally discussed on empirical and theoretical grounds. They are false if the remedy that they suggest is in fact not a suitable means for solving the problem envisaged. They are in need of further refinement if alternative and potentially preferable problem solutions can be shown to exist. And they provide irrelevant advice if the addressee at whom they are directed is not interested in solving the problem in question.

Its normative individualism does not turn constitutional economics into a normative economics any more than its interest in solving human problems turns an engineering science into a normative physics. What its normative individualism does is to provide a selective focus to the kinds of questions that constitutional economics seeks to answer.[1] It chooses to concentrate its analytical attention on exploring the theoretical issue of how alternative institutional arrangements affect the well-being of the individuals living under those arrangements, and the practical issue of how institutions may be designed so as to further the common interest of the individuals involved. The arguments that constitutional economics advances in answering these questions are, however, refutable statements about matters of fact, not value judgments. To be sure, such statements are of interest – and in this sense 'of value' – only to someone who is interested in the questions that they are supposed to answer. But, again, the fact that their 'value' depends on the interests of the addressee does not make them value judgments as long as they answer the noted questions purely in terms of refutable conjectures about matters of fact.

Another way of describing the analytical focus of constitutional economics – as compared to standard economics – is to say that its principal concern is with the issue of how individuals can realize mutual gains by jointly committing to suitable rules, rules that guide their interaction into socially more productive paths than would otherwise be the case. If, as James Buchanan suggests, the 'gains-from-trade' paradigm is indeed at the very essence of economics in general,[2] constitutional economics can be said to systematically extend the gains-from-trade perspective from the study of voluntary exchange in markets to the 'voluntary exchanges of commitments' that individuals may engage in at the constitutional level by jointly submitting to mutually beneficial rules. While the economics of markets is about how mutual gains can be realized through voluntary exchange of ordinary goods and services, constitutional economics explores the mutual gains that can be had from adopting better rules of the game, in all arenas – economic, social and political – in which individuals interact with each other.

It is instructive to contrast the perspective of constitutional economics with that of traditional welfare economics. Like constitutional economics, welfare economics can be said to belong to the applied branch of economics in the sense that it uses theoretical economic insights in order to propose solutions to practical problems, specifically the problem of how a polity can improve its 'welfare'. In other words, both approaches advance conjectural advice about what kinds of policy measures promise to advance the welfare of the polity concerned. And, because welfare economics defines welfare in terms of individual utilities, that is, the well-being of the individuals involved, it may appear to share the same normative individualism on which constitutional economics is based. Yet there is, as Buchanan has repeatedly stressed, a paradigmatic difference between the two approaches, a difference that he describes as the contrast between the constitutional economist's 'gains from trade perspective' and the welfare economist's 'allocational or maximizing perspective' (Buchanan, 2001: 137).[3]

What is different about the two perspectives becomes apparent as soon as one takes a closer look at the way in which they model the individual and at the nature of the advice that they provide, specifically in regard to the question of who is, explicitly or implicitly, the addressee to whom the advice is directed. Arguing from a gains-from-trade perspective, the constitutional economist looks at individuals as sovereign-choosing agents who, by their actual choices, express what they judge to be in their interest and who, by their voluntary agreement, express what in social matters they consider to be in their *mutual* interest or, in this sense, to be 'welfare enhancing'.

Accordingly, as advisor in matters of 'social welfare' the constitutional economist's analytical focus is on advancing conjectures about how, as politically organized groups, individuals may be able to realize mutual gains, in terms of their own judgment, and, in particular, conjectures about what kinds of collective choice procedures may better enable them to advance their common interests. The addressees of such advice are the individuals themselves, and the test of the adequacy and relevance of the advice is in whether the individuals addressed consider the constitutional economist's suggestions to, indeed, serve their interests, and in whether the factual assumptions implied in the respective conjectures are correct.

By contrast, arguing from an allocational, maximizing perspective, welfare economists look at individuals as preference or utility functions from which they 'read' the utility values that serve as entries in the social welfare function upon which they, in turn, base their judgment on what policy measures can be said to enhance the welfare of the respective polity. In this construction the individual disappears as a sovereign-choosing agent[4] and is reduced to the role of providing the utility measurements that welfare economists use as informational input in their welfare calculations.[5] The analytical problems that welfare economists encounter in deriving their social welfare functions (measuring utility, interpersonal comparison of utility) are well known and need not be recounted here. Even if we assume that all these problems could be satisfactorily solved, the issue that is of principal interest in the present context would still remain, namely, who is supposed to be the addressee of the welfare economist's advice or, in other terms, who – apart from those interested in the theoretical exercise as such – might be interested in being advised about how the welfare economist's aggregate function of 'social welfare' may by maximized. Put in still another way, since, as noted before, applied sciences advise addressees about how they can better solve problems they face, the question that the welfare economist needs to answer is, who do they suppose might care about solving the problem for which they propose solutions. As far as individual citizens as principals are concerned, we can safely assume that they will be interested in proposals for how their own welfare, jointly with that of their fellow citizens, might be improved. They will, however, hardly care for advice on how aggregate social welfare may be enhanced as such, irrespective of whether this increases or decreases their own welfare. As far as politicians, who act as citizens' agents, are concerned it does not seem to be very plausible either to assume that they have a personal interest in heeding the welfare economist's advice, at least not any more than they expect that by maximizing social welfare they can successfully solve problems that they personally care about, such as the problem of advancing their political career. If, however, neither citizens nor politicians can reasonably be assumed to be interested in solving the problem of maximizing social welfare, it is difficult to see to whom welfare economists think they are talking – other than to themselves.[6]

3 CONSTITUTIONAL ECONOMICS AND CONTRACTARIANISM

With its gains-from-trade perspective, constitutional economics adopts a procedural normative standard for judging social matters. By contrast to approaches that, like welfare economics, seek to evaluate social outcomes in terms of attributes of the outcomes *per se*, constitutional economics bases its normative judgment on attributes of the process from which outcomes result.[7] The measuring rod for what can count as 'socially preferable' or 'welfare enhancing' is located in the subjective preferences or interests of the individuals who are involved in the transaction or social arrangement, preferences or interests that they express with their own voluntary choices. It is not because of attributes that they could read from outcomes *per se*, but only because of the fact that they result from voluntary agreement among the participating individuals that the observing economists may conclude that exchange transactions or collective arrangements are welfare enhancing, as judged by the participants themselves. Accordingly, the analytical focus of the constitutional economist's procedural normative judgment has to be on the issue of whether or not the outcome-generating process can reasonably be assumed to be based on voluntary agreement of the parties involved.

In fact, if examined more closely, the economist's standard assumption that market exchange is mutually beneficial or 'efficient' can be shown to ultimately rest on nothing other than the claim that it is based on voluntary agreement of the trading parties. In other words, it is not because of attributes to be found in market outcomes *per se*, but only because of attributes of the process from which they result that economists can infer their 'efficiency'. By market exchange economists do not just mean any kind of exchange transaction, no matter what the circumstances are under which the traders make their choices. Instead, by market exchange they mean trades that are carried out under conditions which can be assumed to assure the voluntariness of the transaction.[8] Even if this is not necessarily reflected in the way they are described in standard textbooks, in the economist's understanding markets are not just places where demand and supply meet, whatever the conditions may be that prevail in these places. Markets are institutionally secured arenas for voluntary trade and voluntary cooperation, arenas within which rules are enforced that aim at preventing the use of coercion and fraud. It is ultimately only on the assumption that markets are, in this sense, arenas for voluntary exchange that economists can base their efficiency claims for market outcomes.

In effect, constitutional economics simply seeks to generalize to all levels of cooperative arrangements the procedural logic that, even if rarely made explicit, is systematically implied in the economist's standard notion of efficiency in market exchange, by consistently extending it from the level of market transactions to the level of collective-political action and, in particular, to the constitutional level at which the rules for the socio-economic–political game are defined.[9] The constitutional economist's central tenet is that a consistent normative individualism requires one to regard voluntary agreement among the parties involved as the ultimate criterion on which alone efficiency claims can be based, in the case of collective action and constitutional choice no less than in the case of ordinary market exchange.[10] What is true for market outcomes is, the economist insists, equally true for political outcomes: whether or not they are welfare enhancing cannot be judged in terms of attributes of the outcomes *per se*, but only in terms of attributes of the processes from which they result, namely the extent to which they can reasonably be assumed to result from voluntary agreement among the individuals involved – if not their agreement to the outcomes themselves, at least their agreement to the decision rules that produce them.

As Buchanan has repeatedly noted, there is an apparent affinity between the constitutional economist's approach to politics and the contract theory of the state in that both derive the legitimacy of the coercive power of government from the voluntary consent of those who are subject to such power. It is in reference to its emphasis on the legitimizing role of voluntary consent that constitutional economics can justly be described as a 'voluntary exchange theory of government'. Such a label is not meant at all to negate the coercive nature of governmental power. It is meant to indicate that a government can claim legitimacy for its power of coercion only if, or to the extent that, such power is granted by, and exercised within the limits of a constitution its citizens voluntarily agree to. The reason for individuals to voluntarily submit to such a constitution is that by their joint commitment to the respective set of rules they can expect to realize benefits that otherwise could not be had or, stated differently, to play a 'better game' than they would in the absence of such joint commitment.[11] In this sense, the label 'voluntary exchange theory of government' is simply supposed to point to the fact that, just as they can realize mutual gains from ordinary market exchange, individuals can realize mutual gains through voluntary exchange of commitments to rules at the constitutional level.[12] And just as efficiency claims for market exchange are contingent on the voluntariness of the traders' choices, efficiency claims for 'constitutional exchange' are equally contingent on whether or not the individuals involved voluntarily submit to the rules in question.

The contractarian perspective that constitutional economics shares with the social contract tradition in political philosophy can be given, and has been given, different interpretations, three of which are of particular interest in the present context because they differ markedly in the line of inquiry that they suggest constitutional economics should pursue. A quite common interpretation of the contractarian perspective, prominently exemplified by John Rawls's *Theory of Justice*, centers around the notion of a 'hypothetical' contract. Authors who adopt this version of contractarianism direct their attention to the issue of what kinds of rules a group of self-interested individuals can be expected to agree upon if they were to make their choice among potential alternative rules under 'ideal' conditions, conditions that are presumed to ensure that the contractual agreement is reached in a voluntary, informed and fair manner. In the case of Rawls's theory it is the conceptual construct of constitutional choice 'behind a veil of ignorance' that is meant to describe ideal conditions under which the contracting parties can readily arrive at a voluntary agreement on mutually advantageous rules because they are both informed and uninformed in ways that eliminate potential sources of disagreement. On the one hand, they are assumed to be perfectly knowledgeable about the general working properties of potential alternative rules such that, in this regard, disagreement because of differing expectations is ruled out. On the other, they are supposed to be perfectly uninformed about any particulars that would allow them to anticipate any specific and differential effects that the chosen rules may have on themselves by contrast to other persons, such that conflicting interests in differentially advantageous rules are excluded as a potential source of disagreement.

Whatever insights the inquiry in what people can be expected to agree upon under 'ideal' conditions – whether what counts as 'ideal' is defined in Rawlsian or in other terms – may generate, it is obvious that they can be of limited value only to constitutional economics as an applied science that seeks to provide advice for how real people may solve their constitutional problems. As noted earlier, advice that an applied science provides will be of relevance only if it informs the addressees of how they may solve a problem they are interested in solving. And the question must be asked of whose problem-solving interest may be served by information about what persons would agree upon under ideal conditions. The hypothetical contract approach has been criticized on the grounds that the insights it produces are of no consequence. And, surely, if constitutional advice is to be of relevance it needs to inform addressees who know who they are about changes in rules that promise to make them better off, relative to where they are, and not about what would be in their interest if they did not know who they are and were placed under hypothetical conditions.

The hypothetical contract construct can be contrasted to two alternative lines of inquiry that one may pursue from a contractarian perspective, lines of inquiry that, as I suppose, promise to lead an applied constitutional economics on to a more productive research path. Instead of conjecturing about what might be agreeable under hypothetical conditions, the constitutional economist may seek to advance conjectures about potential factual agreement, that is, conjectures about what changes in rules would promise mutual gains for all parties involved, compared to the status quo, rule changes that should be agreeable to the parties concerned, given the conditions in which they actually find themselves. Such conjectures are conjectures about constitutional interests that the individuals involved actually have in common, as opposed to conjectures about constitutional interests that they would share under hypothetical conditions. While conjectures of the latter sort hardly qualify as relevant constitutional advice, by providing conjectures of the first kind constitutional economists inform the addressees about how they may come to 'play a better game' among themselves, for the benefit of everybody involved.

Whether the constitutional economists' conjectures about mutually beneficial constitutional changes are in fact true or not depends not only on the correctness of the underlying hypotheses about the factual working properties of rules. It also depends on the addressees' subjective evaluation of the consequences that the rules under consideration are predicted to have. However correct the constitutional economists' hypotheses about the factual working properties of rules may be, if their expectations about what kinds of consequences the addressees themselves regard as beneficial are wrong, their conjectures about welfare-enhancing rule changes will be falsified. *In this sense* the addressees themselves are the ultimate judges on what can count as 'welfare enhancing' in matters of constitutional reform, and their agreement to suggested constitutional changes is the ultimate test of the constitutional economist's conjectures about mutually beneficial reform.[13]

The emphasis on 'in this sense' is important for two reasons. First, because the addressees can, of course, not be considered to be the ultimate judges on the truth or falsehood of the constitutional economist's conjectures about the factual working properties of rules. And to the extent that their rejection of suggested reforms is based on incorrect expectations about how the reforms will actually work, their rejection of the constitutional economist's advice does, of course, not falsify his conjecture that the suggested reform, if adopted, would work out in ways that the addressees would consider mutually beneficial. In such cases, lacking agreement would point to the fact, that additional 'constitutional information' may be needed to allow the addressees to make a better educated choice. The second reason why the emphasis on the 'in this regard' is important is that a failure to find agreement may not be due to the falseness of the constitutional economist's conjectures but to 'blockages' in the existing decision-making procedures that prevent the addressees from reaching an 'agreement'[14] on suggested rule changes that would in fact be in their common constitutional interest, 'blockages' that may exist because of strategic behavior or for other reasons.

I noted above that there are two alternative lines of inquiry that a contractarian constitutional economy may pursue by contrast to the construct of a hypothetical agreement. The above remarks on 'blockages' in the existing decision-making procedures point to the second of these alternative lines of inquiry. Like the first it is concerned with the addressees' *factual* constitutional interests as opposed to constitutional interests that they might have under hypothetical ideal conditions. Yet, while the first line of inquiry is concerned with the issue of which rules may promise to be mutually beneficial and can, therefore, be predicted to be agreed upon among the relevant parties, the second is concerned with the quite different issue of how well potential alternative rules or procedures for choosing rules are suited to enhance the prospects for those rules to be actually chosen or established that serve, in fact, the common constitutional interests of the parties involved. In other words, the applied constitutional economist who pursues this line of inquiry is interested in identifying potential changes in the rules for choosing rules, or in the procedures for establishing rules, that may enable the individuals concerned to more readily and more reliably select and establish among themselves rules that are in their *common* constitutional interests, whatever these constitutional interests may be in substance.

The distinction between, on the one hand, conjectures about which rules may be in the common constitutional interest of a group of persons and, on the other, conjectures about which rules for choosing rules enhance the prospects for common constitutional interests to prevail is an important distinction even if it may appear somewhat subtle. By contrast to the former, the validity of the latter conjectures does not depend on the substantive content of people's constitutional interests, that is, on what kind of rule regime they wish to adopt. They are purely factual conjectures about what procedures for choosing rules make it more likely that rules will be chosen which serve the common constitutional interests of the persons concerned, as opposed to constitutional interests that they may harbor individually and separately but that are in conflict with each other. Whether these conjectures are true or not is to be decided on theoretical and empirical grounds. The persons to whom the constitutional economist addresses his advice may, of course, reject the adoption of rules which he supposes favor the choice of mutually beneficial rules. But such rejection does not prove that the constitutional economist's conjectures are wrong, it only indicates that the addressees of his advice prefer, for whatever reason, other procedures for constitutional choice than those which, according to his conjecture, would improve the chances for their common constitutional preferences to prevail.

4　DEMOCRATIC POLITIES AS CITIZENS' COOPERATIVES

In the remainder of this chapter the general arguments that have been made above about constitutional economics as an applied science and about the advisory role of constitutional economists will be applied to the case of democratic polities. Before turning to this issue, though, it is useful to briefly discuss in more explicit terms the distinction between different levels of collective-political choice – and, accordingly, between different levels of political advice – that has been implicit in the above analysis.

With his distinction between 'the order of rules and the order of actions', Friedrich von Hayek has drawn attention to the systematic interrelation that exists, in terms of the game metaphor, between the ways in which the rules of a game are defined, that is, the 'order of rules', and the kinds of moves that the players will choose in playing the game, that is, the 'order of actions'. With his distinction between 'the constitutional and the sub-constitutional level' Buchanan has pointed to the fact that 'the order of rules' may consist of several layers of rules such that in addition to the rules of the game *per se*, that is, the rules that define what the players may do or not do in playing the game, there are rules for choosing rules and even rules for choosing rules for choosing rules. The former I propose to call 'operating' rules, the latter 'constitutional' rules, 'constitutional' here understood in the sense of 'rules for choosing rules'. Applied to the collective choices that the members–citizens of a democratic polity may make, the Hayek–Buchanan scheme suggests a distinction between three principal levels of choice. There are, first, choices at what one may call the 'allocational level', in the sense of policy choices that directly intervene in the 'order of actions' or the playing of the game, policy choices that seek to correct directly outcomes of the game by correcting allocational choices the players have made. By and large the attention of traditional welfare economics may be said to mainly focus on this level. Its principal ambition is to provide advice for how 'government' may improve social welfare by correcting 'inefficient' allocational choices of private economic agents. Constitutional economics, by contrast, focuses attention on the second and third levels of political choice. Its principal tenet is that, again in terms of the game metaphor, the more adequate strategy for correcting (systematically and not just incidentally occurring) undesirable outcomes of a game is to seek to improve the rules of the game rather than intervening in the playing of the game. This can be done directly by changes in what I have proposed above to call 'operating rules', that is, the rules that define how the game is to be played, and it can be done indirectly by changes in the 'constitutional rules', that is, the rules for changing rules. In what follows I shall refer to constitutional choices of the first kind as 'constitutional choices type I', and to those of the second kind as 'constitutional choices type II'. The ultimate purpose of political choices at all three levels is, of course, to contribute to a desirable order of actions, that is, to make sure that the ways in which the game is played, and the outcomes it produces, serve the interests of the persons involved. Constitutional choices of either type are, in this sense, no less than policy choices at the allocational level ultimately targeted at improving the resulting order of actions. They differ with regard to the level at which they intervene in order to achieve this ultimate purpose.

As has been said before, advice that an applied science provides must, if it is to be of any practical relevance, be directed at an addressee who has an interest in solving the problem for which the advisor suggests a solution. In the case of democratic polities the citizens are, quite obviously, the natural addressees for constitutional advice that seeks to inform about potential mutual gains from trade. Democratic polities can be best described as 'citizens' cooperatives' or, in John Rawls's (1971: 84) terms, as 'cooperative venture(s) for mutual advantage'. Just as the members of cooperative enterprises or voluntary associations are the owners or principals of their joint venture, the citizens of democratic polities are the 'owners' or principals of the polity as a territorially based association. They are the 'sovereigns' with whom the ultimate authority to decide on the polity's affairs resides.[15] There are, to be sure, important differences between democratic polities on the one side and 'ordinary' cooperative enterprises or voluntary associations on the other, among them, in particular, the fact that a polity is not only a territorial but also an inter-generational organization in the sense that new members are typically 'born into the polity' rather then admitted by an express act of voluntary entry. Such differences, however, do not alter the fact that in a democratic polity no less than in any other cooperative enterprise the members–citizens are the sovereigns with whom the ultimate authority to decide upon common affairs rests.

As far as constitutional choices of type I are concerned, that is, the choice of operating rules, contractarian reflections on what rules of the game citizens would agree upon under hypothetical, ideal conditions can, for reasons discussed above, not be expected to result in constitutional advice of practical relevance. Neither the citizens as members–principals of democratic polities nor politicians as their agents can plausibly be assumed to find such information on hypothetical agreements helpful for solving problems they are interested in solving. If constitutional advice is to be of interest for citizens who know who they are and who can anticipate how they, personally, will be affected by suggested rule changes, it has to provide information on how mutual gains may be realized by all parties involved compared to the status quo and given their actual (not their hypothetical) constitutional interest. In other words, if he wants his advice to be of practical relevance the constitutional economist must suggest changes in the rules of the game that, as he conjectures, promise mutual gains for all parties involved, in terms of their own judgment, given their actual interests. Or, stated in yet another way, he has to suggest rule changes that he conjectures to serve the common constitutional interests of the members–citizens of the polity.

The constitutional economist's task as advisor is to examine the existing operating rules for potential 'defects' that prevent citizens from realizing mutual gains that could be had, and to suggest constitutional reforms that may correct for such defects. The ultimate judges on whether or not the rule changes that the constitutional economist suggests do in fact allow for mutual gains are the citizens themselves. Their voluntary and informed agreement is the ultimate test of whether his conjectures about what is in citizens' common constitutional interest are correct or not.[16] Failure to find such agreement proves the constitutional economist's conjectures wrong, if not his conjectures about the working properties of the suggested rules at least his conjectures about what kind of constitutional environment the citizens themselves consider desirable.[17] That the citizens' voluntary and informed agreement is the ultimate test for what is in their common constitutional interest must be emphasized for two reasons. First, even where the relevant decisions are made under unanimity rule, factual, observed agreement, or factual, observed failure to reach agreement, need not be perfectly reliable indicators of what is and what is not in citizens' common constitutional interest but may be due, instead, to insufficient information, strategic behavior and other reasons. Second, collective choices in democratic polities are typically not all made by unanimity rule. As J.M Buchanan and G. Tullock have argued in their foundational contribution to constitutional economics, *The Calculus of Consent* (1962), there are prudential reasons why members–citizens of a democratic polity – as, in fact, members of any cooperative enterprise – may voluntarily choose to give up the veto power that a unanimity rule grants and to agree to decide, instead, their common affairs by majority rule, or even to delegate decisions to representatives or agents whom they authorize to make political choices on behalf of the polity, at any of the three noted levels. In this sense a careful distinction must be made between unanimity as the ultimate legitimizing principle in democratic polities and unanimity as a decision rule for ongoing policy choices. Or, in other words, one must distinguish between the source of legitimacy of a democratic polity's constitutional rules and the content of these rules. While the constitutional rules of a democratic polity can ultimately derive their legitimacy from no other source than the voluntary agreement among its members–citizens,[18] in terms of their content they may very well allow for non-unanimous decision or the delegation of decision-making authority.

The test of whether or not the constitutional economist's suggestions for constitutional reform find acceptance by the actual decision-making procedures that the citizens of a democratic polity have established among themselves can only be a proximate but not the ultimate test of their validity. Such procedures may well allow for the rejection of rules that are, in fact, in citizens' common constitutional interest, and they may allow for the acceptance of rules that are not. Accordingly, if the constitutional economist's proposals for reform fail to find acceptance by the existing decision-making procedures, this must not be taken as the final verdict on the validity of his conjectures on what serves the common constitutional interests of a polity's citizens. It may also be due to shortcomings of, or 'defects' in, the decision-making procedures, that is, in the rules for choosing rules, which prevent reform proposals from being accepted even though their acceptance would be in citizens' common interest. There are reasons, therefore, for the constitutional economist to examine whether there might be such shortcomings or defects in a polity's rules for choosing rules, that is, its constitutional rules, and to look for ways in which they may be corrected. This points to the second level of constitutional choice, namely of constitutional choice type II, at which the constitutional economist may play a role as advisor.

5   CONSTITUTIONAL RULES AND CITIZEN SOVEREIGNTY

In terms of the distinction between operating rules and constitutional rules, the institutions of democracy must be classified under the latter category. Democracy as a system of government is characterized by particular procedures for making policy choices and for choosing the operating rules of a polity, namely procedures that are supposed to promote the common interests of the citizens and that derive their legitimacy from citizens' voluntary consent. This is what the characterization of democratic polities as 'citizens' cooperatives' or as 'cooperative ventures for mutual advantage' is meant to express. Democratic institutions may, therefore, be examined, in particular with regard to their capacity to actually enhance the prospects for a 'citizens' cooperative' to come to adopt mutually beneficial operating rules. And how well democratic institutions perform as procedures for choosing rules may, accordingly, be measured in terms of their capacity to promote citizens' common constitutional interest. This criterion for judging the performance of democratic institutions can be called, as I suggest, 'citizen sovereignty'. To improve democratic institutions means, in terms of this criterion, to make them better instruments for citizen sovereignty, that is, to change them in ways that better enable citizens to realize mutual gains from joint commitment to rules that are in their common constitutional interest, whatever these common interests may be in substance.[19]

The criterion of citizen sovereignty is central to the second capacity in which constitutional economists may serve as advisors in democratic polities, namely in providing information on potential changes in a polity's constitutional rules, that is, in the rules for choosing rules, that enhance the prospects for citizens' common constitutional interests to prevail and, thus, increase the chances for the polity to actually operate as a cooperative venture for mutual advantage. Proposals for reform that the constitutional economists may submit in this regard are, to be sure, subject to the test of whether they will be accepted by the citizens to whom they are addressed, or, more precisely, of whether they pass the existing decision-making procedure by which a citizens' cooperative changes its constitutional rules. But this test is an 'acceptance test' only, not a test of the validity of the constitutional economist's conjectural advice. Whether the constitutional reforms that he suggests are in fact suitable to further citizen sovereignty is to be judged on empirical and theoretical grounds. The polity's sovereign citizens are, of course, entitled to opt for other constitutional rules than those which, according to the constitutional economist's conjecture, would allow for more citizen sovereignty. But their refusal to follow the constitutional economist's advice does not prove his conjecture wrong. It only proves that, for whatever reason, the citizens prefer not to follow his advice.[20]

The constitutional economist's advice for how to improve democratic institutions in terms of citizen sovereignty can actually come in two versions – weaker and stronger. As the weaker version I consider advice about potential changes in the procedures for choosing rules that – by comparison to the existing procedures – promise to improve the chances for choosing rules that serve individuals' common constitutional interests, relative to the status quo. Such advice takes the existing constitutional rules as the benchmark against which improvement is measured. By the stronger version I mean advice on how the existing procedures for choosing or establishing rules ought to be changed if the aim is to create more conducive conditions for voluntary and informed consent in constitutional choice. As subtle as it may appear, the distinction between the two kinds of constitutional advice is of significance. As noted, in the first case the constitutional status quo is taken as the benchmark against which to judge whether or not suggested constitutional changes promise to allow for more citizen sovereignty. In the second case the constitutional status quo is itself judged against a normative criterion, namely in terms of the extent to which it can reasonably be assumed to be based on voluntary and informed consent of the persons concerned. And constitutional advice of the stronger version is advice for how the procedures by which rules are chosen and established may be changed in ways that facilitate not just the reaching of factual agreement on mutually beneficial rules, but that promote voluntary and informed agreement in constitutional choice.

The relevant analogy here is with the notion of voluntary market exchange discussed above. As noted there, the normative quality or 'efficiency' that economists attribute to market exchange is based on their, explicit or implicit, assumption that markets are institutionally secured arenas for voluntary cooperation. It is because – or, more precisely, to the extent that – the institutional framework within which they take place assures (as far as this can be assured under real-world constraints) their voluntary and informed nature that market transactions can be assigned the normative qualities that the gains-from-trade paradigm emphasizes. Analogously, efficiency may be attributed to constitutional agreements or agreements on rules if – or, more precisely, to the extent that – the conditions under which they have been reached justify the presumption that they are based on voluntary and informed consent of the contracting parties. And just as the constitutional economist can inquire into how the institutional framework of markets may be improved by creating more suitable conditions for voluntary and informed exchange, he may likewise inquire into how at the level of constitutional choice more favorable institutional conditions for voluntary and informed agreement may be created.

The weaker and the stronger versions of the constitutional economist's advice for how to promote citizen sovereignty differ in terms of the reasons why the addressees to whom the advice is given, that is, the citizens of a democratic polity, may want to listen. Advice of the weaker version directly appeals to citizens' constitutional interests, given the constitutional status quo. It informs citizens about potential changes in the existing procedures for choosing rules that will improve the prospects for mutually beneficial rules to be chosen. Citizens who believe such advice to be correct have prudential reasons to agree to the suggested constitutional changes because they promise to make them better off, jointly with their fellow citizens. In this sense the weaker version can surely be expected to be of practical relevance. It informs about possibilities for solving a problem that its addressees, the citizens, presumably have an interest in solving. Apparently, the same cannot be said about advice of the stronger version. Advice of this kind does not appeal to citizens' given constitutional interests but refers, instead, to the normative standard against which the constitution of a citizens' cooperative should be measured, namely that it is legitimized by the voluntary consent of the members–citizens of the polity. It suggests changes in the procedures for choosing rules that one should adopt if one wants to create more suitable conditions for voluntary and informed constitutional choice and, thus, conditions that can lend more credence to the claim that a democratic polity's constitution is based on voluntary and informed acceptance on the part of its citizens.

Since advice of the stronger version does not appeal to interests of its addressees but to a normative principle, namely the legitimizing force of voluntary and informed agreement, it may perhaps seem that advice of this kind is subject to the same charge as the welfare economist's advice, namely not to be tuned to the interests of real persons but to be directed to an imaginary, benevolent dictator who is interested in the normative principle as such. I do not consider this charge to be justified, nor would it be justified, in my view, to charge the inquiry into suitable conditions for voluntary and informed constitutional choice with committing the same mistake as the hypothetical contract approach, namely to speculate about what hypothetical people would agree upon under hypothetical conditions instead of conjecturing what may be mutually beneficial for real people, given the situation they are actually in. To start with the latter charge, there is a fundamental difference between speculating about the content of hypothetical contracts and seeking to identify institutional provisions that may, under real-world constraints, create more conducive conditions for voluntary and informed constitutional choice. While information on the content of hypothetical agreements is, presumably, of little interest to people who know who they are, information on what may enhance voluntariness in constitutional choice may well be of interest to real citizens, to the extent, at least, that they are interested in living in a polity that can claim to be based on the voluntary and informed consent of its citizens. And this brings me to my answer to the first charge, for citizens of democratic polities there are indeed, as I suppose, good reasons for having an interest of this kind.

With advice of the stronger version, the constitutional economist reminds citizens of democratic polities of the normative foundation on which their polity as a citizens' cooperative is based. He informs them about possibilities for constitutional reform that, as a matter of normative consistency, they should consider if they want to secure better preconditions for their polity to actually operate as a cooperative venture for mutual advantage. Such advice is not at all directed at an imaginary benevolent dictator but at the citizens themselves. It tells them what provisions they may jointly adopt if they wish to enhance voluntariness in matters of constitutional choice, provisions that – in terms of A.O. Hirschman's (1970) classification – may strengthen their voice or their exit options.[21] Apart from reasons of normative consistency, a prudential reason for citizens to follow such advice is that a democratic polity can be expected to be more stable and robust against changing circumstances the more its constitutional foundations can be assumed to be based on the voluntary and informed consent of its citizens.

6   CONCLUSION

As an applied science, constitutional economics inquires into how people may realize mutual gains from joint commitments or, in other words, how they may come to play 'better games' among themselves by exchanging commitments to suitable common rules. The citizens of democratic polities as 'cooperative ventures for mutual advantage' are the natural addressees for the kind of advice that such an applied constitutional economics may be able to provide. The focus of the above analysis has been to draw a distinction between two different levels at which constitutional economists may provide advice to citizens of democratic polities in matters of institutional–constitutional choice. The first level concerns, as I have called them, the *operating* rules and the second level the *constitutional* rules, that is, rules for choosing rules. Advice on operating rules is based on conjectures about which among alternative rules are better suited, in terms of their working properties, to result in mutual advantages for the members–citizens of a polity. Such conjectures have two kinds of components, namely hypotheses about the factual working properties of rules on the one hand and, on the other, assumptions about what, in terms of final outcomes, the citizens concerned will find preferable. While the citizens to whom advice for reforms in operating rules is addressed are, to be sure, the ultimate judges on the latter, they cannot be considered the competent judges on the validity of the constitutional economist's conjectures on the factual working properties of rules. Advice on constitutional rules is based on conjectures about which among potential alternative procedures for choosing rules provide better chances for citizens' common constitutional interests to prevail. The validity of such conjectures is to be judged in terms of empirical and theoretical arguments, not in terms of citizens' preferences, even though, of course, it is up to citizens as the sovereigns of democratic polities to decide upon whether they wish to follow the constitutional economist's advice in such matters.

NOTES

1. As J.M. Buchanan (1999a: 41f.) states his view of the constitutional economics research program: 'I am simply proposing, in various ways, that economists concentrate attention on the institutions, the relationships, among individuals as they participate in voluntary organized activity, in trade or exchange, broadly considered'.
2. Buchanan (1999a: 36): '[T]hat mutual gains can be secured through cooperative endeavor, that is, through exchange or trade . . . is the one important truth of our discipline'.
3. Buchanan describes the difference between the two perspectives in terms of their respective definitions of 'market failure'. From the gains-from-trade perspective, market failure 'means that there exist unexploited gains-from-trade, and the economist diagnoses such failure by identifying the barriers that prevent the potential gains from being exploited' (Buchanan 2001: 137). By contrast, from the maximizing perspective, market failure 'implies inefficiency in resource usage, and the economist performs his diagnostic task when he identifies departures from those conditions that must be satisfied to ensure optimality' (ibid.). Accordingly, the allocationist economist 'calls explicitly for a shift in allocation, independent of direct reference to the institutional setting' (ibid.), the gains-from-trade economist 'calls, quite simply, for a removal of the barrier' (ibid.).
4. As Buchanan (1999a: 34) notes: 'If the utility function of the choosing agent is fully defined in advance, choice becomes purely mechanical. . . . [A] computer can make all of my choices for me'. This is, in fact, what Walras and his followers intended to achieve in representing the individual as a utility function. As Walras (1874[1954]: 256) noted: 'In our theory each trader may be assumed to determine his own utility or want curves as he pleases. Once these curves have been determined, we show how prices result from them under a hypothetical régime of absolutely free competition'. And, as Georgescu-Roegen (1971: 343) reports, Walras's successor to the Lausanne chair, Vilfredo Pareto, stated, in quite similar terms, that once we have obtained 'a photograph of his tastes . . . the individual may disappear'. As a comment on this quotation (as reference for which he cites V. Pareto, 'Mathematical economics', *International Economic Papers*, No. 5, 1955, p. 61) Georgescu-Roegen (1971: 343) remarks: 'The individual is thus reduced to a mere subscript of the ophelimity function $\Phi_i(x)$'.
5. Buchanan (2001: 138): 'The allocational economist defines an individual strictly in terms of a preference or utility function. . . . In this analytical construction, efficiency or optimality in resource use is defined in terms of individual values, but these values are "disembodied"'. For a critique of the implicit collectivism of the 'social welfare function' approach, see Vanberg (2005: 10ff.).
6. The argument spelled out above is, of course, little more than a restatement, albeit from a somewhat different perspective, of the well-known Wicksell–Buchanan charge that welfare economists act as if they were proffering policy advice to an imaginary benevolent despot (Buchanan, 1999d: 456).
7. Buchanan (1999b: 204): 'Whereas the "social welfare function" approach searches for a criterion independent of the choice process itself . . . the alternative approach evaluates results only in terms of the choice process itself'.

8. Buchanan (1999a: 38): 'The "market" . . . is . . . the institutional embodiment of the voluntary exchange processes that are entered into by individuals in their several capacities'.

9. Buchanan (1999a: 39): 'The task of the economist includes the study of all such cooperative trading arrangements which become merely extensions of markets as more restrictively defined'.

10. Buchanan (1999c: 248): 'One of the great advantages of an essentially economic approach to collective action lies in the implicit recognition that "political exchange", at all levels, is basically equivalent to economic exchange. By this we mean simply that mutually advantageous results can be expected from individual participation in community effort'.

11. Buchanan (1999b: 204): 'Since it is carried out only after general agreement, collective action is essentially voluntary action. State or governmental coercion enters only insofar as individuals, through collectively imposed rules, prevent themselves from acting as they would in the absence of such rules'. On this issue, see also Buchanan (1999a: 39).

12. Buchanan (1977: 136): 'Economists . . . are specialists in exchange . . . When they observe a social interaction, they interpret the results in exchange terms, as possibly emerging from voluntary action. To the extent that results can be fitted into the exchange pattern, economists can infer that *all* parties secure gains, as these gains are measured in terms of the participants' preferences and not those of the observer. . . . This explanatory-evaluative task for the economist may be extended from the simplest to the most complex institutional structures' (original emphasis).

13. Buchanan (1977: 137): 'The observing economist can suggest ways and means through which improvements may be made by agreement among all parties, and the test of his hypothesis lies only in agreement itself'.

14. 'Agreement' is put in quotation marks here because it is meant to denote not only unanimous group decisions but any kind of collective decisions that are made according to decision-making rules that themselves are based on voluntary agreement among the members of the group.

15. Rawls (1999: 577) describes 'democratic citizenship in a constitutional democracy' as 'a relation of free and equal citizens who exercise ultimate political power as a collective body'.

16. Buchanan (1999b: 207f.): 'In a sense, the political economist is concerned with discovering "what people want." The content of his efforts may be . . . summed up in the familiar statement: *There exist mutual gains from trade.* His task is that of locating possible flaws in the existing social structure and in presenting possible "improvements." His specific hypothesis is that mutual gains do, in fact, exist as a result of possible changes (trades). This hypothesis is tested by the behavior of private people in response to the suggested alternatives. Since "social" values do not exist apart from individual values in a free society, consensus or unanimity (mutuality of gain) is the only test which can ensure that a change is beneficial' (original emphasis).

17. As noted earlier, the citizens as the addressees of constitutional advice, of course, cannot be considered the relevant judges on whether or not the constitutional economist's conjectures on the factual working properties of alternative rules are true. Such conjectures have to be judged on empirical and theoretical grounds, not in terms of preferences.

18. As Mueller (1998: 173) notes with regard to the unanimity principle: 'It provides a normative underpinning to the constitution in that the assumption of unanimity combined with that of individual rationality implies that the institutions of the constitution must be expected to advance the interests of *all* citizens. The basic institutions of the polity are not designed to allow one group of individuals to exploit another' (original emphasis).

19. Buchanan (1999d: 461): 'Improvement in the workings of politics is measured in terms of the satisfaction of that which is desired by individuals, whatever this may be, rather than in terms of moving closer to some externally defined, supra-individualistic ideal'.

20. Because it would not add anything of systematic relevance, I do not discuss here the fact that such refusal may be due to 'defects' in the actual procedures by which a democratic polity chooses its constitutional rules and that, therefore, one may ask for these procedures, in turn, whether they could not be improved in terms of their capacity to promote citizen sovereignty. Following this line of reasoning would mean that the constitutional

economist may have to shift his attention to the level at which the 'rules for choosing rules for choosing rules' are chosen.
21. These are, for instance, institutional provisions that fall under the rubric of 'competitive federalism' (see, for example, Vanberg, 2000 and 2001: 7ff.).

REFERENCES

Buchanan, James M. (1977), 'The use and abuse of contract', in J.M. Buchanan, *Freedom in Constitutional Contract*, College Station, TX: Texas A&M University Press, 135–47.

Buchanan, James M. (1999a), 'What should economists do?', in *The Collected Works of James M. Buchanan*, Vol. 1, Indianapolis, IN: Liberty Fund, 28–42.

Buchanan, James M. (1999b), 'Positive economics, welfare economics, and political economy', in *The Collected Works of James M. Buchanan*, Vol. 3, Indianapolis, IN: Liberty Fund, 191–209.

Buchanan, James M. (1999c), 'The orthodox model of majority rule', in *The Collected Works of James M. Buchanan*, Vol. 3, Indianapolis, IN: Liberty Fund, 247–61.

Buchanan, James M. (1999d), 'The constitution of economic policy', in *The Collected Works of James M. Buchanan*, Vol. 3, Indianapolis, IN: Liberty Fund, 455–68.

Buchanan, James M. (2001), 'Economists and the gains-from-trade', in *The Collected Works of James M. Buchanan*, Vol. 19, Indianapolis, IN: Liberty Fund, 135–52.

Buchanan, James M. and Gordon Tullock (1962), *The Calculus of Consent: Logical Foundations of Constitutional Democracy*, Ann Arbor, MI: University of Michigan Press.

Georgescu-Roegen, Nicholas (1971), *The Entropy Law and the Economic Process*, Cambridge, MA and London, UK: Harvard University Press.

Hirschman, Albert O. (1970), *Exit, Voice and Loyalty: Responses to Decline in Firms, Organizations, and States*, Cambridge, MA: Harvard University Press.

Mueller, Dennis C. (1998), 'Redistribution and allocative efficiency in a mobile world', *Jahrbuch für Neue Politische Oeuonomie*, **17**, Tuebingen: J.C.B. Mohr, 172–90.

Rawls, John (1971), *A Theory of Justice*, Cambridge, MA: Harvard University Press.

Rawls, John (1999), 'The idea of public reason revisited', in J. Rawls, *Collected Papers*, Cambridge, MA and London, UK: Harvard University Press, 573–615.

Vanberg, Viktor J. (2000), 'Functional federalism: communal or individual rights?', *Kyklos*, **53**, 363–86.

Vanberg, Viktor J. (2001), *The Constitution of Markets: Essays in Political Economy*, London and New York: Routledge.

Vanberg, Viktor J. (2005), 'Market and state: the perspective of constitutional political economy', *Journal of Institutional Economics* **1**, 23–49.

Walras, Léon (1874[1954]), *Elements of Pure Economics: Or the Theory of Social Wealth*, Homewood, IL: Richard D. Irwin (reprinted 1984 by Orion Editions, Philadelphia, PA).

7. Diffuse and popular interests versus concentrated interests: the fate of environmental policies in divided government

Giorgio Brosio

1 INTRODUCTION

According to a popular view in the literature on pressure groups, popular and diffuse interests are destined, on frequent occasions, to succumb to concentrated interests. This should be even more likely in systems of divided government, such as presidential and/or bicameral systems. Divided government favours the prevalence of the status quo, since it compounds the difficulties of finding an agreement on new policy formulations, when the two chambers and/or different branches have divergent views on the issues at stake.

Environmental policies could represent in principle a case where concentrated interests prevail over diffuse interests. In fact, while environmental policies are surely a response to diffuse and popular interests, they impose huge costs on industrial firms to install technologies that reduce the emissions of pollutants. Firms are potentially capable of resisting successfully the introduction of environmental policies and legislation. The costs of organizing producers into an effective lobbying group are quite small. Producer organizations already exist and can easily be employed on a new front. The same can be said of labour in the concerned firms. We are thus in the typical position where producers, and their allies, can outbid consumers and no, or only weak legislation, can be expected.

The reality, however, is that a substantial amount of environmental legislation has been enacted in most countries, particularly in the industrialized ones with divided government systems, and the division of government does not seem to have been relevant. This chapter provides an illustration of the emergence of environmental legislation and an explanation of this emergence. It is structured as follows. In Section 2, the arguments for the prevalence of concentrated interests are presented with reference to the characteristics of environmental policies. Section 3 is devoted to the illustration of why divided government, in particular bicameralism, tends to favour the status quo, thus making even more difficult the introduction of legislation favouring diffuse and popular interests. Section 4 provides evidence of the introduction of environmental legislation in a group of developed countries. Section 5 gives an explanation for this occurrence. Section 6 concludes.

2   BENEFITS AND COSTS OF ENVIRONMENTAL POLICIES: POPULAR VERSUS CONCENTRATED INTERESTS

Less air pollution, diffusion of protected areas and conservation of wildlife benefit almost everybody in the population. These policies provide collective goods that are in general consumed more or less equally by all individual citizens. Individual benefits from a cleaner environment are longlasting.

Present-day environmental problems tend to be global, rather than local in scale. They have cumulative rather than immediate effects. To appreciate them fully, people have to discount them. They are not easy to monetize and in some cases uncertain, given the disagreements among scientists and experts have doubts about the effectiveness of given instruments in solving the problem at stake. When uncertainty about future benefits is huge and present costs are substantial, one could even label environmental policies as unpopular, making their introduction more difficult, but still possible.[1]

The counterpart for firms of benefits to individuals are costly investments in alternative technologies to reduce the emission of pollutants. There may be some dissension among firms – some have lower costs than rivals and could exploit the environment regulation to oust rivals from the market. Things could become even worse, when we consider that business and labour traditionally enjoy a privileged position within the political party system of advanced democratic systems. While business interests find traditional sympathy with right/centre coalitions and parties, labour has the traditional support of left-wing coalitions and parties.

Environmental groups could, in principle, reverse the balance. Their number and strength has grown considerably in the last decades. Proportional electoral systems, when present, have allowed the birth of Green parties. Everywhere, non-profit organizations, both national and international (with national branches), have mushroomed. Their proliferation is the typical response that political entrepreneurs give to collective action problems in democracies. With a substantial budget and a large membership they are in a position to influence legislation. However, environmental groups are thought in general to be economically weaker (although this no longer seems to be the case in some countries, notably the US; see Shellenberger and Nordhaus, 2004) and possibly less cohesive than labour and business interest groups and thus less influential in lobbying.

The theory of interests groups and its combination with divided government would provide very grim predictions on environmental legislation.[2]

In reality a substantial amount of environmental legislation has been enacted in most countries, particularly in the industrialized ones. However, according to staunch supporters of the interest groups theory, the simple presence of legislation does not overturn their theory. Supplementary explanations have been advanced in its favour, and we shall examine them in turn.

First is the so-called 'conspiratorial' theory based on differentials in costs of environmental compliance between firms. In other words, more-efficient firms could exploit strict environmental legislation to impose unbearable costs on less environmentally efficient firms, forcing them to exit the market. The view that firms exploit strategically environmental policies has been advanced by Buchanan and Tullock (1975) and has received considerable attention in the literature, especially from the point of view of the choice of the instruments for enforcing environmental standards (see Jaffe et al., 1995; Oates and Portney, 2001).

A close relative of the conspiratorial theory is the interpretation of environmental legislation as a symbolic gesture to please the general public. This legislation may be quite severe, but it will be softened during the implementation process, that is delegated to administrative agencies (the environmental protection agencies: EPAs). According to this theory, business lobbies and labour do not have the strength and/or the willingness to oppose environmental legislation, while legislators prefer to shift the blame elsewhere, that is, to delegate enforcement to specialized agencies. This combination of strict legislation and delegation of implementation can satisfy the general public and concentrated interests, who perceive that with the capture of the agency they will reverse the result of legislation.

Finally, interest group theory could also be based on consumers. Rent-seeking legislation could in this case have originated in the strong interest for environmental amenities expressed by upper-middle class individuals.

Most of these supplementary explanations of the power of concentrated interests are only partially convincing. For example, the strength of the conspiratorial theory is weakened by the very large number of firms concerned, which complicates and questions the enacting of legislation that favours some of them at the expense of the others (see Pashigan, 1984; Jaffe et al., 1995 and provides evidence for the US). In fact, legislation should be tailored to the internal characteristics of each sector. It also sounds implausible that the general public can be deceived by a legislation that, while officially furthering the public interest, is in reality targeted to maintain the interests of the producers, or worse the interests of a selection of them.

Similar weaknesses are attributable to the view that stringent regulations will be rendered ineffective through capture of the enforcement by concentrated interests. The view is disputed even in the US, where state EPAs depend on the federal EPA, making them more vulnerable to capture. It looks more implausible, on evidence grounds, in other systems where EPAs depend on state/regional governments. One can observe, in fact, disparities in the degree of enforcement. In general, enforcement is higher and more efficient in richer states and regions, a fact that can be explained more easily with reference to productivity levels or to citizens' preferences than to the power of the lobbies. Moreover, as McCubbins et al. (1987) explain in their paper on administrative procedures, most of American environmental legislation (at least the legislation in force at that time) contains procedural mechanisms that protect their content against watering down during the implementation stage.

Even consumer rent seeking is better applied to the conservation of natural resources, such as the forest of the American West or the Amazonian forests, than to legislation restricting the emission of pollutants.

3   DIVIDED GOVERNMENT AND THE PREVALENCE OF THE STATUS QUO

3.1   Efficient Results

The introduction of environmental policies requires a change of the (legislative) status quo, a change to which collective actors have to agree. These actors are referred to in the literature as 'veto players'. Veto players are specified in a country by the constitution (the president, the lower and upper houses, the supreme court) and by political parties. The number of veto players is higher in presidential and/or bicameral systems, which are typical examples of divided government. To simplify the matter, I shall refer to one category of divided government: bicameral systems.

According to the theory of bicameralism (Levmore, 1992; Riker, 1992a, 1992b; Tsebelis and Money, 1997), this system produces two efficient results: (a) more stable outcomes, and (b) better legislation.[3] I shall focus on the first result. Stability of outcomes means the prevalence of the status quo and it derives from the compounded difficulty there is in a bicameral system to find an agreement on new policy formulations, when the two chambers have divergent views concerning their preferred outcomes.

Stable outcomes associated with bicameralism also derive from the reduction of voting cycles (Brennan and Hamlin, 1992; Riker, 1992b; Hammond and Miller, 1987).[4] Riker gives a huge weight to this outcome: 'When majority A (with cycling) adopts a motion opposed by majority B, then there is a clear instance of majority tyranny. Naturally, this leads to instability' (1992b, p. 166).

The second efficiency gain, stressed by the literature, derives from the lengthier process needed for introducing new legislation. The prevalence of the status quo in bicameral systems has its counterpart in longer debates and more refinement of legislation since the two chambers can make wider and better use of information. A bicameral legislation implies more scrutiny and evaluation by a broader range of opinion and knowledge. In other words, with a bicameral system it is harder to introduce changes in the existing legislation, but once the changes have been introduced they will be of a better quality than with a unicameral system.

It has also to be noted – and this is quite relevant for this chapter – that divided government provides greater access to legislation to different groups of the society, increasing the opportunities for competition. Competition has generally been recognized as one of the biggest merits of divided government. Since Montesquieu's *Défense de P'Esprit des lois* (1748), separation of powers in every public sphere refers essentially to competition and to the fact that citizens have more alternatives to satisfy their aspirations. With divided government and bicameralism, when citizens, or a group of them, perceive that they have no access to one branch of government, or to one chamber, they can try to have access to the other branch, or to the other chamber. Divided government and bicameral systems contribute to establishing a level playing field, increasing the chances of distinct interests being represented in the decision-making process.

Figure 7.1 illustrates the basic points about stability of legislation, which means the prevalence of the status quo. The setting is that of two chambers and a two-dimensional policy space framework. Legislators (and thus parties and party coalitions that aggregate them) have concave (that is, weighted Euclidean) preferences. This means that the utility that each chamber majority derives from a given policy decreases the further it is located from the ideal point. Preferences are depicted by the somewhat elliptical indifference contours, $I_L(SQ)$ for the lower and $I_H(SQ)$ for the higher chamber. This shape simply reflects that, while each chamber likes a mix of policies, it gives more weight to one policy dimension than to the other. L (lower) and H (higher) are the 'ideal points', that is, the mix that the majority of each chamber prefers over all other mixes and that it would choose in a unicameral system. L attaches more importance to A, the policy measured on the vertical axis, while H is more attached to B. SQ is the

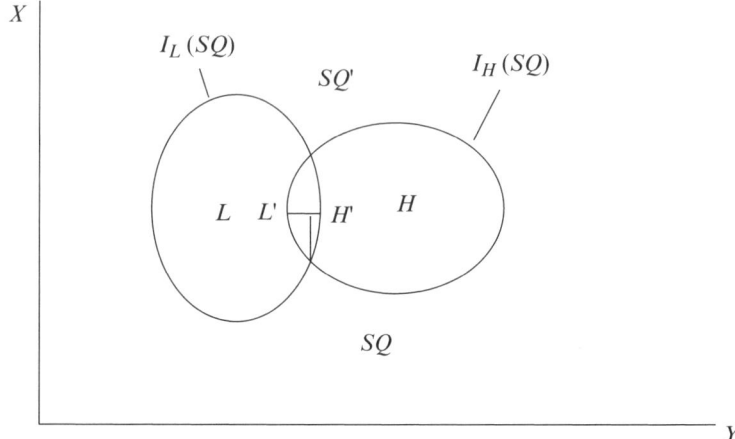

Figure 7.1   Prevalence of the status quo with a bicameral system

status quo, the present dimension of both policies. First, consider how a unicameral system would work. *SQ* will move towards *L*, which becomes the new ideal point. Every point situated inside the indifference contour is preferred to the status quo – disregarding, for simplicity, how the preferences of a multiplicity of members can be reduced to a single point.

Let us now introduce a second chamber. If not perfectly congruent with *L*, it will have a new ideal point, *H*. Preferences are shown by the contour passing through *SQ*. If alone, *H* would move to its ideal point. With a bicameral system the changes from the status quo are constrained within the space determined by the intersection of the two indifference contours: $I_L(SQ) \cap I_H(SQ)$. The bicameral system is more stable. Furthermore, every point on segment *SQSQ'* is preferred by both chambers: any change of the policy it represents is efficient. When *SQ'* is reached, the other policy dimension will be determined by bargaining within the two chambers. Segment *L'SQ'* is the locus of possible solutions. Each chamber has to cede something to the other: bicameralism requires compromise agreements between the (majorities of) two chambers – which is why it is typical of federal and consociational democracies. As mentioned above, the prevalence of the status quo depends on the distance between the ideal points of two chambers and thus on the size of the win set, that is, the set of outcomes that can replace the status quo.

Before continuing the analysis it is important to stress that stability of legislation, the prevalence of the status quo, can be liked, or it can be disliked. When pollution reaches an unbearable level for the population and a new more stringent regulation is needed, the prevalence of the status quo is without doubt a liability. It can, however, become an asset when the public gets distracted from environmental issues, and powerful lobbies ask for a reduction of the standards that were introduced in the past. An example is provided by the present pressures for the reduction of excises on petrol and diesel. The same applies to increased access to interested persons and groups. Divided government and bicameralism provide access both to the good guys and to the bad guys, and it is not possible to discriminate among them.

3.2 Necessary Conditions for Stability and Quality of Legislation

Most of the properties of bicameral systems, particularly the prevalence of the status quo, are subject to the simultaneous existence of two distinct conditions: 'non-congruency' and 'symmetry' (according to the terminology introduced by Lijphart, 1984).

Non-congruency means that the two chambers are selected according to different criteria.[5] Non-congruency makes it possible for the two chambers to have different majorities *vis-à-vis* the policies they legislate.

Symmetry means that both chambers legislate in the same areas (policies) and have the same procedural rights.[6] With perfect symmetry both chambers can initiate legislation and both approve each bill with the same majority required (as in the case of the US Congress and the Italian parliament).

Some form of non-congruency is almost the norm. In fact, most bicameral systems are designed with a view to introducing non-congruency. Symmetry is much less frequently found and perfect symmetry is an exception rather than the rule, making the combination of total non-congruence and perfect symmetry a rare occurrence.

However, the prevalence of the status quo requires non-congruency and only some symmetry, more specifically power of legislation in the same field, while some asymmetry in procedural rules is compatible with the stalling and stopping of legislation.

3.3 Arrangements that Ensure Non-congruence

There are many constitutional arrangements that ensure non-congruence; in other words that ensure that the two chambers will have different majorities:[7] (i) electing/appointing the two chambers at different times; (ii) combining different electoral systems; (iii) combining the democratic with the federal principle; and (iv) combining selection by popular election with a corporatist appointment system (such as the appointment of the propertied classes to the traditional upper houses). Moreover, these mechanisms can be combined.

In the real world, the choice between these systems and their combinations is dictated by a host of considerations that go beyond non-congruence. The two easiest systems, in terms of ensuring non-congruence, are the first and the last ones, which are the least popular. With distinct time schedules for elections, non-congruence requires a change over time of voters' preferences, which is a frequent occurrence. The size of the change needed depends on the electoral system: it needs to be bigger with proportional representation than with a majoritarian system. The selection of a chamber according to the corporatist principle has fallen out of favour, but can ensure a clear non-congruence in view of possibly diverging voting patterns by social classes if they are selected with a view to stressing their diverging interests.

3.4 Combinations of Electoral Systems

Non-congruence can be ensured by combining two different electoral systems, such as, for example, a proportional representation (PR) system for the first chamber and a majoritarian system, such as a first-past-the-post (FPTP) system, for the second one.

A combination of FPTP and PR would bring non-congruency if there is malapportionment (districts that elect a single member have a different size in terms of voters) and if the voting patterns, more precisely the choice of parties by voters, are geographically different.[8] It could also occur with coalition games.

3.5 Democratic and Federal Principles (in Federal and Highly Decentralized Systems)

In most federal and highly decentralized systems the second chamber provides some representation to the territories. This is called the 'federal principle'. According to this principle the number of seats in the second chamber is not related to the population, but to the number of territories with some lumpiness. There are different versions of the federal principle. With the 'pure' federal principle,[9] federated states send a delegation to the second chamber. The size of the delegation can vary (big states may have a higher number), however, each member has to cast her/his vote as a delegation, meaning that legislation needs a majority of states for approval.[10] The American Senate provides a milder version of the federal principle, where each state sends an equal number of senators, who are elected by popular vote at different times, with the whole state being the electoral district.

The pure federal principle when combined with the democratic principle in the first chamber has a high potential for non-congruence. As was the case with the combination of PR and FPTP systems, non-congruence is also in this case ensured by diverging geographical voting patterns and by malapportionment, which in its pure form – each state has the same representation – is the essence of the federal principle.[11] There is also non-congruence if the state delegations or representatives do not vote according to the discipline of the party for which they were elected. Variations in the preferences within each party are also important for introducing non-congruence.

If the previous analysis is correct then, because of malapportionment[12] a combination of the federal and democratic principles should provide substantially the same results in terms of non-congruence as a combination of PR and FPTP systems.[13] In the real world, however, the federal principle introduces a bias towards more conservatism than the FPTP system, because frequently small federated states have a more conservative electorate, being mostly rural (as with the small Swiss cantons). But while in federal and decentralized systems the combination of federal and democratic principles is rather the rule, unitary countries tend to avoid the opposition between PR and FPTP systems.[14]

Appendix Table 7A.1, provides some indirect evidence. The table shows how the representation of political parties has changed over recent decades, passing from the first to the second chamber. The pattern seems to be that changes are bigger in federal than in non-federal countries. As a consequence, there should be a greater stalling and stopping impact on legislation in federal systems, than in non-federal ones.

3.6 Arrangements that Facilitate Access to Legislation

Electoral systems and the combination of democratic and territorial representation also impact on the access to legislation. PR systems give easier access to small and/or single-issue parties, whose voters are not geographically concentrated. The typical example is Green parties, which emerged in a number of continental European countries with PR (or mixed) systems. FPTP systems disfavour small parties with non-concentrated voter constituencies – the Greens would be barely represented with this system – but favour representation of concentrated interests. These are the typical, business and labour lobbies of the environmental issues, but it could also be the case of large groups of individual voters affected by big environmental problems in their district.

Also, territorial representation could expand access, if the states or regions that represent the districts on which the second chamber is built are sufficiently small and of equal size. This would allow the 'voice' of the inhabitants of those areas, who are particularly affected by some environmental problem, or who have strong environmental concerns, to be brought within the legislative sphere.

3.7   Veto Playing and the Internal Organization of Legislatures

Stopping and stalling legislation also depends on how distinct chambers are internally organized. In turn internal organization, such as the setting up of committees and the delegation of powers to them, is usually the responsibility of each chamber with almost no constitutional regulation. There is little literature (with the exception of Tsebelis and Money, 1997) on the internal organization in bicameral systems. Diermeier and Myerson (1999) observe that in presidential–congressional systems (in essence in the US) committees have a veto power that is absent in most parliamentary systems. This is because of competition between distinct veto players. More precisely, in parliamentary systems the consonance of majority between the parliament and the cabinet reduces the opportunity of divergent choices – the destiny of parliament is tied to the destiny of the cabinet. In presidential systems, the chambers have a destiny and interests that are separate from those of the executive. Thus, chambers have incentives to set up their internal organization in a way that increases their bargaining power; for example, by assigning veto power to their committees. But why should constitutions remain silent about such a crucial delegation of powers to parliament?

4   THE EMERGENCE OF ENVIRONMENTAL LEGISLATION IN INDUSTRIALIZED COUNTRIES

This section presents a short reconstruction of the emergence of environmental legislation in a group of industrialized countries. I rely basically on the important work of Vogel (1993) for the illustration of the cases of Japan, the United Kingdom and the US.

Vogel describes how in Japan the introduction of environmental legislation was for a long time forcefully resisted by the LPD, the ruling party at the central level, despite the worrying levels of pollution in the urban areas (three-quarters of total industrial production was concentrated on only 1 per cent of the land). In fact, the LPD drew most of its support from the rural areas, whereas the main opposition party, the Socialists, had close links with organized labour. Thus, most demands were addressed to, and partly satisfied by, local governments. In the late 1960s and early 1970s, popular pressure intensified and a large number (more than 3000, although all of them small) of environmental groups were created. Opposition parties and the media became strong advocates of environmental control policies. The first major pollution law was approved by the National Diet in 1967. Increasing mobilization of citizen activists forced the ruling party to act. In a special session of the Diet in 1970 – the 'Pollution Diet', as it was known – 14 major pieces of environmental legislation were passed. Nor, according to Vogel, did this special session remain a unique event. The Diet approved an important piece of environmental legislation during each of the following sessions. Now Japan has standards of environmental protection quite close to those of the US.

Britain (also illustrated by Vogel, 1993) had much earlier traditions of environmental concern, but also traditions of air and other pollution in urban areas. The first law on air pollution control was passed in 1956, and its origins have to be traced back to the 'unusually nasty fog' ('smog') that settled over London in the winter of 1952. The most important pieces of legislation were passed in the 1970s. Again, according to Vogel, environmental disasters such as the *Torrey Canyon* spill of a huge quantity of oil off the coast of Cornwall in 1966 prompted the membership of local and national environmental groups and induced political parties to become active defenders of the environment.

In the US during the 1950s and the 1960s, environmental protection was mostly a concern of the states. Environmental groups although present were not as strong as their British counterparts. Moreover, the federal system represented a restraint to federal legislation. The first important piece of legislation, the Clean Air Act, was passed in 1963. The late 1960s witnessed a radical shift of public concern about the environment. About 20 million Americans participated in 'Earth Day', on 22 April 1970, to demonstrate their keen interest in stricter environmental policies. The National Environmental Protection Act was passed unanimously in January 1970. Other important pieces of legislation were passed in 1971 and 1972, despite the increasing opposition of interest groups. The influence of public opinion, however, became dominant. As Vogel recounts (1993, p. 256):

> Senator Edmund Muskie, who chaired a powerful Senate Committee with responsibility for environmental legislation, was a leading candidate for the Democratic party's 1973 presidential nomination. Anxious to prevent Muskie from making environmental legislation into a campaign issue, Richard Nixon became a strong supporter of stricter pollution standards.

In the late 1970s and the 1980s, there were some reversals of environmental policies in the three countries, but even under Ronald Reagan and Margaret Thatcher, these periods have been brief. One of Vogel's main conclusions is that: 'the content and the intensity of public opinion has been more important than the structure of political institutions in determining cross-national and intertemporal differences in environmental policies'. In fact, Congress has been relayed by the executive, and vice versa in the US. Parliament has been relayed by the judiciary in each of these three countries, and environmental groups have become a landmark in their political landscape.

The German history of the birth of environmental is slightly different. Until the 1960s, environmental laws, particularly those referring to air pollution, had been promulgated only by the *Länder*. Federal legislation was introduced in a systematic way only in the late 1960s and early 1970s, apparently without the occurrence in Germany of an acute environmental crisis and in the absence of noticeable pressure from the public. Engel and Zimmermann (2007) and the literature on which these authors base their arguments maintain that it was mainly an ideological choice stimulated possibly by an imitation effect; namely the ambition to align Germany to the level of environmental legislation introduced in Japan, the UK and the US.

Green parties came to the fore, later. Only in 1977 did they take part in national elections and only in 1979 did they enter a *Land* parliament (City state of Bremen). The role of public opinion became substantial only in the mid-1970s as a response to a relaxation of environmental standards established in the early 1970s under pressure from industry and trade unions and in the middle of the international oil crisis and economic recession. Since then, Germany has played a leading role in Europe as far as environmental legislation is concerned (Pehle and Jansen, 1998).

Environmental legislation in the Netherlands has followed the prevailing pattern, as shown by Lieffering and Wiering (2007). Until the 1970s there was barely any environmental legislation in the Netherlands and the protection of the environment was almost exclusively a local government responsibility. Environmental associations gained strength during the 1950s and the 1960s, but it was a series of environmental incidents that prompted public concerns and gave rise to an extremely active environmental movement, with many local and national organizations bringing pressure to bear on political parties. Parties became increasingly environmentally friendly and concerned about related issues. The passage of a law on surface-water pollution opened a period of intense reform that brought the introduction of legislation that is considered among the most progressive in the world (see also Hanf and Van de Gronden, 1998).

Italy is somewhat of a latecomer in environmental legislation (see Lewanski, 1998 and Capozza and Garrone, 2007). The first piece of environmental legislation referring to clean air was introduced in 1966 under pressure from local governments and judges, and with very weak environmental groups. The second piece of legislation (on clean water) had to wait for another 10 years. The Seveso accident stimulated an increased public awareness and a demand for environmental protection, although with huge regional differences that probably undermined its strength. Similar incidents across the world – notably Bhopal and Chernobyl – highlighted the issues, as well as advances made in neighbouring countries. Green parties obtained good results in local and national elections. A third piece of legislation, on soil protection and water management was passed in 1989. A crucial factor in speeding up environmental policy was the creation of the ministry of the environment. Italy being a parliamentary democracy, there is congruence between the executive and the legislative and new important legislation is usually initiated by the executive.

The executive also seems to play a similar role in France, particularly after the creation in 1971 of the ministry of the environment (see Breton and Salmon, 2007). A crucial decision, concerning among other things air emissions, had been taken earlier with the onset of the nuclear energy programme (Larrue and Chabason, 1998). Environmental groups became important in the late 1970s. However, they receive public subsidies and are subject to central regulation. This does not prevent them from being vibrant actors, even (or perhaps more forcefully) abroad. The general public has become increasingly concerned about the environment and is exerting more pressure for effective policies. Legislation and innovation in legislation has also been subject to pressure from the European Union.

5   DIVIDED GOVERNMENT AND PUBLIC ASPIRATIONS: LOOKING AT ALTERNATIVE EXPLANATIONS FOR THEIR SATISFACTION

The literature on concentrated interests gives too much weight to them and possibly presents a simplified view of the legislation process. Its results can be determined by the preferences of the public, despite its political weakness, especially in times where a large front with strongly felt preferences for a given policy is established. Farber (1992) provides an illustration of this statement by providing an account of the success of environmental legislation in the US.

Farber makes explicit references to an article by James Pope (1990) about phases of civic republicanism, but his theory also echoes closely Albert Hirschman's *Shifting Involvements* (1982). Hirschman's book tries to explain why individuals (and societies because of mass behaviour) show cyclical patterns in their involvement in the private and public spheres.

Farber's views has a cyclical dimension like Hirschman's. There are periods, such as the 1970s, when public attention to broad long-term and value-charged issues is weak and there are periods – Pope calls them 'republican moments' – when attention and public participation, also taking the form of popular movements and proliferation of voluntary associations, are high. During these periods, legislative attention cannot diverge from the preferences and demands of the general public. Of course, in a representative democracy the demand for public intervention on the environment does not translate automatically into real, non-symbolic, legislation if legislators and political parties are not motivated to become involved. There must be some mechanism that induces legislators to do so. Farber suggests that the main force driving legislation in these phases is legislators seeking credit for major reform.[15]

In fact, although Farber does not model the behaviour of legislators and parties, his approach is a typical supply model of legislation. That is, legislators maximize their expected utility, which derives from satisfaction of being a member of the legislature now and in the future. When they make their decision to vote for or against a given bill, they will balance the opportunity cost of their decision (for example, the support withdrawn by interest groups) against the benefits that their decision will generate on their future chances of re-election, or on their aspirations to a higher position, and against the satisfaction they derive from voting (ideological component of voting).

In a way Farber combines, with reference to those moments when the aspirations of the public are high, the theory of retrospective voting with the theory of ideological voting. The basic idea of the theory of retrospective voting[16] is that the incumbent's performance influences voters' decision. Voters are not interested in policies as such but in results, that is, in actual outcomes. The following statement by Fiorina (1981, pp. 5–6) gives a clear idea of the main message of the theory:

> [C]itizens . . . know what life has been like during the incumbent's administration. They need *not* know the precise economic or foreign policies of the incumbent administration in order to see or feel the *results* of those policies. And is it not reasonable to base voting decisions on results as well as on intentions [that is, campaign promises]? In order to ascertain whether the incumbents have performed poorly or well, citizens need only calculate the changes in their own welfare. . . . If polluters foul food, water or air, something is wrong. And to the extent that citizens vote on the basis of such judgments, elections do not signal the direction in which society should move so much as they convey an evaluation of where society has been [original emphasis].

In the theory of retrospective voting the incumbent is not compared to the challenger, but to a standard, the outcome desired by voters, such as clean air. If air has become substantially cleaner and closer to the aspiration of the voter, he or she will give the support to the incumbent and ignore the promises of the challenger.

As we see, retrospective voting reverses the ideological voting approach, that is, the typical Downsian approach to electoral behaviour. In this

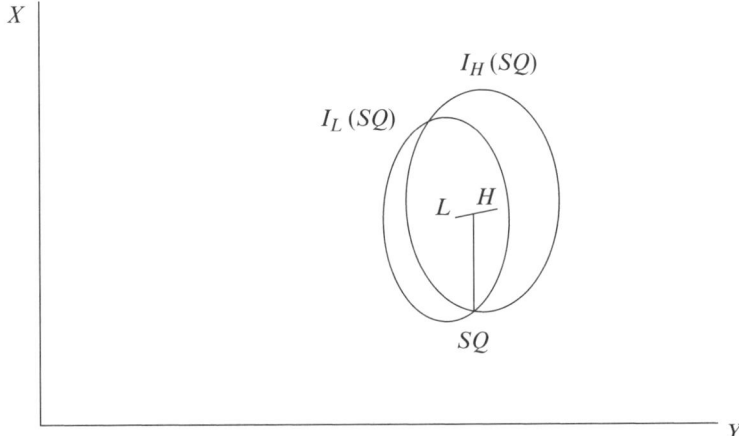

Figure 7.2   When prevalence of the status quo in a bicameral system becomes weaker

approach politicians and parties define and make public their platforms, while ideology is an instrument that summarizes these platforms and makes them accessible to the public. Voters will then decide on the basis of the distance between their views and the spatial location of the platforms of politicians. In other words, voting is decided through a comparison of platforms.

In those peculiar moments when the general public is acutely aware of the urgency of environmental legislation, and when a huge majority favour a tightening of environmental regulation, the differences between re-election and ideological policies become blurred. Legislators have to support bills that will provide real outcomes, because voters can check outcomes. Legislators also have to show unbending commitment to the environment, since the environment in general is high on the preferences of voters. This is shown in Figure 7.2, where the indifference contours now have a similar shape, indicating that both chambers give higher priority to the environment. The ideal points are now very close to each other. In fact they are now situated inside the area of intersection of the indifference contours. This area – the winset over the status quo: $I_L(SQ) \cap I_H(SQ)$ – is now considerably larger than the corresponding area of Figure 7.1.

Environmental groups are in these moments quite powerful as concentrated interest groups, and they are allied with the general public. They can play a crucial role by providing information and, thereafter, in ensuring the implementation of legislation against the attempts by interest groups to capture administration agencies.

6 CONCLUSIONS

As we can see from these examples, diffuse interests are able to prevail and divided government and bicameralism does not appreciably weaken them by delaying policies strongly felt by the general public, such as in our example of environmental legislation. Most of the countries examined – France, Germany, Italy, the Netherlands and the US – exhibit bicameralism. The US and to a smaller extent Germany have both non-congruent and symmetric federal systems that fill the conditions for the prevalence of the status quo. However, no appreciable delay in passing environmental legislation is discernible in comparison with the other countries. The US has another crucial feature of divided government: the presidential executive. In principle, the veto power of the president could further delay environmental legislation. Japan and Britain are unicameral and have an FPTP system that is in principle unfriendly to diffuse interests.

Italy is symmetric but congruent, but within this group is the latecomer in environmental legislation. Bicameralism in the Netherlands is non-congruent with imperfect symmetry. France's bicameral system under the Fifth Republic has shown frequent non-congruence. This is because, while the composition of the second house has remained relatively stable – reflecting the traditional French conservatism – the first chamber has shown considerable variation. In fact, non-congruency forces the shuttling of legislation between the two chambers and has increased (according to Tsebelis and Money, 1997, p. 129) the power of the Constitutional Council.[17]

A lot of imitation, more precisely of spatial interaction at the international level, is clearly visible. Major incidents that influenced legislation took place in different and very distant countries. As I have already noted, voters do not compare incumbents with challengers but with standards that are not only their desired outcomes, but also what other countries have already achieved. When a large and compact[18] majority of voters demand what is considered essential legislation, institutional constraints, such as bicameralism, lose their impact.

Summing up, we observe the introduction in the last decades of substantial environmental regulation in most industrial countries. The genesis of this legislation shows many similarities, in terms of time, since most of it took place in the 1980s and in 1990s, and in terms of response to an alerted public. The introduction of environmental legislation can be conceived as a response by parties and individual legislators to deeply felt aspirations of voters, which induce the former to disregard the appeals by concentrated interests. Voter sensitivity to a higher environmental quality is heightened by particular occurrences, such as massive environmental disasters. In response, legislators of different persuasion become fervent supporters of environmental causes. Moreover, the increased access provided by the existence of two distinct chambers to people and groups interested in legislation on the environment can help to overwhelm the tendency to maintain the status quo.

The prevalence of the status quo is a liability when the general public feels it urgently needs legislation that would fix major problems in society. It can become an asset when public awareness *vis-à-vis* the environment declines and the legislation stage is left to the involvement of interest groups, as in the current situation in some industrialized countries, notably the US. Even active environmental groups cannot suffice.

NOTES

1. Salmon (1993) explains that democratic systems can and do cater to unpopular policies.
2. For example, Fredriksson and Millimet (2005) in a paper on pollution taxes and bicameralism assume right away that environmental lobbies plainly succumb to other organized interests.
3. Bicameralism has two additional *political* properties: supermajority and restraints to the agenda setter. When representation differs between the two chambers, the making of a decision requires a broader majority than with a single chamber. In turn, a broader majority implies lower external decision costs. The argument holds particularly for Westminster-type systems where both the executive and the legislative are governed by the same majority and, more in general, this property of bicameralism is more evident when compared with a unicameral system based on a system of district elections with a first-past-the-post system. In such a system, a party which wins 51 per cent of the districts with 51 per cent of the votes in each will have a majority of seats with only 26 per cent of the total vote. Under bicameralism, unless the second chamber replicates the first one exactly, a party needs to obtain a larger share of the total vote to be allowed to govern. Ideally, with totally different modes of selection it will take one-half of the votes to control both houses of a legislature (Buchanan and Tullock, 1962; Hammond and Miller, 1987; Cooter 2000). However, supermajoritarianism is also ensured by other institutional arrangements of separation of powers, such as, for example, presidentialism, or supreme court jurisdictional review.
4. The problem of the agenda setter has been elaborated by Levmore (1992). Basically, when voting cycles are possible, in other words when no alternative is a Condorcet winner, the power of the agenda setter in a single chamber system of determining the result is enhanced. To determine the result according to her/his own preferences, the agenda setter can orchestrate the vote of the alternatives. In a bicameral system, the agenda setter's preferred alternative has to be approved by the second house. This means that it needs to win against all alternatives. Unless there is collusion with the second chamber 'bicameralism can be understood as an antidote to the manipulative power of the convener, or agenda setter, when faced with cycling preferences' (Levmore, 1992, pp. 147–8).
5. For example, the Italian senate is quite congruent since its main differences with the first chamber are that: (i) senators have to be more than 40 years old (25 years for the first chamber) and (ii) voters have to be more than 25 (18 for the first chamber). On the other hand, the German, South African and Canadian second chambers are *non-congruent*, their members being selected by the subnational governments (Germany and South Africa) or by the central government (Canada).
6. The two chambers may have features of symmetry, such as, for example, voting confidence in the executive and appointing officials. These are disregarded here, although they can in principle impact on (environmental) legislation.

7. The existence of different majorities between the two chambers may also be due to a lack of party discipline. This derives, in turn, mainly from the electoral systems. Party discipline can also vary according to the issues at stake. In democratic systems, voting discipline is lifted when chambers have to decide on issues that are highly divisive inside parties.

8. Suppose, for example, that there are three single-member districts, which form a national constituency. The Red Party gets 60 per cent of the vote in the first district, 51 per cent in the second and 40 per cent in the third, while the Blue Party gets 40, 50 and 60 per cent, respectively. There are 5000 voters in the first, district, 10,000 in the second and 15,000 in the third. With FPTP the Red Party will get two seats and govern the first chamber, while the Blue Party will have a majority of seats with PR and govern the second chamber.

9. This principle characterizes bicameralism in Germany, South Africa and Ethiopia.

10. Additional features of the German second chamber are that state governments and not members or delegations are initiators of legislation, and that delegations can be changed for each single piece of legislation according to its object, with the result that the second chamber works each time on a committee basis.

11. In Germany and in the period prior to unification, there were approximately 16 years of similar majorities in the two chambers, 10 years of dissimilar majorities and 15 years of big coalitions (see Koenig, 2001).

12. However crucial, malapportionment is not the unique origin of non-congruence.

13. With a pure federal principle there is an additional reason for non-congruence, in that there is an inducement for state delegations to decide independently from party discipline.

14. Italy, for example, switched from a pure proportional system in both chambers (in theory there was an FPTP system in the Senate that was completely ineffective) to a mixed system in both chambers where 75 per cent of their members are now elected according to FPTP and the remaining 25 per cent according to PR.

15. This should be especially true for the American Senate, where prominent members have presidential aspirations. There are at least two such cases in the recent history of American Senate: senators Edmund Muskie and Al Gore who established themselves as 'Mr Environment'.

16. This theory was first outlined by V.O. Key (1966). Accounts are given by Fiorina (1981).

17. Vogel mentions how the Japanese ruling party, the LDP, was extremely harsh with the inhabitants of the most polluted urban areas who were demanding a cleaner environment, sending in the police to quell the unrest.

18. The Netherlands and Sweden, for example, have some of the most advanced environmental legislation. At the same time these countries enjoy some of the most equal distributions of personal income, making them more susceptible to demands for a more stringent environmental legislation (Marsiliani and Renström, 2000 stress the impact of equal distribution on environmental preferences).

REFERENCES

Brennan, Geoffrey and Alan Hamlin (1992), 'Bicameralism and majoritarian equilibrium', *Public Choice*, **74**: 169–79.

Breton, Albert and Pierre Salmon (2007), 'France: forces shaping centralization and decentralization in environmental policymaking', presented at the first Alghero Seminar of the Environmental Governance in Decentralized Setting, forthcoming in Albert Breton, Giorgio Brosio, Silvana Dalmazzone and Giovanna Garrone (eds), *Environmental Governance: Country Studies*, Cheltenham, MA and Northampton, USA: Edward Elgar.

Buchanan, James and Gordon Tullock (1962), *The Calculus of Consent*, Ann Arbor, MI: Michigan University Press.

Buchanan, James and Gordon Tullock (1975), 'Polluters' profits and political response: direct controls versus taxes', *American Economic Review*, **64**: 139–47.

Capozza, Ivana and Giovanna Garrone (2007), 'Italy: towards responsibility sharing in environmental protection', presented at the first Alghero Seminar of the Environmental Governance in Decentralized Setting, forthcoming in Albert Breton, Giorgio Brosio, Silvana Dalmazzone and Giovanna Garrone (eds), *Environmental Governance: Country Studies*, Cheltenham, UK and Northampton, MA, USA: Edward Elgar.

Cooter, Robert (2000), *The Strategic Constitution*, Princeton, NJ: Princeton University Press.

Diermeier, D. and R. Myerson (1999), 'Bicameralism and its consequences for the internal organization of legislature', *American Economic Review*, **89**: 1182–96.

Engel, Stephanie and Melanie Zimmermann (2007), 'Environmental institutions in Germany: leader or laggard?', forthcoming in Albert Breton, Giorgio Brosio, Silvana Dalmazzone and Giovanna Garrone (eds) *Environmental Governance and Decentralization*, Cheltenham, UK and Northampton, MA, USA: Edward Elgar.

Farber, Daniel (1992), 'Politics and procedure in environmental law', *Journal of Law, Economics, and Organization*, **8**: 59–82.

Fiorina, Morris (1981), *Retrospective Voting in American National Elections*, New Haven, CT: Yale University Press.

Fredriksson, Per and Daniel Millimet (2005), 'Legislative organization and pollution taxation', mimeo, University of Louisville and Southern Methodist University.

Hammond, T. and G. Miller (1987), 'The core of the Constitution', *American Political Science Review*, **81**: 1155–74.

Hanf, Kenneth and Egbert van de Gronden (1998), 'The Netherlands: joint regulation and sustainable development', in Kenneth Hanf and Alf-Inge Jansen (eds), *Governance and the Environment in Western Europe. Politics, Policy and Administration*, London: Longman, pp. 152–80.

Hirschman, Albert (1982), *Shifting Involvements: Private Interests and Public Action*, Princeton, NJ: Princeton University Press.

Jaffe, Adam, Steven Peterson and Paul Portney (1995), 'Environmental regulation and competitiveness of U.S. manufacturing: what evidence tells us?', *Journal of Economic Literature*, **33**: 132–63.

Key, V.O. (1966), *The Responsible Electorate: Rationality in Presidential Voting 1936–1960*, Cambridge, MA: Belknap Press.

Koenig, Thomas (2001), 'Bicameralism and party politics in Germany: an empirical social choice approach', *Political Studies*, **49**: 411–37.

Larrue, Corinne and Lucien Chabason (1998), 'France: fragmented policy and consensual implementation', in Kenneth Hanf and Alf-Inge Jansen (eds), *Governance and the Environment in Western Europe. Politics, Policy and Administration*, London: Longman, pp. 60–81.

Levmore, S. (1992), 'Bicameralism: when are two decisions better than one?', *International Review of Law and Economics*, **12**: 145–62.

Lewanski, Rudolf (1998), 'Italy: environmental policy in a fragmented state', in Kenneth Hanf and Alf-Inge Jansen (eds), *Governance and the Environment in Western Europe. Politics, Policy and Administration*, London: Longman, pp. 131–51.

Lieffering, Duncan and Mark Wiering (2007), 'Netherlands: an integrated participatory approach to environmental policy-making', presented at the first Alghero

Seminar of the Environmental Governance in Decentralized Setting, forthcoming in Albert Breton, Giorgio Brosio, Silvana Dalmazzone and Giovanna Garrone (eds), *Environmental Governance: Country Studies*, Cheltenham, UK and Northampton, MA, USA: Edward Elgar.

Lijphart, A. (1984), *Democracies: Patterns of Majoritarian and Consensus Government in Twenty-one Countries*, New Haven, CT: Yale University Press.

Marsiliani Laura and Thomas I. Renström (2000), 'Inequality, environmental protection and growth', Center for Economic Research, Tilburg University, No. 3.

McCubbins, Mathew, Roger Noll and Barry Weingast (1987), 'Administrative procedures as instruments of political control', *Journal of Law, Economics and Organization*, **3**: 243–77.

Oates, Wallace and Paul Portney (2001), *The Political Economy of Environmental Policy*, Washington, DC: Resources for the Future.

Pashigan, Peter (1984), 'The effect of environmental legislation on optimal plant size and factor shares', *Journal of Law and Economics*, **27**: 1–17.

Pehle, Heinrich and Alf-Inge Jansen (1998), 'Germany: the engine in European environmental policy?', in Kenneth Hanf and Alf-Inge Jansen (eds), *Governance and the Environment in Western Europe. Politics, Policy and Administration*, London: Longman, pp. 82–109.

Pope, James (1990), 'Republican moments: the role of direct popular power in the American constitutional order', *University of Pennsylvania Law Review*, **27**: 1–27.

Riker, W. (1992a), 'The justification for bicameralism', *International Political Science Review*, **13**: 101–16.

Riker, W. (1992b), 'The merits of bicameralism, commentary to Levmore', *International Review of Law and Economics*, **12**: 163–8.

Salmon, Pierre (1993), 'Unpopular policies and the theory of representative democracy', in Albert Breton, Gianluigi Galeotti, Pierre Salmon and Ronald Wintrobe (eds), *Preferences and Democracy*, Dordrecht: Kluwer Academic Publishers, pp. 13–40.

Shellenberger, Michael and Ted Nordhaus (2004), 'The death of environmentalism: global warming politics in a post-environmental world', www.thebreakthrough.org/images/Death_of_Environmentalism.pdf.

Tsebelis, G. and J. Money (1997), *Bicameralism*, Cambridge: Cambridge University Press.

Vatter, Adrian (2005), 'Bicameralism and policy performance: the effects of cameral structure in comparative perspective', *Legislative Studies*, **11**: 194–215.

Vogel, David (1993), 'Representing diffuse interests in environmental policymaking', in K. Weaver and Bert Rockman (eds), *Do Institutions Matter? Government Capabilities in the United States and Abroad*, Washington, DC: Brookings Institution, pp. 237–71.

Table 7A.1 Average difference in party representation between the first and second chambers in a sample of bicameral countries, 1971–1996

	Switzerland	Netherlands	Belgium	Austria	Spain (1977–96)	Italy	France
Extreme Left	–2.0	+0.3	–0.5	–	–4.0	–1.3	–2.7
Green	–2.5	+0.7	–0.4	–2.1	–	–0.7	–
Left	–13.2	–4.3	–1.7	+0.7	–0.1	+4.0	–10.8
Liberal	+10.4	+0.6	+0.6	–7.0	–	–2.7	+12.1
Conservative	+14.2	+4.1	+1.3	+7.1	+1.6	+4.0	+3.2
Extreme Right	–3.9	–0.3	–0.2	–0.2	–	–2.4	–0.6

	Germany	Ireland	UK	USA	Canada	Australia	Japan
Extreme Left	–0.9	–	–	–	–	–	–
Green	–2.8	–0.4	–	–	–	–	–
Left	+4.7	–0.7	–18.0	–	–9.4	–4.0	–0.4
Liberal	–8.6	–1.6	+7.4	–5.5	+17.7	+6.3	+0.9
Conservative	+7.6	+3.0	+14.1	+5.0	–12.3	+4.3	–4.7
Extreme Right	–	–	–	–	–	–	–

Source: Drawn from Vatter (2005, p. 196). Original sources are listed there.

8. Should the democratic model be applied to non-governmental organizations and firms?

Pascal Salin

1   INTRODUCTION

'Democracy' is the taboo word of our time. It tends to be the single crite-rion by which humane institutions and organizations are evaluated. Its importance is such that it has obtained an ethical dimension: being demo-cratic is good, being non-democratic is bad. There is even a shift in the meaning of the word since, for instance, democratizing education just means extending education to a wide category of people and not only organizing education according to democratic processes. However, let us keep the concept with its strict meaning, namely a system in which a col-lective decision is adopted through voting, for instance with a majority rule.

Given the importance given to the democratic character of institutions in the modern world, it is not surprising that many people consider it desirable to apply democratic rules to as many organizations as possible, beyond the public sphere for the working of which they have been initially designed. Thus, it is claimed that firms, associations and even, perhaps, the family ought to be managed according to democratic principles. At first glance this seems to be very attractive: why, for instance, would wage earners, who are con-cerned by what will happen in their firm, not be associated with decisions that can affect them? Why, in non-profit organizations – such as a university – would those who are concerned by the correct working of their institution not participate in decisions? Such general ideas are at the source of much legisla-tion which obliges firms to accept representatives of wage earners on their board or which organize universities so that professors, students and members of the administration democratically elect representatives for the various committees and boards and/or appoint their president.

However, in spite of this positive prejudice, the extension of the democra-tic principle to all these humane organizations outside the public sphere com-pletely changes their very nature in a way which can be incoherent – and, therefore, be a threat to their functioning – or which can even be dangerous, as we shall demonstrate in this chapter, but first (Section 2), let us consider the problem of the role played by the democratic principle in the working of public organizations (which, to simplify, we shall call 'the state'). We shall proceed to an analysis of the proper role of democracy in firms (Section 3) and will then briefly consider the case of other non-governmental organizations (Section 4). Section 5 concludes.

2   DEMOCRACY, LIBERTY AND PROPERTY

A democratic state is a state in which voting procedures are used either directly to take a decision or indirectly to appoint representatives who, in turn, are entitled to take decisions in the name of citizens. Thus, democracy concerns the functioning of the state and, from this point of view, democratic and non-democratic states, for instance dictatorships or authoritarian regimes, form two ends of the spectrum. In-between one may imagine different degrees in the democratic character of the state.

Now, beyond the rules concerning the working of the state, there is another and more important problem which concerns the limits of the state. From this point of view, one may oppose the systems that are respectful of individual liberty – and therefore of private property – and those that are not and which can be called totalitarian systems. Here again, in-between, different intermediary situations – implying various degrees of individual liberty – can be distinguished.

Now, these criteria – democratic versus non-democratic on the one hand and liberal systems versus totalitarian ones on the other – do not coincide. A dictator can be – but is not necessarily – totalitarian and one can even imagine at the extreme the existence of a dictator who is perfectly respectful of individual liberty. In some sense such was the imaginary figure of the 'enlightened despot' in the eighteenth century. Similarly, a democracy can be more or less respectful of individual liberty and it may even be tyrannical or totalitarian. Tyrannical democracies exist whenever, for instance, 51 percent of voters decide to take the property or the liberty of the other 49 percent, which is a rather frequent occurrence. This means that the democratic character of the state is not a sufficient criterion to evaluate this state, which also means that it cannot be a satisfactory criterion to evaluate any other humane organization. Thus, democracy cannot be considered as a universal criterion. Before examining the more or less democratic characteristic of a state, one ought first to evaluate to what extent the state is respectful of individual liberty. At the limit, if ever the state had no power at all, there would be no reason to care and to wonder whether it was a democracy or a dictatorship: why should we be anxious about the existence of a dictator without any power over individuals?

Thus, democracy can be antinomic to individual liberty and there is one fundamental reason for that. In fact, the basic system which has to be solved in any society consists in allocating scarce resources. Potentially, claims on these resources are unlimited and one has to find a way to limit them and to make them compatible. In other words, one has to define property rights, since, whenever someone holds a property right on something, all other individuals are excluded from using it. Thus, any social system is designed in order to determine those who pay – that is, are abandoning part of their property – and those who receive property rights. As is well known, a liberal order implies that property rights arise from acts of creation and that they are individually defined, which does not prevent people from pooling their resources and deciding a collective use of them according to commonly accepted rules. In a free society people themselves decide to what extent they want to create new property rights, to use them, to exchange them and to acquire new ones. The liberal order is the only conceivable coherent social system, because it makes it impossible for different persons to claim the ownership of one single piece of property: as far as property rights are individually defined and protected, there is no ambiguity regarding ownership, and exclusion and conflicts are impossible.

Therefore, why should one introduce any other decision-making process, for instance a democratic process by which resources could be transferred from some people to others according to the will of a majority? As we have already mentioned, individuals can voluntarily decide to pool a part of their resources and to determine their allocation according to some majority rule. We shall come back to this form of democracy later on. But the state – as a monopolist of legal constraint – obliges some citizens to abandon part of their resources and distributes them to others.[1] Now as these resources are not legitimately owned, in that sense the link between ownership and creation has been broken by the emergence of constraint, some other process for deciding the allocation of these resources has to be found. Under an authoritarian regime, the despot decides these transfers of property. Under a democratic regime, some of the citizens decide the transfers according to a majority rule.

Thus, as regards the private sphere – in which property rights on resources are linked to their creation – the process of decision is perfectly clear and there is no room for any democratic rule, except in cases voluntarily decided by individuals. With regard to the public sphere, resources are pooled, so that property is collective, which, in fact, means that resources belong to everyone and no one in particular. But, as far as exclusions have to be defined, a collective decision rule has to be defined and democracy may play its role. Certainly democracy can be preferred to dictatorship,[2] but the problem of democracy is of secondary importance compared to the problem of determining the frontier between the private and the public spheres: it is only as far as resources are not fully owned privately that the problem of democracy may arise.

Recent history brings a clear illustration of these problems. The collapse of the communist regimes in Europe and Russia has been a shift from a totalitarian regime to a system more respectful of individual freedom. But it has mainly been interpreted as a return to democracy, as if the whole life of individuals had to be politicized. Obviously, this interpretation has been particularly adopted by people who favor state interventionism.

This means that the democratic character of an institution must be considered as a secondary criterion in comparison with the only significant one – that related to the degree of individual freedom and to the role played by private property. In other words, far from being the ultimate criterion in social affairs, the role of democracy has to be considered whenever purely individual solutions cannot be used. We have already stressed that individuals quite often choose collective decision-making processes and they may use democratic solutions. As regards the state, it would certainly be going beyond the scope of the present chapter to discuss the possible justifications for its existence. Theoretically, the best justification is the one given by the theory of public goods, but it remains debatable and there are reasons to believe that public goods do not exist. Anyhow, let us assume that some public goods exist and have to be provided. To that extent, one may evaluate the merits of a democratic solution. This means that democracy, far from being a first-best solution for a fair and coherent working of societies, is a second-best solution, whenever it is believed that better solutions – the definition of individual property rights – cannot be used.

But, whenever individual property rights can be defined and protected, there is necessarily a conflict between a liberal order based on these property rights and democratic solutions. In fact, as we have already stressed, a liberal order is the only coherent social system. It is not coherent to add to this system another decision system by which people decide on the distribution of resources which they do not hold. This is the very general reason why – as we now try to demonstrate – it is dangerous to introduce democratic solutions in non-governmental organizations.

3   DEMOCRACY IN FIRMS

Democracy is already present in firms, associations, condominiums and other non-governmental organizations. In order to evaluate the role it is playing (or the role it could play) we mainly have to consider to what extent it is compatible with a correct definition of property rights. Let us first focus on the case of firms, before considering other organizations in the next section.

The place of democracy in firms has sometimes been increased by legislation which, for instance, obliges big corporations to introduce 'worker participation', as is the case in Germany or – at least in public firms – in France. And in many countries there are debates about the necessity for extending it under the pretext that workers contribute to the process of production of firms, so that it is fair that they also contribute to the decision-making process. In fact, worker participation can take two different forms: a distribution of shares to workers and/or the introduction of elected representatives of workers in the deciding boards of the firm. In this chapter we shall largely consider the second aspect.

In order to evaluate the possible consequences of such a reform, we should bear in mind a clear view of the nature of the firm. A firm is something very abstract since it can be defined as a set of contracts. If the firm is a corporation, there is an initial contract by which owners of resources pool their resources together and transform their individual property rights into property rights on a collective pool of resources. As far as there is such a change, there is a necessity to decide on some collective decision-making process. The rule that has spontaneously emerged from history is not a unanimity rule, since it appeared that there was a risk that no decision be taken in such a case. Therefore, the normal rule is either a majority or a qualified majority rule. In that sense the shareholders constitute a democracy, but the working of this democracy does not conflict with the definition of property rights for two reasons:

- first, voting rights are proportional to property rights; and
- second, these initial shareholders, as well as those who will later join, freely enter into the democracy (and can leave it as well). They know that there is a risk that they do not agree with the decisions adopted by a majority of shareholders and that these decisions may decrease the value of their shares. But they also know that the working of the democracy of shareholders will not deprive them of their property by means they would consider as illegitimate, that is, contrary to their own will (since they have freely accepted the risks linked with the participation to this pool of property rights).

Later on, contracts will be signed with wage earners, lenders of funds, suppliers and customers. The price of goods and services obtained or sold in all these contracts is certain. Once all contracts have been honored (the owners of the firm have paid their debts and received what was due to them), the shareholders get a residual return, if any, which is called the profit. It is well known that there is a specialization of tasks in the firm, since, for instance, there is always a risk in production and someone has to bear the burden of this risk. The solution which emerged spontaneously from history consists in shifting the risk mainly to shareholders – and because they bear this risk they are entitled to make productive decisions, since their profits depend on the quality of their decisions. But other solutions could be imagined and have been tried in history. They have probably been abandoned because they could not allow a precise definition of property rights.

For instance, one could imagine that isolated workers decide to pool their efforts and part of their resources, because they rightly consider that they would be more efficient by cooperating in a common organization than by staying isolated and exchanging their output. In such a case, there would not be an entrepreneur, and the workers would be risk takers. Once more, there would necessarily be collective problems to be solved, as regards both the choices to be made for production and the distribution of the final output. And the solutions to these problems could be based both on a priori rules and on collective decision-making processes.

If there is no a priori rule concerning the distribution of the final output, there is a risk of conflicts, since it is unlikely that unanimity could be obtained. Therefore, the distribution of the output is made by violent means – and there is no chance that the organization can last – or it is made by some democratic process which would be more efficient and would make it possible for the organization to survive. Thus, either the distribution of the output between workers would be decided by some majority rule or it would be decided by an individual or a group of individuals democratically elected by the workers. In such a case all those who agreed to cooperate are members of a democracy. But it is quite certain that those who do not obtain what they expected will be frustrated. In fact there is absolutely no guarantee that a decision taken according to a majority rule would be both fair and efficient. This creates a risk that the organization might break down, some workers being unsatisfied by what they get.

It would therefore be both fairer and more efficient to decide the distribution of the output by using a priori rules which would allow the percentage of the final output that will be obtained by each worker to be determined in advance. This example is interesting since it shows that a democratic solution is needed only as far as a problem is not solved by an a priori rule and it even shows that a democratic process is less fair and efficient than a system of rules (at least if the rules are correctly defined). The democratic solution is the last recourse solution to avoid conflicts, whenever other solutions have not been adopted for one reason or another.

However, in the hypothetical case we are analyzing, even if a priori rules have been adopted as regards the distribution of the output of the mutual firm, it does not solve all problems. Collective decision-making problems appear if, for instance, a new worker enters into the firm or if one is fired. Moreover, decisions have to be taken with regard to the production: how to organize it, which markets to reach, what to invest and so on. Rules are not sufficient for that and because there is no specialization of roles in such a firm, all workers are potential deciders. Once more, as there cannot be unanimity, decisions have to be made according to some majority rule and for a large part of its activity the firm is a democracy.

However, one may wonder why the traditional capitalist firm has been preferred historically to the category we just analyzed, that of a mutual firm? Is it not precisely because one is obliged to use democratic processes in a mutual firm more frequently than in a traditional capitalist firm? 'Inventing' the entrepreneur[3] can be considered as a great innovation which makes it possible to get rid of most democratic processes in the firm.

Thus, democratic processes may be the second-best solution when first-best solutions cannot be adopted, and they are certainly better than third-best solutions such as violence and arbitrariness. But one ought always to look for institutional solutions which make it possible to avoid democracy. This means that all legislation which is aimed at introducing more democracy in firms ought to be rejected.

In order to better illustrate this idea, let us consider the working of the capitalist firm. As we have already said, there are limited applications of the democratic principle in corporations, since, for instance, the shareholders choose by majority rule the members of the board who, in turn, elect the chairman by majority rule. But, by doing so, the shareholders are freely using their property rights and, anyhow, there is certainly no other way to run a corporation (obviously, when the firm is owned by a single person, democracy is not necessary). Now, let us imagine that representatives of the wage earners are introduced into the board of a firm, either because shareholders voluntarily decided it or because the state has obliged firms to do so. Many arguments can be opposed to such a type of organization (and it may be because these arguments have been implicitly recognized that owners of firms do not adopt them whenever they are not obliged by the state).

The most powerful argument seems to be the following one. A contract is the most fantastic tool that humankind has found in order to reconcile diverging individual interests. Thus, the seller of a good would like the highest possible price, the purchaser would like the lowest possible price.

But they can find a price which is satisfactory for both and both benefit from their contract (if not, they would not do it). This can certainly be applied to the case of a wage contract: there are a priori antagonistic interests between a wage earner and an entrepreneur, but they can find an agreement and they benefit from it. Now, let us imagine that a lot of wage contracts have been signed in a firm between wage earners and shareholders (or their representatives) and that representatives of wage earners are introduced in the board along with representatives of the shareholders, because of a specific legislation which makes this system compulsory.

The consequences of such a system can be logically deduced as soon as one has correctly understood the nature of a firm. Wage earners can leave their firm at any time, voluntarily or not, with limited consequences on the value of their human capital. On the one hand, if they should leave, they would try to obtain higher wages thanks to the experience they had accumulated in the previous firm; on the other, they might have a very specific role which could not be valued as highly elsewhere. Anyhow, they do know that there is a certain probability that they will leave the firm in the future. Therefore, it is in their interest to try to get short-term benefits, even if it is at the expense of longer-run benefits. As far as worker representatives can influence strategic decisions, they may be inclined to favor increases in present wages, more comfortable working conditions or all sorts of various benefits, at the expense of investments. At the limit, one might imagine that the very capital of the firm is progressively eroded by the claims of wage earners. Thus, the extension of democracy in the firm introduces a bias in favor of the short run in comparison to the long run. The rate of growth of the firm is reduced, as well as the rate of profit and, therefore, the incentive for people to invest in the firm. If this kind of democracy is compulsory in all the firms of a country, the rate of growth of all firms is lower and the welfare of all citizens is increasing less rapidly.

The owners of the firm are in a completely different situation, since they cannot 'leave' the firm. To be sure, they can sell their shares, but the value of these shares depends on expectations about future profits. If ever a system of worker participation does reduce the profitability of the firm, the selling price of the shares is also reduced. In some sense the owners of a firm are 'trapped' in it. This is one reason why it is legitimate to say that they get the profit. It is also a reason why the owners of a firm are more inclined than anyone else to choose the future rather than the present.

The harmful results of introducing compulsory democracy in firms are a consequence of the fact that it creates a structure of decision which is incompatible with the one which would naturally emerge from the free interplay of different individuals through contracts. It arbitrarily changes the structure of rights and, therefore, the incentives of the different participants in the firm. A firm is not and cannot be a democracy. This is fundamental, because it is a bundle of contracts and not an institution, and it is meaningless to try to manage a set of contracts in a democratic way. More precisely, it is true, as we have already said, that there are normally some 'islands of democracy' in a firm, for instance in the case of shareholders. Democracy works in that case because the contracts between the shareholders are contracts of cooperation and not contracts of exchange: they decide to pool their resources in order to reach a *common goal*. The existence of this collective pooling necessarily implies adopting collective decision-making processes. In contrast, wage earners and shareholders (or lenders of funds and shareholders) sign exchange contracts. Their interests are antagonistic and they find contractual conditions – for instance prices – which are acceptable for all of them. But it is a dangerous fiction to believe that these conditions can be found through democratic processes which give illegitimate rights to some people over others (for instance, by allowing wage earners to decide upon the use of resources which belong to shareholders).

These being the consequences of wage-earner participation, it is doubtful that shareholders would freely decide such a representative system if they were not obliged by the law. In fact, they readily understand that it implies an increased degree of risk, in so far as they do not know exactly how these representatives would behave on the board and they can suspect that they would be tempted to prefer short-term benefits to long-term ones. It is more likely that they could admit or even desire a participation in profits rather than a participation in decisions. To this end, they may decide in the working contract that part of the return obtained by a wage earner would be conditional, for instance on the amount of profits. The reason for that is quite simple: in so far as the shareholders are the main beneficiaries of profits, it is in their interest to try to maximize profits, even if they have to abandon a small part of it. Profit sharing may stimulate the wage earners and induce them to be more productive. However, in a large corporation, every wage earner has a very marginal influence on the final result and each one knows that he/she will get, as a recipient of profit sharing, an infinitesimal part of profit. Therefore, profit sharing can produce only insignificant incentives for wage earners to improve productivity. This is certainly less true for those who are in a high position, since the link is more direct between their own efforts and the improvement in the management of the firm and its results. This is why stock options exist and why they are normally attributed to only a limited number of wage earners who are placed in a high position. Such a solution is more desirable than democracy both for the owners of the firm and for their high-rank managers.

Above we discussed the existence of 'islands of democracy' in firms, for instance with regard to shareholders. But other islands may exist quite legitimately and efficiently. For instance, wage earners may believe that it is more profitable or easier for them to negotiate their contracts on a collective rather than on an individual basis. Therefore, they will adhere to trade unions which will be in charge of defending what is felt to be the common interests of wage earners. And as it implies collective decision making, it is quite natural that representatives of the wage earners be elected through a democratic process in order to represent these common interests.[4]

Until now we have considered only the relations between those who cooperate in the firm in order to produce its output, namely wage earners and shareholders. But we may also consider the relations between the firm and its customers. From this point of view it is once more interesting to make a comparison between the firm and the state. As regards the state, the voters in a democracy are not those who produce 'public goods and services' (civil servants and politicians), but the citizens, that is, those who pay for these goods and services and who receive them. In other words the voters are the 'customers' of the state. Thus, those who would like firms to work in a way similar to that of the state – considered as the best system of organization – ought not to recommend 'internal democracy' – that is, participation of wage earners to decisions – but 'external democracy', that is, the democratic control of the customers over the producers. However, it is quite justified to create such a democratic control of state decisions, since the state is the only organization which benefits from an absolute and definitive monopoly position, no one being authorized to compete with it. Therefore, democracy is introduced in order to limit the arbitrary power of the state and to try to help citizens to reveal their needs as customers of the state. But this process of control and of transmission of information is very imperfect, since citizens can rarely express their choices (usually once every four, five or six years) and they are asked to choose between a very limited number of bundles, each composed of a very great number of public goods and services. In addition, they are even not certain that these bundles will be delivered to them. It is obvious that, on the free market, where producers are free to enter and the customers can express their choices at any moment and for any good or service, there is a much closer correspondence between the structure of production and the structure of wants. Therefore, it would be foolish to replace the sophisticated non-democratic way by which individuals express their choices on the free market by the terribly imperfect process of a democratic decision. This is also a reason to leave decisions to the free interchange of will on the market, whenever it is possible, rather than to the working of any democracy.

We have a significant example of such confusion in the management of universities. Universities are firms producing education services and their customers are the student. But according to the prejudices of our time, it is quite often decided by the law – for instance in French universities – that they are to be managed along democratic lines. But the voters are not only the producers (professors and members of the administration), but also students, that is, the customers, and they elect representatives who take strategic decisions. As no one is an owner of a university, the voters and their representatives tend to make decisions which give them short-run benefits and not decisions which could maximize the value of the university and of the services it can supply.

Let us go back to the problem of internal democracy in the firm. Saying that there is no democratic participation of workers in the decisions of the firm does not mean that they are not participating in decisions. In fact, a well-functioning capitalist firm is a firm in which every wage earner participates in the process of production – and, therefore, in the numerous processes of decision making – but according to the capacities, specializations and roles of each of them. It is a very sophisticated system of participation. Introducing a democratic representation of workers in such a firm through the election of representatives to committees and boards, creates a risk that the normal and sophisticated system of participation be more or less destroyed. This risk is increased by the fact that, quite often, those who are candidates to such positions are individuals who cannot realize great achievements in production because of their lack of competence or motivation. By being elected as a representative of others, they find a way to get power and consideration. In fact it is meaningless to pretend that someone can be 'represented' by someone else. In that sense democracy is always a fiction, since it disregards the infinite diversity of personalities. It may have some meaning in a beehive in which most units have about the same role and the same behavior, but not in a society composed of human beings, for instance in a firm which is successful as far as it is possible to use each worker according to his/her specificity. Those who make a plea for worker participation have a collectivist view of societies and they consider that individuals can be interchangeable.

4   ASSOCIATIONS, CONDOMINIUMS, FAMILIES . . .

The ideas we have just developed can easily be applied to non-governmental organizations other than firms, and it is not necessary to devote too much time to them. Let us first consider the case of associations. They exist just because some people have common interests and they consider that they will be more efficient by coordinating their efforts than by trying to achieve them individually. Typically associations are producing 'public goods', that is, goods and services which are supplied for the benefit of all members without any individual appropriation. Such a pooling may be the result of a technical impossibility to individualize activities or rather the result of an explicit will of members who consider that it would not be efficient to market the goods and services supplied by the association. From this point of view the working of an association is very similar to that of the state and it is quite natural that it is organized under the form of a democracy. Nevertheless there is a big difference between both sorts of organizations: members of an association freely decide to become members and not to leave (exit is easy), whereas whenever an individual is located in a given place, he/she is obliged to be a citizen of the state which has jurisdiction over the given area. Therefore, while associations bring together individuals with common interests, citizens are people with diverging interests and it is possible, in this latter case, for a coalition of citizens to plunder several other categories of citizens through democratic processes.

It is also significant that, in an association, those who vote are the members and not the wage earners who have possibly been hired by the association. It has been recognized that democracy was a satisfactory form of management only as long as it implied collective decisions by people who have common interests. Moreover, an association is producing goods and services mainly for its members and not for the general public, contrary to what is usual for firms. Now, it is also true that property rights are very vague in an association and, from this point of view, it is an inferior form of organization, compared with a firm. It is clear that the firm has been selected in history as the best productive structure. Associations exist to the extent that collective needs do exist and constitute a limited part of the life of their members. Moreover, nowadays, associations are quite often hidden extensions of governments which allow them to survive thanks not to the contributions of their members, but to public subsidies.

Condominiums are also collective forms of organization and they are also democracies. However, in this case, property rights are clearly defined, at least on a significant part of the condominium. But inhabitants find that it is easier to consider that some parts of the condominium be collective goods (for instance, a lane or a lift). When somone enters into a condominium by buying a flat or a house, he/she knows that decisions concerning the common part of the condominium will be taken according to a democratic rule. But that person enters freely into the condominium and can freely leave at any time. In that sense democracy is 'desired'.[5] From this point of view, there is a great difference between the way a condominium is managed and the way a city is managed. In the first case only those who own property rights have voting rights and their voting rights are proportional to their property rights. All owners of properties know that the investments of the condominium give more value to their property so that they can ask a higher price if ever they sell it or a higher rent if ever they rent it. On the contrary, the voters who, for instance, choose the members of a city council, are not only owners, but also tenants. There are opposing interests and the tenants may use the democratic process in order to extract the maximum amount of wealth from the owners in the short run. They know that they can move freely from one city to another and they do not care as much as owners would do about the increase in the market value of the properties. This consequence of the democratic process is very similar to the one which exists when wage earners have voting rights in a firm (choosing short-run benefits).

A final example of a non-governmental organization is the family. If ever democratic processes were used in a family – implying that all decisions would be taken according to a majority rule both by parents and children – there would certainly be inconsistencies between these decisions and those which would result from the existing property rights. In fact property rights are rather precise in a family, since resources are created by the efforts of the parents and they belong to them. The parents freely choose to transfer a part of these resources to their children. Moreover, teaching children that a family is not a democracy can be a good principle for education.

5   CONCLUSION

With regard to collective decisions, a unanimity rule is the only universally acceptable rule. But it is obvious that unanimity can rarely occurs. Therefore, one is obliged – as long as it is felt that it is impossible to get rid of the collective decision-making process and as long as authoritarian decisions are not accepted – to use a democratic rule. But it must be clear that the democratic rule – for instance, the majority rule – is only a second-best rule. In fact, the majority rule is used only because when a majority of voters makes a decision it is logically impossible that an incompatible decision also be taken (contrary to what would happen if a decision could be taken by, for instance, only 40 per cent of voters). But it has no scientific or moral value: if 51 per cent of voters decide to kill someone or to steal that person's property, their decision is not justified because it is a democratic decision. Therefore:

- instead of trying to extend the scope of democratic decisions, one should consider whether a better definition of property rights would

not rather rid us of collective decisions and, as a consequence, of democratic processes; and
- democracy, whenever it exists, ought to be the result of free choices and not imposed by the state.

In short, instead of wondering to what extent non-governmental organizations ought to imitate the decision-making processes of the state, one ought to wonder to what extent the tasks presently performed by a democratic state could not be fulfilled by private contracts, that is, according to non-democratic processes.

NOTES

1. The state may directly transfer resources from one to the other. But what happens when it creates a new good or service? Production cannot be obtained from nothing and the process of production of state goods necessarily implies using resources which have been obtained by legal constraint. Thus, in that case too, there is a transfer of resources from those who had to abandon their property rights to the original resources to those who receive the final good or service.
2. I deliberately write 'democracy can be preferred to dictatorship' and not 'democracy has to be preferred to dictatorship' because – even if I prefer democracy – I consider that it is a personal value judgment which will not be considered here. What about the choice between a tyrannical democracy and a benevolent dictator?
3. By so saying we implictly refer to an assumption made by Frederic Bastiat, who assumed that workers who have created a sort of mutual firm discover that it would be profitable for them to 'hire' an entrepreneur who would bring equity capital, take the burden of risk and organize the production. See P. Salin, 'The firm in a free society: following Bastiat's insights', *Journal of Libertarian Studies*, **16** (3), summer 2002, pp. 1–18.
4. Here, too, it is necessary to make a distinction between spontaneous, desired democracy and compulsory democracy due to labor laws.
5. It is true that one can also leave a country, but the scope of choices is much more limited since there are a limited number of countries in the world.

9. Citizenship and democracy in international organizations

Bruno S. Frey and Alois Stutzer

1 IS DEMOCRACY POSSIBLE IN INTERNATIONAL ORGANIZATIONS?

One of the foremost scholars in political science, Robert A. Dahl (1999), takes a strong position with respect to whether international organizations can be made (more) democratic: 'whatever kind of government may prevail in international organizations it will not be recognizably democratic' (p. 20). 'Democracy' is understood to be a 'system of popular control over government policies and decisions' (p. 20). Dahl applies this skepticism to international organizations in general, not only to specific cases (p. 23). He calls his argument 'simple and straightforward':

> In democratic countries where democratic institutions and practices have been long and well established and where, as best we can tell, a fairly strong democratic political culture exists, it is notoriously difficult for citizens to exercise effective control over many key decisions on foreign affairs. What grounds have we for thinking, then, that citizens in different countries engaged in international systems can ever attain the degree of influence and control over decisions that they now exercise within their own countries?

This clear position does not mean that Robert Dahl or other skeptics with respect to democracy in international organizations (for example, Schmitter, 1997) would not *wish* to see a greater say of the citizenry in the international sphere. They are well aware that, under the prevailing conditions, the issues and decisions taken are remote from the lives and experiences of ordinary citizens, who therefore lack the required knowledge. As a consequence, important foreign policy decisions are in most cases taken by the policy elites (p. 24). But 'we have no reason to believe that the views of elites are in some demonstrable sense objectively correct'. Indeed, the 'public debate is one-sided and incomplete, and in the end the views and interests of the political leaders and activists prevail' (p. 27).

While Dahl – and many international relations scholars[1] – are most skeptical about democracy in the international sphere, he nevertheless argues with respect to any international organization that 'we should not only subject its undemocratic aspects to scrutiny and criticism but also try to create proposals for greater democratization and insist that they be adopted' (p. 34).

This chapter advances such a proposal. It starts from the premise that international organizations perform important and indispensable roles in our world today, taking over allocative, redistributive and stabilizing functions. However, the existing international organizations are characterized by a fundamental democracy deficit and lack democratic legitimacy. We propose institutional measures to increase the direct participation possibilities of the citizens of an international organization's member countries. Due to the sheer number of citizens involved, it is not feasible to let all of them decide on every single constitutional question. Rather, trustees should be selected by a random mechanism. This guarantees that the electorate is represented in a totally fair way. The trustees are given the right to start initiatives and to vote in referendums on issues related to an international organization's constitution. They can also recall executives when they are dissatisfied with their behavior. The trustees are thus understood as citizens of international organizations having rights and obligations. The random mechanism proposed for selecting the trustees is indeed unusual. However, its potential in constitutional design is supported by scientific research, as well as by historical examples.

To show the practicality of the proposed democratization of international organizations, the various elements are specified, such as the number of citizens to be chosen as trustees, and the number of years for which they are elected. These specifications are only exemplary; they can and should vary from one international organization to another. In particular, there are large differences in the number of member countries in international organizations ranging from regional associations to organizations like the United Nations. Moreover, there is a range of types of international governance organizations with some having 'charter'-based bodies and others 'contract'-based bodies. Independent of these differences, an important requirement proposed is that of a double majority: in order to change or amend an international organization's constitution, there must be a majority among all the trustees participating, as well as a majority of member countries approving a proposal.

The construction of the international organizations existing today, especially in their executive function, remains initially unaffected. Citizens' participation rights via their trustees do not substitute for these functions. The major difference to existing constitutions is that the randomly selected trustees have the final say. The executives of international organizations must obey the constitutional changes adopted by the trustees. The power given to the trustees can be expected to have a significant effect on the behavior of the agents in international organizations. The executives would be subject to the control of the citizens of the member states. This would induce both a higher responsiveness to the preferences of the people and greater efficiency. Moreover, they would be given democratic legitimacy, which would improve citizenship behavior.

We are well aware of the fact that our proposal is not ideal, therefore possible counterarguments will be discussed. But many points of criticism are due to lack of familiarity with institutions of direct democracy. Based on the experience with the working of initiatives, referendums and recall, many of the counterarguments are shown to be doubtful.

Section 2 presents our basic argument. The following section sets out the necessary institutional features. Section 4 discusses the crucial element of random mechanisms in the political sphere. The advantages and disadvantages of our proposal are discussed in Section 5. Section 6 offers concluding remarks.

2   THE PROPOSAL

In order to overcome the insufficient democratic foundation and efficiency of international organizations we propose to empower the citizens of the member states to have a say in the decisions made. To deal with the frequently considerable number of citizens involved, the voting body is reduced to a size allowing voting to proceed in a manageable manner. This is achieved by selecting a restricted number of persons via a random mechanism, giving each citizen of a member country the same chance of being chosen. The random choice of a subset of the citizenry allows for taking advantage of citizen participation while keeping transaction costs low. In order to reflect the equality of member countries in international organizations, the same number of citizens is selected from each nation, for example 10,000.[2] The appointment is for several years (five years in order not to coincide with most national legislative periods).[3] The citizens selected in this way will now be referred to as 'trustees' in order to indicate that they carry a special responsibility, and that they have an incentive to be trusted by the community of citizens as a whole. The trustees are identified, so that they can be addressed both by individuals and groups interested in having the particular international organization pursue a certain policy. Becoming a trustee of an international organization is thus understood as an extension or generalization of citizenship (see Frey, 2003 on citizenship: organizational and marginal (COM)).

Trustees may vote by using either the postal system or e-mail (provided e-voting is secure). The more e-voting is introduced and becomes the standard way to participate politically, the larger the percentage of citizens selected as trustees can be. However, when choosing the number of trustees, it must be taken into account that citizens are not overburdened with too many mandates as trustees (for different organizations). Trustees are given the right to vote on issues of content, as is the case in semi-direct democracies. The institutions existing in the governing bodies of the respective international organizations remain in force. The governing body is still responsible for making day-to-day decisions and executing policies. The major difference to the international organizations existing today is that the vote by the trustees would be binding for the executive bodies: they must undertake what the trustees have decided according to the international organization's constitution or charter.

By definition, the random mechanism assigns an equal probability to each citizen of a country being chosen as a trustee. The random selection may, in practice, be undertaken by using any appropriate mechanical system (such as lots) or computer programs. The underlying population from which the trustees are selected can be taken from the voting registers of the countries that are members of the particular international organization, assuming that these countries are (at least formally) democracies. Where the voting register and/or the selection mechanism is doubtful, the international organization should be given the constitutional right to send observers in order to guarantee that appropriate procedures are applied.

3   INSTITUTIONAL FEATURES

The trustees selected by lot can exercise their rights and determine the international organization's policies in two different ways:

1. They can initiate votes on issues of content (*initiatives*) or on people (*recall*). Both a successfully launched initiative and a recall force the managers of the international organization concerned to hold a vote among all the citizens selected.

    An initiative enables trustees to put an issue on the political agenda of an international organization. The demands are directed explicitly against the political establishment represented in the international organization's assembly or executive.

    Recall allows for the dismissal of whichever executives of the international organization the trustees deem unreliable, ineffective, corrupt, or unwilling to undertake the policies described by the international organization's constitution.

Whether such votes are frequent or rare is to a large extent determined by the signature requirement. The signature requirement can be defined as a total minimal number across nations. However, it can also include minimal numbers of signatures within a percentage of countries, or restrictions for the maximum duration of time between the point of time an initiative/recall is announced and the point of time the signatures are deposited.[4]

We propose a signature requirement of 10 percent of the total number of trustees. Moreover, in order to give a counterweight to the possible dominance of a single country or a group of countries, a minimum percentage of member countries must reach this signature requirement (we propose one-quarter of the member countries). This double-signature requirement prevents an initiative from being undertaken by a few countries, or even one country, in isolation.

2. Trustees can vote in a *mandatory referendum* applicable to major issues, such as changes in the ground rules (the constitution) of the international organization. Mandatory referendums thus serve a controlling function because, if successful, they overrule the decisions taken by the executive and the legislative bodies. We propose that changes in the constitution require the trustees' approval.

For an initiative or recall to be successful, or a constitution to be amended by a referendum, a majority of trustees has to approve the proposals. In order for constitutional changes to be adopted, some qualified majority may be required, and we propose a simple double majority: more than half of all the trustees exercising their voting right must vote for the change. In addition, more than half of the member countries must approve the proposal.

The content of initiatives is not restricted. However, proposals are made for changes in the constitution of an international organization. Recall of the management of international organizations can be applied to politicians and public officials. Assigning a signature quorum faces a trade-off. The lower the quorum is, the larger the uncertainty among the managers, inducing them to take a short-term view. The higher the quorum is, the stronger is the position of the managers. The less discretionary room the managers have, the less threatening is such management power to the interests of the citizens in the member states. In some cases, the tasks of the international organizations are so precisely defined that the managers are severely restricted. If that happens, the quorum for recall can well be high. In other cases, the managers are, to a large extent, able to determine the organization's activities by themselves, in which case a stricter restriction on the threat of recall is desirable.

Instruments of direct democracy have a long tradition.[5] They refine the form of democracy based on representation and indirect political participation via elections. Direct democracy (or, more precisely, semi-direct democracy) does not substitute for parliament, government, courts and all the other features of representative democracies. Likewise, it does not substitute for the executive or the assembly of an international organization. Instead, it transfers the final rights for determining issues to the citizens or trustees. There is extensive knowledge in political science, law and economics about the workings of direct democracy at the state and federal levels.[6] Some of the consequences to be expected from our proposal are based on this research and are discussed in the following section.

4 RANDOM MECHANISMS IN POLITICS

4.1 Applications Today and in the Past

The random mechanism has rarely been used in the public realm.[7] But there are several examples where random procedures have been used:

First, they can be used as a strategy in decision making. An important example is conscription for military service. In the 1970s, the US government, for instance, used a lottery based on birthdays to determine which men were drafted into the army in order to fight in Vietnam. Draft lotteries were also used during the two world wars, both in the United States and in several European countries. Every eligible man should have an equal probability of being chosen.

Second, random mechanisms can be used as a strategy to choose decision makers. The best-known example today is the choice of persons to form a jury in serious criminal cases, such as murder, but sometimes also in civil cases. Criminal juries are of major importance in Anglo-Saxon countries, but they also exist on the European continent, especially in Scandinavia. While professional judges are certainly more knowledgeable, the major reason to randomly select jurors is in order that justice be perceived as fair. Persons drawn by chance from the whole population are seen to be, on average, more honest than some professional judges, and to reflect more closely the moral standards of the population. Moreover, fairness may lie in being heard and judged by ordinary people drawn from the whole population.[8]

Third, there have been important cases in the past in which random selection has been used. Classical democracy in Athens in the fifth and fourth centuries BC, which is still a model for today, used random selection as a central feature (see, for example, Engelstad, 1989; Hansen, 1991; Manin, 1997). The Assembly, which every one of the between 30,000 and 60,000 citizens could attend, took the most important decisions. Its business was prepared by the Council of 500 members, composed of 10 groups of 50 members each. Each group was chosen by lot from one of the 10 tribes of Athens. Each group took a turn as the Committee (*prytany*), and the order in which this was done was determined by lot. The persons presiding over the Assembly, the Council and the Committee were chosen by lot on the day they met. In addition, most public officials were chosen randomly. The only exception was when competence was considered fundamental for a particular office, such as the military officers and financial officials who were elected. Moreover, not all citizens could become randomly selected officials. They had, for instance, to be at least 30 years old. They were also subject to an assessment when selected, as well as at the end of their respective terms of office.

It is likely that other ancient Greek city-states used similar random mechanisms to select their politicians and public officials, but little is known about the respective rules. However random choice is well documented for medieval Italian city-states. It played a large role, particularly in Florence between 1328 and 1530, where the six to 12 members of the city government (whose terms were quite short, sometimes being only of two months' duration) were chosen by lot from the volunteers running for office. Their ability to do the job was scrutinized by a group of aristocrats and citizens. The latter were again selected by lot. Random mechanisms were also extensively used in other Italian city-states, such as Bologna, Parma and Vicenza, as well as in Barcelona. It was used in Venice until the city's independence was terminated by Napoleon in 1797. The selection process for the doge was very complex and, at each stage, involved random elements (see Knag, 1998). First, 30 members of the Great Council, composed of several hundred members, were selected randomly and then reduced to nine by another draw. These persons elected a new group of 40, which in turn were reduced to 12 by yet another draw. These 12 persons in turn elected a new group of 25, which was again reduced by a random mechanism to nine. This was repeated several times. Only then did a group of 41, none of whom could have been chosen previously, elect the doge. In the 1900s in San Marino, a similar procedure was used to select the state's two governors from the 60-member council (Carson and Martin, 1999: 33).

4.2 Proposals Involving Random Mechanisms

In the scholarly literature, many suggestions have been made to use random mechanisms in social decision making because of its attractive features.

It suffices to refer to some examples directly relevant for the proposal advanced here.

Random dictator

Out of the total electorate, one person is chosen by lot to act as a dictator for a specified period. This proposal seems to be rather awkward, but there are some good arguments in its favor (Elster, 1989: 86–91). Random election is the only system not making it in the people's interest to misrepresent their preferences, in particular by appearing to be more honest and less egoistic than they in fact are. In contrast, all elections provide an incentive to the contenders to present a too favorable image of themselves to the voters. Another advantage is that the institution of a random dictator selects an 'ordinary', representative, member of the citizenry, and thus prevents professional politicians with their special interests taking over. These advantages are also directly relevant for the random selection of citizens in charge of international organizations.

The institution of a random dictator also has some obvious disadvantages. The persons chosen as temporal dictators have no opportunity to learn from experience. The public bureaucracy, with its long and extensive experience, tends to accumulate considerable power and, when taken to the extreme, can dominate the citizens selected. In contrast to selection by lot, regular elections and re-elections have the advantage of making the incumbents accountable to the voters. As was already taken into account in the classical Athenian democracy, random selection is inefficient in those areas of governance where the office holders have to exhibit special competence.

Probability voting

Random selection can be combined with voting on issues. In the simple case of there being two alternatives, a vote is taken and the winner is then determined by using a random mechanism, whereby alternatives are attributed probabilities according to the percentage of votes they received. If alternative A receives 70 percent of the votes (and seven red balls), and B 30 percent (and three blue balls), then alternative A is chosen if, for example, a random draw from a receptacle with the ten balls results in the selection of a red ball. If a blue ball is randomly drawn, alternative B is the winner (Frey, 1969; Intriligator, 1973).

Voting by veto

In this decision-making system (Mueller, 1978), each person puts forward one alternative, and there is also the status quo alternative. In each round of voting, one voter can veto one of the alternatives. The sequence in which the voters can act in this way is determined by lot. Whichever alternative remains, that is, is not vetoed by anyone, is the winner.

Random selection in a representative democracy
From the voting populace, a random sample is chosen to form a national legislature (Mueller et al., 1972). Selection is through stratified sampling in order to ensure the representation of people with certain characteristics, as well as to prevent the overrepresentation of minority preferences. There is no stratified geographic sampling, as one goal of the proposal is to overcome pork-barrel activities.

4.3   Advantages and Disadvantages of Random Selection

As is true for all social decision-making mechanisms, random selection has its strengths and weaknesses. Only the most important ones are mentioned here (for a fuller discussion see Elster, 1989: 103–22; Carson and Martin, 1999: 34–8).

Major advantages are:

- A random selection is fair in the sense that every person gets an equal chance of being selected.[9] If the random mechanism is correctly applied, no other consideration, such as income, status or political connections plays any role.
- The selection is totally representative as, after a number of draws, the persons chosen exactly reflect the underlying population of voters. No particular gender, race, religion or any other group is favored.
- Decisions by lot are easy to undertake and are universally applicable. A common method of deciding between two issues is to toss a coin. When there are more issues involved, balls are put into an urn, and then one or more balls are selected either mechanically or by a person (these procedures are well known from lotteries, and are regularly shown on TV).

There are also important actual or presumed disadvantages:

- The random method seems to lack 'rationality', in the sense that no reason for a particular choice is given. But individuals seem to have an innate need to attribute a reason to a certain choice. Having no reason for a selection leaves a feeling of dissatisfaction. The interpretation of random mechanisms being aimless, haphazard and indifferent derives from this.
- The persons chosen tend to have a reduced obligation to take the task they are chosen for seriously. Exactly because they are chosen

indiscriminately, they can hardly pride themselves on having been selected because of their intelligence, dedication, efficiency or knowledge. As a result, the intrinsic motivation to perform well might be reduced (this is a kind of 'crowding-out effect', see Frey, 1997b).

While this argument rings true, it is of lesser importance in reality than one might expect. Even purely randomly selected persons, after a short time, tend to attribute positive features to themselves, once they have been selected. At least, to some extent, they believe that their choice has been 'god's will' (an aspect crucial in Athenian democracy, see Elster, 1989: 50–52) or, in a secularized society, that it at least has some unknown deeper meaning behind it.

These advantages and disadvantages should not be considered in isolation. They need to be compared to the advantages and disadvantages any other social decision-making system has (following a comparative institutional analysis). This chapter argues that the advantages of random selection are particularly strong for the selection of representative citizens to overview international organizations. While the disadvantages certainly cannot be dismissed, they are in this particular application reckoned to be of minor importance compared to the disadvantages of using other social decision-making mechanisms.

5   EVALUATING THE PROPOSAL

5.1 Advantages

Selecting voters randomly from the population of citizens of the member countries belonging to an international organization has several important advantages over other ways of approaching the issue.

Democratic control by the citizens is strengthened
The democracy deficit now characterizing international organizations is overcome by giving citizens direct participation rights. This enables them to not only react to what the management of an international organization proposes, but also to exert agenda-setting power.[10] Initiatives and referendums are an effective means of controlling the management of international organizations. This power can be exercised by the citizens directly, but also indirectly by non-governmental organizations and spontaneously arising groups. They gain institutionalized access via the trustees to make their demands known. To a lesser extent, they are induced to go out on the streets and demonstrate, or are even forced to resort to violent action.

Moreover, these non-state actors, who claim to speak on behalf of the people, have to convince the trustees that they are campaigning for a good cause, and that they do more than pursue their own self-interest.

Legitimacy and citizenship behavior

The democratization of international organizations gives them a measure of general acceptance which otherwise cannot be attained. The citizens of the member countries, aware that they are fairly represented in the organizations' decision-making process, are motivated to provide international public goods, or at least to politically support their provision. An example would be international agencies for the improvement of global environmental goods (such as combating global warming), which are today essentially technocratic units without much, or any, democratic basis. They act far removed from the citizens. In a system of randomly selected voters connected to such organizations, the citizens in the various member countries start to feel an incentive and obligation to participate in the joint effort. An important route is the general discussion generated among the citizens, whether they are selected or not.[11] On the one hand, citizens are informed by non-governmental organizations (mostly via the mass media, in particular TV and radio). On the other, citizens have an incentive to involve their trustees in discussions about the issues to be decided by the respective international organization. The public discourse from the grassroots level, as well as from specialists, serves to strengthen the willingness to participate in the provision of international public goods.[12] Decisions on international agreements taken by the citizenry gain substantial legitimacy. It becomes costly for single governments of member countries to step back due to short-term interests, although no direct enforcement of the agreements is possible. Not sticking to these agreements cannot easily be justified by too high costs for the population, if a majority of selected citizens actually approved them.

Decentralized information

Another important advantage of direct participation rights by trustees is their gathering of information from lower levels. This information is less filtered and distorted than that coming from the organization's bureaucracy, which tends to be biased by the self-interest of the executives and the other employees.

5.2   Possible Disadvantages

All social decision-making systems have some weaknesses; there is no such thing as an ideal system. This also holds for the random selection of citizens, who have extended democratic participation rights in international organizations. But, as will be argued, many of these shortcomings are not as serious as they initially appear to be.

Trustees' capacities

It may be thought that the randomly selected trustees do not have the necessary skills to make decisions concerning an international organization's business in a reasonable and effective way. By definition, the selected citizens only have average education and may therefore be perceived to be ill prepared for the task. This argument goes to the roots of political decision making. Democracy is based on the principle that citizens, on average, are capable of making political decisions in a reasonable way. They have one great advantage over professional politicians and bureaucrats: they know their own preferences better and are therefore able to express them better politically. Moreover, there is the fundamental principal–agent problem in politics: the professional politicians *should* act in the interests of their principals, the citizens, but they have only limited incentives to do so. In a representative democracy, the professional politicians are responsive to the citizens' preferences, especially at election time. Empirical evidence demonstrates that, at other times, the actions undertaken by the professional politicians deviate substantially from the citizens' wishes.[13] In the extreme, the politicians 'exploit' the voters by pursuing policies according to their personal or party ideologies, follow the interests of well-organized and financially well-endowed pressure groups, or decide in their own favor (see Brennan and Buchanan, 1980, 1985). For instance, they accord themselves special privileges (for example, immunity from laws) or material benefits (such as generous compensations and pensions, sumptuous expense accounts, cars and planes at their free disposal). With direct participation rights of the citizens, these problems arise to a lesser extent. Econometric studies show that citizens can make well-reasoned political decisions. Indeed, the more extensive citizens' direct participation rights are, the better is the public economy run. For instance, the relationship between public expenditures and revenue is better controlled, so that the public debt per head is lower. It has also been shown that per capita income is higher because the public sector is better run, and that even self-reported subjective well-being is higher.[14]

Lack of information

A related argument claims that randomly selected citizens are not well enough informed and are therefore at the mercy of bureaucrats. First of all, it must be said that the same applies even to professional politicians; public officials always have more information at their disposal, because they have often been in charge of particular issues for a much longer period of time. It should also be noted that the randomly selected citizens tend to rise to the challenge and can collect the information necessary for making reasoned decisions. Such information need not be very detailed: what matters are the fundamental issues to be decided on. Citizens need to be able to draw on the knowledge of experts, whose job it is to provide detailed information. Moreover, empirical evidence shows that it would be a mistake to take the present level of information about the issues related to international organizations as given. Rather, the amount of information consumed is endogenously determined and is higher when citizens have more extensive political rights (Benz and Stutzer, 2004). It can thus be expected that the randomly chosen citizens are capable and willing to learn the information necessary to perform their task adequately.

Inadequate incentives

It may also be argued that the trustees are not really motivated to participate in the international organization's decision making. But a high participation rate should not be taken as a value in itself. What matters is that the selected citizens participate in the initiatives, referendums and recalls when important issues are at stake. Such behavior provides clear signals to the international organizations' management that they are effectively controlled by the citizens and cannot simply do what is in their own interests. Most people will consider it an honor to be selected as a citizen with actual voting rights to an international organization, and will therefore have an incentive to participate.

Misperceived fairness

The citizens may perceive the random selection of trustees as unfair and therefore tend to reject it. In the private realm, there is indeed considerable resistance to random decisions. Several studies analyzed the allocation of scarce private goods in situations of excess demand. In a survey among the population, the use of a random decision mechanism has been considered to be less fair than alternative social decision-making mechanisms such as 'first-come, first-served', an allocation by the commune, or even than the use of the price system (Frey and Pommerehne, 1993; see also Wortman and Rabinowitz, 1979; Erez, 1985). Such resistance where rationing is concerned certainly has to be taken into account. In the public sphere, potential resistance can probably be overcome by showing the citizens the advantages of random selection, in particular the guarantee that every citizen is treated equally. People can also be informed that random systems are used, and generally accepted, in many areas relating to their personal lives as, for instance, in the hugely popular national lotteries, where the mechanism used is extensively shown at prime TV time.

Missing democratic tradition

An organization's member countries may have little or no experience with democracy. While the random mechanism can probably be controlled from outside, this is less likely to be the case for the underlying list of the electorate, and the communication of who has been selected. But, most importantly, the selected citizens in such a country will be induced, or forced directly, to follow the will of the country's government. This is unfortunate, but our proposal does not claim to be able to transform non-democratic governments into democratic governments. If, indeed, the citizens are forced to act as government pawns, the situation is no worse than today, where the delegates of international organizations are directly selected by the respective non-democratic governments. However, the random selection of trustees may even give them a measure of independence with respect to their own government, not least because they decide jointly with selected citizens in democratic countries. Such joint experiences may (under the most favorable conditions) even initiate a step towards democratization.

Exploitative decisions

Giving the citizens in the member countries of large international organizations participation rights may be seen as opening the door to the majority of the poorer members being able to exploit the minority of the richer members. Of course, the possibility already exists under present conditions that the delegates of the poorer nations may find a majority to burden the richer member states. However, such proposals are unlikely to be successful. To some extent, the double majority required to effect a corresponding change in the constitution prevents the adoption of such proposals. The trustees in the various countries would be alerted to the fact that such a constitutional change would provoke the countries concerned and would provide reasons for leaving the respective international organization. It is therefore in the self-interest of the trustees to be careful in this respect.

6   CONCLUDING REMARKS

International organizations form an indispensable part of global governance. They are necessary in providing global and international public services. They certainly fulfill a need, reflected in the rapid growth since the end of the Second World War in the number of different organizations, the number of employees and the budgets at their disposal.[15] The services provided refer to all three classical functions of government: international organizations are active in the allocation of resources in the form of global or international public goods and services, the redistribution of income and the stabilization of the global economy.

International organizations, however, lack a democratic citizenry. While there is the idea of a global civil society, there is no blossoming citizenry so far in international governance. Therefore, international organizations cannot, in general, be seen to consist of democratic institutions based on the consent and will of the citizens. This is in contrast to a favorable development at the national level. The number of national governments that may be considered to be democratic, or nearly democratic, has increased considerably in the last century (Freedom House, 1999). Compared to the development at the national level, international organizations are thus lagging behind. There is a 'democracy deficit', and 'democratic legitimacy' is either inadequate, or even lacking altogether. Decision making in international organizations is far removed from the citizens' preferences. There is, at best, an indirect and weak link, via democratically elected national parliaments and governments. In most cases, the delegates are sent by the member countries to particular international organizations and are determined by the national bureaucracies. Only in the case of international organizations, deemed particularly important by the government, are the delegates determined by a political rather than a bureaucratic process. The decision-making processes in the international organizations themselves are largely shaped by issues to do with bureaucracy or power, again far removed from democratic influences.

The lack of democratic decision making in international organizations, however, has a negative effect on the provision of public goods and services. Such organizations have often been observed, and accused of being dominated by the narrow self-interest of their employees. They are taken to be open to corruption, and to disregard the interests of both the taxpayers financing these activities and the persons receiving them. The activities are undertaken in an inefficient and wasteful way. As a result, the allocative, redistributive and stabilizing functions undertaken by international organizations leave much to be desired.[16]

However, many such accusations against international organizations are unfair because they compare the actual way they function with an ideal situation in which they would perform in a perfect way. If this standard is applied, *all* institutions must be considered to work badly. The same charges can be made against national governments, non-governmental organizations, and even private corporations (see the recent flurry of excessive managerial compensation, distorted bookkeeping and open fraud, for example, Frey and Osterloh, 2005). A more appropriate approach must compare the behavior of international organizations to similar existing institutions, such as national governments. International organizations then appear in a more favorable light.

However, the fundamental weakness of today's international organizations – the democracy deficit – remains. It involves a lack of responsiveness to the preferences of the citizens, with regard to both the provision of outcomes and the application of decision-making processes. Therefore, to strengthen citizens' participation rights in international organizations, we see it as a value in itself, as well as a means for reducing inefficiency (broadly conceived). The argument thus combines procedural *and* outcome considerations.[17]

Instead of providing a positive analysis of international organizations (a task which has been attempted in Frey, 1984, ch. 8; 1997d; Frey and Gygi, 1990, 1991; Vaubel and Willett, 1991), this chapter puts forward a *proposal* for increasing the direct participation possibilities of the citizens of an international organization's member countries. We propose that they are given the right to start initiatives, to vote in referendums, and to recall executives. As, at least at the present time, it is impossible to have all citizens participate in such referendums, we propose using a random mechanism in order to select those citizens who could then exercise these direct democratic rights (they are referred to as 'trustees'). This idea may seem to be rather unorthodox, and may perhaps even appear to be unrealistic. We readily admit that we do not expect our proposal to be adopted rapidly and to be widespread. But we would like to draw the attention of a skeptical reader to three aspects:

1. our proposal should be considered in the light of the current problems international organizations face. For instance, the United Nations finds it extremely hard, if not impossible, to make even minor reforms;
2. our proposal could serve as a general indication of what direction a useful reform might go in; and
3. it does not appear to be totally out of the question that newly founded international organizations might adopt a constitution giving citizens more rights. Due to strongly entrenched interests, it seems less likely that already established international organizations would be able and willing to grant citizens more power in the near future, but it cannot be excluded long term.

NOTES

1. But there are also other political scientists arguing that international organizations can be democratized. Prominent examples are Archibugi and Held (1995); Held (1995). See also

Hewson and Sinclair (1999); Keohane and Nye (2000); Nye and Donahue (2001); Kahler and Lake (2003); Kaul et al. (2003).

2. We are aware that weighting is a possibility. The number of trustees could, for example, be proportional to the size of the population or financial contributions. Our proposal, however, is based on current practice in many international organizations to give equal weight to each member country. It thus protects small countries, which would lose any influence in formal decisions if the size of the population would be the basis for selecting trustees. The proposal, however, is not just giving in to the status quo by simply taking over the distribution of power. Rather, giving equal weight to small countries counteracts their incentive to free ride, which is stronger than for the large countries that are decisive for the provision of international public goods.

3. There is, of course, a trade-off here. The shorter the term in office, the larger the number of preferences represented via random selection. But this has the disadvantage that the selected citizens are less capable of getting informed about the activities of the particular international organization. The more important experience and factual knowledge are, the longer the term should be.

4. Alternatively, signing an initiative or recall can be granted to every citizen, whether selected or not. In this case, signature requirements should be substantially increased.

5. See, for example, Magleby (1984); Cronin (1989); Butler and Ranney (1994); Frey (1994); Kirchgässner et al. (1999).

6. For reviews of the literature, see, for example, Bowler and Donovan (1998), Kirchgässner et al. (1999), Gerber and Hug (2001), Matsusaka (2004) and Frey and Stutzer (2006).

7. Extensive discussions of the use of the random mechanism in politics are provided by Elster (1989, ch. II) and Carson and Martin (1999). They refer to much additional literature.

8. In reality, neither the draft nor juries are chosen in a perfectly random way. See Elster (1989: 93–103) Carson and Martin (1999: 20–21, 26–30).

9. Of course, this only holds for ballots with equal probabilities, which are the general rule. But it is quite possible to assign a person, or group of persons, more weight, for example, they can be given two or three times as much weight. But the argument continues in the sense that no other considerations enter into the matter.

10. The crucial importance of agenda setting is discussed in McKelvey (1976) and Romer and Rosenthal (1978).

11. For the role of political discourse in multilateral organizations, see Verweij and Josling (2003).

12. See the experimental results with public goods games, demonstrating that pre-play communication, and even identification of the persons involved, raises the willingness to contribute to the provision of public goods considerably. See Bohnet and Frey (1999) and the extensive survey by Sally (1995). A cross-section econometric analysis for Swiss cantons suggests that the more extensive the citizens' direct participation rights are, the higher tax morale is, and therefore the lower tax evasion is (Pommerehne and Weck-Hannemann, 1996; Frey, 1997a). See also Torgler (2005).

13. See, for example, the evidence on political business cycles in Frey (1997c) and Mueller (2003, part IV).

14. See Kirchgässner et al. (1999) and Frey and Stutzer (2000), as well as the literature mentioned in note 12.

15. On the growth of international organizations according to size and number, see, for example, Vaubel et al. (2003) and Union of International Associations (2004).

16. For a review of the pathologies of international organizations, see, for example, Barnett and Finnemore (1999).

17. The procedural aspect of democratic political decision making is emphasized in research on participatory democracy (see, for example, Pateman, 1970; Thompson, 1970; Mansbridge, 1983; Barber, 1984). An introduction to the concept of procedural utility is provided in Frey et al. (2004). The argument of (in)efficient outcomes is based on reasoning developed in public choice or new political economy (see, for example, Frey, 1978; Mueller, 1997, 2003), and more specifically on constitutional economics (Buchanan and

Tullock, 1962; Frey, 1983; Brennan and Buchanan, 1985; Mueller, 1996; Cooter, 2000) and on new institutional economics (North, 1990; Furubotn and Richter, 1997).

REFERENCES

Archibugi, Daniele and David Held (eds) (1995), *Cosmopolitan Democracy, An Agenda for a New World*, New York: Harcourt Brace.
Barber, Benjamin R. (1984), *Strong Democracy: Participatory Politics for a New Age*, Berkeley, CA: University of California Press.
Barnett, Michael N. and Martha Finnemore (1999), 'The politics, power and pathologies of international organizations', *International Organization* **53**: 699–732.
Benz, Matthias and Alois Stutzer (2004), 'Are voters better informed when they have a larger say in politics? Evidence for the European Union and Switzerland', *Public Choice* **119**(1–2): 31–59.
Bohnet, Iris and Bruno S. Frey (1999), 'The sound of silence in prisoner's dilemma and dictator games', *Journal of Economic Behavior and Organization* **38**(1): 43–57.
Bowler, Shaun and Todd Donovan (1998), *Demanding Choices: Opinion, Voting, and Direct Democracy*, Ann Arbor, MI: University of Michigan Press.
Brennan, Geoffrey and James M. Buchanan (1980), *The Power to Tax: Analytical Foundations of a Fiscal Constitution*, Cambridge: Cambridge University Press.
Brennan, Geoffrey and James M. Buchanan (1985), *The Reason of Rules. Constitutional Political Economy*, Cambridge: Cambridge University Press.
Buchanan, James M. and Gordon Tullock (1962), *The Calculus of Consent: Logical Foundations of Constitutional Democracy*, Ann Arbor, MI: University of Michigan Press.
Butler, David and Austin Ranney (eds) (1994), *Referendums around the World: The Growing Use of Direct Democracy*, Washington, DC: AEI Press.
Carson, Lyn and Brian Martin (1999), *Random Selection in Politics*, Westpoint, CT and London: Praeger.
Cooter, Robert D. (2000), *The Strategic Constitution*, Princeton, NJ: Princeton University Press.
Cronin, Thomas E. (1989), *Direct Democracy: The Politics of Initiative, Referendum and Recall*, Cambridge, MA: Harvard University Press.
Dahl, Robert A. (1999), 'Can international organizations be democratic? A skeptical view', in Ian Shapir and Casiano Hacker-Cordon (eds), *Democracy's Edges*, Cambridge: Cambridge University Press: 19–36.
Elster, Jon (1989), *Solomonic Judgements*, Cambridge: Cambridge University Press.
Engelstad, Fredrik (1989), 'The assignment of political office by lot', *Social Science Information* **28**(1): 23–50.
Erez, Edna (1985), 'Random assignment, the least fair of them all: prisoners' attitudes toward various criteria of selection', *Criminology* **23**(2): 365–79.
Freedom House (1999), *Freedom in the World: 1999–2000: The Annual Survey of Political Rights and Civil Liberties*, New York, NY: Freedom House.
Frey, Bruno S. (1969), 'Wahrscheinlichkeit als gesellschaftliche Entscheidungsregel', *Wirtschaft und Recht* **21**: 14–26.
Frey, Bruno S. (1978), *Modern Political Economics*, London: Martin Robinson.

Frey, Bruno S. (1983), *Democratic Economic Policy*, Oxford: Blackwell.

Frey, Bruno S. (1984), *International Political Economics*, Oxford and New York: Basil Blackwell.

Frey, Bruno, S. (1994), 'Direct democracy: politico-economic lessons from Swiss experience', *American Economic Review* **84**(2): 338–48.

Frey, Bruno S. (1997a), 'A constitution for knaves crowds out civic virtues', *Economic Journal* **107**(443): 1043–53.

Frey, Bruno S. (1997b), *Not Just for The Money: An Economic Theory of Personal Motivation*, Cheltenham, UK and Lyme, USA: Edward Elgar.

Frey, Bruno S. (ed.) (1997c), *Political Business Cycles*, Cheltenham, UK and Lyme, USA: Edward Elgar.

Frey, Bruno S. (1997d), 'The public choice of international organizations', in Mueller (ed.): 106–23.

Frey, Bruno S. (2003), 'Flexible citizenship for a global society', *Politics, Philosophy and Economics* **2**(1): 93–114.

Frey, Bruno S., Matthias Benz and Alois Stutzer (2004), 'Introducing procedural utility: not only what, but also how matters', *Journal of Institutional and Theoretical Economics* **160**(3): 377–401.

Frey, Bruno S. and Beat Gygi (1990), 'The political economy of international organizations', *Aussenwirtschaft* **45**(3): 371–94.

Frey, Bruno S. and Beat Gygi (1991), 'International organizations from the constitutional point of view', in Vaubel and Willett (eds): 58–78.

Frey, Bruno S. and Margit Osterloh (2005), 'Yes, managers should be paid like bureaucrats', *Journal of Management Inquiry* **14**(1): 96–111.

Frey, Bruno S. and Werner W. Pommerehne (1993), 'On the fairness of pricing – an empirical survey among the general population', *Journal of Economic Behavior and Organization* **20**(3): 295–307.

Frey, Bruno S. and Alois Stutzer (2000), 'Happiness, economy and institutions', *Economic Journal* **110**(446): 918–38.

Frey, Bruno S. and Alois Stutzer (2006), 'Direct democracy: designing a living constitution', in Roger Congleton and Birgitta Swedenborg (eds), *Democratic Constitutional Design and Public Policy, Analysis and Evidence*, Cambridge, MA: MIT Press, pp. 39–80.

Furubotn, Eirik G. and Rudolf Richter (1997), *Institutions and Economic Theory: The Contribution of the New Institutional Economics*, Ann Arbor, MI: University of Michigan Press.

Gerber, Elisabeth R. and Simon Hug (2001), 'Legislative response to direct legislation', in Matthew Mendelsohn and Andrew Parkin (eds), *Referendum Democracy: Citizens, Elites and Deliberation in Referendum Campaigns*, New York: Palgrave: 88–108.

Hansen, Mogens Herman (1991), *The Athenian Democracy in the Age of Demosthenes: Structure, Principles and Ideology*, Oxford: Basil Blackwell.

Held, David (1995), *Democracy and the Global Order: From the Modern State to Cosmopolitan Governance*, Stanford, CA: Stanford University Press.

Hewson, Martin and Timothy Sinclair (eds) (1999), *Approaches to Global Governance Theory*, Albany, NY: State University of New York Press.

Intriligator, Michael D. (1973), 'A probabilistic model of social choice', *Review of Economic Studies* **40**(4): 553–60.

Kahler, Miles and David A. Lake (eds) (2003), *Governance in a Global Economy: Political Authority in Transition*, Princeton, NJ: Princeton University Press.

Kaul, Inge, Pedro Conceicao, Katell Le Goulven and Ronald U. Mendoza (eds) (2003), *Providing Global Public Goods: Managing Globalization*, New York and Oxford: Oxford University Press.

Keohane, Robert O. and Joseph S. Nye (2000), *Governance in a Globalized World*, Washington, DC: Brookings Institution.

Kirchgässner, Gebhard, Lars Feld and Marcel R. Savioz (1999), *Die direkte Demokratie: Modern, erfolgreich, entwicklungs- und exportfähig*, Basel et al.: Helbing & Lichtenhahn/Vahlen/Beck.

Knag, Sigmund (1998), 'Let's toss for it: a surprising curb on political greed', *Independent Review* 3(2): 199–209.

Magleby, David B. (1984), *Direct Legislation: Voting on Ballot Propositions in the United States*, Baltimore, MD and London: Johns Hopkins University Press.

Manin, Bernard (1997), *The Principles of Representative Government*, Cambridge: Cambridge University Press.

Mansbridge, Jane (1983), *Beyond Adversary Democracy*, Chicago: University of Chicago Press.

Matsusaka, John G. (2004), *For the Many or the Few: The Initiative, Public Policy, and American Democracy*, Chicago: University of Chicago Press.

McKelvey, Richard D. (1976), 'Intransitivities in multidimensional voting models and some implications for agenda control', *Journal of Economic Theory* 12: 472–82.

Mueller, Dennis C. (1978), 'Voting by veto', *Journal of Public Economics* 10(1): 57–75.

Mueller, Dennis C. (1996), *Constitutional Democracy*, Oxford and New York: Oxford University Press.

Mueller, Dennis C. (ed.) (1997), *Perspectives on Public Choice: A Handbook*, Cambridge, New York and Melbourne: Cambridge University Press.

Mueller, Dennis C. (2003), *Public Choice III*, Cambridge: Cambridge University Press.

Mueller, Dennis C., Robert D. Tollison and Thomas D. Willett (1972), 'Representative democracy via random selection', *Public Choice* 12: 57–68.

North, Douglass (1990), *Institutions, Institutional Change and Economic Performance*, Cambridge and New York: Cambridge University Press.

Nye, Joseph S. Jr. and John D. Donahue (2001), *Governance in a Globalizing World*, Washington, DC: Brookings Institution.

Pateman, Carol (1970), *Participation and Democratic Theory*, Cambridge: Cambridge University Press.

Pommerehne, Werner W. and Hannelore Weck-Hannemann (1996), 'Tax rates, tax administration and income tax evasion', *Public Choice* 88: 161–70.

Romer, Thomas and Howard Rosenthal (1978), 'Political resource allocation, controlled agendas and the status quo', *Public Choice* 33(4): 27–43.

Sally, David (1995), 'Conversation and cooperation in social dilemmas – a meta-analysis of experiments from 1958 to 1992', *Rationality and Society* 7(1): 58–92.

Schmitter, Philippe (1997), 'Is it really possible to democratize the Euro-polity?', in Andreas Føllesdal and Peter Koslowski (eds), *Democracy and the European Union*, Berlin: Springer: 13–36.

Thompson, Dennis F. (1970), *The Democratic Citizen: Social Science and Democratic Theory in the Twentieth Century*, Cambridge and New York: Cambridge University Press.

Torgler, Benno (2005), 'Tax morale and direct democracy', *European Journal of Political Economy* 21(2): 525–31.

Union of International Associations (ed.) (2004), *Yearbook of International Organizations: Guide to Global and Civil Society Networks. Volume 1: Organization Descriptions and Cross-References*, Munich: Saur.

Vaubel, Roland, Axel Dreher and Ugurlu Soylu (2003), 'Staff growth in international organizations: a principal–agent problem? An empirical analysis', Mimeo, University of Mannheim.

Vaubel, Roland and Thomas D. Willett (eds) (1991), *The Political Economy of International Organizations: A Public Choice Approach*, Boulder, CO and Oxford: Westview Press.

Verweij, Marco and Timothy E. Josling (2003), Special Issue: 'Deliberately democratizing multilateral organization', *Governance: An International Journal of Policy, Administration, and Institutions* **16**(1): 1–21.

Wortman, Camille B. and Vita C. Rabinowitz (1979), 'Random assignment: the fairest of them all', *Evaluation Studies Review Annual* **4**: 177–84.

10. Law and economic development: common law versus civil law

Francisco Cabrillo

1 INTRODUCTION

There is relatively ample literature based on the notion of demonstrating the superiority of common law, with its origins in medieval England and furthest developments in the United States, over the civil law system, on which the majority of the European and Latin American countries as well as numerous others around the world are based. There is plentiful room to discuss the validity of this position. The main objective of this chapter is not to offer a complete overview of this discussion, but rather to analyse economic development, based on market economy and industrialization, centred around the two major themes of private law: contract law and tort law. We shall look at some of the most interesting features in the evolution of these two branches of the law in the United States and Spain, the former a common law country, the latter belonging to the civil law tradition.

The thesis put forward in this chapter, based around the analysis of the aforementioned is the following: both civil and common law systems have followed a parallel evolution, searching for similar objectives and adapting themselves to the ideas and dominant values present at historical moments in Western society. Moreover, the *Zeitgeist*, and in many cases dominant values in a given society, conditioned legal evolution to a larger degree than internal structures present within a specific judicial system.

In accordance with this interpretation, neither the principle of freedom of contract nor the remaining legal institutions that have permitted economic development in the Western world are specific characteristics of common law. And, more importantly, a common law system does not guarantee a sounder defence of free market principles than civil law. Put differently, there are no sound arguments that demonstrate that judge-made law better positions itself to defend the market economy than legislation passed by parliament or legislative assemblies.

In Section 2 some ideas about the development of the civil and common law systems are presented. Section 3 deals with contract law in both common and the civil law. In Section 4, tort law and administrative regulation as instruments for industrialization are discussed. Finally, Section 5 presents a brief set of conclusions.

2   CIVIL LAW AND COMMON LAW

Comparative analysis of the development of the administration of justice within the common law and civil law systems has received ample attention in the literature after some studies argued in favour of the superiority of the common law system over its civil law counterpart.[1] There are two basic arguments put forward to defend this idea. The first relates to what is considered to be the superiority of common law as an instrument for the defence of individual liberty and democracy. The second, alternatively, emphasizes the supposedly superior capacity of common law in achieving economic efficiency. Although the literature offers numerous authors that have advanced one of the two above arguments, we shall look at the work of two – Friedrich von Hayek and Richard Posner – as proponents of these two arguments, respectively.

Hayek's opinions concerning common law and the role of judges in England are interesting for numerous reasons. First, few economists have shown such an interest in the role played by judicial institutions in the development of a free and prosperous society. Indeed Hayek was not just a great economist but also one of the leading legal philosophers of the twentieth century. Second, Hayek himself was trained in the continental system; his enthusiasm for common law came from time spent in England and the discovery of a model of social institutions that was very different from what he had learned in his initial academic training in Austria. For Hayek, the foundations for superior freedom that British citizens enjoyed over their European continental counterparts were a result not of the separation of powers, as was thought by Montesquieu, but common law. In his opinion, the English institutional system was superior because common law had not been created by political volition and furthermore was administered by judges and courts that had acquired a high degree of independence from the political branch. In this system, not only is legislative power independent from government, but it is also limited by law over which it has no control.[2]

Common law fits well into Hayek's model of 'abstract norms of behaviour'. He asserted that common law is not just a collection of loosely bound cases, although this could be the interpretation of a continental jurist reading a work such as Blackstone's *Commentaries on the Law of England* (Blackstone, 1765–69). In his opinion, common law, rather, consists of a collection of general principles to be explained and developed by judges in their decisions. It is also interesting to note that for Hayek, the role of the judge was not to find efficient solutions to particular problems in the sense of maximizing social utility, but rather to ascertain whether or not behaviour corresponded with previously established legal principles (Hayek, 1973, 85–8).

However, many lawyers and judges in the common law tradition would be quite sceptical about Hayek's ideas. From our point of view it is especially interesting to recall certain ideas about common law and the role of public policy formulated by Judge Oliver Wendell Holmes throughout his extensive career. Holmes is probably the most relevant North American jurist in history. He not only made important contributions to resolving particular cases but also addressed the significance of common law *per se*. His interpretation of the role that general principles play in common law was quite different from Hayek's. In Holmes's interpretation of common law, general propositions do not decide concrete cases and opinions are based more on a judgement or intuition than a general proposition.

Holmes was very interested in the economic effects of the law; and his view of the future of legal theory is well known, namely: 'For the rational study of the law the black-letter man may be the man of the present, but the man of the future is the master of statistics and the master of economics'. Does this phrase have a meaning beyond the obvious necessity of having today some knowledge of economics in order to understand the law, or in Holmes's own words, that 'every lawyer ought to seek an understanding of economics?'.[3] In *The Path of the Law* (1897) Holmes established a clear relationship between the evolution of the law and the social problems that legal rules and judges should solve. He criticized judges for not recognizing their duty 'of weighing considerations of social advantage'. In fact he thought that law is no more than a concealed, half conscious battle on the question of legislative policy. The law, in his opinion, is open to reconsideration upon a slight change in the habit of the public mind. And some of the basic principles of social and economic life – the principle of free competition, for instance – may vary in different times and places.[4]

Posner and some literature in the law and economics tradition also defend the superiority of common law, but their arguments are very different from Hayek's, since they are based on the idea of efficiency. In this approach the doctrines developed in the different fields of the common law induce people to behave efficiently by creating property rights, and protecting them through remedies. In a well-known paper, Landes and Posner (1987), tried to illustrate the efficiency of common law in terms of a well-known concept of tort law, the Hand Formula. Accordingly, a person or company should be held liable for an accident if the cost of preventing it is less than the expected cost of the accident, that is the product of the damage and the probability that an accident would result. So this rule places liability on the party better able to prevent or minimize the damage. And contract law would do the same in the case of unforeseen contingencies that make the performance of a specific contract impossible. The superiority of common law would therefore be based on its assumed superiority in finding efficient solutions to some of the main questions involved in the development of private law.

There is, however, cause to doubt the soundness of the notion of superiority of common law from an efficency perspective. Bentham's criticisms regarding the legislative function of the courts and the stability of principles based on the system of *stare decisis* or the subjection of judges to precedent, are now more than 200 years old (Bentham, 1776[1988]). And to cite but another example as a means of demonstrating critical opinions regarding basic aspects of common law, one need only look at Roscoe Pound when he criticized the adversary system as having contributed to a 'sporting theory of justice' and defended the idea that administrative courts would surely be more efficient than common law courts in the resolution of many types of cases (Pound, 1906).

More recently it has been argued that in reality both systems have acted efficiently, allowing for the development of prosperous economies (for some examples, see Rubin, 2000). To wit, if the aim is to adapt the law to socially changing economic realities, it is not easy to say which of the two systems is superior. In support of the common law one can put forward that judges are continuously creating law, which permits a better adaptation of legal principles to changing situations. However, one may also argue that the application of the principle of *stare decisis* can have the opposite effect. In reference to the civil law system, the principle of respect for statutes would appear to reduce the possibilities of adapting the law to a changing society; in reality, however, a statute can be modified without great difficulty in the majority of cases. As an aside, the widespread notion that within civil law systems a single word by the legislature can render entire law libraries useless appears to raise more the problem of legal stability than the difficulty of adapting laws to new situations.

It is further important to emphasize the idea that the separate and varied evolution of both systems is more related to different historical realities than to different views of what should be the main objectives of the law. In fact it is not difficult to prove that the evolution of both models reflects a search for efficiency in institutional design. Both within the civil law as well as the common law system changes have been introduced in order to find solutions for situations not appropriately being dealt with. Judges in common law countries and parliaments in civil law countries have often tried throughout history to reach similar goals.

If one had to mention a single differentiating characteristic between the two systems, it is, without doubt, the different role associated with judicial precedent. In this sense, nothing better defines the model of continental civil law than the well-known Justinian maxim '*non exemplis sed legibus iudicandum est*' (courts must adjudicate on the strength of the law not the case). This consideration clearly grants a more limited role to judges in the allocation of resources in an economy. This Justinian position, however, was not a product of real innovation, but rather the continuation of a far more ancient tradition. In Roman law, judges from the beginning were not the basic elements in the administration of justice, this role being assigned to 'jurists'. Without understanding the influence of these jurists, it is impossible to understand the evolution of civil law systems up to the present day. These jurists were legal assessors to the parties and the judges that had to resolve a conflict. They interpreted the law, and with the passage of time had their opinions put down in writing, leading to the development of authentic legal rules and influencing to a great extent the entire development of the judicial system. Some of these legal assessors acquired such importance that their opinions became binding for the courts, and, as a result, had the authentic force of the law. In comparison with the jurists, the role of the judge was of relatively less importance. Judges were initially selected by the parties for the resolution of a specific case, and in exercising their function needed to consult the jurists. Looking at the role of the judges and jurists in diverse judicial systems from a historical perspective, one can unearth a rule, according to which the relevancy of one of the groups is inverse to the other. Wherever judges have formed a prestigious professional group – as has been the case in England from the thirteenth century – the role that jurists occupy has been small. In those cases, however, where judges lack technical expertise – as was the case in the Roman Republic and Empire or in Germany prior to the eighteenth century – the jurists have been the authentic protagonists in the process of developing legal rules.

Naturally, this rule may have some exceptions and its strength is not the same in every country. In the civil law countries the weight of academic doctrine in the development of law has been larger, for instance, in Germany than in France. Moreover, Sir William Blackstone, who was a key figure in the diffusion of common law in England and its extension to the colonies, was a 'jurist', since he was a law professor at Oxford University. It should be remembered, however, that Blackstone was the first professor to teach English law at a university, and his appointment did not take place until as late as 1758. The European continental tradition was markedly different, with law being taught in the university from the Middle Ages. Moreover, the structure of Blackstone's *Commentaries* was criticized precisely because it lacked legal theory – in the continental law meaning of the term – and the work had very much the feeling of a practical guide, to serve as a manual to understanding the principal matters of English law for judges, lawyers, and even persons not versed in the law.

In the Italian universities of the early Middle Ages, the tradition of Latin jurists would be continued, to a large extent, by academic scholars, so-called '*glossators*'. Their work would quickly spread to other universities in continental Europe, permitting the recuperation of Roman law and becoming the basis of a judicial system – with contributions from canon law and new mercantile law – culminating in the process of codification in the nineteenth century, whose final objective was to organize and systematize the law in accordance with well-established rational principles. If the Roman law was a basic element to build a model of economic relations based on the principle of exchange with voluntarily formed contracts, the recovery of this tradition in the Middle Ages and in the Renaissance allowed the development in this age of the Italian mercantile republics. The economic development of Venice, Genoa or Florence in this period would not have been possible without an efficient body of laws and an administration of justice that offered security to economic agents.

Later on, the idea of the existence of individual natural rights that could be understood in a purely rational way and incorporated into legal texts helped to ensure the success of the idea of the necessity of codes based in the organizing power of the reason that judges and courts should obey. Codification should assume, in principle, a clear restriction in the discretion afforded to continental judges. The old idea that the judge's principal mission was to serve as the mouthpiece of the law becomes more lucid, as the law and its application become more precise. In this sense, there can be no doubt that the codes, beginning in the nineteenth century, offered a clear guide for the behaviour of the courts. Codification was not easy in many countries and generated internal tensions and numerous conflicts between a conservative approach in defence of local laws and those in favour of unification of national law, which a code of general application clearly demands. Legal unity was achieved in a diverse manner and at a varied pace in different countries. The French *Code Civil* of 1804 became the model to be followed by all countries in the path towards codification. In Spain this process manifested itself in a languid fashion, whereby the power of local laws ensured that a code did not emerge until 1889, 85 years after the French codification, and more than 60 years after the country introduced its first commercial code, which in substance related more to the practices of merchants than to local traditions.

From our perspective it is necessary to emphasize the fact that, in civil law countries, the development of markets was precisely one of the main aims of codification. It was considered that if the supremacy of the code over local law and local judges could be affirmed, a double objective could be reached. On the one hand, an authentic national market could be created, a goal not easily reached without a general law superior to the local regulations which created distortions in the economic marketplace. On the other, a decisive advance could be made towards the principle of freedom of contract which had been hindered by the presence of local privileges of every type.

3 CONTRACT LAW

One of the key features often put forward to support the view that common law is superior to civil law is the supposedly greater support it offers to the principle of the autonomy of contracting parties, or in other words, freedom of contract. To many continental lawyers, however, this view has always appeared somewhat surprising, given that the principle of freedom of contract served as a great inspiration for the wording of civil codes in Europe in the nineteenth century, beginning with the French *Code Civil* in 1804. This position is unmistakably manifest in later codifications, such as the Spanish civil code of 1889, where article 1255 establishes with clarity the principle of liberty of contract, establishing that contracting parties may create their own agreements, clauses and conditions as the parties see fit, as long as they do not run counter to the law, morals or public order.

It is certain that if one analyses the evolution of legislation post-codification, one can bear witness to how, on the one hand (i) the principle of contractual freedom has been losing importance, and how, on the other (ii) legal scholars and judges have discredited it as the basic principle of the legal system. In reference to point (i), it makes sense to interpret a good part of the laws passed over the last century as a departure from the civil code and the principle of freedom of contract which inspired it. From laws that regulate labour relations to those that seriously limit freedom on many different contracts, new regulations have been introduced as a means of social redistribution in favour of certain social groups. Individual volition is thus, to a large extent, replaced by collective interest principles.

With reference to the second point, it is sufficient to look at some of the books studied by lawyers and judges. The extensive work by J. Castán, *Derecho Civil Español, Común y Foral* (National and regional Spanish civil law), without doubt the most studied textbook on civil law ever in the history of Spain, may serve as an example. In his introduction to the analysis of contract law, Castán had no doubt in affirming: 'it must be confessed that civil law in many points concedes excessive respect to private conventions to the detriment of equality and moral demands' (1967, 375). Regarding what he considered to be the future of contractual agreements, he unsurprisingly suggested: 'One need succeed the old individualist dogma of the autonomy of volition with the rule of the principle of intervention' (p. 376). Moreover, Federico de Castro, surely one of the key specialists in civil law in Spain in the twentieth century, argued that the principle of freedom of contract in the performance of services led to 'scandalous extremes' (de Castro, 1968, 58). In his interpretation of the role played by the liberal Spanish jurists, dominant when the civil code was formulated, he voiced the following: 'the legal dogma that has been dominant up to now attempts to dry out legal precepts, depriving them of moral sap, putting them at the services of the calculative safety of traders and financiers' (p. 40). This position was naturally compounded with the view that there is a need to abandon the individualist view of the law and replace it by a version that favours the notion of 'community'.

One may make a similar evaluation of the decisions handed down by courts, which have recognized the loss in importance of contractual freedom. This can be seen, for example, in a decision handed down by the Supreme Court in 1946:

> [If] one reviews legislation since the passing of the civil code, one soon realizes that legal evolution is commandingly moving down the path towards a greater infiltration of social and ethical elements, which in both a general and absolute manner discipline private law relations, imposing upon them a public character at the expense of the principle of freedom of contract.[5]

There can be little doubt therefore that civil law systems, of which the Spanish one may be considered representative, have been gradually moving away from the position where decisions taken within markets are the principal means for allocating productive resources in an economy. But is the historical experience of common law really different? According to Posner: 'in settings in which the cost of voluntary transactions is low, common law doctrines create incentives for people to channel their . . . actions through the market' (1998, 272). But one can suggest that developments against the principle of freedom of contract also occurred in the common law system; and that the evolution of the North American legal tradition in the past century was quite similar to the European experience, bar differences in institutional settings.

American law witnessed, in the twentieth century, an important change regarding freedom of contract. Over a long period the Supreme Court overturned numerous economic and social laws on the grounds that they ran counter to freedoms constitutionally protected by the Fifth and Fourteenth Amendments. Later, however, the Supreme Court abandoned this process of revising statutes, which in turn would lead to a serious restriction on many economic activities based on the principle of contractual freedom. Moreover, local, state and federal authorities could now regulate economic activity with no restriction other than discrimination or arbitrariness. The most representative defence of freedom of contract by the US Supreme Court in the twentieth century is probably the case of *Lochner v. New York* (1905). The Supreme Court in Lochner ruled that it was contrary to the constitution to limit the maximum working hours in the bakery sector to 60 hours a week and 10 hours a day. In the final decades of the nineteenth century, however, the Supreme Court accepted on various occasions the constitutionality of regulatory laws in economic activity. One could also cite previous cases: for example, the case of *Munn v. Illinois* 1876, where a Chicago-based firm that refused to apply for a state licence as a warehouse owner and accept its regulation lost its case in the Supreme Court on the grounds that there was a public interest in the warehouse sector.

Thirty years later, Lochner constituted a reaffirmation of the principles of classical jurisprudence from the nineteenth century, and for this reason was harshly criticized by those who considered this position to be unsustainable, given existing economic conditions and the changes that the North American economy had been experiencing. Holmes's dissenting vote in Lochner, perhaps the most famous dissenting vote in the history of North American legal history, would constitute an authentic manifesto for those in favour of what became known as the progressive approach to the problem. The liberty of a citizen to do as he likes as long as he does not interfere with the liberty of others to do the same – wrote Holmes – is itself interfered with by many laws and regulations, from school laws to every state or municipal institution that takes his money whether he likes it or not. Reducing freedom of contract was, therefore, not a new principle. 'The Fourteenth amendment does not enact Mr. Herbert Spencer's Social Statics'.[6]

The position of judges and law professors is similar. Only four years after Lochner, Roscoe Pound published his famous article 'Liberty of contract' (1909). In this article, Pound attacked the application of the principle of contractual freedom in US courts from two standpoints: first because, in his opinion, this was not a traditional principle in US law; and second, because it assigned the false impression of equality between the parties in contractual relations. In his opinion, previous legal doctrine had exaggerated the relevance of the principle of freedom of contract and had, contrarily, downplayed the importance of public interest. Individualism should, accordingly, be surmounted by a more social vision of legal relations.

The specific circumstances and legal tradition were undisputedly different from those found in Spain and other civil law countries, but legal doctrines in both countries showed clear signs of convergence. Opposition to the principle of freedom of contract would gather strength in the years following and the Supreme Court in the 1930s would further reel it in. In *Nebbia v. New York* (1934), for instance, the Supreme Court refused the right to sell some merchandise at a price agreed by both buyer and seller, thus endorsing a law passed by the State of New York establishing a minimum price for milk, with the aim of helping farmers who had experienced a strong fall in the price of this product. Many other cases could be mentioned. In fact one can find in either system an evolution in both law as well as legal theory towards the reduction of contractual freedom in favour of regulatory ideas, presented as a step towards progress and modernity. Principles of freedom of contract became subordinate to other principles based on ethics and moral values, thus reducing contractual freedom in favour of a redistribution of gains for the benefit of weaker contracting parties.

If contract law in civil law countries has been moving away in a general form from the principle of freedom of contract, there can be little doubt that labour relations specifically constitute one of the most highly regulated areas of economic activity. Furthermore, one can also observe significant parallels between both civil and common law systems, particularly with regard to growing regulation, as well as the timeframe in which these regulations transpired. The Spanish civil code at the time of its introduction included a section referring to the regulation of the labour market. It was limited to only five articles (arts 1583 to 1587). Of these, three regulated the relationship between master and servant and the other two were limited to prohibiting unfair dismissal in specific contracts before the termination of the work. All other factors were to be governed according to the aforementioned principle of freedom of contract.

Attempts to regulate specific aspects of labour relations, such as the duration of a working day, were the object of discussion, being criticized by exponents of the principle of contractual freedom. Thus, the economist Laureano Figuerola (1991, 39) argued for free agreement of employers and employees in fixing the number of working hours and thought that an eight-hour law would be the first step towards socialism. But the tendency towards regulation began to assert itself with the passage of time. And what is more important, it was accepted that labour relations were of a unique nature, which demanded that they be regulated by specific laws, and could in no case be governed by the principle of freedom of contract as found in the civil code.

Legal evolution in common law countries was not very different. In the United States, labour relations also constituted one of the most important arguments for attacking the principle of freedom of contract. The idea that labour relations did not fit the same principles as the majority of contracts also made headway in the United States. Following a tradition started in continental Europe, the National Labor Relations Board (NLRB) was created in 1934 with the objective of arbitrating in collective agreements related to working conditions. With the Wagner Act in 1935, the position of the labour unions was reinforced, and because it was written into the framework of the commerce clause, this law gave power to the Federal Congress to regulate labour relations. In the case of *NLRB v. Jones and Loughlin Steel Corp.* (1937), the Supreme Court accepted – in a five to four decision – that 'manufacturing' was 'commerce' so the powers of federal government were reinforced in this field.[7] What in civil law countries was achieved through statutes passed by parliament, in the US was done through the substitution of common law by statutes with the help of the Supreme Court.

4 TORT LAW

Throughout most of the Western world, the nineteenth century was the century of industrialization. And in this process, an important part was played by the legal body in the way of laws and regulations. According to Coase's theory, in a world with no transaction costs and with well-defined property rights, situations of conflict would be solved efficiently by agreement between the parties. But in a real world of confused property rights and positive transaction costs, laws and courts of justice play an important role since they exert a direct influence on the economy.

It has been pointed out that in the analysis of economic problems such as those raised by tort law, the strict theory of market failures gives only a partial view, and often a misleading one at that. In these cases what usually happens is that the market, indeed, fails; but, at the same time, the laws of private property which are a prerequisite for the functioning of the market also fail. It is very rare that we find ourselves faced with a simple alternative between the free market and public regulation. The problem is, rather, the option between two forms of control, both proceeding from public authority: private law and administrative regulation (Posner, 1998, 401). This distinction is especially relevant for this section since it discusses how, throughout the nineteenth century, tort law and administrative regulation were modified so as to encourage industrialization. In this idea, countries coincided which were very different in themselves and which, furthermore, had distinct judicial systems.

After much controversy throughout the 1970s and 1980s, many econo-mists and legal scholars think that the civil legal system during the nine-teenth century in the United States clearly evolved in favour of the interests of industry. This transformation, however, was not achieved by means of a substantial modification of the laws that regulated industrial activity, but rather through a significant change of the legal interpretation of tort law. This concept is generally known as 'Horwitz's theory' but it has, in fact, been developed and studied by numerous historians.[8] The main idea is that common law gradually stopped applying the strict liability rule, which prevailed in the period prior to industrialization, and started to examine claims for damages caused by industrial installations following the negli-gence rule. It is not hard to understand why this change in the liability rules could have an important effect both on resource allocation and on income distribution. According to the strict liability rule, the person or company that causes an accident should pay the cost of the damages produced, inde-pendent of whether or not they have taken the necessary measures to try to avoid such an accident taking place. Under this rule the manufacturer who, for example, causes a fire accidentally in the land adjacent to his factory, or who causes losses in agricultural production in the farms bordering his property because of badly controlled smoke emissions, should indemnify the injured parties. However, the legal decision would be quite different in a claim for damages in which the negligence rule was applied, since in this case the factory owner would have to indemnify the injured parties only if he had not taken reasonable precautions.

For those who defend the theory of the change in liability rules in the US legal tradition, the judges were not neutral in the application of tort law but rather applied a utilitarian criterion which, in the language of welfare eco-nomics, allowed the external costs generated by a process of industrializa-tion to be transferred partially to third parties. In other words, the American judges assumed a pro-industrial economic ideology in their interpretation of civil liability.

Apparently the story was quite different in continental Europe, since eco-nomic policy in the civil law countries followed a stricter regulating, inter-ventionist tradition than the one existing in Great Britain and the United States. It is not surprising, therefore, that the encouragement of industrial-ization by the legal community should take a different shape from that in the Anglo-Saxon world. But the goals were similar. Thus, we could talk of a 'continental model' where industry would also be favoured by laws, but where administrative regulations would play the more dominant role.

Although the legal system in continental Europe was dominated by administrative regulation regarding the creation of new industrial establishments, one should not overexaggerate the differences between the two models since both coincided on two important points.[9] First, administrative regulation also began to appear in the Anglo-Saxon countries. Second, the change in legal interpretation of tort law from strict liability to a negligence rule was *not* necessary in civil law countries, such as France and Spain where, from the beginning, the civil codes upheld the negligence rule as a general principle.

The attitude of mistrust shown by the authorities of the *ancien régime* towards the damage caused by industrial establishments is well known. As in other countries, Spain underwent fundamental change in the course of the nineteenth century, in which central government adopted a decidedly favourable attitude towards manufacturers as far as third-party damages were concerned. An important legal text in this respect is the Law of 8 June 1813 on the 'Freedom of establishment of factories and trades'. The declared objective of this legal text was 'to remove the obstacles which until now have hampered the progress of industry'; and in it not only were the examinations for admittance to the industrial trades and the obligation to belong to a guild eliminated, but also a background was established of general freedom in the creation of factories in the townships of the monarchy, without the requirement of either permission or a licence: 'as long as the policy regulations are followed which have been adopted or which may be adopted for the health of these townships' (Alcubilla, 1887, vol. V, 3). However, it seems that this general rule of freedom of establishment soon clashed with the allocation to local administrations of the authority over the creation of factories for reasons of health within their respective municipal boundaries. It was precisely the interpretation of this law in favour of the manufacturers that was one of the legal means used by central government to encourage the creation of factories.

But disagreements between manufacturers and town councils regarding the authority of the latter to regulate the establishment and functioning of factories broke out quite frequently in the nineteenth century. Furthermore, manufacturers presented complaints in response to the opposition they frequently encountered in establishing new industries. These complaints were used as the reason for the government to take a new step in favour of the manufacturers with the promulgation of new laws to facilitate the establishment and development of useful industries and 'to overcome prejudices which science does not accept'. The legislators lamented the 'systematic opposition of certain people and businesses to give momentum to industry and to labor, the true axis on which reform for the future has to revolve' (ibid., 6).

Thus civil law countries' legislators made use of administrative procedures to encourage industrialization, while a similiar objective was pursued in the United States by applying the negligence rule. Both administrative and civil laws took into account the advantages that the new industries and technology offered to social welfare and sought formulas by which the affected third parties would pay a part of the external cost. Throughout the nineteenth century, as was noted above, Spanish law also upheld, with very few exceptions, the principle of negligence, so that interesting similarities can be found between Spanish cases and the decisions reached by the British and North American courts which are often quoted to support the theory of the industrialist tendency of common law in that century.

For instance, the Spanish courts maintained the thesis that the railways inevitably gave rise to accidents and risks, and that it was the obligation of the railway workers to take the necessary measures to avoid these dangers. But if accidents occurred even when such measures had been taken, the companies could not be held responsible for what had happened. In this sense, we could mention the Spanish Supreme Court's decision of 30 May 1865. It denied the appeal for annulment presented by a landowner in Burgos against the decision of the Court of Appeals of that city. The Court had acquitted the Isabel II Railway Company of the damages caused by a fire in a gorse thicket on the property of the appellant. Since the railroad crossed the appellant's land, the engines started a fire on more than one occasion, causing considerable damage. The landowner claimed compensation before the Court of Appeals of Burgos, but the railway company fought the case. They argued that they recognized that the engines caused the fires, but they claimed that the engines were only working in keeping with their nature and that the fires had been completely unavoidable and beyond the control of the engine drivers. The Supreme Court accepted this reasoning and pointed out that, since no carelessness or blame on the part of the engine drivers had been proved, there were no grounds for imposing the payment of compensation to the aggrieved party.[10] The Spanish Supreme Court ruled similarly on many occasions. To cite another example, let us look at the case resolved by the Supreme Court in its decision of 3 June 1901. On this occasion, an engine had caused a fire in a nearby haystack while manoeuvring in a station. The court applied the law mentioned above and ruled that there was no blame or negligence on the part of the engine driver. It pointed out, moreover, that the haystacks had been placed near the railway line without any agreement that would limit the right of the company to use the line, and in full knowledge of the constant use that was made of the railway line and of the consequent risk to the merchandise.[11]

The opinions of the British and American courts in that period were not very different. Economists familiar with Coase's theory will now find themselves on well-known ground. As an example, there are two interesting North American cases in which the judges' arguments coincided with the enthusiasm for industrialization which we have seen reflected both in the text of the Spanish law referred to above and in the Spanish Supreme Court decision mentioned earlier. The first of these court decisions was in reference to the explosion in a factory which caused damage to a neighbouring farm. In 1873, a judge in New York State ruled in the case of *Losee v. Buchanan* that 'society has to have factories, machines, dams, canals and railways. These installations are called for to satisfy the multiple needs of the people and form the basis of our civilization'. He went on to add that if any damage was caused to a third party's property because of an accident, the factory owner could not be held responsible for it (Hovenkamp, 1983, 687). Some years later we find a similar opinion in the case of the *Georgia Railroad and Banking Co. v. Maddox* (1902), where the judge ruled that if a railway station had been authorized and was appropriately run, the people who lived in the vicinity could not sue the company for damages since these were the inevitable results of the very existence of the railway system itself (Coase, 1988, 129).

5 CONCLUSIONS

The main thesis of this chapter is that most of the changes that took place in the legal systems both in the civil law countries and in the common law countries in the twentieth century should be understood more as the expression of the *Zeitgeist* and the new system of values that gained strength during the course of the nineteenth and twentieth centuries in the Western world. The two main fields of private law, contracts and torts, have been studied in order to check whether the specific characteristics of the common and the civil law were responsible for substantial differences in these two legal systems. More similarities than differences have, however, been found. In contract law both systems were based on the principle of freedom of contract in the nineteenth century. Moreover, reforms in both systems were introduced in the twentieth century as a means of achieving redistribution of income, whereby the principle of private interest was replaced by moral and common interest ideas.

Nineteenth-century tort and administrative law shows that the belief in technical progress and industrialization as the driving force for prosperity and happiness for all humankind had spread throughout the Western world; and the varying legal systems simply supplied answers to a common worry. It is not a coincidence that new consumer preferences in the second half of the twentieth century caused major modifications in regulations of dangerous activities and in the liability rules. When the main objective is industrialization, the negligence rule and tolerant administrative regulation are the legal implements to be applied. But when, as nowadays, the value of such assets as clean air and a healthy environment increase even at the cost of more expensive production techniques and a slowing-down of the rhythm of industrial growth, we should not be surprised at the increase in restrictive administrative regulation and a recovery of the strict liability rule. No big differences can be found in this respect in civil and common law countries.

NOTES

1. For a good bibliography on this topic, see Rubin (2000).
2. Hayek defends the superiority of the common law in several of his works; but his most systematic analysis is in Hayek (1973), vol. 1, ch. 4, 'The changing concept of law'.
3. Holmes, 'The path of the law' (1897), in Holmes (1992, 170 and 174).
4. Ibid., 167–8.
5. Spanish Supreme Court, Decision of 2 April 1946.
6. Holmes, Dissenting vote in *Lochner v. New York* (1905), Holmes (1992, 305–7).
7. For a good analysis of the role of the Supreme Court in judicial review of social and economic legislation, see Siegan (1980).
8. See especially Horwitz (1977). An analysis of this theory can be found in Schwartz (1981) and Hovenkamp (1983).
9. The criticism of A.V. Dicey (1885) to any administrative regulation as the opposite of the rule of law greatly exaggerated the differences between the common and civil law systems and helped to sustain the idea of two incompatible legal models.
10. Jurisprudencia civil (1901, 921–3).
11. For a general view of the role of administrative and tort law in nineteenth-century Spain, see Cabrillo (1994).

REFERENCES

Alcubilla, M. (1887), *Diccionario de la Administración Española. Compilación de la novísima legislación española, peninsular y ultramarina en todos los ramos de la Administración Pública*, Madrid.
Bentham, J. (1776 [1988]), *A Fragment on Government*, Cambridge: Cambridge University Press.
Blackstone, W. (1765–69), *Commentaries on the Law of England*, 4 vols, Oxford: Clarendon Press.
Cabrillo, F. (1994), 'Industrialización y derecho de daños en la España del siglo XIX', *Revista de Historia Económica*, **12**(3), 591–609.
Castán, J. (1967), *Derecho Civil Español Común y Foral. III. Derecho de obligaciones*, Madrid: Reus.
Coase, Ronald (1988), 'The problem of social cost', in *The Firm, the Market and the Law*, Chicago: University of Chicago Press, 95–156.

de Castro, F. (1968), *Compendio de derecho civil*, Madrid: Reus.

Dicey, A.V. (1885), *An Introduction to the Study of the Law of the Constitution*, London: Macmillan.

Figuerola, L. (1991), *Escritos económicos*, Madrid: Instituto de Estudios Fiscales.

Hayek, F.A. (1973), *Law, Legislation and Liberty*, Vol. 1: *Rules and Order*, London: Routledge.

Holmes, O.W. (1992), *The Essential Holmes*, edited by R.A. Posner, Chicago: University of Chicago Press.

Horwitz, M. (1977), *The Transformation of American Law (1780–1860)*, Cambridge, MA: Harvard University Press.

Hovenkamp, Herbert (1983), 'The economics of legal history', **67** *Minnesota Law Review*, 645–97.

Landes, W.M. and R. Posner (1987), *The Economic Structure of Tort Law*, Cambridge, MA: Harvard University Press.

Posner, Richard A. (1998), *Economic Analysis of Law*, 5th edn, New York: Aspen.

Pound, R. (1906), 'The causes of popular dissatisfaction with the administration of justice', **40** *American Law Review*, 729.

Pound, R. (1909), 'Liberty of contract', **18** *Yale Law Journal*, 454.

Rubin, P.H. (2000), 'Judge-made law', in B. Bouckaert and G. De Geest (eds), *Encyclopedia of Law and Economics*, Volumes, Cheltenham, UK and Northampton, MA, USA: Edward Elgar, pp. 543–58.

Schwartz, G.T. (1981), 'Tort law and the economy in nineteenth century America: a reinterpretation', **90** *Yale Law Journal*, 1717–75.

Siegan, B.H. (1980), *Economic Liberties and the Constitution*, Chicago: University of Chicago Press.

PART III

Voting Issues

11. A reformulation of voting theory

William A. Niskanen

1 INTRODUCTION

Our standard theory of voting behavior – the core of public choice – is a mess! The theory of voter behavior is asymmetric with the theory of candidate behavior. And more important, the theory does not explain some of the more important changes in the outcomes of American elections. This is not a new observation. Samuel Huntington (1950), Morris Fiorina (1974), Richard Fenno (1977) and Sam Peltzman (1984) were among the most vocal critics of the median voter theorem, arguing that divergent platforms are needed to adequately explain political behavior. But none of these distinguished scholars offered a coherent competing theory of voting behavior. This chapter summarizes a major problem of the standard theory of voting behavior, develops an alternative theory based on a joint determination of voter and candidate behavior, and presents some evidence from recent elections that is more consistent with the alternative theory.

2 A MAJOR PROBLEM WITH THE STANDARD THEORY OF VOTING BEHAVIOR

The standard theory of voter behavior is dramatically asymmetric with the theory of candidate behavior. (For a good recent summary of the standard theory, see Munger, 2001.) Voters are assumed to make a *joint* determination of *whether* to vote and *for whom* to vote, based on their understanding of the issue positions of the alternative candidates. Candidates, in contrast, are represented as assuming that voters have made a decision whether to vote that is invariant to the issue positions of the candidates but that their decision for whom to vote is still open and is dependent on these issue positions. The assumptions about the sequence with which the candidates' issue positions are revealed are also asymmetric: voters are assumed to know the issue positions of the candidates when they make a decision whether to vote, whereas candidates are assumed to know the preference distribution of those who vote before they choose and

announce their issue positions. When the decision *whether* to vote is
invariant to the issue positions of the candidates, a candidate does not risk
losing votes from his (or her) party base, and there is a strong incentive to
choose issue positions close to that of the alternative candidate, gaining
two net votes for every swing voter that he attracts. Only in this case (plus
the usual assumptions that voter preferences are single peaked on all issues
and that there are only two candidates) do both candidates have an incentive to choose issue positions close to the median preferences of those who
vote. An encouraging result, perhaps, suggesting that the variance of the
issue positions among our elected representatives is lower than the variance of voter preferences, reducing the bargaining costs of the compromises necessary to govern. The problem is that this result does not seem
consistent with the evidence.

3   AN ALTERNATIVE THEORY OF VOTER AND CANDIDATE BEHAVIOR

In a prior article on these issues (Niskanen, 2004), I concluded that 'Public
choice scholars need to rebuild voting theory to incorporate the effects of
a candidate's issue position on both the decision to vote and the choice
among those who decide to vote'. That is what I try to do in this section.

   We shall start with the following two equations describing the conditions
that determine the number of votes for the candidate of the left and of the
right, respectfully,

$$V_L = a - b(L - L_M)^2 - c(L - R)^2, \qquad (11.1)$$

and

$$V_R = d - e(R - R_M)^2 - f(R - L)^2, \qquad (11.2)$$

where

   V_L = total votes for the candidate of the left,
   L = position in issue space of the candidate of the left,
   L_M = position in issue space of the median potential voter on the
          left,
   R = position in issue space of the candidate of the right,
   V_R = total votes for the candidate of the right, and
   R_M = position in issue space of the median potential voter on the
          right.

The issue space is represented by a scale from 0 through 100, with 0 representing the position of the extreme left and 100 the extreme right. The first squared term in each equation represents the votes that a candidate loses, primarily by potential voters choosing not to vote, by choosing a position in issue space different from the party base. The second squared term in each equation represents the votes that a candidate loses, primarily to the other candidate, by choosing a position in issue space different from the other candidate. The challenge for each candidate is to choose a position in issue space such that the marginal votes gained by attracting swing voters is equal to the marginal votes lost by members of his own party choosing not to vote.

The following two equations describe the conditions that determine the vote-maximizing position in issue space for each of the two candidates:

$$L = (bL_M + cR)/(b + c), \tag{11.3}$$

and

$$R = (eR_M + fL)/(e + f). \tag{11.4}$$

The candidate of the left, for example, is pulled toward his party base by the ratio $b/(b + c)$ and to the issue position of the candidate of the right by the ratio $c/(b + c)$. If either candidate is confident that he knows the issue position of the other candidate, his own equation is sufficient to determine his own vote-maximizing position in issue space. More generally, however, both candidates choose a vote-maximizing position in issue space on the assumption that the other candidate does also, in which case their positions are jointly determined. In this case, equations (11.3) and (11.4) must be solved jointly to determine both **L** and **R**. This leads, for example, to the following equation for **L** that does not include the specific issue position of the candidate of the right:

$$L = [b (e + f)L_M + ceR_M]/[(b + c)(e + f) - cf], \tag{11.5}$$

and the level of **L** from this equation can then be inserted into equation (11.4) to determine the level of **R**.

The primary lessons from this model of the behavior of voters and candidates may best be illustrated by a quantitative example. For the example presented in Table 11.1, the coefficients **a** and **d** (the magnitude of the respective party bases) are both set equal to 200, L_M (the issue position of the median potential voter on the left) at 40, and R_M (the issue position of the median potential voter on the right) at 60. Table 11.1 then presents the effects of separately varying the coefficients **b** and **c** from 0.5 to 1.5, leaving

Table 11.1   *Effects of varying voter responses to differences in a candidate's issue position from the party base and the other candidate*

Variables	0.5	1.0	1.5
b			
L	50.0	46.67	45.00
R	55.0	53.33	52.50
V_L	125	111.11	106.25
V_R	150	111.11	87.50
c			
L	44	46.67	48.57
R	52	53.33	54.29
V_L	152	111.11	87.50
V_R	72	111.11	134.69

all other coefficients set at 1. The effects of varying the coefficients **e** and **f** are symmetric with those illustrated.

This table illustrates the following major patterns from this model, in each case given the assumed values of the coefficients **a, d, L_M** and **R_M**:

- When the coefficients **b, c, e** and **f** are all equal to 1, the vote-maximizing position of both candidates are a symmetric *difference* from the median position in issue space, the votes for each candidate are equal, and the voter participation rate (given these coefficients) is 55.6 percent.
- An increase in the votes lost by choosing an issue position different from the median of the party base (such as the illustrated increase in the coefficient **b** relative to the coefficients **c, e** and **f**) pulls the issue positions of *both* candidates (in this case) toward the left, reduces the voter participation rate of both parties, and increases the *relative* vote (in this case) for the candidate of the left.
- An increase in the votes lost by choosing an issue position different from that of the other candidate (such as the illustrated increase in the coefficient **c** relative to the coefficients **b, e** and **f**) pulls the issue position of *both* candidates (in this case) toward the right, and increases the *relative* vote (in this case) for the candidate of the right.

Another pattern of the model (not illustrated by Table 11.1) is the effect of a shift in the median issue position of the party base. A change in L_M in the direction of R_M, for example (a move to the right), shifts the issue position of *both* candidates to the right, increases the vote for both candidates, *but does not change the relative votes for the two candidates.* Again, increasing the coefficients **e** and **f**, or reducing R_M would have just the opposite effects.

4 SOME RELEVANT EMPIRICAL TESTS

The primary condition that seems inconsistent with the standard theory of voter behavior is the increased polarization of Congress. David Broder, a leading political commentator, summarized this condition in a January 2, 2003 column in the *Washington Post*, observing:

> Party caucuses on both sides of the Capitol have become more cohesive internally and further apart from each other philosophically . . . with almost every session, (there are) fewer moderates or progressives on the Republican side and fewer conservatives among the Democrats – especially when it comes to fundamental economic and social questions and the role of government in American life.

Broder based this observation on an analysis of the 'Party Unity' scores calculated and reported each year by the *Congressional Quarterly*. These scores are the percentage of roll-call votes in which a majority of Republicans oppose the position of a majority of Democrats and the percentage of votes that each member has voted with the party majority on these votes. In the same column, Broder reported:

> When I averaged the year-by-year results for both chambers, I found the percentage of partisan-divide-roll calls has gone from 39 percent in the 1970s to 47 percent in the 1980s to 58 percent in the 1990s.
> Even more striking is the growth in cohesion – call it discipline or philosophical agreement – within both party caucuses. In the 1970s, on partisan roll calls, the average member of Congress backed the party position 65 percent of the time. In the 1980s, the average degree of partisan loyalty rose to 73 percent; and in the l990s, to 81 percent. In the past two years, it has been 87 percent.

Since Broder wrote this column, the Party Unity scores increased to the highest level in five decades in 2003, only to decline slightly in 2004 (Poole, 2004).

My own contribution to empirical tests of this issue has been an analysis of the votes for Congress in 2002 and 2004, my study of the 2002 election concluding: 'U.S. elections are increasingly biased against *moderates*', (Niskanen, 2004, original emphasis). My null hypothesis, again, is that the most vulnerable incumbents in these two congressional elections were moderates. My measure of the moderation of Republican incumbents is their Americans for Democratic Action rating. Similarly, my measure of the moderation of Democratic incumbents is their Americans Conservative

Table 11.2   Were the vulnerable incumbents more moderate than other incumbents?

	Year	Sample	Score		S.D.	t-ratio
			Median	Mean		
Senate	2002					
Vulnerable		6	30	24.00	13.13	
Nonvulnerable		21	10	12.19	9.90	
Difference			20	11.81	5.78	2.04
Senate	2004					
Vulnerable		3	16	17.00	2.65	
Nonvulnerable		22	17.5	17.27	11.16	
Difference			−1.5	−0.27	2.83	−0.10
House	2002					
Vulnerable		18	12	22.06	23.16	
Nonvulnerable		368	5	11.34	14.59	
Difference			7	10.72	5.51	1.94
House	2004					
Vulnerable		15	20	23.00	20.40	
Nonvulnerable		318	5	11.51	13.28	
Difference			15	11.49	5.32	2.16

Union rating for the same period. Very few incumbents were defeated in either election, so I defined the vulnerable incumbents as those who won less than 55 percent of the major party popular vote in their states or districts. Even by this measure the samples of vulnerable incumbents were surprisingly small. The samples of nonvulnerable incumbents exclude those that had no major party opposition candidate. I test this hypothesis for both the Senate and the House for both 2002 and 2004 by a difference-of-means test. The results of these tests are summarized in Table 11.2.

In the congressional election of 2002, the vulnerable incumbents in both the Senate and the House had significantly higher scores (ratings by the standards of the other party) than the nonvulnerable incumbents. In the congressional election of 2004, the scores of the vulnerable and nonvulnerable Senate incumbents were not significantly different, but the vulnerable House incumbents again had a significantly higher score than the nonvulnerable incumbents.

For the congressional election of 2004, I also carried out one other test to determine whether there was a significant relation between the ratio of the vote for the incumbent to the vote for the candidate of the major opposition party and the 'moderation score' of the incumbent, again excluding those incumbents who had no major party opposition candidate. Consistent with the findings presented in Table 11.2, there was no such relation for Senate incumbents but a highly significant *negative* relation for House incumbents.

Most of these tests, in summary, indicate that a favorable ranking by the standards of the other party makes an incumbent *more* vulnerable by reducing the ratio of their popular votes relative to that for the candidate of the major opposition party. At the same time, there seems to be little risk for most incumbents to be considered a moderate, because the average incumbent in the 2004 congressional election received around twice as many popular votes as their major party opposition candidate. For most incumbents, their first election to Congress is close to a lifetime appointment.

All in all, I suggest, my alternative model of voter and candidate behavior is a better explanation of the major recent changes in American elections than the standard model. One major change is the increased polarization of Congress, as summarized above. Another major change has been the increased attention of Republican candidates to energize their party base, rather than to reach out to a broader range of uncommitted voters. For example, the focus of the 2004 Bush campaign, as described by political scientist Morris Fiorina (2004), was:

> [to get out] the votes of a few million Republican-leaning evangelicals who did not vote in 2000, rather than by attracting some modest proportion of 95 million other non-voting Americans, not to mention moderate Democratic voters who could have been persuaded to back a genuinely compassionate conservative.

There will still be those who claim that the median voter theorem is a sufficient explanation of voter and candidate behavior *within* each constituency and that the increased polarization of Congress reflects an increased polarization of policy preferences *among* states and congressional districts. That may be true, but I doubt it. A study by political scientists Melissa Collie and John Mason (2000) found that the variance of votes in Congress is more polarized than the variance of opinion in the electorate. A major recent book by Fiorina (Fiorina et al., 2004) concludes that it is the political activists who are polarized, not the public. He asserts (Fiorina, 2004) that

> political elites do not take extreme positions because *voters* make them. Rather, by presenting them with polarizing alternatives, elites make voters appear polarized, but the reality shows through clearly when voters have a choice of more moderate alternatives . . .

An analysis of county-level data from the 2004 election by political scientists Philip A. Klinkner and Ann Hapanowicz (2005) shows only slight increases in geographic and political segregation, with no evidence that strongly partisan counties became more so between 2000 and 2004. And an analysis of panel data from US states over the 1963–2002 period by economist Andrew Leigh (2005) found that there are surprisingly few differences in policy settings, social outcomes and economic outcomes under Democrats and Republicans.

5   CONCLUSION

My reading of this evidence is that the behavior of American voters and political candidates leads to a larger polarization of American politics than is consistent with the median voter theorem. The evolutionary biologists, interestingly, describe this type of pattern – where two regional subspecies develop contrary characteristics when they compete for resources – as 'character displacement'. Over time, this pattern of behavior will lead to an evolutionary reduction in the moderates in both parties and an increasing divergence of the issue positions of the two major parties. This pattern will also make it more difficult for Congress to govern. More issues will be subject to partisan deadlock, more issues will be decided by near party-line votes, and a reduction of the moderates in both parties will make it more difficult to achieve the bipartisan consensus that is necessary for a major reform to be approved and to survive a change in the majority party. For different reasons, Congress is becoming more like the Italian parliament – more partisan, a reduced ability to address major reforms, and an increased centralization of political power in the executive. Not a happy thought.

REFERENCES

Broder, David (2003), 'Don't count on bipartisan niceties', *Washington Post*, 2 January.
Collie, Melissa P. and John L. Mason (2000), 'The electoral connection between party and constituency reconsidered: evidence from the U.S. House of Representatives, 1962–94', in David W. Brady, John E. Cogan and Morris P. Fiorina (eds), *Continuity and Change in House Elections*, Stanford, CA: Stanford University Press/Hoover Institution Press.
Fenno, Richard F. (1977), *Home Style*, Boston, MA: Little, Brown.
Fiorina, Morris P. (1974), *Representatives, Role Calls, and Constituencies*, Lexington, MA: Lexington Books.
Fiorina, Morris P. (2004), '*What* culture wars?', *Wall Street Journal*, 14 July.
Fiorina, Morris P., Samuel J. Abrams and Jeremy C. Pope (2004), *Culture War? The Myth of a Polarized America*, New York: Pearson Longman.
Huntington, Samuel (1950), 'A revised theory of American party politics', *American Political Science Review*, **44** (3), 669–77.

Klinkner, Philip A. and Ann Hapanowicz (2005), 'Red and blue *déjà vu*: measuring polarization in the 2004 election', *The Forum*, **3** (2), Article 2.

Leigh, Andrew (2005), 'What's the difference between a donkey and an elephant? Using panel data from U.S. states to estimate the impact of partisanship on policy settings and economic growth', Draft Working Paper, Canberra: Australian National University.

Munger, Michael C. (2001), 'Voting', in William F. Shughart II and Laura Razzolini (eds), *The Elgar Companion to Public Choice*, Cheltenham, UK and Northampton, MA, USA: Edward Elgar, pp. 197–239.

Niskanen, William A. (2004), 'U.S. elections are increasingly biased against Moderates', *Cato Journal*, **23** (3), 463–67.

Peltzman, Sam (1984), 'Constituent interest and congressional voting', *Journal of Law and Economics*, **27**, 181–210.

Poole, Isaiah J. (2004), 'Party unity vote study: votes echo electoral themes', *Congressional Quarterly*, distributed by the office of the House Democratic whip Steny Hoyer.

12. Informational limits to public policy: ignorance and the jury theorem[†]

Roger D. Congleton

1 PUBLIC CHOICE AND PUBLIC POLICY

The positive, or scientific, strand of the public choice research program attempts to analyze how democratic institutions operate and the extent to which its various theories explain real democratic policy choices. It addresses such questions as: to what extent does electoral competition determine public policies? Are interest groups able to operate behind the scenes in a manner that distorts public policies away from those preferred by voters, and are there substantial resources invested in those activities? Are majoritarian outcomes dominated by institutional agenda setters, moderate voter interests, or chance? In addition to the positive literature, there is a normative literature that analyzes the quality of public policy decisions made and the institutions under which political competition takes place. Do the properties of democratic decision making imply that budgets and deficits are too large or too small, too oriented toward special-interest groups, or too favorable to moderate voter interests to the detriment of others? Are there agency problems within the executive branch of government that legislative oversight fails to solve? How well do governmental agencies implement and enforce legislative decisions? Both these strands of the public choice literature focus attention on the *institutional* limits of political decision making within democracies.

This chapter addresses a somewhat different, although perhaps more fundamental, limitation of democratic policy making. Suppose that all the normative agency and stability problems analyzed by the mainstream public choice literature are solved with institutional reforms. How well would democracy work in this case, given the *information limits* of voters?

† An earlier version of this chapter was published in the *Journal of Economic Policy Studies*, 2(1–2), 2005, pp. 3–15. Reprinted with kind permission of the Japanese Economic Policy Association.

There is considerable survey evidence that voters know very little about government policies or the backgrounds and personalities of important governmental officials. If the information possessed by a typical voter determined public policies, even the best democratic government imaginable would adopt policies that are far from perfect, because voters know so little about the details of public policy issues. Indeed, if democratic outcomes were based entirely on the limited information available to a 'typical voter', democratic policies would evidently be doomed to endless mistakes and failure. Yet, for the past century, democratic regimes have outperformed their authoritarian counterparts. How is this possible?

This chapter demonstrates that electoral competition under majority rule aggregates voter information in a manner that allows far better candidate and policy choices to be made via elections than would be possible if policies were made directly by a 'typical' voter. In particular, Condorcet's jury theorem implies that majoritarian outcomes are often better informed than are any of the participating voters. However, if democracy aggregates information better than most people recognize, there are also limits to the information-aggregating ability of majority rule that limit the scope of effective democratic policy. These limits are also explored below.

The principal methodology of the chapter is simulation. Section 2 simulates elections in which 'slightly informed' voters cast votes for political candidates that differ in quality. These simulations demonstrate that majority rule can greatly reduce the impact of the limited information sets that most voters use to appraise the relative merits of candidates. Section 3 explores the extent to which different kinds of information problems may affect democratic public policy choices. These results suggest that the information-aggregating power of majority rule is quite sensitive to the kind of informational constraint faced by voters; thus, policy decisions may be better in some areas than in others.

The models used in the simulations are mathematically tractable in the limit as electorates and the number of elections approach infinity; consequently, the analysis could have been based on mathematical results, rather than simulations. However, modern democracies have had far fewer national elections than necessary to make asymptotic relationships relevant for the present analysis. Even longstanding democracies have had fewer than 100 national elections, and many have had fewer than 20. Moreover, majority decision making is often used in settings in which there are very few voters, as within committees. Thus, asymptotic results are less relevant for understanding how majority rule operates in ordinary political settings than are the small-sample results developed in this chapter. Simulations allow such small-sample results to be computed and also provide useful illustrative 'pseudo data' that are often easier to understand than are the results of limit theorems.

Overall, the simulation analysis suggests that the informational efficiency of majority rule is much greater than skeptics allow, although it tends to be reduced significantly by voter ignorance.

2   DEMOCRACY AS AN INFORMATION AGGREGATION DEVICE

There is a long, although somewhat sparse literature that attempts to analyze how information problems affect political decision making. For example, the early Italian school of public finance attempted to analyze the effects of information biases, what came to be called 'fiscal illusion', on public policies (Puviani, 1897, 1903). The Italian school argued that politicians exploit voter ignorance by using taxes that were difficult for ordinary individuals to assess, while exaggerating the benefits of government programs and downplaying their costs. A related problem was tackled by Downs (1957) and Tullock (1972), who attempted to analyze voter incentives to be well informed. Both Downs and Tullock argued that voters would gather little information about public policy, because their decisions were very unlikely to affect electoral outcomes. As a consequence, voters might systematically underestimate the benefits or costs of public policy, because of entirely rational decisions to economize on information.

Rational ignorance, loosely defined, provides a possible microfoundation for fiscal illusion and mistaken public policies. As noted above, survey data is largely in accord with these predictions. Voters rarely know the names of important political figures below presidential or prime ministerial levels and are often confused about which candidates or parties favor particular policies (Neuman, 1986).

A parallel literature, rooted in Condorcet's jury theorem (1785), suggests that uninformed voting is not a major problem for democracies. The statistical properties of medians combined with electoral competition among political parties implies that voters may not need very much information for democracy to yield 'correct' policy outcomes. Lupia and McCubbins (1998) argue that party labels have enough informational content that voters rarely mistakenly vote for the 'wrong' candidate. Wittman (1995) argues that information problems are no worse in political markets than they are in private markets. These papers and others that more directly explore the implications of Condorcet's jury theorem suggest that the policy choices made by majority rule tend to be far more accurate than one would expect based on survey evidence of voter knowledge.

This divergence of opinion reflects two different ideas about the meaning of 'rational ignorance'. Elementary statistical theory implies that even a small sample is sufficient to allow individuals to form unbiased (although imprecise) estimates of most causal relationships. Democratic outcomes, thus, would not be systematically biased even in cases in which voter information is very limited as long as the data collected are accurate or are accurately filtered. That literature concludes that the source of fiscal illusion, if it exists, cannot be the result of the finite samples implied by models of rational search (Stigler, 1961). Voters can radically economize on policy-relevant information without undermining the accuracy of majoritarian decisions or the viability of democratic policy formation.

On the other hand, Congleton (2001) suggests that fiscal illusion and other forms of biased expectations are not the results of small datasets, *per se*, but rather consequences of complete ignorance of policy-relevant information. That is to say, if voters economize on information costs by collecting no data about a subset of policy-relevant parameters, voter information is incomplete in a different sense from that analyzed by the jury theorem literatures. Such voters are ignorant, rather than slightly informed, about relevant policy parameters and implications.

Confusion on this point exists because the Downs and Tullock discussions of rational ignorance are not clear about what is being 'sampled' by voters, and, thus, what is meant by rational ignorance. When information about relevant parameters is not available, not gathered, or not analyzed, biased expectations are very likely. Indeed, Congleton (2001) demonstrates that voter ignorance implies that unbiased estimates cannot generally be formed by even the most conscientious and rational voter.

3 SIMULATED ELECTIONS AND THE INFORMATION-AGGREGATING POWER OF MAJORITY RULE

In order to analyze the properties of median-voter estimates in a setting of limited information, a computer program was written to simulate election outcomes in settings in which voters economize on information in various ways. The model assumes that two candidates (or parties) compete for elective office and that their platforms have completely converged to the median voter's ideal point. In such cases, the electoral problem for voters is to decide which candidate is more competent, that is, more trustworthy, intelligent, or creative. Some candidates will perform better than others in unanticipated emergencies and will more faithfully represent voter interests in the secret negotiations among members of parliament.[1]

Suppose that it is well known that the quality of candidate i is a linear function of one observable characteristic, E (perhaps experience) and one unobservable characteristic, H (perhaps honesty or intelligence).

$$Q_i = H + bE_i, \tag{12.1}$$

where E_i and u_i are specific values for candidate i. For the purpose of the simulations, both E and H are assumed to be uniformly randomly distributed among candidates. The observable quality indicator of the distribution of candidates, E, is assumed to be distributed between E_L and E_H, with mean zero. The unobservable indicator of candidate quality, H, of the distribution of candidates is assumed to be composed of a deterministic and stochastic component, $H_i = a + u_i$, with the distribution of u_i for the set of potential candidates being uniformly distributed between h_L and h_H with mean zero. Parameters a and b are unknown to voters and have to be estimated.

For the purposes of the first series of simulations, assume that voters are slightly informed. Voters acquire the smallest dataset that allows them to estimate the quality of candidate relationship. The smallest dataset that can be used to estimate equation (12.1) consists of two data points. One of these data points is assumed to be in common. Each voter is assumed to know the quality, Q, and value of the observable characteristic, E, of the incumbent. The other data point varies among voters. Each voter is assumed to know the quality and observable characteristic of a single 'reference politician' from the past, although all voters are assumed to have information about different politicians. Such differences may reflect regional or family differences or simply the random distribution of knowledge about political history. Voters use their two data points to estimate a and b. They estimate the challenger's quality by substituting his or her observable characteristic, E^c, into their estimated candidate quality equation. The estimated quality of the challenger will vary among voters, because voters use different datasets for their estimates.

Figure 12.1 illustrates the variation in estimated quality that can emerge when voters estimate challenger quality using small, but different, datasets. Note that in the case depicted, differences in reference politicians cause voters to disagree substantially about the relative quality of the current incumbent and challenger, even though they completely agree about the meaning of 'quality' and the quality of the incumbent. (Imagine, for example, using Thomas Jefferson or Jimmy Carter as reference politicians, with George Bush as the incumbent.) In Figure 12.1, differences in the estimated quality of the challengers cause Voter 2 to favor the incumbent over the challenger and Voter 1 to favor the challenger over the incumbent.

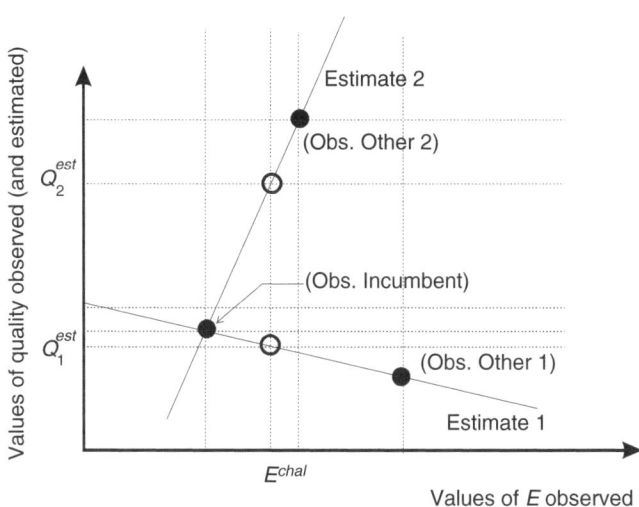

Figure 12.1   Variation in voter estimates of candidate quality for voters with different datasets

In practice, the range of estimated candidate quality will vary substantially when voters use small, but private, datasets to estimate candidate quality, because nearly every data point will be influential. It is this variation in individual experience (data about past candidates), rather than variation in ideology or preferences, that generates the different rankings of candidates in the simulations below.[2]

3.1   Simulated Elections and the Power of the Jury Theorem

Consider the distribution of estimates that result in the case in which reference candidates are drawn randomly from a distribution in which their observable characteristic is uniformly distributed:

$$E \sim U(-10, 10)$$

and their unobservable characteristic, H, is uniformly distributed as

$$H = -4 + u, \text{ with } u \sim U(-2, 2)$$

These distributional assumptions together with the assumption that $b = 0.4$ characterize the quality of candidate function used for the simulations:

$$Q = -4.0 + 0.4E + u \qquad (12.2)$$

Each voter knows Q and E for the incumbent and a different reference candidate from this distribution. These data are used to estimate (a) the mean value of the unobserved variable, and (b) the rate at which the observed quality indicator generates candidate quality. (In a series of simulated elections, the values of E and H for the incumbent and challenger are also drawn from this distribution.)

To illustrate the information-aggregating ability of majority rule, consider the case in which the challenger has observable characteristic $E^c = 4$ and unobservable characteristic $H = 4$. Voters, of course, do not know these values, but can assess challenger quality by estimating the quality of candidate function and using their knowledge of the observed quality indicator, E^c. Figure 12.2 depicts a truncated scatter diagram of parameter estimates from a population of 101 voters with completely accurate data about the incumbent and a reference politician from the past. (The top 10 and lowest 10 percent of the estimates are dropped to make the scatter diagram clearer.)

Note that the *median voter* has a very accurate estimate of the underlying quality of candidate function. The center of mass for this distribution of estimates is approximately at $A = 4$ and $B = 0.4$, the actual parameters of the candidate quality function used in the simulation. The median estimate together with the observed quality indicator of the challenger, $E^c = 4$, implies that the median voter's estimate of the challenger's quality is -2.39. The actual quality of the challenger, in this case, is $-2.4 = -4 + 0.4(4)$.

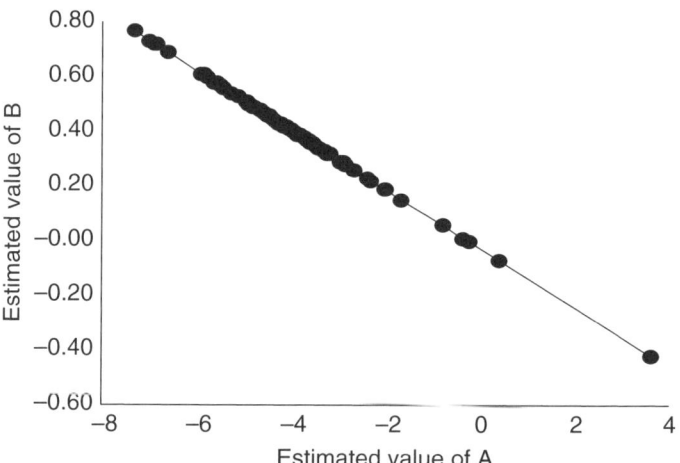

Figure 12.2   Distribution of A, B estimates

The median voter is not always this accurate, because the unobserved quality component, u_i, generally takes values different from zero, but such accuracy is common in the simulations. The entire range of estimated quality for the challenger varies enormously, from $+47$ to -32. Many of these estimates are actually impossible, because they lie outside the actual distributions from which candidates are drawn, but are nonetheless consistent with voter experience! Within the 'moderate' 80 percent of the electorate tabulated in Figure 12.2, estimated challenger quality varies less, but the range of opinion is still considerable, from $+2$ to -5.

Note that the accuracy of the median voter's estimate is not produced by any assumed informational advantage of the median voter. He or she has only two data points, as is true of the other voters. One of the data points is the same for all voters and the other is drawn from the same distribution of reference candidates. The median voter's accurate assessment is entirely caused by his or her position in the middle of the distribution of voter estimates. The median estimate of a and b is an unbiased and extremely accurate estimator in the present informational environment, although individual voter estimates are not very accurate.

Moreover, the size of the electorate does not matter very much, in spite of the extremely limited information base used by voters to assess candidate quality and the wide range of voter estimates of candidate quality. The average difference between the median estimate and the average true value is less than 2 percent in each of the election series. The standard error of the median estimate of challenger quality falls only slightly as the size of the electorate increases. That is to say, median estimates rapidly approach the prediction limits determined by the underlying stochastic nature of challenger quality even in small electorates, as is typical of many committees. The power of the jury theorem is clearly evident in these simulations.[3]

3.2   Ignorance and the Limits of the Jury Theorem

The above simulations assume that voters are well aware of the underlying quality of candidate relationship and gather some data about both candidate quality and the observable characteristic of challengers. In many cases, however, voters will choose to remain completely uninformed about a subset of relevant parameters in order to economize on information. Ignorance implies that some useful parameters go unestimated, and other parameter estimates may therefore be systematically biased (Congleton, 2001). Ignorance, thus, creates another kind of informational challenge for majoritarian policy making. Unfortunately, it is a problem that is not necessarily solved via the jury theorem.

The next series of simulations analyzes the power of majority rule to aggregate information in cases in which estimated candidate quality is not only widely dispersed, but also systematically biased as a consequence of voter ignorance.

The choice setting modeled above allows the electoral effects of three types of ignorance to be analyzed. First, voters may completely understand the underlying quality of candidate relationship, but decide to economize on information by gathering no information about the observable candidate quality characteristic, E. Such rationally ignorant voters might approximate E with its expected value, namely 0, and base their assessment entirely on the unobservable variable, H. These voters vote for the incumbent only if they believe that the incumbent is of above-average quality. They vote for the challenger if the incumbent is of below-average quality, because they expect the challenger to be of average quality, $E(Q^c) = E(H^c) = a$. Of course, whether a particular incumbent is considered to be above or below average depends on the reference candidate used by a particular voter to estimate a.[4]

Second, voters may decide to economize on information by ignoring the effect of the unobservable variable, H, and focusing all of their attention on the observable variable, E. This form of ignorance may be a rational choice undertaken with complete knowledge of the model or the result of natural ignorance if variable H is simply unknown to a subset of voters. In either case, such voters implicitly assign H the value 0 and use information about E to estimate the quality of candidate function $Q = bE$, and assess the relative quality of candidates. Given the very limited datasets assumed in this chapter, b can be estimated as $(Q^0 - Q^c)/(E^0 - E^c)$.

Third, voters may decide to remain completely ignorant (or be naturally ignorant) about both observed and unobserved determinants of quality. In this case, voters choose among incumbents and challengers in a manner uncorrelated with expected performance in office. They might, for example, vote expressly on the basis of regional affiliation, joke-telling ability, or height. For the present purposes, it is assumed that such voters randomly attribute 'quality' to the incumbent and challenger and therefore vote randomly for and against the incumbent. Because their votes are cast randomly, they do not systematically affect electoral outcomes, although they may contribute to electoral mistakes in a given election. These voters, unlike the other two types of rationally ignorant voters, do not have biased assessments, but totally uninformed ones.

Table 12.1 summarizes the results of eight simulated series of elections. In each simulated election, incumbents and challengers are drawn from the distribution characterized in equation (12.2). Voters then estimate the quality of candidate function, as indicated above, and use those estimates

*Table 12.1 Electoral mistakes in populations of poorly informed and
rationally ignorant voters*

Range of u	Slightly informed electorate	Rationally ignorant of B electorate	Rationally ignorant of H electorate	Rationally uninformed electorate	Overall electoral mistakes
Simulations: 100 elections, with 202 slightly informed voters, and 101 of each type of rationally ignorant voter					
+/−0.1	0	27	35	40	0
+/−1.0	5	28	34	55	5
+/−2.0	13	17	33	48	14
+/−4.0	28	31	37	45	23
Simulations: 100 elections, with 51 slightly informed voters, and 51 of each type of rationally ignorant voter					
+/−0.1	1	25	54	49	28
+/−1.0	5	19	34	55	24
+/−2.0	15	27	49	43	38
+/−4.0	21	24	36	51	32

to assess challenger quality and vote. They vote for candidates with the higher estimated quality. Electoral success is determined by majority rule. An electoral mistake occurs if the majority chooses the inferior candidate.

Two populations of voters composed of all four types of voters are simulated. The first includes relatively more of the relatively informed voters used in our first series of simulations than of the three types of rationally ignorant voters. The second includes equal numbers of all four types of voters. To distinguish the mistakes induced by rational ignorance from those associated with irreducible uncertainty about candidate quality, elections are simulated for four ranges of the unobserved quality variable, u.

The simulations demonstrate that there is a systematic increase in mistakes made by majorities in every group and by the electorate as a whole as the variance of u increases. The more difficult it is to assess candidate quality, the more errors tend to be made. However, there is an even larger increase in the number of electoral mistakes made by electoral majorities as the proportion of rationally ignorant voters increases. The error rates in the second series of estimates (tabulated in the bottom half of the table) are much greater than in the first (tabulated in the top half).

Overall, the results suggest that rational ignorance has effects on the efficiency of democratic decision making that may be even more important than the difficulty of the estimation problem faced. However, even in the case in which the range of the unobservable variation in candidate quality (u) and the electorate composition are the least favorable to democratic decision making, majority rule still reduces the problem of voter efforts to economize on information. The overall majority choice is less error prone than are the majorities in two of the three ignorant subpopulations, although it is generally far more error prone than is the majority of the group that collects a small amount of comprehensive information. (The last column generally has fewer errors than all but the first column.)

The simulations demonstrate that majoritarian errors are jointly determined by the irreducible estimation error generated by unobservable variables and the relative size of the rationally ignorant subpopulation of voters. The greater the irreducible stochastic element of the phenomena to be estimated, the more mistakes an electorate is bound to make. Similarly, the greater the fraction of voters who are ignorant, whether naturally or rationally, the more mistake prone is majoritarian policy making. Both these information problems limit the extent to which democracies can enact policies that systematically advance the interests of the median voter, and both imply that elected officials and public policies will necessarily be imperfect when voters rely on very constrained datasets.

3.3   Public Policies and Voter Ignorance

The results suggest that democracy will work best in policy areas in which voters have reasonably broad, if shallow, datasets. This tends to be true, for example, of pure public goods or readily observable externality problems, about which voters have direct experiential knowledge. In such cases, majoritarian decisions are likely to be effective, in the sense that public policy systematically advances the interests of the majority or at least that of the median voter. In other public policy areas, ignorance will be more commonplace, which implies that the ability of majority rule to overcome voter information constraints is substantially reduced. Public policies in such areas will be error prone. The more widespread is voter ignorance, the more likely public policies are to worsen rather than increase the welfare of the median voter.

Note also that, consistent with the simulation results, essentially all well-functioning democracies have a variety of policies in place that reduce ignorance. Such policies as public education, a free press, the publication of policy information and data sources, and even subsidies for social science and policy analysis all tend to reduce ignorance. And, moreover, all are longstanding policies. The simulations suggest that without such policies, democratic governance would be far less effective, because policy and candidate choices would be far more error prone.[5]

Nonetheless, it is clear that more could be done to assure transparency and to induce more dissemination of policy-relevant information in most democratic polities. For example, secrecy could be reduced and decision-making processes made more transparent. Institutions such as bicameralism and referenda may also be used to help encourage broader public debate.

4   CONCLUSIONS: INFORMATIONAL LIMITS TO PUBLIC POLICY

This chapter has explored the informational limits of policy formation in well-functioning democracies. In cases in which just a bit of complete information is readily available and median voter results obtain, majority rule will make remarkably accurate policy decisions even in cases in which voters have very little information. However, democratic decision making remains imperfect even in the most benevolent of the circumstances examined, because uncertainty about the future implies that electoral mistakes cannot be completely avoided. Unexpected events and unobservable features of candidate talents and proclivities imply that electoral errors are unavoidable, because the future consequences of alternative policies and alternative candidates can only be partially predicted.

In more realistic settings in which voters are only partly informed about the significant variables or dimensions of the dataset, electoral errors tend to be larger. Voter ignorance undermines the power of the jury decision by introducing systematic (but largely unpredictable) biases into the electoral process. Rationally ignorant voters are far more error prone than 'sample-constrained' voters, and, as a consequence, so is democratic decision making.

However, the 'jury theorem' effect can substantially reduce the extent to which electoral errors are generated by rationally ignorant voters, if there are a sufficient number of unbiased voters in the electorate. Overall, however, the results suggest that the informational limits of effective public policy are jointly determined by the aggregating properties of majority decision making, the underlying uncertainty of the problems being addressed, and the extent and distribution of voter ignorance.

Such information-based mistakes may be the ultimate limit of democratic public policy. This is not because imperfect information is the only problem faced by democratic polities. A broad strand of the public choice literature indicates that there are a variety of agency and institutional problems associated with political decision making, as noted above. However, imperfect information is a more intractable problem. Given perfect information, competitive elections, and a symmetric distribution of voter interests; most agency problems would be solved democratically, as voters demand and candidates deliver appropriate institutional reforms. Without a relatively broad information base, these institutional solutions may not be adopted, either because they are neglected by rationally ignorant voters or because of errors in judgment about their need or effectiveness.

In non-stochastic models of elections, the proper scope of government is usually assumed to be determined by the median voter's goals and financial constraints. However, clearly informational limits also are relevant. The proper domain of democratic policy is partly determined by the relative effectiveness of markets and democratic institutions as instruments for advancing median-voter goals. If policies are to be limited to those which advance the median voter's true interests, the domain of public policy should be limited to areas in which majority rule can effectively aggregate both voter preferences and knowledge. Informational limitations may well be the binding constraint.

Both markets and governments have to address a wide range of information problems (Coase, 1937; Hayek, 1945). In both cases, existing institutions and existing informational policies will also affect the proper domains of private and collective action, because they affect the relative effectiveness of private and collective means of advancing individual goals. Clearly, consumers and markets occasionally make mistakes, although the informational trade-offs between the two systems cannot be directly analyzed here.

The present chapter demonstrates that democratic governance will be less effective than implied by models that ignore informational problems, although it will be far more effective than might have been expected given the knowledge base of typical voters. The results suggest that democratic decision making will be more effective in some areas than in others, because the extent of voter information varies across areas. In areas in which voters have some direct knowledge of the consequences of public policy, policies are likely to be quite effective. In other areas of policy, biases and mistakes will be commonplace.

NOTES

1. The point here is to simplify the analysis rather than to argue that this exact convergence actually takes place. However, note that considerable convergence takes place within most electoral systems among viable parties. For example, the political platforms of the Democrats and Republicans in the United States are much more similar to each other than they are to the platforms of the Libertarian or Green parties.
2. Although no empirical tests of this assumption are undertaken in this chapter, it seems likely that a significant portion of the variation in real-world assessments of candidates also reflect differences in information. It is informational differences that potentially allow

persuasion to operate among friends and neighbors and in organized political campaigns (which are largely based on the subsidized dissemination of information about the candidates and their policies).

3. Additional simulations of the power of the jury theorem are available from the author on request. Electoral decisions in several informational environments were simulated below to discover some of the small-sample properties of majority decision making. Small-sample properties are more relevant for understanding the performance of well-functioning democracies than the asymptotic relationships used in most theoretical work, because most longstanding democracies have had fewer than 100 elections for important federal offices. This relatively short history limits the relevance of mathematical proofs based on the central limit theorem or asymptotic properties of estimators.

4. This electoral behavior is assumed in many theoretical models of uninformed voters. See, for example, Persson et al.'s (1997) analysis of divided government.

5. The simulations also suggest that informative policies are far more important for democracies than they are for dictatorships. This may partly explain the fact that democracies tend to have far more informative policies in place than dictatorships.

REFERENCES

Coase, R.H. (1937), 'The nature of the firm', *Economica* **4**, 386–405.

Condorcet, M. (1785), 'Essai sur l'application de l'analyse a la probabilité des décisions rendues à la pluralité des voix', Paris: Imprimerie Royale.

Congleton, R.D. (2001), 'Rational ignorance and rationally biased expectations: the discrete informational foundations of fiscal illusion', *Public Choice* **107**: 35–64.

Downs, A. (1957), *An Economic Theory of Democracy*, New York: Harper & Row.

Hayek, F.A. von (1945), 'The use of knowledge in society', *American Economic Review* **35**: 519–30.

Lupia, A. and M.D. McCubbins (1998), *The Democratic Dilemma: Can Citizens Learn What They Need to Know?*, Cambridge: Cambridge University Press.

Neuman, W.R. (1986), *The Paradox of Mass Politics: Knowledge and Opinion in the American Electorate*, Cambridge, MA: Harvard University Press.

Persson, T., G. Roland and G.E. Tabellini (1997), 'Separation of powers and political accountability', *Quarterly Journal of Economics* **112**: 1163–202.

Puviani, A. (1897), *Teoria della Illusione Nelle Entrate Publiche*, Perugia.

Puviani, A. (1903 [1973]), *Teoria della Illusione Finanziaria*, Milan: Instituto Editoriale Internazionale.

Stigler, G. (1961), 'The economics of information', *Journal of Political Economy* **71**: 213–25.

Tullock, G. (1972), *Toward a Mathematics of Politics*, Ann Arbor, MT: University of Michigan Press.

Wittman, D.A. (1995), *The Myth of Democratic Failure*, Chicago: University of Chicago Press.

13. Democratic decision, stability of outcome and agent power, with special reference to the European Union

Manfred J. Holler and Stefan Napel

1 INTRODUCTION

In *The Economics of Public Choice*, McNutt (2002, pp. 282ff.) refers to a so-called 'Holler–Steunenberg' model. Since we presume that it is largely unknown to most public choice scholars, this chapter will discuss the roots of this model and further elaborate on its theoretical frame and potential of application. The model derives from a contribution by Bernard Steunenberg (1994), entitled 'Regulatory policymaking in a parliamentary setting', and a comment of one of the present authors (Holler, 1994), both published in the *Jahrbuch für Neue Politische Ökonomie*. Sections 2, 3 and 4 are basically identical with this comment. Section 5 contains an extension and discusses decision making in the European Union.

In a nutshell, the model demonstrates the impact of procedural rules to determine the political outcome in a democratic setting in which agents (bureaucrats or policy makers) are controlled by their principal(s) by means of voting. Steunenberg shows that in order to understand a specific regulatory policy we have to take into consideration the preferences of the agent and of its principal, the legislature, as well as the procedural rules of parliamentary decision making even if the parliament turns out not to decide on a bill concerning a given issue. In this chapter, we shall summarize his application of proposal-veto rule and the gatekeeping procedure and the implications for decision making which follow from this procedure.

In Steunenberg (1994) single-peaked preferences are assumed. Holler (1980, 1982, 1994) demonstrates for a standard incumbent-opposition simple-majority voting model that, even if the preferences of the voters are non-single peaked, a subgame perfect equilibrium can be derived such that the incumbent can see its most-preferred alternative win despite a second-mover advantage of the competitor. Here it is assumed that the candidates are interested in both the policy outcomes and the winning of incumbency. The analysis shows that there is a chance for a rather stable policy arrangement despite the fact that voter preferences are non-single peaked and incumbency may change over time. If changing policy implies substantial transaction costs then it could be socially beneficial that candidates are interested in winning the election – in addition to benefiting from the policy outcome. This implication of the model in Holler (1980, 1982, 1994) is quite different from the standard result in the case of non-single-peaked voter preferences which suggests that the winning policy will change from one election to another.

The selection of procedural rules discussed in this chapter is, to a large extent, rather arbitrary and the results cannot necessarily be generalized or directly applied for alternative procedural rules. In fact, this is immediate from a comparison of the rules discussed. In order to give more substance to the choice of rules we shall discuss similarities to stylized versions of decision making in the European Union. The discussion confirms the eminent importance of the procedural rules for the outcome of decision processes and therefore for the understanding of what we observe in the political arena.

2 THE MESSAGE OF THE STEUNENBERG PAPER

Steunenberg (1994) examines agent policy making in a parliamentary system. The agent (that is, the policy maker) can be thought of as the government, the central bank, the university system and so on. The underlying policy-making procedure implies that the proposal of the agent will be realized and that the existing statutory policy will prevail unless the legislature agrees to implement an alternative policy, usually by means of a law. Thus, on the one hand, the parliamentary system may force the agent to change its position by the threat of introducing a bill which constrains its policy or, on the other, even select an alternative agent, and thereby a new policy. By this, the agent's policy depends on the procedural rules of the legislature and on the preferences of its members.

A change in the agent's regulatory policy is therefore not necessarily the result of a change in the agent's preferences: it may be initiated by changes in the preferences of, for example, the members of parliament, even if the House has not taken any decision which has visibly constrained the agent's policy. Correspondingly, the legislature's decision will depend on the agent's policy: when the legislature decides on an alternative policy, the latter will be designed and decided with reference to the existing policy. By this, the agent has in general an influence on the legislature's decision even when the agent's policy is rejected.

The conclusion is that, in order to understand a specific regulatory policy, we have to take into consideration the preferences of the agent and of the legislature as well as the procedural rules of parliamentary decision making even if the legislature did not decide on a bill concerning this issue.

Steunenberg models the strategic interaction of agent and legislature in the decision making on regulatory policy as a game which builds on the following basic assumptions:

1. The set of players N consists of agent a and the set M containing the legislators. The players are characterized by ($A1$) single-peaked preferences with respect to a one-dimensional policy space with A as the most-preferred position of agent a, ($A2$) the fact that 'none of the players prefers that its decision is overturned', and ($A3$) complete information, that is, players know the game tree.[1]
2. The alternative procedural rules are the 'proposal-veto game' and the 'gatekeeping game'.[2] The status quo is characterized by policy x represented by agent a. In the *proposal-veto game* ($A4$) a member of M may propose an alternative policy y. One or more members of M are players with veto power. They decide whether they will accept the bill y given the existing policy x. If y is not vetoed then y is accepted and x is dismissed. In the *gatekeeping game* ($A5$), the set of players N includes a gatekeeper g who has the power to initiate a bill y. This bill is going to be decided by the legislature, summarized as player p, with reference to existing policy x as the alternative. Bill y can be amended by player p to a bill y. Given single-peaked preferences and simple majority voting, the most preferred position of p can be identified with the median of M.

Steunenberg's analysis proceeds to combine alternative preference profiles of the players, in principle only constrained by single peakedness, with alternative structural rules. The structural rules define the strategy sets of the players. Subgame perfect Nash equilibrium is applied as the solution concept. This is an adequate choice. The problem lies in the abundance of structural alternatives combined with a multitude of preference profiles. Steunenberg's solution to this problem is to select specific cases and to derive from them some generalizations for policies and regulation in unicameral and bicameral parliamentary systems.

If we accept this analytical procedure, while being aware of its limitation, then, in the gatekeeping game, we get the result that if some player only functions as gatekeeper g, the set of successful x-policies, X^0, is likely to be larger than for the case that the initiator of a bill y is also voting on this bill. Note that p will select y' as the final decision if g proposes y. However, g will not propose y and thus accept x, if g weakly prefers x to y'. Thus agent a can avoid a legislative process which results in y', if a chooses an x such that g weakly prefers x to y'. If such an x exists and a prefers this x to y', then x will be the accepted policy. If several such policies exist, then agent a will choose the x which is closest to its most preferred position A. The more extreme the preferences of g, the larger the discretion of the agent a in the choice of x.

In the proposal-veto game, the preferences of the left- and right-most extreme voters determine X^0, and thus agent a's discretion in the selection of x. Obviously, a can avoid that its policy x will be challenged by a proposal y if x is identical with the most-preferred policy position of one of the veto players. However, even if x is identified with a position between the most-preferred policy positions of two veto players, an alternative y will always be less preferred than x by at least one veto player and therefore vetoed. The conclusion is that the proposal-veto procedure gives substantial leeway to the policy of an agent and only rules out policies which are outside the interval between the most-preferred positions of the left- and right-most extreme members of the set of veto players.

3 DISCUSSION OF STEUNENBERG'S MODEL

The above analysis suggests that the gatekeeping procedure puts a tighter constraint on the policy of an agent than the proposal-veto procedure, and therefore includes a higher degree of control by the legislature. Steunenberg's analysis captures only a small selection of all structural settings (combinations of voting rules, hierarchy of decision bodies, initiative power and so on) which can be found in parliamentary systems and determine the strategy sets of the voting games under consideration. There are alternatives which include more or less control than the procedures discussed here. Obviously, there is a larger selection in voting procedures than veto and majority voting. And whether the initiator of a bill may vote on it, or act as a gatekeeper only, may depend on the bill itself or on the decisions of other players. To conclude, we have to be careful in generalizing the derived results. This warning also holds because even within the setting which Steunenberg has chosen, only a subset of structural alternatives has been discussed. It seems, however, that the author has selected the most interesting cases.

Another degree of freedom which Steunenberg uses rather selectively is the one-dimensional single-peaked modelling of *preferences*. Even within the constraints of single-peaked preferences, a multitude of preference profiles can be chosen and some of them produce quite diverse results within identical structural settings. Again we take it that the author has selected the most interesting cases.

Of course, the assumption of single-peaked preferences in one dimension is rather strong. Whenever a distribution of a fixed (positively valued) sum of income or wealth is considered, preferences are not single peaked and majority voting on the sharing leads to cyclical majorities if the voters benefit from shares of the 'cake' (see Ward, 1961). In other words, the core of the distribution game is empty. If we consider distributional effects to be an important aspect of public decisions then the assumption of single peakedness is a substantial constraint to the model presented in Steunenberg's paper.

One can rightly argue that single peakedness in one dimension is an adequate point of departure, justified by tradition, although in general reserved to voters and not necessarily assumed for the members of a committee, and by the fact that it produces the famous median-voter result. However, the author himself introduces a second dimension into the preferences of the players: none of the players likes to see his/her decision overturned, and if it does happen then the final payoffs to a player are reduced. The impact of the incumbency objective (that is, winning a majority of votes) on the selection of the policy x however, is, not discussed. Since it remains unsaid whether there is a trade-off between winning and the selected position, we cannot derive any conclusion which takes the incumbency objective into consideration.

Steunenberg's modelling also fails to take into consideration the re-election target of the politicians (cabinet members and members of parliament: MPs). Even if we assume that the preferences of the voters are perfectly represented in the preferences of the MPs, an extreme MP might hesitate to veto a bill y, which is alternative to the policy x, if this reduces the probability of him/her being re-elected.[3] If parliamentary candidates are uncertain about the choices that voters will make, the median position, or a position not too far from the median, regains importance with respect to the choices of the candidates' platforms and thus to the outcome of the election (see Enelow and Hinich, 1984; Lafay, 1992). Consequently, in the proposal-veto model, MP i may hesitate to veto a bill y if it is closer to the median, although x might be closer to i's preferred position than y. Given some degree of uncertainty on candidate platforms or voters' preferences, it seems likely that the agent's level of discretion on the choice of x is smaller than in Steunenberg's model if the MPs are interested in getting re-elected.

If we keep the re-election target in mind (and perhaps even problems of representation) then the multitude of models and results which can be derived from the basic building blocks discussed above will be further increased. This is likely to be counterproductive with respect to the explanatory power of the approach. The discussion highlights that results given in Steunenberg's paper can be generalized only with great care.

4 INCUMBENT-OPPOSITION MODEL AND NON-SINGLE-PEAKED PREFERENCES

The following model derives from Holler (1982, 1994). It introduces two issues into the analysis which have been identified as a possible shortcoming in Steunenberg's modelling, preference to win and non-single-peakedness, and discusses the impact of this modification in a standard incumbent-opposition model. It will be interesting to find out whether this setting implies more or less control of the agent than the alternatives discussed in the previous sections.

We have chosen the incumbent-opposition model because in this setting it seems adequate to assume that decision makers are interested in winning an election. More specifically, we assume that there are two candidates, the incumbent a and the opposition g, that are characterized by utility functions $u_1 = (m, p)$. Here $m \in M = \{0, 1/2, 1\}$ expresses the probabilities of the incumbent winning, which is assumed to be 1/2 in the case of the indifference of the decision makers or in the case of non-decisiveness (ties) in the voting body, and $p \in P = \{u, v, w\}$ where P describes a *discrete* set of alternatives (policies platforms and so on). The incumbent and opposition can be identified with agent a and gatekeeper g, respectively. Both, however, are assumed to have preferences of the u_i-type. Moreover, there are three voters 1, 2 and 3 (or respective groups of voters of equal numerical strength); their preferences on the set P are non-single peaked and ordered as shown in Figure 13.1.

Given the preferences illustrated in Figure 13.1, g can always win a two-to-one majority of votes, and thus defeat x by selecting some y, if a presents x first and g knows x when choosing y. This illustrates the well-known 'Condorcet paradox'. However, let us assume that a's ranking on the set p is $w > u > v$ and g's ranking on the set P is $u > v > w$ while their ranking on the elements of M is $1 > 1/2 > 0$.

Agent a decides on policy x by solving the decision problem of g for alternative own choices of x (represented by u^*, v^* and w^* in Figures 13.2 and 13.3). The potential best reply set, illustrated in Figure 13.2, shows the outcomes which derive from the choices of a and g for the given preferences.[4] If a chooses w^* and g selects v, voters 1 and 2 will vote for v and 3 will vote for w (see Figure 13.1). Thus g will win a majority of votes ($m = 1$) and v will be the policy outcome. The ranking of g on the pairs (m, p) is illustrated in Figure 13.2. For example, g prefers the outcome $(1, v)$ to $(1, w)$

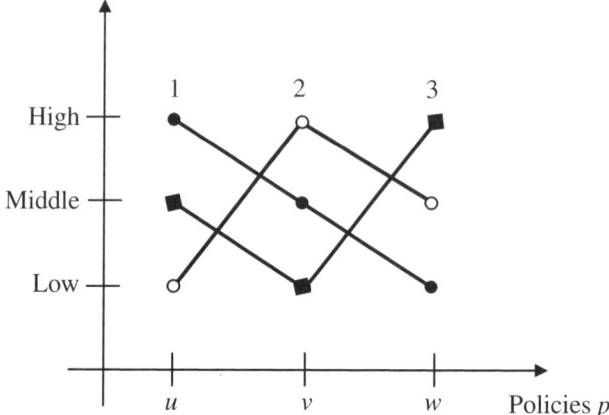

Figure 13.1   Set of non-single-peaked preferences

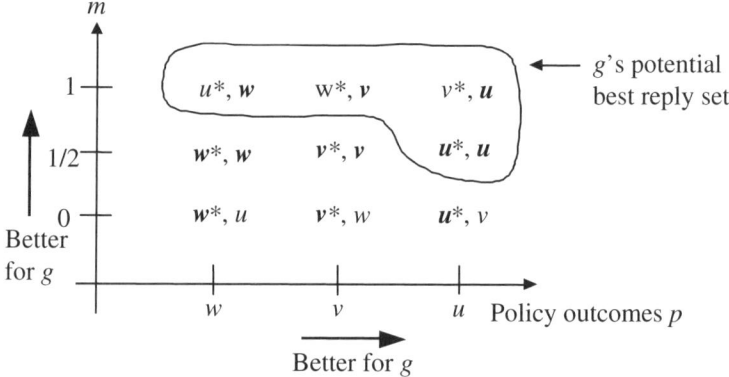

Figure 13.2   Best reply set of the opposition g

which results from the choices (u^*, w). However, g prefers (1, u), which results from the choices (v^*, u) to (1, v).

Given $m = 1$, Figure 13.2 reflects the Condorcet paradox: g will win with certainty and no x exists which can prevent g from winning. The pair (u^*, u) says that both a and g select policy u and thus there is a 1 in 2 chance of each of them winning the election.

Obviously, seen from the perspective of incumbent a, there are elements in the potential best reply set of opposition g that are dominated by another element in this set. Figure 13.3 illustrates a's evaluation of the elements contained in g's potential best reply set. Given a's preferences, (w^*, v) and (v^*, u) are clearly dominated by (u^*, u) and (u^*, w). Thus, we can conclude that

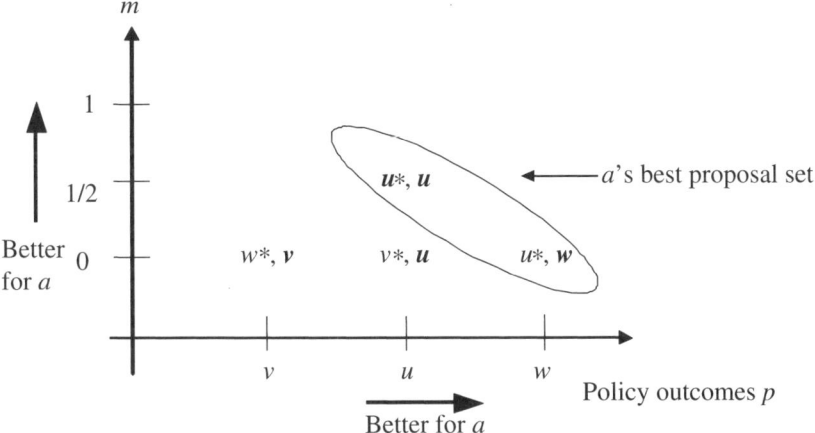

Figure 13.3   Best proposal set of incumbent a

a will propose policy u^*. Whether *g* accommodates and proposes an identical policy or whether it selects *w* to defeat the proposed policy u^*, is a question of *g*'s preferences on (u^*, u) and (u^*, w). If we abstract from the case that *g* is indifferent as regards these two alternatives, then the policy outcome is uniquely determined and corresponds to a subgame perfect equilibrium.

More generally, every finite sequential-move game of perfect information has a *unique* subgame perfect equilibrium if all players have strict preference orderings over the possible outcomes. This follows by backward induction.

Note that social preferences, that is, political outcomes, are not cyclical although we dropped the assumption of one-dimensional single-peaked preferences and considered politicians' preferences on incumbency. Note further that the policy outcome could be *u*, irrespective of whether *a* or *g* is winning the election. Thus we conclude that there is a chance for a rather stable policy arrangement despite the fact that voter preferences are non-single peaked and incumbency may change over time. If changing policy implies substantial transaction costs then it could be beneficial from a social point of view (that is, welfare enhancing) that candidates are interested in winning the election (in addition to benefiting the policy outcome). The platform *u* can function as a substitute for the median position which is not defined for cyclical preferences. This implication of the above model is quite different from the standard result in the case of non-single-peaked voter preferences, which suggests that the winning policy will change from one election to another.

Holler (1982) analyses all 36 cases which result from combining the possible preferences of incumbent a and opposition g if the preferences of the two candidates have the structure of any of the three preference orders given in Figure 13.1. Each best proposal set of the corresponding incumbent-opposition game contains two undominated alternatives. One of these alternatives is characterized by a pair of identical policies. This implies that there is a chance that the policy will be the same, irrespective of the candidate who wins a majority of votes and thus incumbency. In the case discussed above, this of course presupposes that both candidates prefer $(1/2, u)$ to winning a majority 'with certainty' but having to propose something less preferred than u. The latter possibility characterizes the second undominated alternative in the best proposal set.

From the analysis of 36 cases in Holler (1982) we can conclude:

1. There is a second-mover advantage in the incumbent-opposition game: being the first to present a proposal can never be preferred to being the second. If the proposal a is acceptable to g, because it ranks high in g's preference order, then the latter can select an identical proposition, thereby gaining a 50 per cent chance of winning the election. If the proposal of a is not acceptable to g, because it ranks low in g's preference order, g can present a different proposal and win a majority of votes.
2. There are combinations of the candidate's preference orders on $P = \{u, v, w\}$ such that the outcome of a presenting a proposal first and g second are identical to the outcomes of a presenting a proposal second and g presenting a proposal first.

5   APPLICATION TO EU DECISION MAKING

This section introduces the main institutions of the European Union (EU) and provides a rough sketch of the rules according to which they interact. One finds variations of the proposal-veto and gatekeeping games at several levels. Although the decision procedures always differ somewhat from the games discussed above, the same basic principles determine their outcomes. The above models, chosen from a large set of alternatives, are thus instructive examples and provide insights into a relevant subset of real-world policy making.

The three key players who determine EU decisions which then apply to the EU's currently 25 members are the Commission, the Council of Ministers, and the European Parliament.[5] The Commission comprises 25 members, one from each member state. Commission members are appointed jointly by the Council and the Parliament for a renewable term of five years, generally within six months of the EU-wide parliamentary elections.[6] The Commission is chaired by a president, who is in fact nominated before all other Commission members and holds a veto right over the remaining nominations. One can expect its members to hold views as diverse as those held within other political institutions, but there are tight bounds on the extent to which internal differences may be publicly expressed. This possibly explains why the Commission is usually treated as a unilateral player in formal analysis of EU decision making.

All commissioners are assigned individual portfolios, such as agriculture, health, competition policy and so on. On most issues, commissioners have considerable leeway and each may, in fact, be viewed as an agent for the full college of commissioners. If there is no consensus on a given issue within the Commission, the EC Treaty prescribes that decisions are to be taken by simple majority. So any policy y chosen by an individual commissioner within its portfolio can be overturned by a majority of other commissioners so that the status quo x prevails. This is analogous to Steunenberg's proposal-veto game, with the difference that an entire 'veto coalition' is necessary to block alternative proposals y advocated as replacements for x by Commission members.

The Commission in aggregate is an agent serving two principals, Council and Parliament. It unilaterally decides on many day-to-day issues, for example, in competition policy, along the so-called 'administrative route', and makes any first proposal in the EU's various legislative processes ('legislative route'). Both routes confer great powers and moreover the Commission has some discretion in selecting between them. Since the Commission may be prompted to initiate legislation by either Council or Parliament, it has no gatekeeping power *de jure*. But it may convincingly be argued that the reality is different.

The European Parliament (EP) currently comprises 732 members (MEPs). The Treaty gives a particular number of seats to each of the 25 member states.[7] Parliamentary decisions typically require just a simple majority. But only with a two-thirds majority of votes (cast by an absolute majority of MEPs), can the EP force the college of commissioners to resign before its term expires. It may thus unilaterally abandon the agent shared with the Council. One might conclude that, in analogy to the discussion in Sections 2 and 3, this imposes constraints on the Commission's scope to exercise discretion regarding its policy decisions x. But neither in practice nor in theory do they seem likely to bind, at least not in the aforementioned sense that a preference shift within the EP actually induces a policy shift of the Commission without any proper EP decision. The reasons are, first, the demanding two-thirds majority requirement and, second, that although the EP may unilaterally dispose of a given college of commissioners, it cannot unilaterally appoint a new one. Napel and Widgrén (2006a) conclude from a game-theoretic analysis of the appointment procedure that it is in fact almost exclusively the Council which determines the political composition of a new Commission. Parliamentary constraints on the Commission's behaviour can thus be expected to be very rare.

The Council of Ministers comprises the 25 national heads of state or government or, for more specific policy areas, the respective ministers of agriculture, education and so on. It is widely regarded as the most powerful institution in the EU. The Council is chaired by the member holding its rotating presidency. This member is commonly expected to define EU priorities during its six-month presidency. It thereby acts as an agenda setter and at least a temporary gatekeeper in the spirit of above analysis.

Decisions in the Council need to be taken either unanimously or by a qualified majority. The actual qualified majority rule is rather complex and involves three dimensions. First, there have to be at least 232 votes out of 321 (about 72.2 per cent) in favour of a proposal, with 29 votes each for France, Italy, Germany and the UK, 27 votes each for Poland and Spain, and so on. Second, these votes have to be cast by a simple majority of member states. Third, the 'yes' votes have to represent 62 per cent of the total EU population.

Council members and MEPs can be regarded as jointly making up the set M of legislators considered in Section 2. They do not merely appoint and possibly replace their agent, the Commission, but interact with it according to several alternative decision procedures specified in the EC Treaty. The two main ones are the *consultation procedure* and the *codecision procedure*.

The consultation procedure was introduced in the Treaty of Rome in 1957 and was the only way of taking decisions in the European Community until the Single European Act came into force in 1987. It involves actual decision making only by the Commission and the Council. The EP has the right to express its opinion on the issue under discussion, but that is it. In general, the Council can request the Commission to undertake any studies that the former deems desirable for the attainment of the common objectives, and then to submit to it an appropriate proposal (Art. 208 of the EC Treaty). Decision making under the consultation procedure is then formally started by the legislative proposal submitted by the Commission to the Council. If it is to replace the status quo, this proposal has to be accepted by the Council with either qualified majority or unanimous consent as determined by the Treaty (depending on the proposal's policy domain). It is possible that at the time the latter can involve no legislation at all regarding the concerned issue. As an alternative to either accepting the Commission proposal or confirming the status quo, the Council can also amend the Commission's proposal and pass this amendment without requiring the Commission's consent. However, such an amendment necessitates unanimity in the Council (regardless of the issues policy domain). This gives substantial agenda-setting powers to the Commission very similar to the above proposal-veto game.

Strategic analysis of the consultation procedure can be conducted by backward induction, analogous to Steunenberg's investigation or that of the incumbent-opposition game. Let us focus on the version requiring only a qualified majority to accept the Commission's proposal. Then, if one assumes single-peaked preferences over a single-dimensional policy space, the equilibrium outcome of the procedure (making suitable tie-breaking assumptions) corresponds to one of three cases, depending on actors' ideal policy positions and the legislative status quo. First, the Commission can propose its own ideal point and the Council accepts it by the required majority (since a qualified majority prefers it to the status quo and at least one Council member would lose from an amendment). Second, the Commission cannot get its own ideal point but proposes the policy closest to it such that a qualified majority prefers the proposal to the status quo and at least one Council member would lose from any amendment. This will then be passed by a qualified majority. Third, if no policy exists that is weakly preferred to the status quo by a qualified majority in the Council or if such an alternative exists but is worse than the status quo in the eyes of both the Commission and at least one Council member, then the Commission proposes the status quo; it will then be confirmed or, rather, any attempt to pass an amendment will fail.

This equilibrium prediction reveals considerable powers for the proposal-making agent, the Commission, even though it cannot technically keep the legislative gates closed. It may have to live with a new policy x' deemed worse than the status quo x in the case that *all* Council members prefer to move, say, to the right while the Commission is weakly to the left of x. But even in this case, by making the left-most of the Council members' positions its own proposal x' to prevent worse (falling under the above-mentioned second case), it exerts considerable power.[8]

The above predictions presuppose single-peaked preferences and, more critically, that policy decisions about whether and how the status quo x is to be changed are isolated across different policy dimensions. If – as it transpires after any EU summit meeting – Council members can engage in logrolling and can trade their respective endorsement of policies across issues that affect their individual utility asymmetrically, then the agent's, that is, the Commission's, power is weakened relative to its main principal, the Council. In particular, opportunities to prevent a Council amendment by choosing the proposal such that at least one Council member prefers the Commission's stated position to any internal change shrink drastically. This indicates that consideration of preferences that are non-single peaked (as in Section 4) is not merely necessary to understand the stability of policies; rather, it is desirable in order to get a more accurate picture of real-world institutions that seem to rarely take two decisions in isolation from each other.

It emphasizes our earlier point about the importance of the procedural rules for the outcome of decision processes that even with single-peaked preferences and no logrolling, or formation of long-run coalitions and so on, the powers of the Commission are highly restricted in all the legislation passed by the codecision procedure. The latter was introduced by the Maastricht Treaty in 1992 and initially applied to 15 areas of Community activity. Its current version came into force in May 1999, as specified in the Treaty of Amsterdam. Presently, it pertains to 43 areas – including the internal market, environment, transport, public health, education and research, and the Regional Development Fund. This notably excludes agriculture, taxation and competition, which all fall under the domain of the consultation procedure.

The codecision procedure – just as consultation – is initiated by a policy proposal of the Commission. This can, however, be quite easily amended in potentially up to three readings by the EP and the Council. First, the EP can approve the Commission proposal or replace it by simple majority with an amended version of its own. Then, the Council either approves the proposal on the table or initiates a second stage of decision making by making further amendments. This new proposal – the Council's 'common position' in EU parlance – is either approved by the EP by simple majority, or again amended. The Commission in this case comments on the amended proposal. By giving a negative opinion the Commission can require the Council to decide unanimously if the EP's proposal is to be passed immediately. However, if the Council does not pass the EP's proposal with whatever majority is required, the so-called 'Conciliation Committee' represents another chance to seek a change to the status quo, with neither an additional unanimity requirement nor another special role for the Commission. The Committee is composed of all 25 members of the Council (or typically their civil-servant delegates) and an equal-size delegation of MEPs. The Commission attends meetings and helps to draft compromise proposals as and if requested by the Council and the EP. If the Council and the EP agree on a compromise, it is submitted to a third and final reading in both institutions involving only the usual majorities.[9]

The strategic interaction between Commission, Council and Parliament under the codecision procedure is analysed in great detail by Napel and Widgrén (2006b), again assuming isolated decisions and single-peaked preferences. They conclude that the EP can be expected to have rather negligible influence on policy outcomes, whereas the Commission's preferences play no role at all. First and foremost, it is the Council's on average rather conservative aggregate position that determines a change of the status quo.

Of course, the actual execution of whatever regulation or directive is passed is again delegated to the Commission and/or national legislatives and executives. This again comes with all the issues regarding sensitivity to procedures and preferences discussed above. Note, however, that while outcomes can be very sensitive to the choice of the decision procedure, *fixing* a procedure in a treaty or constitution results in stable policies.[10] In our discussion, this meant a unique (subgame perfect) equilibrium outcome for any given profile of single-peaked preferences. And, as illustrated by Section 4, the generic uniqueness of subgame perfect equilibrium in sequential-move games with finitely many stages also ensures stable outcomes much more generally.

Based on the results of Section 4, a possible conjecture is that the influence of the Commission and the EP increases if preferences are non-single peaked and decisions are not taken in isolation, or that we see more logrolling in the Council. A critical observer may argue that we already see enough logrolling to conclude that the Council thereby dwarfs the influence of its rival decision-making bodies.

NOTES

1. In as much as information is imperfect because of simultaneous decisions (that is, moves), the corresponding subgames have a unique equilibrium and the outcome is well determined, given rational decision making.
2. Steunenberg (1994) also analyses policy making in a bicameral system which is characterized by 'extended procedural rules'.
3. In a multi-party setting, the choice of a median-voter position does not necessarily concur with vote maximization (see Selten, 1971; Breyer, 1987; Hermsen and Verbeek, 1992).
4. These preferences result from applying the dominance relation, but do not consider trade-offs between m and p. For example, in g's perspective, u dominates v as a response to a's choice of u (denoted by u^* in Figure 13.2). However, winning for sure ($m = 1$) with w, that is *ceteris paribus* the least desirable policy for g, may potentially be preferred to responding with u resulting in outcome u (indicated in bold in Figure 13.2) but only $m = 1/2$.
5. A fourth one is the European Court of Justice, which we shall ignore in our discussion.
6. Particularly in ordinary press coverage, the term 'Commission' is used not only for the actual college of 25 commissioners but also their roughly 25,000 staff in the Brussels head offices, the Luxembourg offices and elsewhere. We focus on the former. Of course, the latter are also subject to interesting principal–agent problems in line with the discussion in Sections 2 and 3.
7. The European Parliament is more commonly divided along ideological rather than national lines. It is thus a truly supranational body.
8. Its strategic power is here of a preventive or destructive kind, that is, it can block all alternatives to the right of x'. In the case of the Council being entirely on the opposite side of the status quo, the creative influence of the Commission is zero: small or moderate shifts in its own ideal position would *not* translate into a different outcome; lobbyists

would address the left-most Council member rather than the Commission. See Napel and Widgrén (2004) for a conceptualization of strategic power as outcome sensitivity with respect to a player's possibly utility-maximizing behaviour.

9. Three of the 43 codecision policy areas require unanimous Council decisions irrespective of the Commission's actions.
10. Clearly, the problem of fixing a procedure is by itself a collective choice problem whose outcome is sensitive to the procedure applied to solve it. Transaction costs of negotiations (over the procedure which is used to agree on a procedure which is used to agree on a procedure which . . .) in practice seem to prevent the infinite regress that would theoretically be possible.

REFERENCES

Breyer, F. (1987), 'On the existence of the political equilibrium in a three-party system with plurality voting', in M.J. Holler (ed.), *The Logic of Multiparty Systems*, Dordrecht: Kluwer, pp. 113–27.

Enelow, J. and M.J. Hinich (1984), *The Spatial Theory of Voting: An Introduction*, Cambridge: Cambridge University Press.

Hermsen, H. and A. Verbeek (1992), 'Equilibria in multi-party systems', *Public Choice*, **73**, 147–65.

Holler, M.J. (1980), 'What is paradoxical about the voting paradox?', *Quality and Quantity*, **14**, 679–85.

Holler, M.J. (1982), 'The relevance of the voting paradox: a restatement', *Quality and Quantity*, **16**, 43–53.

Holler, M.J. (1994), 'Regulatory policymaking in a parliamentary setting: comment', in Ph. Herder-Dorneich, K.-H. Schenk and D. Schmidtchen (eds), *Jahrbuch für Neue Politische Ökonomie*, Vol. 13, Tübingen: Mohr-Siebeck, pp. 66–71.

Lafay, J.-D. (1992), 'La théorie probabiliste du vote', *Revue d'économie politique* **102**, 486–518.

McNutt, P. (2002), *The Economics of Public Choice*, 2nd edn, Cheltenham, UK and Northampton, MA, USA: Edward Elgar.

Napel, S. and M. Widgrén (2004), 'Power measurement as sensitivity analysis – a unified approach', *Journal of Theoretical Politics*, **16**(4), 517–38.

Napel, S. and M. Widgrén (2006a), 'The European Commission – appointment, preferences, and institutional relations', CEPR Discussion Paper, Centre for Economic Policy Research, London.

Napel, S. and M. Widgrén (2006b), 'The inter-institutional distribution of power in EU codecision', *Social Choice and Welfare*, **27**, 129–54.

Selten, R. (1971), 'Anwendung der Spieltheorie auf die politische Wissenschaft', in H. Maier, K. Ritter and U. Matz (eds), *Politik und Wissenschaft*, Munich: C.H. Beck, pp. 287–320.

Steunenberg, B. (1994), 'Regulatory policymaking in a parliamentary setting', in Ph. Herder-Dorneich, K.-H. Schenk and D. Schmidtchen (eds), *Jahrbuch für Neue Politische Ökonomie*, Vol. 13, Tübingen: Mohr-Siebeck, pp. 36–57.

Ward, B. (1961), 'Majority rule and allocation', *Journal of Conflict Resolution*, **5**, 379–89.

14. The unequal treatment of voters under a single transferable vote: implications for electoral welfare with an application to the 2003 Northern Ireland Assembly elections

Vani K. Borooah*

1 INTRODUCTION

The single transferable vote (STV) is a method of voting that allows voters to rank candidates (as opposed to parties) in order of preference. Under STV, each voter is allowed to write a number against the name of each candidate listed on the ballot paper, where this number expresses the voter's preference for the candidate: the most preferred candidate has a '1' against his/her name, the next most preferred a '2', and so on. The first stage of the count is to ascertain the total number of first-preference votes for each candidate. Any candidate who has more first-preference votes than the 'quota'[1] is immediately elected. If no candidate achieves the quota, the candidates with the lowest number of votes is eliminated and the second preferences on his/her ballot papers are assigned to the remaining candidates. If a candidate is elected at a particular count, the surplus votes (that is, votes in excess of the quota) are redistributed, according to the subsequent (or 'next available') preferences on the ballot papers, to the remaining candidates.[2] National parliamentary elections in Ireland (Sinnott, 1993 provides a good analysis) – and elections to the Assembly and to local district councils in Northern Ireland – are underpinned by STV. It is also used in Malta and for elections to the Tasmanian – and the Australian Capital Territory – Legislative Assembly.

The rationale for the STV method is twofold. First, each ballot paper is capable of expressing the preference ordering of voters over *all* the candidates though, needless to say, voters – by truncating the ordering – may express preferences over only a subset of the available candidates. Second, the preference rankings of the voters are taken into account in determining the successful candidates. This occurs because when a candidate is elected at a count – or when a candidate with the lowest number of votes is eliminated, in the event of no election at a count – votes are transferred to the candidates next in the order of preference on the successful (or eliminated) candidate's ballot papers.[3]

However, an anomaly of the method is that when a candidate (or candidates) is elected at the first count, the transfer of votes to the remaining candidates is effected by examining the second preferences of *all* the ballot papers of the elected candidate(s). However, for candidates elected at subsequent counts, only the transfers made at the count at which they were elected are examined for subsequent preferences. This rule for effecting transfers creates two classes of voters. Some voters – 'further-preference' voters – after declaring their preferences across the candidates, have a range of their preferences taken account of in determining the successful candidates. For other voters ('first-preference-only' voters), it is only their first preference votes which influence the election outcomes, their remaining preferences being ignored. This is what is meant by the 'unequal treatment of voters' under STV. How this discriminatory treatment comes about – and the voters who comprise the 'further-preference' and 'first-preference-only' groups – is discussed in the next section. Suffice it to say here, the value of the STV method is diminished by the fact that all voters are not treated equally. As a corollary of this, there may be a case for supporting alternative election methods which, while allowing voters only a limited expression of their preferences across candidates, ensures that all votes count equally towards the electoral outcome. In other words, it can be argued that, if electoral welfare depends on both the full expression of preferences by voters *and* the equal treatment of all voters, there may well be a trade-off between 'full expression' and 'equal treatment'. The purpose of this chapter is to analyse the nature of such a trade-off and to apply it to results from the (STV-based) elections of November 2003 to the Northern Ireland Assembly.

2   THE ANALYTICAL FRAMEWORK

There are N voters in a constituency from which, without loss of generality, six members are to be elected[4] using the method of STV. The (Droop) quota is, therefore, $Q = (N/7) + 1$: any candidate receiving Q or more votes, at any count, is deemed to be elected. If C represents the set of candidates, let V^r_X represent the number of votes counted for $X \in C$ at the Rth count, where

V_X^1 – the number of votes counted for X at the *first* count – represents the number of *first-preference* votes received by the candidate.

2.1 Case 1: A Candidate(s) Is Elected at the First Count

Suppose that X, at the first count, receives votes equal to, or in excess of, the quota ($V_X^1 \geq Q$) and is, therefore, elected. The 'surplus' of X, denoted S_X, is the excess of votes received over the quota: $S_X = V_X^1 - Q \geq 0$. This surplus is then to be distributed over the remaining candidates.

Let $V_{Xj}^1 (>0)$ represent the number of voters – of the V_X^1 voters who had X as their most preferred candidate – who ranked j ($j \in C, j \neq X$) as their *second-preference* candidate and let $V_{X0}^1 \geq 0$ be the number of X's *non-transferable* votes (that is, votes received by X in which no further preference was expressed). By definition:

$$V_X^1 = \sum_{j \neq X} V_{Xj}^1 + V_{X0}^1. \tag{14.1}$$

Now define the proportions:[5]

$$\pi_{Xj}^1 = V_{Xj}^1 / V_X^1. \tag{14.2}$$

Then, at the second count, candidate j ($j \notin X$) receives the proportion π_{Xj}^1 of X's surplus of S_X votes. Consequently, the transfers to candidate j (denoted T_{Xj}^2), *made at the second count*, from the surplus votes of X are computed as:[6]

$$T_{Xj}^2 = \pi_{Xj}^1 S_X. \tag{14.3}$$

If, at the first count, another candidate, Y, was also elected, each of the remaining candidates j would receive transfers from Y – computed analogously to transfers from X – as $T_{Yj}^2 = \pi_{Yj}^1 S_Y$. Consequently, at the end of the second count, the votes counted for candidate j are:

$$V_j^2 = V_j^1 + T_j^2, \tag{14.4}$$

where T_j^2 represents the total of transfers received by j from *all* the candidates who were elected at the first count.

In the Republic of Ireland, the T_{Xj}^2 and T_{Yj}^2 ballot papers, representing the transferred votes to j from, respectively, X and Y, are drawn randomly from the total of V_{Xj}^1 and V_{Yj}^1 ballot papers in which voters, after giving their first preference to X and Y, respectively, gave j their second preference. In Northern Ireland, *all* the V_{Xj}^1 and V_{Yj}^1 second-preference ballot papers are transferred to candidate j at the appropriate fractions of their value.[7] This difference in procedure between the two parts of Ireland has no implications for the votes received by any of the candidates at this count, but it does have implications for subsequent counts when later preferences may have to be counted. This is because while all the V^1_{Xj} and V^1_{Yj} ballot papers have the same second preference (namely, candidate j), they will quite likely differ in terms of subsequent preferences.

2.2   Case 2: A Candidate(s) Is Elected at the Second or Later Count

Suppose that a candidate, X, *after receiving transfers from earlier counts*, is elected at the $r = R$th (> 1) count. These transfers may come either from candidates elected or eliminated at previous counts.

If no candidate was elected at the previous count $(R-1) \geq 1$ – because none achieved the quota Q – then the candidate with the lowest number of votes is eliminated and *all* of his/her votes are distributed to the other candidates. Since the candidate was eliminated at count $R-1$, it is the Rth preference on that candidate's ballot that is the relevant ('next available') preference.

Suppose, without loss of generality, that Y received the lowest number of votes at the $(R-1)$th count, in which no candidate was elected. Then Y is eliminated at that count and the votes counted for the remaining candidates – of which X is one – at the subsequent – Rth – count are:

$$V^R_X = V^{R-1}_X + T^R_{YX}, \tag{14.5}$$

where T^R_{YX} are the transfers received by X at the Rth count from Y, the candidate eliminated in the previous count.[8]

On the other hand, the transfers to X could have come from the surplus votes of a candidate (or candidates) elected at the previous $(R-1)$th count. Irrespective of how these transfers arrive, since $V^R_X > Q$, X is elected at the Rth (> 1) count and X's surplus votes ($S_X = V^R_X - Q$), are then tranferred to the remaining candidates.

Now the votes counted for X at the Rth count are the sum of X's votes at the first count (V^1_X) and the transfer votes received by X at subsequent counts ($T^r_X, r = 2, ..., R$):

$$V^R_X = V^1_X + \sum_{r=2}^{R} T^r_X. \tag{14.6}$$

Then X's surplus is distributed among the remaining candidates by calculating, for each of the remaining candidates j, the proportion of the transfer votes that X received *at the count at which he/she was elected –* which, in this case is the Rth count – which had candidate j as their 'next available preference' (that is $(R+1)$th) preference. Let σ_{Xj}^R denote this proportion.

At the end of the $(R+1)$th count, each candidate j receives a total of T_{Xj}^{R+1} transfer votes from the surplus votes of X where:

$$T_{Xj}^{R+1} = \sigma_{Xj}^R S_X. \tag{14.7}$$

If, at the Rth count, another candidate, Y, was also elected, each of the remaining candidates j would receive transfers from Y – computed analogously to transfers from X – as $T_{Yj}^{R+1} = \sigma_{Yj}^R S_Y$. Consequently, at the end of the $(R+1)$th count, the votes counted for candidate j are:

$$V_j^{R+1} = V_j^R + T_j^{R+1}, \tag{14.8}$$

where T_j^{R+1} represents the total of all transfers received by j at the $(R+1)$th count.

3   THE RELATIVE IMPORTANCE OF DIFFERENT VOTERS

Lying at the source of these surplus transfers, described above, is/are the candidate(s) elected at the first count (that is, those whose first-preference votes exceeded the quota) for it is he/she/they who triggers the chain of surplus vote transfers. If X was elected at the first count, then *all* the votes received by X are inspected in effecting the transfer of his/her surplus at the second count to the remaining candidates.

However, the distribution of the surplus votes of a candidate, Y – elected at a later count – to the remaining candidates at the next count, are drawn *entirely* from the transfer votes received by the elected candidates at the count at which they were elected. Consequently, once Y has been elected, the subsequent preferences of those voters for whom Y was the most preferred candidate play no role in influencing subsequent results. In contrast, as long as candidates are elected at successive counts, the subsequent preferences of those voters for whom X – who was elected at the first count – was the most preferred candidate play a role in influencing subsequent results.

In that sense, while all voters are treated equally in terms of first-preference votes, it is the subsequent preferences of voters who plumped for a candidate(s) who was elected at the first count that thread their way into later counts. The subsequent preferences of voters whose most-preferred candidates were eliminated also matter since these preferences show up as votes for the remaining candidates.[9] But the subsequent preferences of those voters who gave their first-preference vote to a candidate who was elected, but *not* at the first count – as well as the subsequent preferences voters who gave their first-preference vote to a candidate who was neither elected nor eliminated[10] – *are entirely disregarded*. This anomaly springs from the fact that vote transfers under STV are effected solely by reference to the votes received by elected candidates at the count at which they were elected.

Table 14.1 shows that in the November 2003 elections to the Northern Ireland Assembly – conducted using STV – only 28 per cent of voters gave their first-preference votes to candidates who were elected at the first count, and only 18 per cent of voters gave their first-preference votes to candidates who were eliminated during the counts: such voters are termed 'further-preference' voters because their preferences – beyond their first preference – influence the electoral outcome. Conversely, 46 per cent of voters gave their first-preference votes to candidates who were elected at later counts, and 8 per cent of voters gave their first-preference votes to candidates who were *not* eliminated during the counts. Consequently, over half (54 per cent) of voters at the elections influenced the electoral outcome *solely* through their first-preference vote; their further preferences were ignored. Such voters are termed 'first-preference-only' voters.

Voters comprising the 'further-preference' group constituted two extreme subgroups. At one extreme, there were those voters who supported (that is, gave their first-preference votes to) strong candidates who were elected at the first count: a little over 28 per cent of all voters at the elections fell into this category. At the other extreme of the 'further-preference' group were those who supported weak candidates who were eliminated before the election was concluded: nearly 18 per cent of voters were in this category. 'First-preference-only' voters also comprised two subgroups. There were those who supported candidates who were strong enough to be elected, but who lacked the necessary support to be elected at the first count: nearly 46 per cent of all voters were in this category. There were also those who supported candidates who did not have enough support to be elected, but who were not weak enough to be eliminated before the election was concluded: such persons comprised 8 per cent of all voters.

Northern Ireland has four main parties. Of these, two – the Democratic Unionist Party (DUP) and the Ulster Unionist Party (UUP) – represent unionist aspirations for Northern Ireland to remain within the United Kingdom and two – Sinn Féin (SF) and the Social Democratic Labour Party (SDLP) – represent nationalist aspirations for a united Ireland. In addition to these four big parties, there are a range of smaller parties

Table 14.1   Percentage of voters whose full range of preferences influenced electoral outcomes in Northern Ireland's 2003 Assembly elections

	Percentage of voters giving 1st preference to candidates elected at first count	Percentage of voters giving 1st preference to candidates elected at later counts	Percentage of voters giving 1st preference to candidates who were eliminated	Percentage of voters giving 1st preference to candidates who were neither eliminated nor elected
Belfast East	50.8 (UUP: 20.9; DUP: 29.9)	30.9	13.4	4.9
Belfast North	46.9 (DUP: 29.4; SF: 17.5)	33.8	15.0	4.3
Belfast South	17.2 (UUP: 17.2)	55.6	20.3	6.9
Belfast West	18.9 (SF: 18.9)	56.0	16.0	9.1
East Antrim	31.4 (UUP: 16.7; DUP: 14.7)	33.1	27.7	7.8
East Londonderry	No election at first count	63.7	29.3	7.0
Fermanagh South Tyrone	No election at first count	71.4	19.1	9.5
Foyle	46.5 (SDLP: 16.7; DUP: 15.0; SF: 14.8)	23.7	20.8	9.0
Lagan Valley	34.2 (UUP: 34.2)	41.2	16.6	8.0
Mid Ulster	36.8 (DUP: 18.5; SF 18.3)	44.3	10.2	8.7
Newry & Armagh	48.6 (DUP: 17.1; SF: 16.0; UUP: 15.5)	32.5	10.2	8.7

Table 14.1   (continued)

	Percentage of voters giving 1st preference to candidates elected at first count	Percentage of voters giving 1st preference to candidates elected at later counts	Percentage of voters giving 1st preference to candidates who were eliminated	Percentage of voters giving 1st preference to candidates who were neither eliminated nor elected
North Antrim	52.2 (DUP: 19.8; DUP: 17.9; UUP: 14.5)	30.5	10.2	7.1
North Down	No election at first count	64.4	27.3	8.3
South Antrim	18.9 (UUP: 18.9)	51.4	18.2	11.5
South Down	15.0 (DUP: 15.0)	53.3	23.0	8.7
Strangford	38.1 (DUP: 22.9; UUP: 15.2)	40.5	13.6	7.8
Upper Baan	21.1 (UUP: 21.1)	54.6	15.2	9.1
West Tyrone	29.2 (Ind: 14.8; SF: 14.4)	44.5	15.6	10.7
Northern Ireland	28.4	45.8	17.5	8.3

Note: DUP = Democratic Unionist Party; UUP = Ulster Unionist Party; SF = Sinn Féin; SDLP = Social Democratic Labour Party; Ind = Independent.

clubbed together in this study under the rubric 'Other parties'. With this background, one may examine the division into 'further-preference' and 'first-preference-only' voters in terms of party support.

Table 14.2 shows that of the 177,944 voters who gave their first-preference vote to the DUP, 44 per cent (77,478 voters) cast their votes for DUP candidates who were elected at the first count. Similarly, of the 156,931 voters who gave their first-preference vote to the UUP, 43 percent (66,741 voters) cast their votes for UUP candidates who were elected at the first count. Consequently, nearly a half of unionist voters were 'further-preference' voters whose further preferences percolated through the

Table 14.2 'Further-preference' voters in Northern Ireland, by party support, Northern Ireland Assembly elections, November 2003

Constituency	Number of voters giving first preference to party elected at first count				
	DUP	UUP	SF	SDLP	Other parties
Belfast East	9,254	6,459	–	–	–
Belfast North	9,276	–	5,524	–	–
Belfast South	–	5,389	–	–	–
Belfast West	–	–	6,199	–	–
East Antrim	4,544	5,175	–	–	–
East Londonderry	–	–	–	–	–
Fermanagh South Tyrone	–	–	–	–	–
Foyle	6,101	–	6,036	6,806	–
Lagan Valley	–	14,104	–	–	–
Mid Ulster	8,211	–	8,128	–	–
Newry & Armagh	8,125	7,347	7,595	–	–
North Antrim	16,630	6,385	–	–	–
North Down	–	–	–	–	–
South Antrim	–	7,066	–	–	–
South Down	6,789	–	–	–	–
Strangford	8,548	5,658	–	–	–
Upper Baan	–	9,158	–	–	–
West Tyrone	–	–	6,019	–	6,158
Total 'first-count' votes	77,478	66,741	39,502	6,806	6,158
Total first-preference votes	177,944	156,931	162,758	117,547	76,848
Share of further-preference votes in first preference votes	44	43	24	6	8
Share of first preference votes in total votes cast (692,028)	25.71	22.67	23.52	16.98	11.12
Number (and share) of Assembly seats	30/108 (28)	27/108 (25)	24/108 (22)	18/108 (17)	9/108 (8)

subsequent counts, influencing their outcomes. By contrast, only 24 per cent of SF voters – and only 6 per cent of SDLP voters – were in a position to influence electoral outcomes beyond the first count.

The DUP received 15,186 more first-preference votes (representing 2 per cent of the total of 692,028 votes) – while the UUP received 5827 fewer votes – than SF. Yet, the DUP won six more seats – and the UUP won three more seats – than SF. At least part of this can be ascribed to the fact that the preferences of DUP and UUP supporters were more effective in making their way through the electoral system compared to the preferences of SF supporters.

More generally, the fact that voters under STV are treated differently, in terms of how their preferences influence electoral outcomes, may also explain why a perceived weakness of the STV system is its lack of proportionality.[11] Indeed, using Gallagher's (1991) 'least squares' index for disproportionality,[12] the 2003 Northern Ireland Assembly elections returned a value of 3.1 for this index.[13] This represented the same level of disproportionality as Ireland and a higher level of disproportionality than Germany, the Netherlands, Austria, Denmark, Sweden, Italy and Iceland (ibid.).

4   WELFARE IMPLICATIONS OF INEQUALITY IN ELECTORAL INFLUENCE

We suppose that every voter, $i = 1, ..., N$, has a preference ranking over all the candidates. Suppose the election extends over R counts. Let $k_i = 1, ..., R$ represent the number of counts at which a preference from voter i's ballot paper is recorded: $1 \leq k_i \leq R$. Hereafter, k_i is referred to as voter i's 'electoral influence': the higher the value of k_i, the greater the influence. At one extreme, if $k_i = 1$, it is only voter i's first preference that matters; at the other extreme, if $k_i = R$, voter i's preferences are taken into account in all the counts. For the 'first-preference-only' group of voters (defined in the previous section), $k_i = 1$ since, by construct of STV, every (first-preference) vote is counted at the first count. For 'further-preference' voters, $k_i > 1$.

We assume that the utility (U) a voter derives from participating in an STV-based election depends postively on the number of counts at which a preference from his/her ballot is recorded:

$$U = U(k_i). \qquad (14.9)$$

where, by assumption: marginal utility is positive ($U'(k_i) > 0$) but diminishing in k_i ($U''(k_i) < 0$). If electoral welfare, W, is represented as the sum of the utilities of the individual voters:

$$W = \sum_{i=1}^{N} U(k_i), \qquad (14.10)$$

then electoral welfare is maximized under an electoral system in which $k_i = R, \forall i$.

Suppose that, because of the nature of the voting method used, electoral welfare cannot be maximized. Assume that, in the most general case, the vector $\mathbf{k} = \{k_i\}$ represents the distribution of electoral influence across the $i = 1, ..., N$ voters, where $k_i < R$ for some i. The average level of electoral influence under the voting method is:

$$\bar{k} = \sum_{i=1}^{N} k_i. \tag{14.11}$$

In the context of the distinction, under STV, between 'further-preference' and 'first-preference-only' voters, $k_i > 1$ for 'further-preference' voters and $k_i = 1$ for 'first-preference-only' voters. If α represents the proportion of 'further-preference' voters, and $\mu > 1$ represents their average electoral influence (that is, the average number of counts at which their votes were counted) then the average level of electoral influence under STV is $\bar{k} = \alpha\mu + (1 - \alpha)$ and electoral welfare under STV is $W = N[\alpha U(\mu) + (1 - \alpha)U(1)]$.

Following Atkinson (1970), let $k^* \leq \bar{k}$ represent the average level of electoral influence which, if equally distributed across the voters, would yield the same level of electoral welfare as the existing distribution of electoral influence, represented by the vector $\mathbf{k} = \{k_i\}$. In other words:

$$W = N \times U(k^*) = \sum_{i=1}^{N} U(k_i). \tag{14.12}$$

Then k^* may be termed the 'equally distributed equivalent electoral influence'. Atkinson's inequality index may be applied to the distribution, $\mathbf{k} = \{k_i\}$, of electoral influence across the voters by defining the inequality index:

$$I(\mathbf{k}; N) = 1 - (k^*/\bar{k}) = 1 - \left[N^{-1} \sum_{i=1}^{N} (k_i/\bar{k})^{1-\varepsilon} \right]^{1/1-\varepsilon}, \varepsilon > 0 \; \varepsilon \neq 1. \tag{14.13}$$

The parameter ε – which ranges from 0 to ∞, so that the values of $I(\mathbf{k}; N)$ range from 0 to 1 – is a measure of society's aversion to inequality in electoral influence. When $\varepsilon = 0$, society is indifferent as to how a given average of electoral influence (represented by $\bar{k}$) is distributed across the voters: $k^* = \bar{k}$ and $I(\mathbf{k}; N) = 0$. For $\varepsilon > 0$, $k^* < \bar{k}$ and $I(\mathbf{k}; N) > 0$. This means that society would be prepared to adopt a voting method that embodies a lower-average electoral influence than the current method, provided that the reduction in the average value is accompanied by an equal distribution of electoral influence across the voters. The higher the value of the inequality aversion parameter, ε, the smaller will be the value of k^* and the higher will be the value of $I(\mathbf{k}; N)$.

In order to make comparisons of loss (or gain) of welfare across different values of $\bar{k}$, a specific transformation, linking the inequality measure I to the different values of $\bar{k}$, is needed. One obvious transformation is the reverse of the Atkinson transformation which yields the welfare function (Sen, 1973):

$$W = \bar{k}(1 - I), \tag{14.14}$$

which is homogeneous of degree one in the k_i.

The electoral welfare function in equation (14.14) has a natural interpretation: electoral welfare from a given average electoral influence, $\bar{k}$, is reduced by the extent of inequality in the distribution of electoral influence between voters. Given a value of $\bar{k}$, equation (14.14) says that electoral welfare depends upon the degree of inequality in the distribution of electoral influence across voters – as measured by the Atkinson index (I) – and this inequality, in turn, is determined by the inter-voter distribution of average electoral influence *and* upon the degree to which society is averse to inequality in electoral influence.

One may compare electoral welfare under STV to that under a 'naive' method in which only first-preference votes matter: for example, the six candidates in a constituency receiving the largest number of first-preference votes are elected as its representatives. Under STV, $\bar{k} = 1 + \alpha\mu - 1)$ and electoral welfare under STV and plurality – denoted, W^S and W^P, respectively – are, from equation (14.14):

$$W^S = (1 + \alpha\mu - 1)1 - I(\mathbf{k}; N) \text{ and } W^P = 1, \tag{14.15}$$

where, from equation (14.13):

$$I(\mathbf{k}; N) = 1 - \left\{ N \left[\alpha\left(\frac{\mu}{\bar{k}}\right)^\varepsilon + (1 - \alpha)\left(\frac{1}{\bar{k}}\right)^\varepsilon \right] \right\}^{1/1+\varepsilon}$$

$$= 1 - \left\{ N \left[\left(\frac{1}{\bar{k}}\right)^\varepsilon + \alpha\left(\frac{\mu - 1}{\bar{k}}\right)^\varepsilon \right] \right\}^{(1/1+\varepsilon)}. \tag{14.16}$$

Then setting $W^S = W^P$ (from equation (14.15)) yields:

$$[1 + \alpha(\mu - 1)][1 - I(\mathbf{k}; N)] = 1, \tag{14.17}$$

and using the expression for $I(\mathbf{k}; N)$ from equation (14.16), allows one to solve for the degree of inequality aversion (ε^*) which would make STV and plurality be welfare equivalent. In determining the outcome of an election, when $\varepsilon = \varepsilon^*$, society is indifferent between: an electoral method which allows voters a fuller representation of their preferences than simply a single preference, but takes unequal account of these representations; and a method which allows voters a single representation of their preferences, but takes equal account of this representation.

Table 14.3 shows what the outcome of the 2003 Northern Ireland Assembly elections would have been if the 'naive' method had been used to determine the results. The number of seats to the DUP and the SDLP would have remained unchanged at, respectively, 30 and 18. However, the UUP would have won four fewer seats (down from 27 to 23), 'Other' parties would have won one fewer seats (down from 8 to 7) and Sinn Féin would

Table 14.3   Party positions under STV and plurality

Constituency	Number of voters giving first preference to party elected at earliest count									
	DUP		UUP		SF		SDLP		Others	
	STV	PL	STV	PL	STV	PL	STV	PL	STV	PL
Belfast East	2	1	2	3	0	0	0	0	2	2
Belfast North	2	1	1	1	2	2	1	2	0	0
Belfast South	1	2	2	1	1	1	2	2	0	0
Belfast West	1	0	0	0	4	5	1	1	0	0
East Antrim	3	3	2	1	0	0	0	1	1	1
East Londonderry	2	3	2	1	1	1	1	1	0	0
Fermanagh and South Tyrone	1	1	2	2	2	2	1	1	0	0
Foyle	1	1	0	0	2	3	3	2	0	0
Lagan Valley	1	2	3	1	0	1	1	1	1	1
Mid Ulster	1	1	1	1	3	3	1	1	0	0
Newry & Armagh	1	1	1	1	3	3	1	1	0	0
North Antrim	3	3	1	1	1	1	1	1	0	0
North Down	2	2	2	3	0	0	0	0	2	1
South Antrim	2	2	2	2	0	1	1	0	1	1
South Down	1	1	1	1	2	2	2	2	0	0
Strangford	3	3	2	2	0	0	0	1	1	0
Upper Baan	2	2	2	1	1	2	1	1	0	0
West Tyrone	1	1	1	1	2	3	1	0	0	1
Total seats	30	30	27	23	24	30	18	18	8	7

have won six more seats (up from 24 to 30) to make it, along with the DUP, the largest party in the Assembly.[14]

4.1 Diagrammatic Representation

It may be useful to present an intuitive understanding of the approach towards measuring inter-voter inequality in electoral influence, set out in the previous sections, by means of a diagram. Figure 14.1 portrays a world of two voters, 1 and 2, who 'share' a given average electoral influence, $\bar{k}$ to obtain, respectively, k_1 and k_2. The horizontal axis measures k_1 and the vertical axis measures k_2. The sharing equation is $\bar{k} = (k_1 + k_2)/2$ and this is represented by the 'electoral-possibility' line PQ in the diagram. Each point on PQ represents a (k_1, k_2) combination that yields the value $\bar{k}$. At any point on the 45° line $0M$, passing through the origin, $k_1 = k_2$.

Superimposed upon the electoral-possibility line in the diagram are the electoral welfare indifference curves: each curve shows the different k_1, k_2 combinations that yield the same level of electoral welfare, defined in equation (14.10). If the voting system delivers the point X, then the average electoral influence $0C$ is distributed between the two voters so that $k_1 = 0C$ and $k_2 = 0D$. In welfare terms this is equivalent to the outcome at point Y (since X and Y lie on the same indifference curve) at which $k_1 = k_2 = 0B$ where $0B$ is the 'equally distributed equivalent' electoral influence (k^*). The degree of inequality in the voting method, from equation (14.13), is given by $(1 - 0B/0A)$.

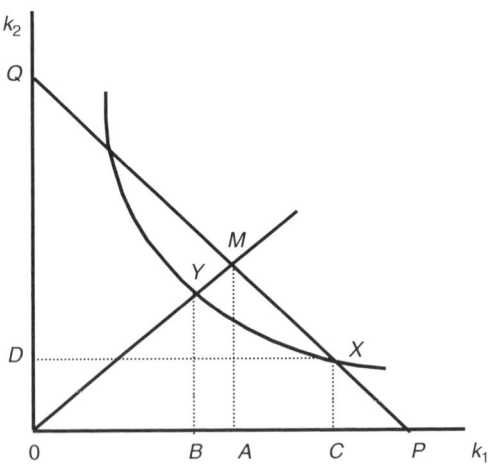

Figure 14.1   Inequality in the distribution of electoral influence

Under STV, $k_1 = \mu$ and $k_2 = 1$ at the point X in Figure 14.1. Under plurality, $k_1 = k_2 = 1$ and this is represented at the point Y in the figure. Since Y and X lie on the same indifference curve, the degree of inequality aversion – as represented by how 'bowed' the indifference curve is – is such as to make plurality and STV welfare equivalent.

5   A PROPOSAL FOR REFORM OF STV

As Section 3 made clear, the unequal treatment of voters under STV arises because, in effecting the transfer of surplus votes of candidates elected at the first count to the remaining candidates, *all* the votes received by the successful candidates are inspected. However, in effecting the transfer of surplus votes of candidates elected at later counts, *only* the transfers received by such candidates, at the count at which they were elected, are inspected. This inter-voter inequality of treatment can be overcome by ensuring that, even for candidates elected at later counts, the transfer of surplus votes is based on an inspection of *all* the votes received by the successful candidates. Call this method 'extended STV' (abbreviated to ESTV). Under ESTV, there would be no change in the way that the surplus of candidates elected at the first count was effected. Nor would there be any change in the analysis relating to the elimination of candidates. However, under ESTV, candidates elected at subsequent counts would have their surplus votes transferred to the remaining candidates in the same way that such transfers are effected for candidates elected at the first count.

Under ESTV, the proportion of the total votes received by X at the Rth count that would accrue to each of the remaining candidates is calculated for each of the remaining candidates, denoted by j, as:

$$\rho^R_{X_j} = V^R_{X_j} / V^R_X, \tag{14.18}$$

where $V^R_{X_j}$ are the number of votes that j would receive from V^R_X, the total votes received by X at the Rth count. The transfers received by j (from X, who was elected at the Rth count[15]) would then be:

$$T^R_j = \rho^R_{X_j} S_X, \tag{14.19}$$

and the total votes counted for j at the $(R+1)$th would be: $V^{R+1}_j = V^R_j + T^R_j$.

In order to effect ESTV, *all* the V^R_X ballots from which X received votes, up to the Rth count, would have to be inspected: the V^1_X ballots listing X as the first-preference candidate would have to be inspected for the second-preference candidate, and the T'_X ballots that listed X as the rth preference candidate would have to be inspected for their $(r+1)$th preference $(r = 2, ..., R)$.

In contrast to ESTV, STV, as discussed earlier, effects the transfer of the surplus of candidates, elected at counts later than the first, only in terms of the transfers received at the count at which they were elected.

6   CONCLUSIONS

Issues relating to equality loom larger in the public consciousness in Northern Ireland – and play a more important role in the making of public policy – than they do elsewhere in the UK. In large measure, this is due to the turbulent history of Northern Ireland where, as is well known, tensions and animosities between the Catholic and Protestant communities have, since the inception of the state in 1920, run deep. Many events have coalesced to produce this state of affairs and some have acquired more prominence in the popular consciousness than others. One event was the abolition in 1922 – by the then government of Northern Ireland, under the prime ministership of Sir James Craig – of proportional representation for local council elections (Bogdanor, 2001). This replacement, at the level both of district council and of parliamentary elections, of proportional representation by plurality election established a Protestant hegemony over affairs in Northern Ireland[16] and the exercise of this hegemony in discriminating against Catholics in public sector employment and housing culminated in the civil rights protests of the late 1960s and thus began the spiral of violence that, notwithstanding the current cease-fire, continues to splutter on.

However, it is the contention of this chapter that by underpinning elections in Northern Ireland – both to district councils and to the Northern Ireland Assembly – by STV, a different kind of inequality has been created. This inequality – which remains largely unremarked and, therefore, is not a cause for public comment – is inequality *between* voters in the way their votes influence the electoral outcome. Under STV, voters with different preferences are treated differently in terms of their impact on the electoral outcome. In essence, STV creates two classes of voters. In determining the list of successful candidates, some voters – 'further-preference' voters – have more than their first-preference vote taken into account, while for other voters – 'first-preference' voters – it is only their first preference that is counted. So, while all voters may express their preferences over all the candidates, such expression is meaningful for only some voters and meaningless for the remainder. If society was averse to inter-voter inequality in electoral influence, it might prefer a voting system which, while allowing voters a more limited expression of preferences, allowed each voter's preferences to count equally towards the outcome of the election.

NOTES

*   I am grateful to John Fitzgerald and George Tridimas for comments though, needless to say, I am solely responsible for any errors.

1.   This quota is also known as the 'Droop' quota and is the analogue of a simple majority in a single-member constituency. A quota is not the same as a 'threshold' since, on the last count, a candidate may be elected without reaching the quota: it is, therefore, a sufficient, but not a necessary, condition for election.

2.   For a fuller discussion of STV, including its merits and demerits, see Hallett (1984), Katz (1984), Amy (1993) and Bowles and Grofman (2000).

3.   For elected candidates it is the votes in excess of the quota that are transferred.

4.   Six members are elected from each of the 18 constituencies to the Northern Ireland Assembly.

5.   By equation (14.1), $\Sigma_{j\neq X}\pi^1_{Xj} \leq 1$, $\Sigma_{j\neq X}\pi^1_{Xj} = 1 \Leftrightarrow V^1_{X0} = 0$. This method of defining proportions where non-transfers are taken into account is used in Northern Ireland. In the Republic of Ireland, non-transfers are set aside and the proportions are defined as: $\pi^1_{Xj} = V^1_{Xj}/(V^1_X - V^1_{X0})$.

6.   Note that, because of the presence of non-transferable votes, the entire surplus of X may not be distributed among the remaining candidates. However, it will be in the Republic of Ireland where non-transfers are set aside.

7.   These fractions are $T^2_{Xj}/V^1_{Xj} = \pi^1_{Xj}S_X/V^1_X = S_X/V^1_X$ and $T^2_{Yj}/V^1_{Yj} = \pi^1_{Yj}S_Y/V^1_Y = S_Y/V^1_Y$.

8.   It is possible, in order to speed the counting, to eliminate more than one candidate at the same count. For example, suppose for three candidates, A, B and C: $V^R_A < V^R_B < V^R_C$, $V^R_C - V^R_B > V^R_A$ and $V^R_A + V^R_B < Q$. Then even if all of A's votes went to B, B would still have the lowest number of votes, after candidate A was eliminated; and even if all of A's votes went to candidate C, C would still not be elected at the next count. Consequently, B is bound to be eliminated at the next count and could, as well, be dropped at the current count.

9.   The only way way the influence of the X voters is broken is if there is no election at a count so that a candidate is eliminated. In that case, subsequent transfers are drawn from the votes of the eliminated candidates.

10.   That is, a candidate who was still in the contest at the count at which the final candidate was elected.

11.   See The Electoral Reform Society, www.electoral-reform.org.uk/voting systems/systems 3.htm.

12.   Defined as: $L = [\frac{1}{2}(\Sigma^K_{k=1} (v_k - s_k)^2)]^{\frac{1}{2}}$, where v_k and s_k are the vote and seat shares of party k.

13.   This was lower than the value of 4.2 for the 1998 Assembly elections.

14.   The degree of disproportionality, as measured by the least squares index would rise to 4.7. However, needless to say, this is not a fair reflection of the outcome under plurality since party strategies in the selection of candidates were made on the basis of STV.

15.   It is assumed, without loss of generality, that no other candidate was elected at that count.

16.   'A Protestant Parliament for a Protestant People' as one Unionist prime minister memorably expressed it.

REFERENCES

Amy, D.J. (1993), *Real Choices/New Choices*, New York: Columbia University Press.

Atkinson, A.B. (1970), 'On the measurement of inequality', *Journal of Economic Theory*, **2**, 244–63.

Bogdanor, V. (2001), *Devolution in the United Kingdom*, Oxford: Oxford University Press.

Bowles, S. and B. Grofman (2000), 'Introduction: STV as an embedded institution', in S. Bowles and B. Grofman (eds), *Elections in Australia, Ireland and Malta under the Single Transferable Vote*, Ann Arbor, MI: University of Michigan Press.

Gallagher, M. (1991), 'Proportionality, disproportionality and electoral systems', *Electoral Studies*, **10**, 33–51.

Hallett, G.H. (1984), 'Proportional respresentation with the single transferable vote', in A. Lijphart and B. Grofman (eds), *Choosing an Electoral System: Issues and Alternatives*, New York: Praeger, 113–25.

Katz, R.S. (1984), 'The single transferable vote and proportional representation', in A. Lijphart and B. Grofman (eds), *Choosing an Electoral System: Issues and Alternatives*, New York: Praeger, 135–45.

Sen, A.K. (1973), *On Income Inequality*, Oxford: Oxford University Press.

Sinnott, R. (1993), 'The electoral system', in J. Coakley and M. Gallagher (eds), *Politics in the Republic of Ireland*, Dublin: PSAI Press, 67–85.

PART IV

Democracy Across the World

15. The pattern of democracy in the twentieth century: a study of the Polity index

Peter Sandholt Jensen and Martin Paldam*

1 INTRODUCTION

The Polity index (Π-index) has provided a measure of democracy/dictatorship for about 52 independent countries since 1900. For a few countries it goes back even further, and over time about 100 countries have become independent and been added. The index is scaled from $+10$ for 'perfect' democracy to -10 for 'perfect' dictatorship.

Figure 15.1 shows the average Π-score for all countries from 1900 to 2003 and for the 52 countries that are covered for most years. For most of the twentieth century, the Π-index has fluctuated around zero. The 52 old countries of the index are dominated by countries in Europe and the Americas with European culture. The 100 new countries are mostly poorer, and have less democracy.

The pattern showed corresponds to our knowledge of a slow increase in democracy in the world. It also shows some well-known crises: the late 1920s and the 1930s represented a swing away from democracy, notably in Europe. In fact, the trend from 1900 to 1972 is of dubious significance, but since then there has been a large increase in democracy in the world.

For the whole of the twentieth century, few variables are available for many countries for the whole of the century, so we shall examine only the following three sets of variables:

- *Set 1: Income and political system change* The long-run development of income is represented by (the logarithm to) gdp, that is, GDP per capita. Income is a catch-all variable, which covers the totality of development in a rather crude way. Political regimes, Π, have much persistence, which is included in two ways: (i) the explained variable, Π_{it}^T, is the average Π for a period of T years, from t to $t + T$; and (ii) the initial value, Π_{t-1}, is used as an explanatory variable.

- *Set 2: Periods*   For reasons to be discussed, we have divided the data into five periods of $T = 20$ years each. An important criterion of validity of our analysis is whether the effects found are stable across these periods. This is formally tested in Table 15.7.

- *Set 3: The 'story' variables: oil, Old West and Islam*   (i) We want to compare two ways of obtaining income: production and resource rent. Oil export is considered the cleanest case of resource rent. (ii) The countries of the West and Islamic countries seem to be diverging in many ways of which one is the form of government as measured by the Π-score. We here speak of the 'Muslim gap'. Consequently, binary dummies are used for three types of countries: major oil exporters, Old Western countries and Muslim countries.

Section 2 considers the theories examined, and Section 3 looks at the data asking how much we can expect these data to say. Section 4 gives a set of ordinary least squares (OLS) estimates, while Section 5 shows that little happens when the estimates are corrected for a set of potential problems. Section 6 gives the conclusions. Finally, Appendix 15A compares the scores of the Polity and the Gastil indices.

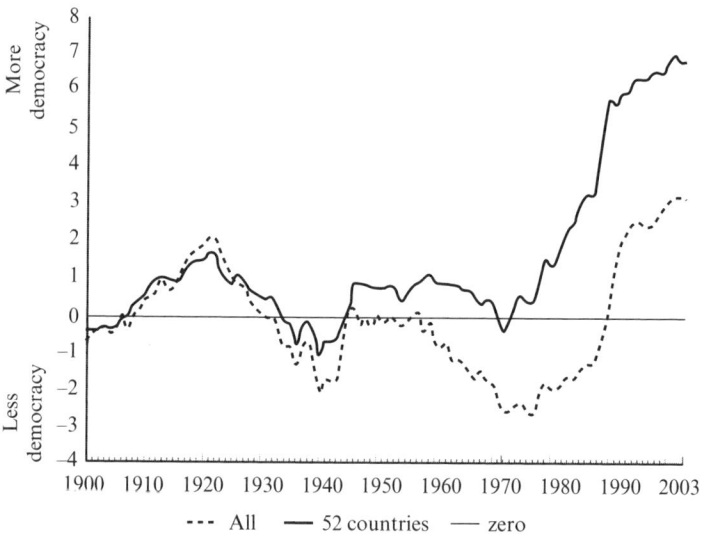

Figure 15.1   Path of the Polity index, 1900–2003

2 THE THEORIES EXAMINED

We consider the complex of theories shown in Figure 15.2. The six solid boxes represent the six variables used. Variables 4 to 6 are binary dummies, which are 1 if the event occurs and zero else:

1. Π_{it}^{20}, average Π-score for each of five periods of $T = 20$ years. Range from -10 to $+10$.
2. Π_{it-1}, initial Π-score for the year before each period starts. Integer range -10 and $+10$.
3. y_{it-1}, log to initial gdp, that is, GDP per capita for the year before each period starts. We use the natural logarithm to the data from Maddison (2003).
4. OW_i, the Old West is Western countries that were already rich in the first period, where 'rich' means that the gdp is above half of the US GDP.
5. Oil_{it}, countries where more than 50 per cent of exports are oil and gas.
6. Mu_i, countries with a majority of Muslims. If it is doubtful whether the criterion is fulfilled (for example, in the cases of Nigeria and Sudan), we use the secondary criterion that the government is Muslim (so that Nigeria is non-Muslim, while Sudan is Muslim).

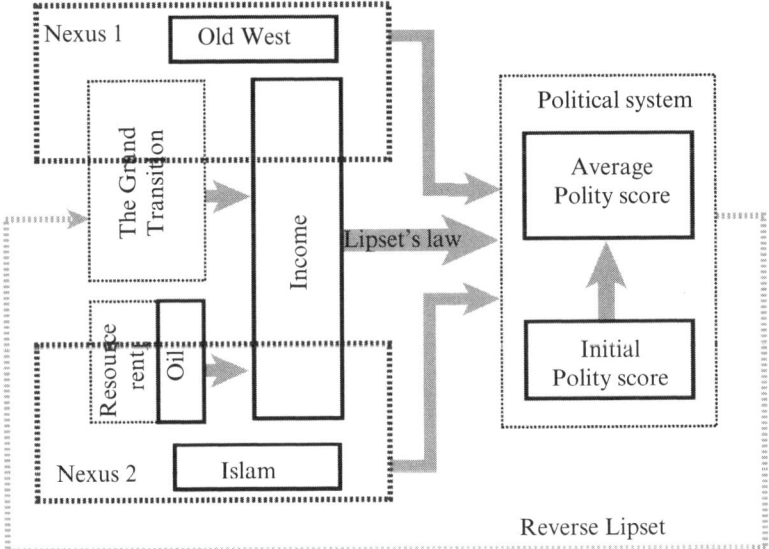

Figure 15.2   Causal structure

The introduction mentions two main problems: the catch-all character of the *gdp* variable used to measure the relation between development and political system, and the strong inertia in political systems. These two problems are connected in two ways:

The first connection is that the following simple relation exists between the estimate of the coefficient to initial Polity β and to income γ:

$$\Pi_{it}^T = \alpha_{(i)}^T + \beta^T \Pi_{it-1} + \gamma^T y_{it-1} + u_i, \qquad \text{as estimated;} \qquad (15.1a)$$

$$\Pi_i^\infty = \frac{\alpha^T}{1-\beta^T} + \frac{\gamma^T}{1-\beta^T} y_i = \alpha^\infty + \gamma^\infty y_i, \qquad \begin{array}{l}\text{gives the implied}\\\text{steady-state values;}\end{array} \qquad (15.1b)$$

$$\Pi_{it}^T = \alpha_{(i)} + \mu^T y_{it-1} + u_t, \qquad \begin{array}{l}\text{as estimated. Here } \mu^T \to \gamma^\infty,\\\text{for large } T_s.\end{array} \qquad (15.1c)$$

If T is small, β becomes large and γ small and vice versa, but we expect $\gamma^\infty = \gamma^T/(1-\beta^T)$ to be fairly stable for some range of T. Equation (15.1c) forces the regression to make the full adjustment to y within T. This is a shortcut, but $\mu^T \approx \gamma^\infty$ if T is sizeable. However, as T grows, the distance to $y_{it}-1$ becomes so large that the estimate loses precision, and the number of observations falls. The choice of T is thus crucial.

The second connection between the effects of initial Polity and income is the statistical consequence of the above. If T is chosen too small, $\beta \approx 1$, and given the time-series variation in the Polity data, the other coefficients will be estimated with low precision. In other words, the unit root in the regression causes the estimates to become nonsense.

The key causal relation modeled is the effect of income on the Π-score. Most of the literature argues that as income goes up, the political system gradually becomes more democratic. This is known as 'Lipset's Law' (after Lipset, 1959, 1994). Lipset himself and several other writers (for example, Przeworski et al., 2000) argue that there may be causality the other way too. On the figure, this is called the 'Reverse Lipset' connection. Column (4) in Table 15.8 below shows that this is a much smaller effect, so in most of this chapter it is disregarded.

As argued in Paldam (2007), we consider the change in political system as a typical part of a whole set of changes known as the 'Grand Transition', where a poor country becomes rich through a complete transformation from low to high productivity. Here the level of education rises dramatically, society becomes secularized, corruption falls, family patterns change, happiness increases and so on. In order to untangle some of the complexity, we divide it into two:

- *The Muslim–Oil nexus*, where we use the two binary dummies *Mu* and *Oil*. They both get negative coefficients in the regressions – also in the other studies of the project. Most, but not all, of the oil countries are also Muslim. Some countries in the Old West group are large oil producers too, but they produce so much that oil does not dominate their exports. In many fields, a gap between the West and the world of Islam is appearing. Figure 15.3 shows the Muslim gap in the Π-score. It is no less than 5.82 points, and it is even larger between the West and the community of Islam. Although the relative movements were unclear before the Second World War where data are thin anyhow, there is a clear upward trend ever since. We study the robustness of the negative coefficient to *Mu* to the initial levels of income and Π, and to oil. In particular, we want to study the dynamics of the gap. It is often alleged that Muslims have values that dominate the ones of democracy. This indicates that the gap is permanent, but others argue that this does not need to be the case and that the gap is thus transitory.

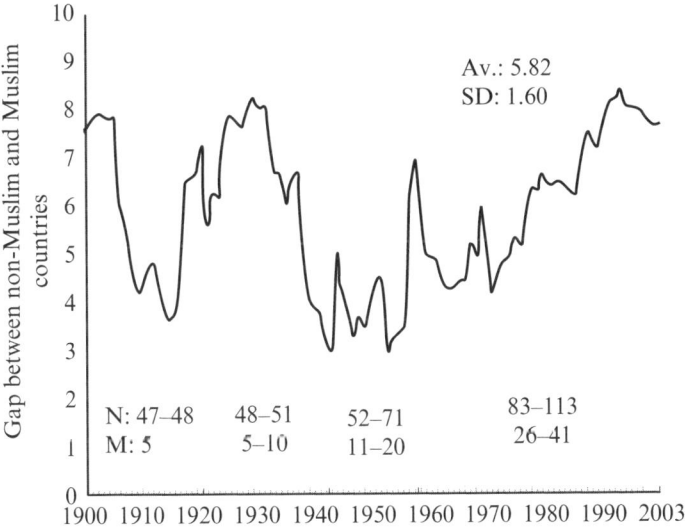

Note: The country composition has changed by a gradual inclusion of more and more countries. From 1900 to 1921 the sample included 47–48 non-Muslim countries and (only) five Muslim ones. Since 1959 the sample has included 83–113 non-Muslim and 26 41 Muslim ones.

Figure 15.3   The Muslim gap *in the Polity data*

- *The Old West nexus* deals with the path dependency caused by an early transition. A hundred years ago, all rich countries were Western, and also democracy originated in the West. So arguably, the West had a *historical* advantage. If we do not control for 'Old West', we shall get an exaggerated effect of income.

As much of the action in the data is connected to the Grand Transition, this introduces a large element of mutual interaction into the reactions. The Grand Transition means that a large number of changes take place simultaneously. If enough variables are included in the relations, they come to contain much collinearity. Therefore, coefficients become significant or insignificant due to small flukes in the series.

We use gdp as the main variable covering the Grand Transition. However, instead of going through the Grand Transition, there is an alternative way of producing a high *gdp*, namely from resource rent. The most extreme type of resource rent comes from oil, where the production technique is fully international and not very labor intensive. The oil dummy is always highly significant and negative. It is hence not enough to be rich to become democratic. It is a product of the complex changes generated by the Grand Transition.

Recently, Acemoglu et al. (2005) demonstrated that the connection between income and democracy is weaker than hitherto believed. When they control for the initial Π-score and fixed effects for countries, the significance of the coefficient disappears in most of their estimates. It is well known that the tool of fixed effects for countries is a powerful test of a cross-country model. It has made many effects vanish.[1] However, in Section 3 we study the relation between the average and the initial level of Π, that is, between Π_{it}^T and Π_{it-1}. Acemoglu et al. work with an average of $T = 5$ years. As will be demonstrated, their T often causes a (near) unit root in the relation, and with fixed effects added everything washes out. With a reasonable size of T, the model proves robust to fixed effects.

It is hence important to study the persistence in the Polity data to determine a proper size of T, and to calculate the effects of the choices.

3   THE DATA: WHAT CAN THEY TELL?

The Polity index is an old project at the Center for International Development and Conflict Management, University of Maryland, with M.G. Marshall, K. Jaggers and T.R. Gurr as the main researchers. The index has gone through several versions, and we use the one presently posted (downloaded in the early fall of 2005). We use the data as posted,

Table 15.1   Some descriptive statistics: the data of the regressions

	Period 1 1901–20	Period 2 1921–40	Period 3 1941–60	Period 4 1961–80	Period 5 1981–00	Total stacked
	Number of observations of the variables					
N	31	34	41	99	124	329
Oil (*Oil*)	1	1	1	10	14	27
Old West (*OW*)	13	13	12	12	12	62
Muslim (*Mu*)	0	0	1	25	35	61
Constant Π*	10	11	16	32	29	98
Of which 10–10*	5	9	12	18	17	61
	Averages and standard deviation of observations					
Polity	2.24	3.00	2.77	−1.40	0.61	0.67
SD	(5.50)	(6.28)	(6.67)	(6.95)	(6.50)	(6.76)
Init Polity	1.42	4.00	0.71	−0.46	−1.94	−0.23
SD	(6.09)	(6.35)	(7.60)	(7.55)	(7.49)	(7.53)
Dif	−0.82	1.00	−2.07	0.93	−2.54	−0.91
SD	(2.71)	(3.22)	(4.94)	(3.59)	(4.36)	(4.30)
Log *y*	7.58	7.74	7.93	7.64	7.98	7.81
SD	(0.58)	(0.52)	(0.55)	(0.85)	(1.30)	(0.89)
Init *gdp*	2287	2633	3222	3004	5182	3746
SD	(1162)	(1341)	(1731)	(2735)	(5647)	4035

Note: * Cases where the average Polity score is equal to the initial one and of these cases where both are 10.

though to get the consistent series for 52 countries from 1900 to 2003, we have filled in a few gaps as best we could. These interpolations are used only in the graphs, not in the regressions.

The *gdp* data are from Maddison (2003). Some countries are covered by the Polity index, but have no *gdp* observations. Unfortunately, this is the case for most Muslim countries before 1960. Table 15.1 gives the dimensions in the data for the different periods.

Note that Western countries are prominent in the long series, while Muslim countries are included for the last two periods only. Altogether, 61 of the observations are of the 10–10 type, where both the initial and the average Π-score are 10. Most of the Old West observations are in this category. When fixed effects for countries are added, these observations are effectively removed, and one end of the income spectrum is greatly reduced.

As discussed, it is important that *T* is chosen within a certain range: if *T* is small, a unit root enters the regression, and if *T* is large, information is lost. We decided to choose *T* = 20 after consideration of the following three persistence measures,[2] where the first two measure the persistence of the cross-country pattern and the third measures the inertia over time:

$\text{Cor}_i(\Pi_t, \Pi_{t+j})$, for $j = 1, ..., 20$,   cross-country persistence function   (15.2a)

$\text{Cor}_i(\Pi_t, \Pi_{t+1}^T)$, for $T = 1, ..., 20$,   cross-country persistence of initial and average Π (15.2b)

$\text{Av}_i[\text{cor}_t(\Pi_{it}, \Pi_{it+j})]$, for $j = 0, ..., 30$,   standard autocorrelation function   (15.2c)

Figure 15.4 shows the three functions. They are calculated for the 52 countries where the data are complete for all periods (with a few interpolations), with the said lags.

The cross-country persistence (15.2a) starts at 0.98 (for $j = 1$) and falls to 0.9 (for $j = 5$), so the correlation between the initial and the average Π-scores is no less than 0.94 for a five-year average. This is too close to a unit root. Even for a 10-year average, the correlation between the average and the initial Π-scores is still 0.9. For a 20-year average, the correlation (15.2b) is 0.85. This is high, but it proves to work, and it still gives 329 observations.

The autocorrelation functions confirm the observation of high persistence. Note the cyclical pattern of autocorrelation in the 13 countries of the Old West. It reflects the fact that a few of these countries (notably Germany) have had one period of dictatorship in the twentieth century. However, in the second half of the century none of the Old Western countries have deviated much from the ideal 10 points, see Figure 15.5.

The figure shows how much the Old West deviates from the average path, which was also depicted on Figure 15.1. Note that once we control for the initial level, the Old West hardly contributes anything to the rise in democracy for the period since 1920, where the series is virtually trendless for these countries.

4   THE BASIC OLS REGRESSIONS

This section presents OLS regressions for the individual periods and for all periods stacked. Section 5 demonstrates that only rather marginal improvements occur when these regressions are re-estimated using estimators that correct for various potential problems.

The model used is a simple exploratory framework between the variables defined at the start of Section 2. All regressions in Tables 15.2–7 have Π_{it}^{20} – the average Polity index for a 20-year period – as the variable explained.

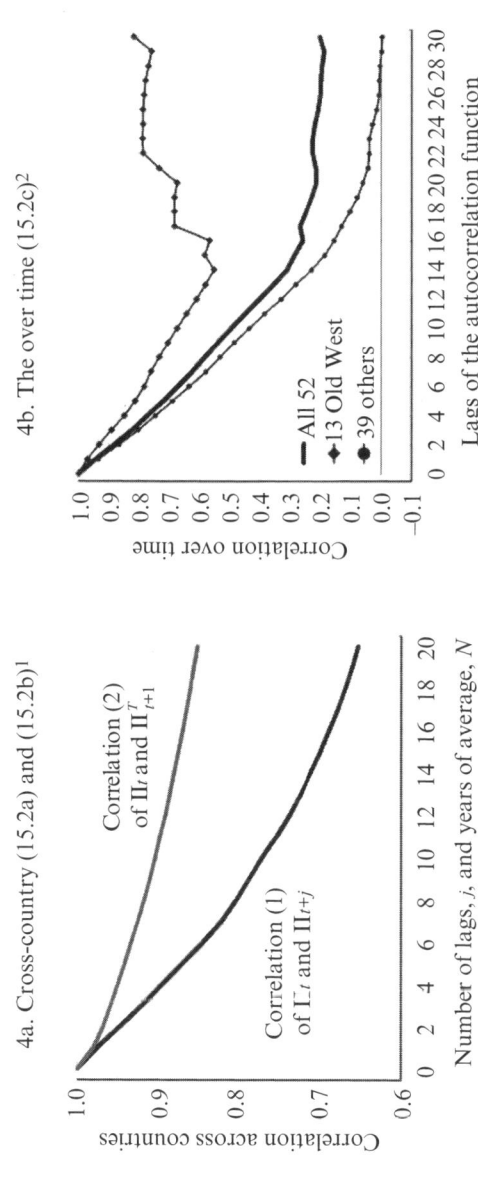

4a. Cross-country (15.2a) and (15.2b)[1]

Correlation (2)
of II_t and II_{t+1}^T

Correlation (1)
of I_t and II_{t+j}

Number of lags, j, and years of average, N

4b. The over time (15.2c)[2]

— All 52
♦ 13 Old West
● 39 others

Lags of the autocorrelation function

Notes:
1. Calculation done after stacking of the observations for the five periods. Every correlation is done on more than 5000 pairs of observations.
2. The autocorrelations are calculated for each of the 52 countries, and three averages are presented.

Figure 15.4   Three measures of persistence in the Polity data

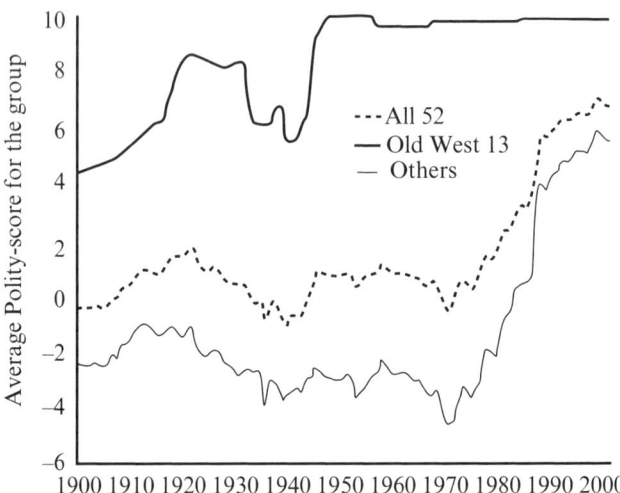

Figure 15.5   Average for the Old West countries

If the constant α is broken up into fixed effects, the subscript i applies – this is only done in Table 15.8:

$$\Pi_{it}^{20} = \alpha_{(i)}^{20} + \beta^{20}\,\Pi_{it-1} + \gamma^{20}y_{it-1} + \lambda_1^{20}OW_i + \lambda_2^{20}Oil_{it} + \lambda_3^{20}Mu_i + u_t.$$

$$(15.3)$$

With this model, we have experimented with the deletion of variables in various combinations and with various estimators. From the model, the steady-state values of the coefficients are estimated by multiplying with $z = 1/(1-\beta^{20})$, so that $\gamma^{\infty} \approx z\gamma^{20}$, $\lambda_1^{\infty} \approx z\lambda_1^{20}$ and so on. We can then examine how robust these estimates are compared to the corresponding ones when the second term, with a lagged initial value of Π, is omitted as explained above.

Table 15.2 shows that when we include only initial Polity and income, everything becomes significant. Also, it appears that the coefficients to the two initial variables, $\log y$ and Π, are fairly constant, but the implied steady-state value of the effect of income is not very stable.

When the full model is estimated – in Table 15.3 – we get much the same picture, and now the implied steady-state effects of income are reasonably stable, around 4 Polity points. In the stacked regressions, all coefficients are forced to be the same. Table 15.4 shows a set of such stacked regressions, with experiments for the three dummies.

When we repeat Table 15.4 without either income or initial Polity (as done in Table 15.5), all story variables obtain significant coefficients with

Table 15.2 OLS cross-country estimates for each 20-year period, and stacked

Explaining av Polity Π_t^{20}	(1)	(2)	(3)	(4)	(5)	(6) Stacked
	Cross-country estimate for 20-year periods					Stacked
	1900–20	1921–40	1941–60	1961–80	1981–00	
Constant	**−19.71**	**−23.48**	**−28.84**	**−14.99**	−5.40	**−12.14**
	(−3.3)	(−2.1)	(−2.4)	(−4.4)	(−1.9)	(−6.1)
y_{-1}, income init	**2.77**	**3.07**	**3.94**	**1.82**	**0.91**	**1.66**
	(3.5)	(2.1)	(2.6)	(4.1)	(2.6)	(56.5)
Π_{t-1}, initial	**0.67**	**0.68**	**0.49**	**0.69**	**0.65**	**0.65**
	(8.9)	(5.6)	(4.5)	(13.8)	(12.9)	(21.6)
R^2 adjusted	0.85	0.77	0.63	0.80	0.68	0.72
N	31	34	41	99	124	329
	Implied steady-state value of the effect of income					
y, long run	8.39	9.59	7.73	5.87	2.60	4.74

Note: Bold estimates are significant. Below each is the *t*-ratio (in brackets).

the signs mentioned. So there is some multicolinearity in the model. When initial Polity, Π_{it-1}, is excluded in Table 15.5, the fit of all other variables increases as it should, and the increase in the constant variables is largest. However, the fall in R^2 is substantial. Note that the long-run effects of income are quite stable. If it is estimated as in Table 15.5, it forces the full adjustment to happen in one period (of 20 years) and it is only 10–20 percent lower.

The conclusions so far are as follows. Income has an effect which is always positive and normally significant. Its size is $\gamma^{20} \approx 1.6$. For $\beta = 0.6$, this implies a long-run effect $\gamma^\infty \approx 4.0$. The scale of y is in (natural) logs to gdp, and it is 'translated' into ratios in Table 15.6. Very poor and very rich countries differ by 50 times. This gives 15.6 points on the Polity scale in the long run. For countries that differ only two or 10 times, it is 2.8 and 9.2 points, respectively, on the Polity scale in the long run – note how long the long run is in this field. The effect of income on the political system is thus substantial, but it takes some time for the full effect to be felt.

The initial Polity index is always positive, significant and stable at around 0.65. The three story variables tell a consistent story: *Oil* is always negative, and, as soon as there are more than one observations, also significant and stable. *OW* is mostly significant, and then always positive and reasonably stable. The least convincing of the three variables is *Mu*. It applies to the last two periods only, where it is negative and mostly significant.

Table 15.3   OLS cross-country estimates for each 20-year period, and stacked (including only initial Polity and income)

Explaining av polity Π_t^{20}	(1)	(2)	(3)	(4)	(5)	(6) Stacked
	Cross-country estimate for 20-year periods					
	1900–20	1921–40	1941–60	1961–80	1981–00	
Constant	−10.16	−14.28	−23.01	−12.92	−10.20	−12.75
	(−1.1)	(−1.0)	(−1.5)	(−3.2)	(−3.7)	(−6.3)
y_{-1}, income init	1.43	1.80	3.12	**1.51**	1.64	1.75
	(1.1)	(1.0)	(1.5)	(2.9)	(4.7)	(6.6)
Π_{t-1}, initial	**0.67**	**0.65**	0.47	0.66	0.54	0.56
	(9.0)	(5.0)	(4.2)	(13.0)	(10.9)	(17.4)
Oil	−2.37	−0.54	−2.22	−1.78	**−5.11**	**−3.70**
	(−1.0)	(−0.2)	(−0.5)	(−1.7)	(−4.8)	(−4.9)
OW	1.62	2.01	2.06	**2.65**	−1.01	**1.63**
	(1.2)	(1.1)	(0.9)	(2.2)	(−0.8)	(2.7)
Mu	n.a.	n.a.	5.72	0.71	**−2.09**	−0.81
			(1.4)	(0.9)	(−2.8)	(−1.5)
R^2 adjusted	0.85	0.77	0.64	0.82	0.76	0.75
N	31	34	41	99	124	329
	Implied steady-state value of the effect of income					
y, long run	4.33	5.14	5.89	4.44	3.57	3.98

Note: See note to Table 15.2.

5   CORRECTIONS OF POTENTIAL PROBLEMS AND A REPLICATION

Models can suffer from many potential problems, but estimators have been developed to deal with many of these. A handful of these estimators are applied in Tables 15.7 and 15.8.

One such problem is residual autocorrelation – that is, the countries differ to the same side from one period to the next, by more than is removed by initial Polity. This is taken into account by the GLS estimate, 'SURE'. When Tables 15.3 and 15.6 are compared, it appears that nearly all *t*-ratios increase in Table 15.7 as they should, and this causes two more coefficients to become significant, but the basic picture is unchanged.

The SURE technique also allows us to test whether we are permitted to make the coefficients the same for all five periods as in the stacked regressions. It appears that we are doing so for all variables except *Mu*. We

Table 15.4   Stacked OLS cross-country estimates

	(1)	(2)	(3)	(4)	(5)	(6)	(7)	(8)
Constant	−12.14	−14.73	−10.28	−11.71	−13.15	−14.34	−9.94	−12.75
	(−6.1)	(−7.6)	(−5.1)	(−5.9)	(−6.5)	(−7.3)	(−4.9)	(−6.3)
y–1, income	1.66	2.04	1.37	1.64	1.79	2.00	1.36	1.75
init	(6.5)	(8.2)	(5.2)	(6.6)	(6.8)	(8.0)	(5.2)	(6.6)
Π_{t-1}, initial	0.65	0.60	0.60	0.62	0.57	0.59	0.58	0.56
	(21.6)	(20.3)	(18.8)	(19.8)	(18.29)	(19.3)	(17.5)	(17.4)
Oil		−4.33			−4.02	−4.01		−3.70
		(−6.0)			(−5.5)	(−5.3)		(−4.9)
OW			2.16		1.62		2.08	1.63
			(3.5)		(2.7)		(3.4)	(2.7)
Mu				−1.64		−0.80	−1.56	−0.81
				(−3.0)		(−1.5)	(−2.9)	(−1.5)
R^2 adjusted	0.72	0.74	0.72	0.72	0.75	0.74	0.73	0.75
N	329	329	329	329	329	329	329	329
			Implied	steady-state	value of	the effect	of income	
y, long run	4.74	5.10	3.43	4.32	4.16	4.88	3.24	3.98

Note: See Table 15.2. If the five periods are allowed different coefficients, the coefficient to income falls by 0.25, and the coefficient to Old West rises correspondingly. The R^2 of the regression increases by 0.02.

have also tied all coefficients at the same time. This tie is accepted, so the deviation of the coefficients to *Mu* is of little importance in the total picture.

It still changes the results very little; however, when we use the loss in R^2 compared to the untied (independent) regressions for each period, the loss is 0.02, 0.04, 0.06, 0.01 and 0.03, respectively. As is also obvious from the changes in the coefficients, it is only in Period 3 that the ties matter to the result. It is also here that one observation for one Muslim country gives a strange result in Table 15.3.

Table 15.8 demonstrates that we can correct the estimates for several additional problems. In order not to drown the chapter in very similar results, we report only re-estimates of the stacked model with all explanatory variables, using various estimators that each correct the regression for one potential problem. Each column is one such regression.

Column (1) is White's correction of the error terms of the regression for heteroscedasticity. The results are virtually unchanged, so heteroscedasticity is not a problem. The same correction has been computed for individual periods, but again, this has little effect.

Democracy across the world

Table 15.5   *Stacked OLS cross-country estimates (with no initial level for the Polity index)*

	(1)	(2)	(3)	(4)	(5)	(6)	(7)	(8)
Constant	−32.47	−34.57	−22.38	−28.27	−25.98	−31.31	−20.01	−23.51
	(−11.9)	(−13.7)	(−8.0)	(−10.7)	(−9.7)	(−12.2)	(−7.5)	(−8.7)
y_{-1}, income	4.24	4.60	2.79	3.83	3.35	4.24	2.60	3.10
init	(12.2)	(14.3)	(7.7)	(11.5)	(9.5)	(13.1)	(7.5)	(8.8)
Oil		−8.27			−6.58	−6.60		−5.18
		(−7.9)			(−6.5)	(−6.1)		(−5.0)
OW			6.76		5.47		6.01	5.21
			(8.1)		(6.8)		(7.5)	(6.6)
Mu				−5.05		−3.41	−4.19	−3.02
				(−6.6)		(−4.4)	(−5.9)	(−4.1)
R^2 adjusted	0.31	0.42	0.43	0.39	0.49	0.45	0.48	0.51
N	329	329	329	329	329	329	329	329
Equation (15.1)	The excess size of the implied steady-state coefficients from Table 15.4							
$(\gamma^{\infty}-\mu^{20})/\gamma^{\infty}$	11%	10%	19%	11%	20%	13%	20%	22%

Note: See Table 15.2.

Table 15.6   *Converting the effects to income into Polity points, and speed of adjustment*

	Coefficient	Size of gaps between incomes					
		1.5	2	3	5	10	50
		Polity points					
Medium term	1.6	0.6	1.1	1.8	2.6	3.7	6.3
Long run	4.0	1.6	2.8	4.4	6.4	9.2	15.6
		Speed of adjustment					
Years		20	40	60	80	100	120
Adjustment	0.6	60%	84%	94%	97%	99%	100%

Note: The relation between the variables is: $4=\gamma^{\infty}=\gamma^{20}/(1-\beta)=1.6/(1-0.6)$.

Column (2) takes the fact that Polity is truncated to lie between −10 and 10 into account. Table 15.1 showed that the corner solution (+10) occurs in no less than 61 of the 329 cases. OLS may thus be inappropriate. Therefore, the model is estimated using the Tobit estimator. The results increase the effect of income a little (as it should), but they are otherwise unchanged.

Table 15.7 SURE estimates for each 20-year period and tests for one coefficient tie

	(1)	(2)	(3)	(4)	(5)	(6) One coefficient tied		(7)
		Cross-country estimate for 20-year periods				Estimate		Wald-test
	1900–20	1921–40	1941–60	1961–80	1981–2000			
Constant	−11.93	−16.69	−23.77	−13.18	−10.43	**−11.74**		Accept
	(−1.4)	(−1.3)	(−1.7)	(−3.4)	(−3.9)	(−5.56)		
y_{-1}, income init	1.68	2.13	**3.22**	**1.54**	**1.67**	**1.66**		Accept
	(1.5)	(1.2)	(1.7)	(3.2)	(4.9)	(6.2)		
Π_{t-1}, initial	**0.66**	**0.63**	**0.43**	**0.65**	**0.53**	**0.59**		Accept
	(9.7)	(5.32)	(4.2)	(13.2)	(10.9)	(20.4)		
Oil	−2.22	−0.69	−2.78	**−1.81**	**−5.13**	**−3.22**		Accept
	(−1.1)	(−0.2)	(−0.7)	(−1.8)	(−4.9)	(−4.7)		
OW	1.43	1.83	2.19	**2.75**	−0.91	**1.22**		Accept
	(1.2)	(1.7)	(1.0)	(2.3)	(−0.8)	(1.9)		
Mu	n.a.	n.a.	5.51	0.66	**−2.13**	−0.73		Reject
			(1.4)	(0.9)	(−3.0)	(−1.4)		
R^2 adj	0.87	0.79	0.64	0.81	0.76			
N	31	34	41	99	124			
	Implied steady-state value of the effect of income							
y, long run	4.94	5.76	5.65	4.40	3.55	4.05		

Note: Columns (1) to (5) allow coefficients to be different. Column (6) shows the key result from six regressions with one tied coefficient. The Wald-test examines whether the tie is accepted.

Table 15.8   Other estimates: White, Tobit and fixed effects for countries and 2SLS

	(1) White	(2) Tobit	(3a)	(3b)	(4) 2SLS
			Fixed effects		
Constant	−12.74	15.81	−28.47	−23.66	−7.92
	(−5.8)	(−6.1)	(−9.8)	(−3.2)	(2.7)
y_{-1}, income	1.75	2.20	3.35	2.94	1.19
init	(6.1)	(7.0)	(7.8)	(7.7)	(3.1)
Π_{t-1}, initial	0.56	0.63		0.25	0.56
	(14.6)	(16.9)		(4.4)	(12.0)
Oil	−3.70	−4.50	0.26	−1.03	−3.44
	(−5.7)	(−5.2)	(0.1)	(−0.4)	(3.9)
OW	1.63	3.78	n.a.	n.a.	1.69
	(3.2)	(4.8)			(2.6)
Mu	−0.81	−0.64	n.a.	n.a.	−1.14
	(−1.5)	(−1.1)			(1.8)
R^2 adj	0.76	0.24*	0.78	0.81	n.a.
N	329	329	293	293	233
	Implied steady-state value of the effect of income				
y, long run	3.98	5.95	(3.35)	3.92	2.70

Note: * Pseudo-R^2, not comparable.

Column (3) allows for country-specific fixed effects. We report panel estimates using the within-groups estimator.[3] Again, the conclusions are unaffected, though the persistence of democracy is lower, as is to be expected from the estimator used. Note that column (3) reports two regressions: (3a) includes fixed effects in the model, and (3b) replaces the initial Polity with fixed effects. It is obvious that the collinearity between the two variables that are accounting for path dependency is large. Also, the use of fixed effect for countries does not permit any constant binary dummy in the regression. We can keep in *Oil* as some countries change from 'non-oil' to 'oil' – however, it is just a couple, so the variable drops in fit.

Column (4) corrects for the potential endogeneity bias. This implies the loss of one cross-section, and it does reduce the size of the coefficient to log y from 1.75 to 1.19. We use the lagged value of initial GDP per capita as an instrument for initial GDP per capita. This reduction is almost significant, but it may be due to a changed sample. However, it does suggest that there is some reverse causality in the relation. The 2SLS regression has no impact on the remaining conclusions.

Finally it should be mentioned that we have replicated everything on the Gastil index for the available period; that is, 1972–2004 (see Paldam, 2005). Fortunately, the Gastil index has slightly less persistence, and for $T = 16$ we get two periods: Period 1 is 1973–88, with 1972 as the initial year. Period 2 is 1989–2004, with 1988 as the initial year. Data are available for 135 and 154 countries, respectively, so $N = 289$. With a conversion of the Gastil scale to the Polity scale (see Appendix 15A), all results also replicate nicely as regards size. The only small deviation from the results is that the variable *Oil* gives slightly weaker results in the Gastil data, while the *Mu* variable gives considerably stronger results. In the Gastil data, all coefficients to *Mu* are significant.

6 INTERPRETING THE RESULTS

The pattern found is simple and clear, and it is constant across the twentieth century. As we have only five variables, we shall go through their effects one by one.

The Polity index contains strong inertia. Political systems do not change very often. Also, countries have a history that matters in a fairly long time perspective. Two methods can be used to account for path dependency: the first is to use the initial level of the index as an explanatory variable, and the second is to use fixed effects for countries. The two methods try to do almost the same, so they have strong collinearity. If the first method is used, the Polity average has to span a considerable period to prevent a near unit root from destroying the regression. If the second method is used, we are unable to use explanatory variables that are constant, such as culture or 'old' history. We have found that in connection with the Polity index, a time unit of 20 years works. This time unit gives a coefficient to initial Polity of about 0.6, so the model can be estimated with reasonable precision.

Income is significant throughout, and gives a substantial effect when the full adjustment has taken place. The Grand Transition gives an increase of 30 to 40 times in income. This increases the Polity index by no less than 12–14 points. However, it is not income as such, but the Grand Transition that matters. The transition to democracy is thus part of the whole process of development, not just an effect of income change.

Another interesting calculation is based on Maddison's estimates of world gdp for the twentieth century: these say that world gdp has increased 4.8 times (that is, 1.6 percent per year) during the whole of the twentieth century. This corresponds to about 6 points on the index. Figure 15.1 shows that is precisely what has happened.

This is visible from the consistently negative sign to the *Oil* variable, and the substantial size of the estimated coefficient. Oil countries are 4 points less democratic than other countries. Countries that have been wealthy throughout the century are all 'Old West', and also democracy emerged in the West. We cannot separate the two historical facts, but we find that the *OW* variable is mostly significant, and when significant it is always positive. It adds 2 points on the Polity scale to be Old West.

We also get a negative effect of Islam, but it is somewhat unstable over time. The *Mu* variable interacts with both the *Oil* variable and the income variable. Muslim countries are only rich if they have oil. When we then include a variable, accounting for path dependency as the initial Polity score, the relation contains too much collinearity, and we are unable to sort out the independent effect of Islam. However, given that Islam is exogenous even in the time perspective of a century, it is reasonable to argue that Islam is causal, and income is more endogenous.

The fact that the data reject that the coefficient is stable gives us some hope that the present divergence between the political systems in the West and those of the Muslim world is transitory only. This brings us back to Figure 15.3, which shows the large divergence that has taken place over the last 50 years. There is, however, an optimistic kink for the last five years.

NOTES

* This chapter parallels Paldam (2007), which examines the Gastil index, and Borooah and Paldam (2007), who use a different technique on the Gastil index. Paldam (2005) replicates the results in this chapter as closely as possible to the Gastil index (converted to the polity scale). Many of the constructive comments we have received to the previous papers are reflected here.
1. Jensen and Paldam (2006) demonstrate how the two most successful models linking development aid to development react to fixed effects. One of the two disintegrates, while the other remains.
2. We could probably have chosen T as low as 15 and as high as 30, and still have reached virtually the same results, so we have used the secondary criterion that an integer should result, when T is divided into 100.
3. The estimator is biased for large N and fixed T for the case of the dynamic model, so our results are at best suggestive.

REFERENCES

Accmoglu, D., S. Johnson, J.B. Robinson and P. Yared (2005), 'Income and democracy', Working Paper, available from: http://econ-www.mit.edu/faculty/index.htm?prof_id=acemoglu&type=paper.
Borooah, V.K. and M. Paldam (2007), 'Why is the world short of democracy? A cross-country analysis of barriers to representative government', forthcoming in *European Journal of Political Economy*.

Jensen, P.S. and M. Paldam (2006), 'Can the new aid-growth models be replicated?', *Public Choice*, **127**, 147–75.

Lipset, S.M. (1959), 'Some social requisites of democracy: economic development and political legitimacy', *American Political Science Review*, **53**, 69–105.

Lipset, S.M. (1994), 'The social requisites of democracy revisited: 1993 Presidential Address', *American Sociological Review*, **59**, 1–22.

Maddison, A. (2003), *The World Economy: Historical Statistics*, Paris: Organization for Economic Cooperation and Development.

Paldam, M. (2005), 'Explaining the Gastil democracy index, using the Polity scale for comparison', Working Paper, School of Economics and Management, University of Aarhus, Denmark.

Paldam, M. (2007), 'The big pattern of democracy. A study of the Gastil Index', forthcoming in A. Marciano and J.-M. Josselin (eds), *Democracy, Freedom and Coercion: A Law and Economics Approach*, Cheltenham, UK and Northampton, MA, USA: Edward Elgar.

Przeworski, A., M.E. Alvarez, J.A. Cheibub and F. Limongi (2000), *Democracy and Development: Political Institutions and Well-Being in the World, 1950–1990*, Cambridge: Cambridge University Press.

APPENDIX 15A   THE RELATION BETWEEN THE GASTIL AND THE POLITY INDICES

The Gastil index from Freedom House is the index for the political system that is used by most economists, so it is worth comparing the two indices. The Gastil index goes from 1972 to 2003, and it is reversely scaled so that it rather measures an absence of democracy. Table 15A.1 gives the scales and an end point consistent conversion of the two. This chapter uses the Polity scale throughout for both Polity and Gastil indices.

Figure 15A.1 compares the average path for the period from 1972 to 2003 for the two indices, when the Gastil index is converted to the Polity scale. The figure shows that the two indices are closely related, though the Polity index is a bit more 'optimistic' than the Gastil index.

Table 15A.1   Comparing the scales of the two indices

Fix points	Polity, P	Gastil, G	Conversions
Full democracy	10	1	$P=(40-10G)/3$
Midway	0	4	$G=4-3P/10$
Full dictatorship	-10	7	

Note: While this conversion is fine at the end points, it is concave in-between, as the Polity index is more optimistic than the Gastil index, see Figure 15A.3 and Table 15A.2.

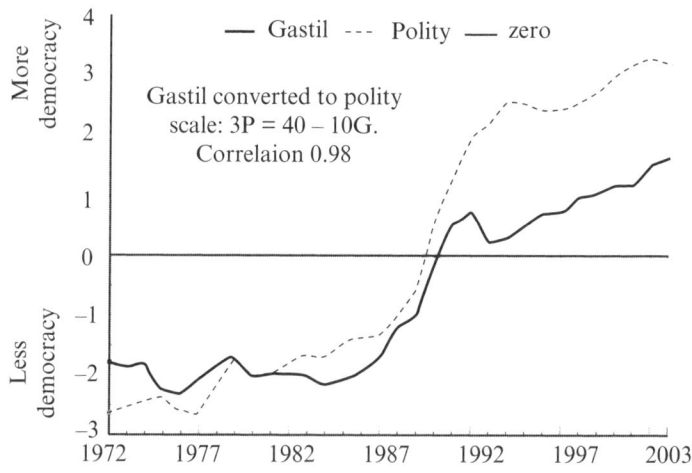

Figure 15A.1   Comparing the path of the averages of the Gastil and Polity indices

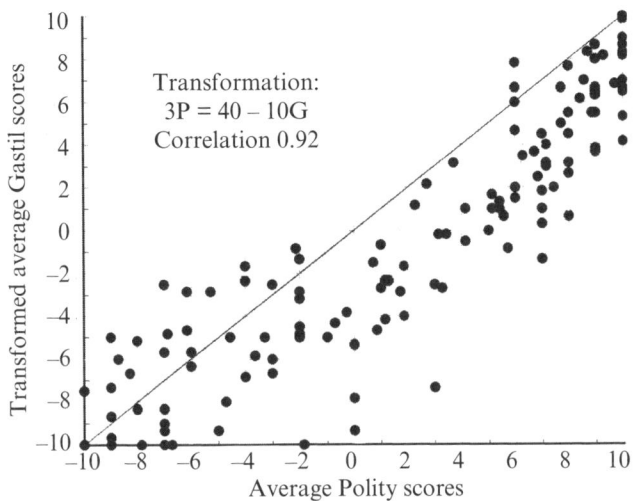

Figure 15A.2   Scatter of observations for the Gastil and Polity indices,
1994–2003

With regard to the individual countries, the two indices are also reasonably well correlated. This is demonstrated in Figure 15A.2, which covers the 1994–2003 period. That is, in the period after the breakup of USSR, where the number of countries covered by both indices is 152. It is at least 25 less for any other decade.

Figure 15A.2 shows that over most of the range, Polity scores are more optimistic, so that even when the end points are the same, the Polity index is on average 2.24 points higher.

Figure 15A.3 shows how the deviations between the two indices are distributed. The distribution is reasonably normal, but some countries deviate considerably.

It is interesting to note the most extreme outliers. Table 15A.2 gives the 10 most extreme deviations. It is unfortunate that large deviations are found for rather substantial countries where the facts are well-known. Perhaps it is understandable that a unique theocratic system such as Iran can generate a large difference in judgment, but it is puzzling that differences which are almost as large emerge for Russia, Indonesia and Turkey.

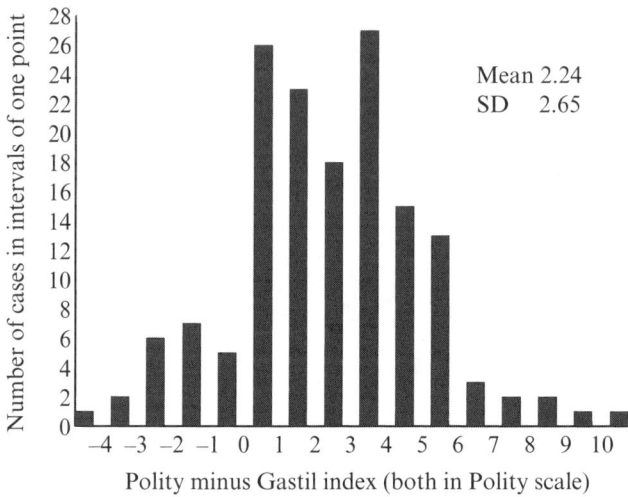

Figure 15A.3   Deviations between the two indices, 1994–2003

Table 15A.2   The most extreme deviations, based on averages, 1994–2003

	Polity	Gastil	Difference	In % of range
Indonesia	3.29	−2.67	5.95	30
Ukraine	7.00	1.00	6.00	30
Russia	5.71	−0.83	6.55	33
Colombia	7.00	0.33	6.67	33
Guatemala	8.00	0.67	7.33	37
Congo Kinshasa	0.00	−7.83	7.83	39
Turkmenistan	−1.86	−10.00	8.14	41
Turkey	7.00	−1.33	8.33	42
Somalia	0.00	−9.33	9.33	47
Iran	3.00	−7.33	10.33	52

Note: The range is the 20 points between perfect democracy (+ 10) and prefect
dictatorship of (−10).

16.   Democracy and low-income countries*

Arye L. Hillman

1   DEVELOPMENT SUCCESS AND FAILURE

Although collective decisions made by voting promise neither justice nor efficient outcomes,[1] democracies can be tempered by constitutions and, we would hope, by ethical norms. There is no controversy that life for a population at large in general is better in democracies than in autocracies. Is democracy, however, a necessity for economic development? There are few cases where development success has been achieved without the accountability of democratic institutions. The prominent case of successful economic development under autocracy is Singapore.[2] The state in Singapore placed paternalistic restrictions on individual behavior to implement what Tremewan (1994) has called 'social control', and also used industrial policy including directed credits to guide and regulate investment. Growth took place with high income equality and private property was protected. It was the mainstay of normative models outside of the public choice framework that government is a benevolent dictator. In Singapore, this was the reality. Paternalistic regulation was, however, quite extensive, and included restraints on individual choice such as banning of long hair on males and disallowing chewing gum. There can be debate about justifications for disallowing long hair on males (ostensibly to avoid sexual confusion but also to preempt public demonstration of teenage rebellion) and whether the discomfort of sitting on other people's chewed gum warrants a ban on chewing gum. The 'social control' was, however, directed at emphasizing education and self-discipline, and establishing a culture of respect for others, and self-reliance.

Singapore has been the exception rather than the rule for development outcomes in autocracies. A general theory of development success and failure however encompasses and explains all observations.[3] High growth was also achieved in Taiwan and South Korea with institutions of governance that at times had attributes more akin to autocracy than to democracy.[4] In China, high growth occurred without the competing political parties of democracy, and with considerable regional diversity and income inequality.

Development failure has been most extensive in autocracies in sub-Saharan Africa. The extensive development failure took place despite the efforts of the World Bank, the International Monetary Fund, and other donors to provide resources for economic development.[5] The development failure was against a background of corruption, both of the low-level bureaucratic type and also at higher levels of government.[6]

Throughout history, there have been 'good' kings and 'bad' kings. The good kings attract attention, expressed in a long heritage of folk songs that attest to how unusual the good kings were.[7] In economic analysis, 'good' and 'bad' autocratic rulers are distinguished by income appropriated for personal benefit: public spending under the bad ruler is reduced by personally appropriated budgetary revenue (Mueller, 2003). Or ways are found outside of the budget to use the authority of the state for personal benefit, through regulation or protection, or other means of creating and extracting rents.

Yet, if the ruler takes a share of the national income, why should the ruler not choose efficiency-enhancing policies that maximize the value of total income? That is, why does the ruler not act in the all-encompassing manner ascribed by Thomas Hobbes to his leviathan? With reasoning similar to Hobbes, McGuire and Olson (1996) proposed the principle of 'encompassing interest' as the basis for a prediction that autocratic rulers will seek efficiency. An autocrat as residual claimant or taking a share of national income should have an encompassing interest in internalizing all benefits from public spending and economic growth or development. Using other terminology (Olson, 2000), we can ask why autocratic rulers do not behave with extended time horizons of 'stationary bandits' but rather as 'roving bandits' who have short time horizons.

Institutions are in part endogenous (the part not embedded in culture). Since the autocrats control the society, why do they not, as was done in Singapore, choose the institutions that will increase national income? That is, why is Singapore not the model for autocratic rulers?

There are, moreover, reasons why autocracy can have advantages over democracy in the quest for economic growth. An autocratic ruler can apply his own time preference to intertemporal allocation and investment, and, being personally satiated in present consumption, might invest more than the population at large would want. There have been cases where present generations have been altogether sacrificed for the future, or at least for hopes for the future. Autocracy can also have an advantage over democracy in the quest for economic growth, because in a democracy policies that result in growth but distribute benefits unequally can be rejected by a majority of voters.[8]

These considerations suggest no reason for the observed general association between autocracy and low growth. Rather, on the contrary, in being free of the constraints of democracy, the autocratic ruler can override the preferences of the population and achieve higher growth than would be achieved in a democracy. Growth can provide unequal benefits that a majority of the electorate, if there were democracy, might reject.

Our question is thus, since the self-serving autocrat should have an interest in maximizing the size of national income or the tax base for government revenue from which he takes his share through personal appropriation, why have the efficient policies and high growth that are predictions of the theory of encompassing interest not been realized, outside the exception of Singapore? Or why have the predictions of the principle of encompassing interest in general failed to be realized?

2 CONTESTABILITY AND THE ENCOMPASSING INTEREST

Hobbes's leviathan rules without contestability by assumption, and by reason of the ruled who perceive their interest in avoiding exposing themselves to each other's base instincts. Regime stability and security are ensured, and resources are not used in contesting the position of the ruler. Within the monarchic systems that existed in most places for most of recorded human history, succession through divine right was similarly intended to set in place disincentives for quests to supplant the monarchs.

However, dynastic monarchies fall, as do autocratic regimes.[9] Rent-seeking theories explain how rents of privileged office attract resources, and minds and abilities, to supplanting incumbents (Tullock, 1989). Incumbents at the same time use abilities and resources in rent-protecting activities.[10]

If successfully challenged, deposed autocrats are rarely permitted to retire peacefully to their estates. Their wealth and their memories of past power pose a continued threat to the new incumbent. The ousted autocrat flees if he can, and places assets abroad in anticipation of the necessity of fleeing.[11]

The encompassing interest is thus compromised by the rents of office and the means of contestability of autocratic government. Loss of the personal authority of government is in general loss of all domestic wealth. The requisites of survival and the dire consequences of displacement tend to make autocrats unpleasant unkind people.

An incumbent can reduce the incentives of challengers by reducing the rents of office. McBride (2005) has proposed that policy 'reforms' in sub-Saharan African autocracies are explained by incumbents making challenges to the regime less attractive. The incentive for efficiency-enhancing policies predicted by the principle of encompassing interest is in that case self-preservation.

Threats to the regime under autocracy need not, however, result in responses that are efficiency enhancing. The consequence of contestability can be increased repression. Economic growth is then impeded because of the use of resources for repression, and the effect of repression on personal incentives of the repressed to be productive.[12]

We have a first reason for failure of the prediction of development success based on the encompassing interest. Attributes of contestability of autocracy expressed in institutions do not allow deposed autocratic rulers claims to property (and perhaps life).

Without appropriate institutions, discovering new natural resources can be socially undesirable.[13] The contestability of natural resource wealth can be accompanied by great cruelty, in particular when the members of contending sides are tribally or ethnically distinct and identifiable.

In oil autocracies, personal wealth of the rulers consists of proceeds from past extracted natural resources plus the oil wealth that waits to be extracted. Personal property rights to the extracted wealth are not secure in the face of a change of regime, and property rights to the non-extracted wealth are not all protected, should there be a regime change.

3   CORRUPTION

Reasons beyond contestability of government under autocracy explain the failure of the principle of encompassing interest. Before proceeding to these additional reasons, background regarding corruption is useful.

3.1   Endogenous Ideology

As noted, 'ideology' and institutions can be endogenous. Lee Kuan Yu in Singapore chose private property distributed among the population. Friedrich von Hayek pointed out (*The Road to Serfdom*, 1944) that autocracy requires the means of control over others. An autocratic ruler has reason to accept, with fervor and enthusiasm, an ideology that centralizes economic and political control. 'Socialism' was correspondingly widely accepted by proclamation as the path to development by the 'strong men' of post-colonial Africa, and also elsewhere in other locations where development failed.[14] Socialism is the most adept system for obtaining personal income from corruption (since all basic economic decisions in life, personal income, employment, accommodation and access to resources depend on decisions of other people). The principle of encompassing interest might predict avoidance of corruption as an 'endogenous' or discretionary policy, because of the incentives for rent extraction and rent seeking when corruption provides incomes that can be unproductively sought. Why then choose an economic system that facilitates corruption or theft within government? If bribes within different levels of government bureaucracy are informal substitutes for formal taxation,[15] why allow corruption rather than choosing private property and market incentives, and behaving as a 'leviathan' government to maximize formal tax receipts?[16]

3.2 Corruption and Income Distribution

The distinction between high- and low-level corruption is important. Bureaucratic or low-level corruption is disadvantageous for corrupt higher-level government officials. Yet low-level corruption is tolerated, or allowed or encouraged in autocratic societies because corruption is a form of income distribution whereby rulers increase incomes of others who are then supportive of the regime that allows their gains from corruption.[17]

A norm underlying the political culture is often that each member of the cabinet or council of ministers has a domain of control that is the source of personal income through the authority of the state. The motivation to achieve high-level office is to receive the financial rents that are associated with the office in government, and also the ego-rents. With such norms of political behavior, there are feelings of neither guilt nor shame in being corrupt. There is rather pride in success. The pride is demonstrated in ostentatious and conspicuous consumption that is evident to all as inconsistent with official incomes.

In such circumstances, corruption impedes the realization of the prediction of the principle of encompassing interest, because of the inhibiting effects of corruption on growth. The corruption sustains regime security, through loyalty of the beneficiaries of corruption.

3.3 Democracy and Corruption

In democracies, being a ruler does not usually ensure great personal wealth. There is a substantial middle class, and the people are in general well off, and in different degrees those unable to provide for themselves benefit from tax-financed welfare programs of the state. Democracies curtail corruption and political venality through the accountability of political competition and a free press. It is a sign of an honest society when politicians are in jail. In autocracies, with few exceptions, rulers are rich and the people are poor, and there is no substantial indigenous middle class. In autocracies, also, it is opposition leaders who are in jail.

Democracy does not ensure absence of corruption. Gains from corruption can be contested through political competition. For example, in Pakistan political competition became a contest between elitist family alignments with geographically concentrated support, and with at times dynastic succession (which has also been present in the democracy of neighboring India).[18] In another example of coexistence of democracy and corruption, democratic change of government, uncommon on the African continent, did not change the self-serving objectives in the government of Kenya. In some states of the former Soviet Union also, corruption coexisted with political competition.

The question is then not so much whether there are democratic institutions and political competition but rather whether the political culture allows personal material reward through government of office.[19]

3.4 Nietzschean Hierarchies

When corruption is pervasive and open, the terminology of 'corruption' seems inappropriate. Corruption suggests an illegal activity that is punished, if revealed, through the legal system. Income from corruption is therefore expected to be furtive and not ostentatiously displayed. Yet, as we have observed, ruling elites and high-level bureaucrats often take pride in ostentatious displays of the income from 'corruption'.

When everybody is corrupt, those who seek to displace corrupt incumbent rulers are themselves corrupt, and will continue to be corrupt if successful in replacing incumbents. In such circumstances, the state is not the instrument of the rule of law. The conditions are present of what I have termed a 'Nietzschean society' (Hillman, 2004a). In a Nietzschean society, personal behavior is devoid of ethics. Whether an act is moral or just is of no consequence for personal behavior, outcomes are determined solely by whether a person is strong or weak, according to what can be imposed on others and what can be resisted.

There is injustice in a Nietzschean hierarchy of strong and weak. Associated incentives also make the society inefficient. The incentive of the weak in a Nietzschean society to be productive is diminished by the likelihood that the strong will take their output. At the same time, the strong are distracted from productive activities by the likelihood that they will find weak people who have chosen to be productive, and whose output or income they can take. The weak have incentives to convince the strong that they are lazy, and that, if they do work, they do not produce very much. Limits on social mobility ensure that the children of the weak will also be weak. Parents then have incentives for cultural transmission of means whereby utility can be achieved through non-appropriable leisure activities.

The inefficiencies of a Nietzschean hierarchy are diminished if the strong adopt the time horizons of stationary bandits who have an interest in the survival of the prey into the future, or have an interest in efficiency because they take from the weak repeatedly over time.[20] The encompassing interest is to act as a stationary bandit. If the strong nonetheless face challenges from others who are strong, then the incentive is to behave as a roving bandit. Another source of compromise of the encompassing interest is thus through incentives not to behave as stationary bandits.

3.5 Nietzschean Transmission through Migration

The weak can escape through emigration, as refugees seeking respite from the strong. Nietzschean hierarchies then influence Western societies. A local society can confront an immigrant society that retains former norms of behavior including, as in the Nietzschean hierarchies that were left behind, diminished incentives for self-reliance and appeal to magnanimity of the strong, who are perceived as the wealthy high-income indigenous society. If, in the previous Nietzschean society from which emigration took place, there was a culture of reliance on episodes of magnanimity of the strong, in the new Western society, the substitute is the conception of the magnanimous welfare state. Perhaps there is a perception that all people, not just the immigrants, are beneficiaries of the magnanimity of the state, and that the state selectively disadvantages the immigrants – or the state may be perceived to disadvantage immigrants' children, who, although offered free-access education, do not succeed scholastically.

The Nietzschean hierarchy is transplanted to local neighborhoods where the physically strong, organized in groups to increase their strength, rule the streets and apartment complexes. Nietzschean principles of physical strong and weak come to apply to the form of protest. Crime or destruction of property is a Nietzschean act.

4 AID AND THE HOSTAGE PROBLEM

It is a natural inclination, and a moral obligation, to help people on whom misfortune has fallen. Aid can be given domestically in high-income countries to local and immigrant populations that have not been successful in integration into local labor markets. Aid is also given to 'poor countries'.

The local aid to immigrant populations can sustain dependence on the state. For foreign aid, the evidence is that aid has been ineffective overall in increasing incomes of poor people in poor countries.[21]

Foreign aid can have the same adverse consequences through rent
seeking as discovery of natural resources. Aid resources might be used for
investment and future consumption, if the rule of law were present to
provide recognized property rights and to make being strong and weak of
no consequence in the determination of beneficiaries of the aid. With
appropriation not recorded in the national accounts, there is no recorded
gain from aid. The aid disappears in unrecorded consumption, or through
capital flight. The aid at the same time decreases growth through the
resources used in contesting claims to aid resources.

The evidence is consistent with the prediction that we would make about
aid to the poor provided through the channel of Nietzschean government.
We expect the aid to be taken by the strong rather than finding its way to
the weak.

There is an associated a hostage problem (Hillman, 2002). The poor (or
weak) are hostages, held by the strong who control the distributional channels of government. The poor are kept poor, so that aid resources provided
for the poor will continue.

We might view appropriation of aid as a tax imposed by the strong on
the aid agencies seeking to help the weak. The international aid agencies
have displayed a willingness to pay the tax. In some cases, the value of the
tax has been computed. It was a claim of the successor to the Suharto government in Indonesia that the tax should be deducted from the debt owed
to the World Bank, on the grounds that the tax (or ransom) was knowingly
paid by the World Bank to the former ruling family and was therefore not
part of the state debt.

'Shocks' can upset development intentions. Van de Walle (2001) concludes from a detailed study of policy implementation in Africa that shocks
have been endogenously contrived by governments so as to maintain the
need for foreign aid and to avoid the continuation of obliged 'reforms' that
were underway before the shock occurred. The poor remain hostages, and
pointing out the shocks is the means of explaining why aid resources have
been ineffective.[22]

Aid of course reaches beneficiaries, in particular when there is close on-
the-ground monitoring of project aid.[23] The Nietzschean strong cannot
take all the aid and expect more aid to be forthcoming.

The hostage problem requires corruption to preempt the poor becoming
self-reliant. There are also direct benefits of corruption, through appropriation of funds for the new projects financed through aid.

The poor as hostages also preempt the growth of a middle class. The
principle of encompassing interest predicts productive investment in infra-
structure and in human capital of the population through health care and
education. The foundations for a middle class would then be put in place.

The middle class would demand political accountability through democratic institutions. Fear of a middle class is therefore an impediment to the realization of the predictions of growth and development based on the 'encompassing interest'.[24]

5 EDUCATION

There is a case based on self-interest of the rich to finance the education of the children of the poor. By being made self-reliant, the children of the poor will in the future contribute to budgetary revenue rather than require welfare payments (Hillman, 2003, ch. 5). Hence, although public education can be inadequate compared to exclusive private schools, there is in general intent in democracies of providing quality education in government schools. Because of the links among education, economic development, the middle class and democracy, the same incentives to provide universal quality education are not present for the rulers of poor countries. Again, the principles of encompassing interest fails.

5.1 Self-financed Education

In different instances, parents in poor countries seek to self-finance quality education for their children. The parents respond to an absent or inadequate government school system by paying school fees.[25] The fees might consist of payment in kind, such as food for the teacher or assistance in maintenance of the school.

Whether parents pay to educate their children depends on demand as well as supply considerations. The supply side is expressed in whether quality government-provided free-access education is available. Willingness to pay for private education also depends on the demand for education, reflected in the evaluation of the benefits of the alternative of child labor. Child labor should, of course, be illegal but is another aspect of failure to provide pre-conditions for development in poor countries.

Demand for education differs for boys and girls. There is a gender bias against girls in many poor countries. Also, girls and sometimes children more generally do not attend school because of the need to care for parents with AIDS, or to care for orphaned siblings.

Where the government has failed to provide quality schooling and the demand is present, payment of user prices or school fees is a means of providing children with an education, and circumventing the government disincentives, or reluctance, or lack of means (since past education policies will have produced poor teachers) to provide quality free-access education.

We find expressions of opposition to private payment for education by poor families in poor countries. Oxfam, one of the more prominent non-governmental organizations, has for example taken the position that poor parents in poor countries should not be permitted to pay privately for the education of their children because education is the responsibility of the government. A market option for education is thereby denied poor families (but not rich families). With autocratic governments not providing quality education, denial of the market option is denial of educational opportunities for children of poor families.

5.2 Social Mobility and Education

Social mobility affects demand for education. Parents perceive little gain from investing in the education of their children, if the education that their children receive is not accompanied by social mobility. The objective of sustaining dominance of the ruler however stands in the way of social mobility. A Nietzschean hierarchy of course impedes social mobility.

5.3 The Content of Education

The content of education also affects economic development. Education that is confined to rote learning of dogma does not provide the attitudes, skills and receptiveness to new ideas and technology required for economic development. Where the government has failed to provide quality free-access education, non-government alternatives do not necessarily provide the requisites for economic development. If children are taught that their beliefs and ways are superior by divine authority, that successes in this world that are due to them have been usurped by others, and that there are rewards from retribution in this world provided in the next world and this is believed, we should not expect successful economic development.

5.4 Skilled Emigration

We have previously noted the consequences of migration of unskilled populations to Western countries. Emigration of skilled people from poor countries is often lamented as disadvantageous for development. It has been noted that returns to human capital in richer foreign countries provide the incentive for investment in education, where possible, in poor countries with little internal social mobility. The 'brain drain' is then beneficial for the people whose education allows legal emigration as skilled self-reliant persons.[26] The autocratic rulers, for whom the presence of an educated population threatens regime stability, also benefit.

6 KNOWLEDGE AND GROWTH

There is reverse causality. Education increases income but also demand for education increases with income. As income increases, the returns to education increase, and learning externalities underlie further growth and increased income.[27] The process of endogenous growth based on education cannot begin when the incentives of government under autocracy are to impede rather than to promote quality education among the population.

Lack of quality formal education prevents technological advances from entering production processes. Transmission of technological change and knowledge is a personalized process, through people learning new ideas and understanding new processes. In the absence of necessary basic educational foundations, the population is not prepared for acquisition and application of advanced new knowledge. Evidence confirms that countries with poor formal education have low incomes and low growth (see Easterlin, 2004).

The conduit for knowledge can be the technical assistance of aid programs. However, aid programs often do not survive the departure of the foreign experts.

Knowledge can also arrive through expatriates who are needed because of the unavailability of local people with requisite knowledge or training. Where basic formal education remains lacking, local people cannot be trained to replace the expatriates.

The expatriates are in general not a threat to the regime. Still, in other cases, when if they stay long enough, or their families arrived generations previously, expatriates do come to be regarded as a threat to the regime, in particular if they continue to educate their children in private or foreign schools. The expatriates may then be expelled and their assets or land appropriated.

In Zimbabwe white farmers stayed in furtherance of a vision of a multi-cultural society where they, like other minority tribes, could be part of the broad society. They lost their farms under a claim of rectification of an unfair or unequal wealth distribution. The white farmers' properties appear in the main to have been taken by members of the ruling elite and not by poor people. At the same time as the white farmers were being evicted from their properties, the makeshift houses of the poor were being destroyed and the people dislocated, in a process termed a 'clean-up operation' but directed against tribal groups that had challenged, by democratic means, the rule of the presiding autocrat. The behavior is Nietzschean. The white farmers were evicted by force through the arrival of the strong on their properties. The homes of the defenseless dissident poor population were destroyed by force.

When the white farmers left their properties, production fell off considerably or ceased altogether. Why did the farms not continue to be productive under the new owners who ceased the farms? Those who appropriated the farms seemingly did not have the requisite knowledge. We might also wonder why the new owners through appropriation did not offer the white farmers contracts to stay on and manage the farms.

7 HEALTH CARE

Different models can be applied to the role of government in health care. There are nonetheless responsibilities of government that are independent of the model of health-care provision.[28] In democracies, governments sponsor and certify immunization of children against standard diseases and protect the public against diseases carried by animals. Contagious and infectious diseases are monitored and controlled as far as possible. In poor countries the government often fails to perform such basic functions. The ruling family and the family of the elites may have access to good personal health care (if required, through evacuation), although they also succumb when public health policy has failed. AIDS, TB and malaria take their toll at all levels of society.

In contradiction to all scientific evidence, a government in Africa declared that HIV is not the proven antecedent to AIDS. Medications against AIDS provided at reduced prices to governments of poor countries have been found re-exported to richer countries. There are dire consequences for young girls in a Nietzschean society when men believe that sexual relations with a virgin will cure them of AIDS.

Malaria is a scourge in some poor countries. In Mozambique, BHP-Billiton, a private publicly traded corporation, eliminated malaria in the region where an investment project is located. Why did the government, which has responsibility for public health, not succeed in eliminating malaria with the external assistance available, while a private foreign company succeeded in doing what the government should have done?

8 THE SUM OF THE PARTS: THE UNITED NATIONS

Consideration of the United Nations is a logical extension of the theme of encompassing interest and personal behavior of rulers and elites in low-income countries.[29] High-level corruption has been revealed at the United Nations. Of course, there should be no inference that everyone in the UN bureaucracy is corrupt. However, people bring with them personal behavioral norms predicated on the political culture of the country that sent them to be part of the United Nations bureaucracy. The composition of UN membership makes corruption within the United Nations bureaucracy predictable.[30] The sum of the parts is the whole. Corruption could only be absent in the United Nations, only if a Thomas-à-Becket effect could be relied upon to prevail.[31]

The World Bank and the International Monetary Fund, which allocate large sums of money, are also international agencies. Yet corruption is rare in these organizations.[32] We might speculate on the outcome, were disbursement of funds at the World Bank and the International Monetary Fund decided on the basis of the same collective decision rules and ethos of leadership as in the General Assembly or in the committees of the United Nations.

9 TERMINOLOGY

Terminology is important. One can refer to 'government' as an institution. 'People in government' acknowledges personal objectives. We speak of 'countries' as aggregates, because of the nation-state and the availability of national accounts and national statistics. However, we could not identify the hostage problem and other internal incentives that inhibit growth and development, if we were not to distinguish the poor or weak from the rich or strong within countries that are in per-capita terms on aggregate poor.

Poor countries were once called 'underdeveloped'. The terminology changed to 'less developed', and then to 'developing countries'. The word 'developing' suggests that improvement is taking place and that perhaps aid resources are being put to good use and should be increased. The terminology belies the instances of persisting development failure.

10 CONCLUSIONS

We have considered why the principle of encompassing interest fails. Conclusions also take us in a number of other directions. We could ask about expectations from more resources provided to the autocratic regimes of poor countries. Or we might ask what we might expect from debt forgiveness: Easterly (2001), after a review of the evidence, has noted a tendency for a 'steady-state' level of debt to be sustained, so, after an episode of debt forgiveness has taken place, the level of debt increases back to the constant long-run level, with in general no economic growth or improvement in the lives of the poor. The effect is the same as that of direct aid: since debt forgiveness is of course also aid. The question perhaps is not what we expect from more aid or debt forgiveness, but why aid and debt forgiveness have continued for autocratic regimes in poor countries.

We have observed that an autocratic ruler faces severe personal losses if displaced from office. Since successful rebellion rarely originates from the poor (see Tullock, 1987), regime security is an incentive to keep the poor in persistent poverty. Through the hostage problem, the continuation of aid and 'debt relief' provides another incentive to keep the poor in poverty. The benefits of preempting a middle class provide further incentives. Autocratic government therefore keeps people poor. Autocratic governments do not deliver quality education and do not provide quality health care. Roads may not be maintained because new aid-financed roads or road recon-struction will provide new opportunities for bribes to government officials, but also maintained roads facilitate the access to markets that increases incomes and initiates the development of a middle class. A middle class that is educated, in good health, and that pays substantial or the major part of taxation, will seek political participation in how taxes are spent and deci-sions of government are made.

In the end, we come unavoidably to the issue of regime change. Yet democ-racy, if achieved, is fragile when political support is regionally based or when ethnic and tribal identities determine the political party that voters support. Sustained democratic institutions require political competition based on competing political platforms of social and economic policies, and not voting outcomes based on a predetermined headcount determined by the size of tribal, ethnic or religious groups, where a minority knows in advance that it will be excluded from government and will in all likelihood be exploited through the 'majoritarian commons'. The complexity of introduc-ing and sustaining democracy can be overwhelming if the minority displaced from power had previously been an elite exploitative faction in the autocracy.

Avoidance of aggression and terror has been the basis for a case for democracy. Democratically elected governments do not initiate aggression and do not willingly harbor terrorists. There is also a case for democracy based on economic growth. The principle of encompassing interest does not give rise to economic growth, and does not result in broad increases in income for the population under autocracy. With the exception offered by Singapore, autocracy is corrupt, imposes a Nietzschean hierarchy, and keeps the broad population poor. High-income private-property egalitar-ian Singapore complicates our conclusions, but not unduly, when we note that the choice of institutions includes a choice between Nietzschean hier-archies and ethical civil societies.

We could proceed to compare China and India, one a single-party state and the other a democracy where government changes. Both have achieved high growth, however, with the beneficiaries selected parts of the population. That comparison is another topic that requires reference to the institutions of the two societies. As noted, in India democracy impeded growth because of electoral concern about the distribution of benefits of growth. In single-party China, the principle of encompassing interest appears to have applied. The future will tell if wide dispersion of the benefits of growth will be consistent with absence of the accountability of democracy.

NOTES

* Prepared for a conference on Problems of Democracy, at Universidad San Pablo Ceu, Madrid, December 1–3, 2005. I thank Chen Kang, Avichai Snir, Yariv Weltzman, Warren Young and participants at the conference for helpful comments.

1. For an introduction to problems of voting, see Hillman (2003, ch. 3).
2. Per capita income in Singapore in 2004 was around $27,000 and in excess of that of Italy.
3. In Singapore the 'outlier' behavior is tied to one person, Lee Kuan Yu. In Spain, King Juan Carlos is interesting in having voluntarily relinquished power after having been brought up by the Caudillo (Franco) with the intent of restoring the monarchy. When Franco died, his close associates turned to Juan Carlos as the intended heir and believed that they could retain the power that they had had under Franco. Once he became king, Juan Carlos introduced democracy to Spain.
4. See Paldam (2003).
5. On the low productivity in poor countries, see, for example, Hall and Jones (1999) and for the account of personal experiences as a World Bank development economist, see Easterly (2001).
6. See Tanzi (2000), and Abed and Gupta (2002). Corruption is in turn an expression of 'political culture', which determines the nature of the personal benefits from political office (Hillman and Swank, 2000). In democracies the benefits principally take the form of 'ego-rents' (that is, the personal satisfaction of partaking in political decisions and holding office within the institutions of the state). In autocracies, the ego-rents are supplemented by personal income and personal wealth from corruption (Aidt, 2003).
7. For the case of good king Wenceslas, for example, see www.songpeddler.com/Georgecat/GoodKingWenceslas_GSkworcow.asp.
8. See Acemoglu and Robinson (2000). An example is the outcome of elections in India in 2005 where a prior opposition party with more populist appeal defeated a government that had presided over high growth.
9. In some autocracies (North Korea, Syria, and various states in Africa) we have seen elements of dynastic rule (which we also observe in some democracies). Dynastic elements are also present in Singapore.
10. In the former Soviet system where personal benefits and personal misfortune were personally designated, a ruler such as Stalin could survive through 'purges' that from time to time systematically eliminated from contention (and from life) those seeking to position themselves to challenge the ruler's incumbency.
11. In the case of a true socialist system, domestic private assets cannot at all be accumulated.
12. Bar-El (2006) formulates a decision problem where the autocrat rationally considers how to assign resources to self-consumption, to improving the well-being of the population and so increasing popularity to reduce support for an opposition, and resources for repressing the opposition.
13. There are exceptions in countries that defy regional norms, such as Botswana.
14. On the 'strong' men of Africa, see Rowley (2000). We shall presently consider consequences of Nietzschean societies where roles are defined by 'strong' and 'weak'.

15. On corruption more generally as a form of taxation, see Shleifer and Vishny (1993).
16. In the case of Singapore the government as residual claimant to taxes was not corrupt. Anti-corruption policies in Singapore introduced in the 1990s included efficiency wages, intended to attract the best and the brightest to the public sector. ('Efficiency wages' refer to high wages that are paid as an incentive to retain the position that provides the wages; the 'efficiency-wage hypothesis' formally explains unemployment as due to Nash equilibrium wages paid by employers in excess of competitive market-clearing wages, to provide employed workers with disincentives to shirk or apply low effort.) Economic theories of 'yardstick competition' propose that neighboring jurisdictions influence the choice of institutions and the behavior of local politicians (for an overview see Hillman, 2003, ch. 9). Political competition was absent in the region when Singapore was achieving its initial economic progress. In neighboring countries, governments were corrupt and the mass of the population remained poor.
17. We can recall the admonition of the late Mobuto Sese Seko, former president of Zaire (now once more the Congo), that 'everyone can steal, but no one should steal too much'.
18. Among the benefits of having been under British colonial rule was the intent of the British to leave behind democratic institutions. The intent was not realized everywhere. Success in sustaining democracy seems, for some reason or other, correlated (albeit not perfectly) with the popularity of the game of cricket. Good cricketing nations have been democratic, while the other post-colonial states, principally in sub-Saharan Africa, were not.
19. Political liberalization when a culture of rent seeking is sustained increases social losses from incentives for unproductive activity. There is increased unproductive competition. See Hillman and Ursprung (2000).
20. For elaboration, see Hillman (2004a).
21. For reviews of the empirical evidence, see Doucouliagos and Paldam (2006).
22. See also Chauvet (2002) on the relation between instability and donor aid responses.
23. When the monitors go home, projects providing benefits to the poor are, however, often not sustained.
24. See Welzman (2005). If the middle class succeeds in introducing democracy, the franchise in general becomes universal and all citizens vote. Mueller and Stratmann (2003) test John Stuart Mill's hypothesis that participation of uneducated or poor parts of the population in the process of collective decision making will reduce the quality of policies and find that, contrary to Mill's concern, political participation of the poor improves outcomes as measured by economic growth.
25. See Hillman and Jenkner (2004).
26. See Beine et al. (2001).
27. As described in theories of endogenous growth, more educated people are more productive when working with other more educated people. Over time the population becomes more productive as better teachers produce better students who in turn become even better teachers.
28. See Hillman (2003, ch. 10).
29. For more detailed discussion, see Hillman (2004b).
30. Also perhaps predictable is the failure to intervene in the Khmer Rouge killing fields, the exit of the United Nations force from Rwanda to allow an unencumbered genocide to proceed, the procrastination that left the indigenous people in the region of Darfur to a plight of murder and rape by agents of the government of Sudan, and more that can be listed, including participation of UN forces in rape.
31. On the Thomas-à-Becket effect, see Hillman (2003, ch. 3). The idea is that respect for the office changes prior principles of behavior of incumbents. So, for example, when King Henry III of England appointed his friend Thomas à Becket to be Archbishop of Canterbury, he expected support from the archbishop. However, Thomas à Becket elevated himself, and changed himself, to abide by the higher principles of the position that he was given to occupy. In the end the king was rid of the 'meddlesome priest'. The Thomas-à-Becket effect is often applied to explain why central bankers can be trusted to behave benevolently, or why government bureaucrats may not follow personal optimizing behavior of budget maximization.

32. When evaluations are made of World Bank or International Monetary Fund policies, corruption is not an issue.

REFERENCES

Abed, George T. and Sanjeev Gupta (eds) (2002), *Governance, Corruption, and Economic Performance*, International Monetary Fund, Washington, DC.

Acemoglu, Daron and James A. Robinson (2000), 'Political losers as a barrier to economic development', *American Economic Review Papers and Proceedings*, **90**, 126–30.

Aidt, Toke (2003), 'Economic analysis of corruption: a survey', *Economic Journal*, **113**, F632–F652.

Bar-El, Ronen (2006), 'Dictators, development, and the realist school of foreign policy', Chapter 3 in 'Three essays on institutions and Public Finance', PhD thesis in economics, Bar-Ilan University, Tel Aviv.

Beine, M., F. Docquier and H. Rapoport (2001), 'Brain drain and economic growth: theory and evidence', *Journal of Development Economics*, **64**, 275–89.

Chauvet, Lisa (2002), 'Socio-political instability and the allocation of international aid by donors', *European Journal of Political Economy*, **19**, 33–59.

Doucouliagos, Hristos and Martin Paldam (2006), 'The aid effectiveness literature: the sad result of 40 years of research', *Kyklos*, **59**, 227–54.

Easterlin, Richard (2004), 'Why isn't the whole world developed?', in Richard Easterlin, *The Reluctant Economist*, Cambridge University Press, Cambridge, pp. 57–73.

Easterly, William (2001), *The Elusive Quest for Growth: Economists Adventures and Misadventures in the Tropics*, MIT Press, Cambridge, MA.

Hall, Robert E. and Charles I. Jones (1999), 'Why do some countries produce so much more output per worker than others?', *Quarterly Journal of Economics*, **114**, 83–116.

Hayek, Friedrich von (1944 [1972]), *The Road to Serfdom*, University of Chicago Press, Chicago.

Hillman, Arye L. (2002), 'The World Bank and the persistence of poverty in poor countries', *European Journal of Political Economy*, **18**, 783–95.

Hillman, Arye L. (2003), *Public Finance and Public Policy: Responsibilities and Limitations of Government*, Cambridge University Press, Cambridge and New York.

Hillman, Arye L. (2004a), 'Nietzschean development failures', *Public Choice*, **119**, 263–80.

Hillman, Arye L. (2004b), 'International collective decision making: the case of the United Nations', Plenary presentation, Mont Pellerin Society, Salt Lake City, August 15–20.

Hillman, Arye L. and Eva Jenkner (2004), 'User payments for basic education in low-income countries', in Sanjeev Gupta, Benedict Clements and Gabriela Inchauste (eds), *Helping Countries Develop: The Role of Fiscal Policy*, International Monetary Fund, Washington, DC, pp. 233–64. Non-technical version published as: 'How to pay for basic education: poor children in poor countries', *Economic Issues*, **33**, 2004, International Monetary Fund, Washington, DC.

Hillman, Arye L. and Otto Swank (2000), 'Why political culture should be in the lexicon of economics', *European Journal of Political Economy*, **16**, 1–4.

Hillman, Arye L. and Heinrich W. Ursprung (2000), 'Political culture and economic decline', *European Journal of Political Economy*, **16**, 189–213.

McBride Michael (2005), 'Crises, coups, and regime persistence in sub-Saharan Africa', *European Journal of Political Economy*, **21**, 688–737.

McGuire, Martin and Mancur Olson (1996), 'The economics of autocracy and majority rule: the invisible hand and the use of force', *Journal of Economic Literature*, **34**, 72–96.

Mueller, Dennis (2003), *Public Choice III*, Cambridge University Press, Cambridge and New York.

Mueller, Dennis and Thomas Stratmann (2003), 'The economic effects of democratic participation', *Journal of Public Economics*, **87**, 2129–55.

Olson, Mancur (2000), *Power and Prosperity: Outgrowing Communist and Capitalist Dictatorship*, Basic Books, New York.

Paldam, Martin (2003), 'Economic freedom and the success of the Asian tigers: an essay on controversy', *European Journal of Political Economy*, **19**, 453–77.

Rowley, Charles K. (2000), 'Political culture and economic performance in sub-Saharan Africa', *European Journal of Political Economy*, **16**, 133–58.

Shleifer, Andrei and Robert W. Vishny (1993), 'Corruption', *Quarterly Journal of Economics*, **108**, 599–617.

Tanzi, Vito (2000), *Policies, Institutions, and the Dark Side of Economics*, Edward Elgar, Cheltenham, UK and Northampton, MA, USA.

Tremewan, Christopher (1994), *The Political Economy of Social Control in Singapore*, Macmillan, London.

Tullock, Gordon (1987), *Autocracy*, Martinus Nijhoff, Dordrecht.

Tullock, Gordon (1989), *The Economics of Special Privilege and Rent Seeking*, Kluwer, Boston, MA and Dordrecht.

van de Walle, Nicolas (2001), *African Economies and the Politics of Permanent Crisis, 1979–1999*, Cambridge University Press, Cambridge and New York.

Welzman, Yariv (2005), 'Corruption, poverty and political exclusion', Paper presented at Silvaplana workshop on Political Economy, Silvaplana, July 14–17.

PART V

Fiscal Issues and Democracy

17. A theory of the democratic fiscal constitution

Francesco Forte and Domenico D'Amico

1 INTRODUCTION

1.1 Rise and Fall of the Benefit Principle

Adam Smith in *The Wealth of Nations*[1] outlined what one may call a 'fiscal constitution' stating 'the four following maxims with regard to taxes in general':

I. The subjects of every state ought to contribute towards the support of government, as nearly as possible, in proportion to their respective abilities; that is, in proportion to the revenue which they respectively enjoy under the protection of the state . . .

II. The tax which each individual is bound to pay ought to be certain, and not arbitrary . . .

III. Every tax ought to be levied at the time, or in the manner, in which it is most likely to be convenient for the contributor to pay it . . .

IV. Every tax ought to be so contrived as both to take out and to keep out of the pockets of the people as little as possible over and above what it brings into the public treasury of the state.

As for the relation between taxes and public goods, a distinction is made[2] between expenses of general benefit to the whole society and the 'local or provincial expenses of which the benefit is local or provincial'. The latter 'ought to be defrayed by a local or provincial revenue'. Smith further distinguished the 'expense of defending the society, and that of supporting the dignity of the chief magistrate' on the one hand, and the expenses 'of the administration of justice . . . of maintaining good roads and communications . . . of the institutions for education and religious instruction' on the other. For the former, the general contribution of the whole society is required: 'all the different members contributing, as nearly as possible, in proportion to their respective abilities'. The latter, in Smith's view, are 'most immediately and directly beneficial' to particular sets of persons, and so could properly be defrayed by fees, tolls or charges.

As one can see, the Smithian 'ability to pay' is defined both in terms of the income of taxpayers and as counterpart of the benefits from the government. But for general expenditures, the benefit principle does not appear so much a criterion for distributing the tax burden as a justification of the tax power. Drawing from this approach, the ability-to-pay principle has subsequently been developed as a criterion of fiscal justice in utilitarian terms and/or perfected as a Benthamite criterion of collective welfare maximization.

And the other Smithian principles of fiscal constitution have been elaborated merely as guarantees given by the state to the citizens, to limit its fiscal powers, not to allow democratic choices in fiscal matters. The modern fiscal constitutions, the Maastricht Treaty included, also appear to have been built with the same view.

1.2 Rebirth of the Benefit Principle in Neoclassical Public Economics and Public Choice

Yet the problem of a consistent theory of the economics of public finance in the general theory of economic equilibrium and dynamics, for a democratic market economy system, remains, both at the positive and at the normative level. Austrian, Swedish and Italian theories of fiscal economy from Sax and Von Wieser to Wicksell to De Viti De Marco and Einaudi have considered taxes, in a democratic market economy, as the subjective tax price for public goods, under the general theory of economic value.[3] The public choice school has renewed this approach, making it more sophisticated and general, and also introducing the seminal field of research of the economics of constitutions.[4] In addition, in the contemporary public finance textbooks, we can find the Lindahl–Samuelson principle that public goods should be supplied until, for each individual, the marginal rate of substitution between private and public goods is equal to his or her personal rate of transformation, that is, to his or her share of their marginal cost.[5] Can the subjective benefit principle assumed in a public choice approach and the Lindahl–Samuelson equation be translated in terms of democratic fiscal constitution rules? Many economists believe that such formulas are merely abstract textbook benchmarks.

1.3 Outline of the Chapter

This chapter aims to show that the formulas may become relevant, in a democracy with market economy, by means of appropriate rules of fiscal constitution. The fiscal constitution should then be viewed not as a mere set of limits to fiscal power but as a set of rules to make operational the subjective law of value in fiscal economy.

The chapter is organized as follows. Section 2 contains an overview of the linkages among neoclassic theory of fiscal economics, public choice and constitutional economics. Section 3, after an examination of Buchanan's constitutional approach to fiscal matters, outlines the constitutional fiscal rules based on the individual choice principle. In Sections 2.1 and 2.2, focusing on the concept of a *democratic* constitution, we question the relevance of the notion of a social welfare function in fiscal matters and what may be called the 'deceptive individualism' of social choice theory with its neglect of institutions. Sections 2.3–5, outlining the neoclassical contributions to fiscal choice theory before Buchanan and Tullock, show that their focus on *ordinary* political decision making hinders the relevance of the subjective benefit principle in fiscal choices; and Section 2.6 deals with the promising steps in this direction made by Buchanan and Tullock's constitutional approach.

In Section 3.1, we show the limits of the constructivist contractarian approach. Section 3.2 then argues for a view of fiscal constitutions as sets of focal conventions transformed in binding rules. With this view, Sections 3.3–9 present basic principles of a fiscal constitution to allow, in the fiscal process, the actual realization of the subjective benefit principle as assumed in a public choice approach and the Lindahl–Samuelson equation – which, therefore, may not be viewed as mere textbook benchmarks. They will provide the institutional frame for applying the general law of economic value in public economy and for sharing the net gains from the supply of public goods, in a way consistent with that law.[6] Section 4 concludes.

2 TAXES AS PRICES OF PUBLIC GOODS IN THE NEOCLASSICAL THEORY, PUBLIC CHOICE AND FISCAL CONSTITUTIONS

2.1 Preliminary Clarifications

The concept of an economic (and fiscal) constitution, as a core of principles on which to build the rules of the game of a democratic society, is a recent innovation.[7] Yet all orderly economies do have a constitution: indeed, a constitution consists of the basic set of institutions governing the political and social interactions among citizens – and even more so in a democratic society recognizing property rights and the market; where the economic–fiscal constitution appears as a (strong) coordination device intended to promote social cooperation and to avoid harmful situations of the prisoner's dilemma type.

But the *binding rules* of a democratic economic constitution appear as an incomplete long-term contract.[8] Our limited rationality, the difficulty of general agreement, the anticipation of opportunistic behaviour and the irrevocability of commitments all contribute to increase the costs of collective decisions *ex ante* and *ex post*. Hence, the constitutions are mostly sets of 'meta-rules',[9] rules to produce other more detailed rules. These rules with constitutional ranking, that is, superior to and constraining ordinary legislation, need not be included in a constitutional charter. Norms with constitutional ranking are found in the common law and in the civil law, in the budgetary law, in the regulations of representative assemblies, in their common practice and, of course, in the cases decided by the High Court.

2.2   Criticism of Social Choice Theory: 'Deceptive Individualism' and Neglect of Institutional Detail

In the second half of the twentieth century, theoretical welfare economics, in search of social 'bliss', focused on the idea of a social welfare function that economists or planners were presumed to derive from hypothetical judgements about how to compare and weigh individual utilities.[10] An all-embracing view of end-states was presupposed, aimed at maximizing the total, by adding together the utilities of the various citizens.[11] In a democratic development of this approach – that is, social choice theory – the social welfare function is supposedly deduced from citizens' individual preferences, in an institutional vacuum. No consideration is given to the fact that, in a free society, such end-state social welfare functions, unlike the individual and collective demand curves for the market, do not have an empirical counterpart. These social welfare functions, even if presented as democratic, cannot be assumed to effectively represent consensual individual choices. They are hypothetical tools of analysis employed by economists. Methodologically, the all-embracing social choice social welfare function, even if conceived as purely individualistic, appears to be an illegitimate concession to an unrealistic theory of unlimited rationality.[12]

However, it would be naive to maintain that the question is merely that of the limits of a methodology of scientific analysis. Indeed, social welfare functions and axiomatic social choice approaches have been instrumental to the rationalization of a paternalistic social welfare state. Here, the basic criterion of fiscal economy, sliding from the individualistic approach, rests on the value-loaded maxim 'from each according to his abilities, to each according to his needs'. In the background there is the figure of an omniscient and enlightened planner, supposedly charged by the majority to pursue a Benthamite happiness.[13]

2.3 Constitutions, Individual Choices and the Subjective Law of Value in Fiscal Economy

Since the nineteenth century, public economy has been seen in terms of *individual* choices. As for fiscal economy, the public choice democratic approach conceives the fiscal relationship between taxpayers and the state in terms of the *subjective* choice principle.[14] Fiscal choices are thus brought under the general law of economic value. The benefit principle, here, is viewed in a procedural subjective context. There may also be room for interdependent utilities, which allow for redistribution via its indirect benefits to the chooser. Freedom of choice in terms of economic value is the test for the proper functioning of the fiscal economy, and the same value test requires leaving to the market all the wants that can be satisfied by private choice. As for collective fiscal choices, voters/taxpayers should judge whether the marginal utility of the supply of public goods is equal to the marginal cost of the taxes paid by them and whether their ratio is equal to the ratio between the marginal utility of the goods purchased on the market and their respective prices. Thus, taxes are (or should be) the fiscal price of public goods, under the same economic laws of value that are at work in the market economy.

Such an approach necessarily requires a basic choice in terms of *democratic* values, that is, freedom of public choices; everybody has an *equal* voting right; a representative government, with institutions of *competitive* democracy, based on *extensive political liberties*, that functions satisfactorily according to the will of the voters. Furthermore, many organizational problems, particularly for fiscal matters, must be dealt with by proper institutions.

2.4 The Paradox of Democracy in Fiscal Matters

There is a crucial problem, however. If every citizen has one vote and wealth differs among them, as usually in a market economy, collective free choices produced by majority voting in the public sector and the individual free choices on the market will reflect different individual powers. Moreover, public expenditures are likely to grow beyond the individual utility of taxpayers.[15] Assuming that median voters with average income decide the result, one may argue that the allocative fiscal equilibrium will reflect the average voters' utility functions.[16] This implies exploitation.[17] Median voters may exploit either the rich or the poor depending on the winning coalition.[18]

The economic equilibrium may be partially restored by tax shifting, taking place immediately and through time. Furthermore, the violation of the law of economic value in public economy is not without sanctions, as a damaging disequilibrium in the economic system is generated.[19] The likely negative micro- and macroeconomic effects may be corrected by a reaction, via the competition between political parties.[20] However, such a restoration of the law of economic value in fiscal matters appears unsatisfactory: the desired solution is given *ex post* only through a painful equilibrium adjustment process. It is not certain, either: it may be hindered by organized interests and an unwieldy bureaucracy.

2.5 Inadequacy of the Wicksellian Solution

A possible solution might appear to be given by Knut Wicksell's fiscal choices under (quasi) unanimity.[21] Here the representatives of voters/taxpayers must agree on a combined public spending–tax proposal that satisfies (nearly) all of them. Therefore, the individual marginal benefit of public goods will generally be equal to the individual marginal burden of taxes, as subjectively assessed by each taxpayer (actually by their representatives). Misallocation by forced redistribution seems to be expelled from the picture, along with all the social issues.[22] Even so, however, as Wicksell himself recognized, unanimity is clearly not appropriate 'when the expenditure is a necessary result of a previously existing obligation and cannot, therefore, be refused'.[23] A dilemma thus arises. The quasi-unanimity rule, by nature, is a time-consuming voting system, but such a scheme would require it to be applied to the budgetary process; that is, in the very circumstances when a choice must be made within a given short time span.

2.6 Decision Making at the Constitutional Level: Towards a Solution of the Difficulties

The way out of the above dilemma is offered by Buchanan and Tullock,[24] who construed the collective political decision making as a 'two-stage' process. In the first stage a democratic constitutional contract sets the basic permanent rules for a free society. The proper voting rule appears to be (quasi) unanimity. Later choices may then be made through a less exacting voting procedure, in so far as it is constrained by the substantive rules of the constitutional contract. Politics, at the constitutional stage, is a positive-sum game, in which long-lasting rules and institutions are chosen under imperfect knowledge of the relevant future personal positions in society. They are therefore expected to be in the general interest. Furthermore, because of its characteristics, constitutional decision making is more resistant to rent-seeking activities than ordinary political processes, and this may help in preventing cumbersome regulations that limit competition.

Analytically, the combined consideration of exploitation and transaction costs in collective choice explains the different voting rules at the two stages, the constitutional and the post-constitutional. The two cost curves are inversely and directly related to the percentage of votes required to take collective action, respectively. For constitutional rules, transaction costs may not increase dramatically because of the delay in agreement, since the contract is not meant to provide for urgent matters. Furthermore, agreement is easier among the different constituents than among the ordinary chooser: due to the very long-run perspective of the decision making, representatives, at this stage, are under a veil of uncertainty about the personal situation of the people they are supposed to represent. They are unable to anticipate either their specific position in society or, therefore, their interests and preferences. Thus, many of them can be *assumed* to converge in favour of average interests. Exploitation costs of not fully agreed decisions, on the other hand, are quite high, since constitutional rules are expected to be everlasting, and quasi-unanimity follows. Note that the rules and institutions laid down in the constitution – if one interprets correctly the generalized positive-sum nature of the constitutional game – may include redistributive mechanisms, provided that they are believed to reduce the risks of all players.

In the post-constitutional stage, the production of rules gives more weight to transaction costs, that is, time efficiency. Implicitly, we have here the recognition of the need of hierarchy in social organization.[25] The weight of exploitation costs is less important, given the constitutional rules that limit the possibility of exploitation by taxation and regulation.

The main seminal innovation of the constitutional approach lies in replacing the misleading dichotomy between rules of choice for allocative and distributive matters[26] with the dichotomy between constitutional contract games and post-contract games played by different actors with their own different utility functions under different circumstances and voting rules.

Another positive consequence of the constitutional approach lies in the solution of Kenneth Arrow's paradox of majority voting.[27] At the constitutional level, because of the (quasi) unanimity rule, the practical relevance of the paradox vanishes. At the post-constitutional stage, where majority rule may be adopted, instability in public choices may be welcome. Indeed, it allows a continuum process of free choices, under the stability of the basic rules of the constitutional contract.[28]

3   A CONSTITUTIONAL BRIDGE BETWEEN THE SUBJECTIVE BENEFIT PRINCIPLE IN FISCAL CHOICE THEORY AND IN THE DEMOCRATIC MARKET ECONOMIES

3.1   Some Critical Remarks on Contractarianism and Constructivism

Per se, a social contract to exit from the brutish anarchic state does not imply universal voting rights and democratic consensus to a free society.[29] Dictatorship or government by a powerful oligarchy cannot be excluded at all.

Unanimity (possibly qualified so as to take account of exploitation and transaction costs) may be adopted for the constitutional rules only after recognition of important substantive general principles in terms of democratic meta-rules, as already hinted in Section 2.3. Behind the exploitation-costs function is the recognition of a market economy society based on extensive private property rights and freedom of enterprise. And behind the unanimity rule is the principle that everybody has the right and the responsibility for the pursuit of their own welfare, in a peaceful society based on individual free choices. Since a general consensus is required, unanimity entails that society is a *consensual* society, based on *cooperation.*

Thus several objections may be raised to a contractarian constructivist approach to the democratic (economic) constitution, starting without any agreed value.[30] Furthermore, the notion of a veil of uncertainty does not appear to be as operational as one could desire.[31] Constitutional disagreement might also arise out of knowledge-based divergences among individuals.[32]

Moreover, the duty to comply with the rules and institutions laid down in the constitution cannot rest on a 'putative' contract. Cooperation is a 'public good'. In the absence of effective external enforcement, each individual has a strong incentive to renege on the cooperative agreement in the hope of free riding on everyone else's efforts. Hence, the members of society are still in need of the 'assurance' that the constitutional contract will be respected. In anticipation of non-compliance, individuals might even judge the 'constitutional deal' unprofitable and deny their consent. The decisive argument for assuming agreement by the large majority, or the quasi-unanimity to the constitution, *ex post* is that compliance with the agreed-on constitution is in the individual interest of most people. Hence *mutuality* follows, as prescribed by the law of the sea, which includes an obligation of mutual aid in case of extreme need, that is, a sort of reciprocity game among a large number of persons.[33]

Furthermore, to ensure that the constitution works *ex post* in the general interest of a large majority of cases, one must assume that the constitutional contract is the result of rational choice under accurate information by 'founding fathers', endowed with full telescopic knowledge, refraining from opportunistic behaviour, despite the basic asymmetry of information that they enjoy.[34] This is barely realistic.[35]

3.2 Constitutions as Focal Conventions Transformed in Binding Rules

To the democratic (fiscal) constitution appears more appropriate a Humean point of view of constitutional rules as convention born in the society and commanding general, if not necessarily universal acceptance. Or, to put it in terms of the contemporary game theory 'focal points of agreement' transformed in binding rules. These rules must have passed a sort of 'spontaneous order' test of (quasi) unanimous consent, since they are agreeable to everyone.[36] In such a perspective, constitutional rules included in legal binding documents are still relevant, though they are mostly the formal recognition of conventions, which develop in a process of trial and error.[37] Some qualifications may be required when considering 'large numbers' settings. In such circumstances the rules are not grounded in everyone's rational expectation that they will be observed out of a common interest (in conformity with the strong Pareto criterion). Rather, they emerge gradually and because of the inconveniences normally arising from their transgression. However, while stability inheres in the idea that a constitutional convention is an equilibrium solution to a repeated game, Pareto optimality does not.[38] To be stable, a convention need not be the most preferred one either *ex ante* or *ex post*. The rules to be formalized in the (fiscal) constitution[39] get a (quasi) general consensus by 'piecemeal' recognition of their usefulness, and formal agreement in the *ex post* stage. Such a process of piecemeal formation and formalization of the fiscal constitution, necessarily resulting in an incomplete contract, implies, by nature, quasi-unanimity – not as a metaphor, but *as a test* for the formal recognition of constitutional rules.

Scholars will then have the task of distilling the likely (quasi) optimal focal rules, relating to taxes as fiscal prices, from the fiscal principles developed by different lines of thought, in different contexts, to promote different interests often hidden under the veil of thick fiscal illusions and Paretian derivations.[40]

3.3 Some New Light on the Subjective Benefit Principle as a Constitutional Principle

'Do we get value for money?' is a disturbing question. Because of the interests involved, resistance to the law of economic value in the fiscal economy, is rather strong. Therefore, any effort to render such a seemingly bookish principle operational, via rules with constitutional ranking, has wide scope and significance.

The first basic principle of a fiscal constitution based on the law of economic value is that taxation and public expenditure of aggregate general government should have a limit, because of their subsidiarity to the market economy. Where to set this limit may be controversial, but here is the dividing line between two possible constitutions for the fiscal economy, the public choice constitution and the paternalistic and/or 'dirigiste' one.

Some widely accepted fiscal rules, usually thought of as rules for sound fiscal policy, do have their rationale in the benefit principle of taxation. Typically, this is the case for two basic interdependent rules, required to implement the law of economic value in the fiscal economy in an intergenerational perspective. These rules are the principle that general government deficits should not exceed a given percentage of GDP, except in specific circumstances, and the related provision that these limited deficits can be admitted only for capital expenditures which benefit future generations – where the word 'benefit' is not unreasonable and provided that one cannot finance them by raising private funds.

Another rule of the same kind is that taxes should be universal, because 'everyone benefits from public expenditure'. Related to this is the principle that tax powers and universality in taxation, for any level of government, ought to be defined in terms of the benefit principle, that is, in relation to the persons and properties that benefit from the public expenditure of that level of government.

3.4   The Subjective Benefit Principle and Government Budgets

Other rules of the fiscal constitution, needed to enforce the law of subjective economic value in the fiscal economy, are also generally listed as principles of sound budget management, but they are rarely applied effectively. Such are the two interdependent rules requiring fiscal transparency and the publishing of detailed and clear information on public budgets.

Some budget rules of a fiscal constitution based on the benefit principle run contrary to 'taboos' of sound budget management. Earmarking of taxes, though clashing with a traditional principle requiring unity of the budget, ensures that taxes are indeed a *quid pro quo* for the benefits of given expenditures. Gasoline taxes should be earmarked for highway expenditures, if they are conceived as prices of highway services. The universality of the budget of any given government also seems to be a wrong principle. Social security contributions should be put in a separate budget in order to allow full operation of the benefit principle, with pensions strictly related to the contributions paid by different social security taxpayers.

3.5 The Subjective Benefit Principle and the Multiplicity of Taxes and Levels of Government

The benefit principle of taxation rules out a single-tax system, since different expenditures are beneficial to different aspects of economic and social life. Thus, property taxes on real estate may be viewed as the fiscal price for the costs incurred by the government to provide urban infrastructures. Consumption taxes have their justification in the expenses of central and local governments that are beneficial to private consumption.

In this connection, the benefit principle implies also other important principles with constitutional ranking: an extensive articulation of levels of government and fiscal federalism with a plurality of taxes. The multiplicity of governments provides ample room for the application of the subjective law of value in taxation, as a result of individuals freely choosing their most preferred 'fiscal club'. It also allows strategic behaviour, however, a risk with which a tax constitution has to deal properly.

3.6 The Subjective Benefit Principle and Representative Democracy in Fiscal Choice

Extensive amending powers of the parliament, as an expression of the preferences of voters, have to be admitted under the subjective benefit tax principle. The existence of a constitutional limit to budget deficits and of other constraints in the fiscal constitution should make it difficult to exploit the minority through these amending powers. The rules for the approval of amendments should meet the Wicksellian requirement that any new or additional expenditures or reductions in taxes should be accompanied by the indication of the means to pay for them, via reductions in other expenditures or increases in other taxes. The presence of two chambers, with a different composition, both responsible for passing the annual budget, implies a sort of qualified majority voting rule. Hence, bicameralism appears a sound constitutional principle, contrary to the common view that requiring the approval of both chambers may be a 'waste of time'.

3.7 The Subjective Benefit Principle and the Systemic Biases of the Fiscal Constitution

The free choice fiscal constitution based on the subjective benefit principle will require other principles, which one may define as *systemic biases*, that is, obligations to provide evidence for reasons to act contrary to them.

First, in every case that is not clear cut, the market should be preferred to the fiscal economy. This principle requires that production of the goods supplied by the government should be left to the market rather than included in the public sector, unless the opposite choice is clearly to be favoured. Indeed, this is a logical corollary of the principle that the demand and supply of public goods should be subject to the same law of economic value as the demand and supply of goods in the market. However, the case is to be judged not from the point of view of private businesses, which have a natural interest in extending their area of supply, but from the point of view of the taxpayer/consumer of public goods.

Second, if taxes are the price for public services, it follows that, for free public goods, the right of consumers to choose will prevail. The domain of this principle, which is often applied through 'vouchers', could be quite wide: from the area of education, with school choice, to that of public health services and such art merit goods as museums, theatres and so on.

A third related bias of the fiscal constitution based on the subjective benefit principle is that in favour of pricing as against taxing, to finance the provision of public goods suitable to be divided into units of consumption, provided that doing so does not infringe the principle of equality of basic opportunities or of mutual aid in extreme need, required by our democratic constitution. Thus, toll roads should be preferred to free roads. Charges for health services (which may be reduced, for particular categories) should be applied extensively. Fees would be required for non-compulsory education, with exemptions only for the less well-off and for those who deserve free education, on the grounds of the positive external effects of their education.

By the same token there should be a bias for taxes based on the benefit principle, also outside the area of social security, as far as one cannot effectively provide these goods by pricing. We have already mentioned the gasoline and motor vehicle taxes as the price for highway services. But one could also include environmental taxes and specific fees for compulsory public services.

3.8   The Subjective Benefit Principle, Tax Proportionality versus Progressivity

How much mutuality is desirable cannot easily be defined at the constitutional stage. One should remember, however, that *ex post* acceptance of the constitution rests on a perception that it is in the general interest.

The order of a market economy sets a limit to mutuality, since the law of economic value for the public economy implies that redistribution cannot exceed a given individual and collective level. Thus, another fiscal issue of constitutional relevance that can be solved, in the light of the benefit principle, is that of progressive personal taxation versus a general proportional tax or a flat-rate tax. According to some theories, progressive taxation may be justified on the basis of the benefit principle, as a consequence of the decreasing marginal utility of income. Such an argument may hold at low levels of income, for both the individual and the regional income distribution, because public services may be considered a sort of superior consumption good.[41] It is not convincing, however, for the upper brackets of the income distribution. Here one may justify modest top rates and a system of regressive taxation, by combining direct taxes with an important taxation on consumption. On the other hand, a flat income tax modified only with deductions for lower-income brackets does not seem appropriate, because it does not take into account the different mutuality duties of different taxpayers, sharing the common gains arising from cooperation. A certain progressive graduation of the general personal income tax in the upward direction seems unavoidable, if one agrees that mutuality inside the benefit principle characterizes this model of fiscal constitution. It is clear, however, that the law of economic value rules out high progressive tax rates, since they are likely to exceed the inframarginal rents of public services.

Violation of the principle of limited taxation on individuals and firms implies that the restoration of this law will be accomplished by market forces leading to capital flight, delocalization and reduction in economic growth.

3.9   The Subjective Benefit Principle and the Criteria for Redistribution

In the worlds of de Tocqueville and Wicksell, under simple majority rule, the supply of public goods may be irrationally extended beyond what is required by the marginal benefit allocative rule, because the majority will impose their tax cost on the minority. However, if the subjective marginal utility principle is to determine the optimal allocation of public goods, a constitutional agreement will be reached to the effect that redistribution, in any case, should be *chiefly* performed through money transfers. Note that such an arrangement does not imply a negative income tax. On the contrary, if one accepts that the constitution includes specified duties of mutuality, it seems reasonable to try to meet the preferences of those who have to bear the burden of the transfers related to these duties. Thus, we would expect to have minimum old-age pensions for those who are not able to get a contributory pension and free healthcare for those who are not able to pay social contributions or charges for health services.

A second related fiscal constitution principle in redistributive matters has to do with specific wants that are instrumental in ensuring equality of basic opportunities and with merit wants generating positive externalities: a case for free universal education.

4   SUMMARY AND CONCLUSIONS

What we have done is to show that the subjective benefit principle of fiscal economy, in spite of widely held contrary beliefs which seem to belong to the family of Paretian derivations, may be rendered meaningful by general and operational rules of a fiscal constitution, both inside and outside the constitutional charter. The fiscal constitution based on the law of economic value, viewed in a cooperative-game context, does not represent the only possible fiscal constitution, from both a positive and a normative point of view. This is very true. But one can hardly argue that a democratic society firmly grounded in a market economy competitive system might choose different fiscal rules conforming to that principle.

Furthermore, the resulting inconsistencies may lead to disequilibria of various kinds. A suggestion for further research!

NOTES

1. Adam Smith, *An Inquiry into the Nature and Causes of the Wealth of Nations*, Book V, 'Of the Revenue of the Sovereign or Commonwealth', Chapter II, 'Of the Sources of the General or Public Revenue of the Society', Part II, 'Of taxes'.
2. In the Conclusion of Book V, Chapter I, 'Of the Expenses of the Sovereign or Commonwealth'.
3. See below, notes 14, 17, 19 and 21.
4. See below, notes 7 and 27.
5. See Paul A. Samuelson, 'The pure theory of public expenditure', *Review of Economics and Statistics*, **36** (1954), 387–9; 'Diagrammatic exposition of a theory of public expenditure', *Review of Economics and Statistics*, **37** (1955), 350–56.
6. If the taxes were merely based on the equilibrium between marginal costs of the public goods supplied and their aggregate demand by the various individuals, under increasing cost, a rent would emerge in favour of the suppliers, that is the bureaucracy and the politicians in control of the government. When the considered public goods have non-rival supplies, if taxes are merely based on the equilibrium between marginal costs of the goods supplied and their aggregate demand, some individuals shall become free riders because their demand at the collective demand equilibrium point is zero. See Francesco Forte, *Manuale di scienza delle finanze*, Chapter 1, Part II, § 2, 3 and Chapter IV, §6 (Milano: Giuffrè, 2007).
7. Recent general works pertaining to constitutional economics include: José Casas Pardo and Friedrich Schneider (eds), *Current Issues in Public Choice* (Cheltenham, UK and Northampton, MA, USA: Edward Elgar, 1996); Dennis Müller, *Constitutional Democracy* (Oxford: Oxford University Press, 1996) and Robert D. Cooter, *Strategic Constitution* (Princeton, NJ: Princeton University Press, 2000). The beginnings of an economically oriented study of constitutions and institutions generally can be traced back to some articles (written in the 1950s and the 1960s) by James Buchanan and to the

classical volume that he co-authored with Gordon Tullock. See James M. Buchanan, 'Positive economics, welfare economics, and political economy', *Journal of Law and Economics*, **2** (1959), 124–38; 'Politics, policy, and the Pigovian margins', *Economica*, **39** (1962), 17–28; 'The relevance of Pareto optimality', *Journal of Conflict Resolution*, **6** (1962), 341–54; James M. Buchanan and Gordon Tullock, *The Calculus of Consent: Logical Foundations of Constitutional Democracy* (Ann Arbor, MI: University of Michigan Press, 1962). A limited sample of contributions to constitutional economics by different scholars (some also disagreeing with the dominant line of research) should include: Peter Bernholz, 'Freedom and constitutional economic order', *Zeitschrift für die gesamte Staatswissenschaft*, **135** (3) (1979), 510–32; 'A general constitutional possibility theorem', *Public Choice*, **51** (1986), 249–65; 'The implementation and maintenance of a monetary constitution', *Cato Journal*, **6** (2) (1986), 477–511; Bruno Frey, 'Economic policy by constitutional contract', *Kyklos*, **32** (1979), 307–19; Russell Hardin, 'Why a constitution?', in *The Federalist Papers and the New Institutionalism*, eds. Bernard Grofman and Donald Wittman (New York: Agathon Press, 1989), 100–120; Dennis Müller, 'Constitutional rights', *Journal of Law, Economics, and Organization*, **7** (1991), 313–33; 'The importance of uncertainty in a two-stage theory of constitutions', *Public Choice*, **108** (2001), 223–58; Peter C. Ordeshook, 'Constitutional stability', *Constitutional Political Economy*, **3** (1992), 137–75; Richard A. Posner, 'The constitution as an economic document', *George Washington Law Review*, **56** (1987), 458–68; Barry R. Weingast, 'Constitutions as governance structures: the political foundations of secure markets', *Journal of Institutional and Theoretical Economics*, **149** (1993), 286–311. For a recent two-volume introduction to the main themes of constitutional political economy, see Stefan Voigt (ed.), *Constitutional Political Economy* (Cheltenham, UK and Northampton, MA, USA: Edward Elgar, 2003).

8. On the relevance and uses of the notion of 'incomplete contract' in economics, see: Oliver Hart and Bengt Holmstrom, 'The theory of contracts', in *Advances in Economic Theory*, ed. Truman F. Bewley (Cambridge: Cambridge University Press, 1988), 71–155; Oliver Hart and John Moore, 'Incomplete contracts and renegotiation', *Econometrica*, **56** (1988), 755–85; Oliver Hart, *Firms, Contracts, and Financial Structure* (Oxford and New York: Oxford University Press, 1995); Eric Maskin and Jean Tirole, 'Unforeseen contingencies and incomplete contracts', *Review of Economic Studies*, **66** (1999), 83–114; Oliver Hart and John Moore, 'Foundations of incomplete contracts', *Review of Economic Studies*, **66** (1999), 115–38; Jean Tirole, 'Incomplete contracts: where do we stand?', *Econometrica*, **67** (1999), 741–81. The theoretical approach based on incomplete contracts may be seen as a development of the earlier transactions costs literature, on which see, for example, Oliver Williamson, *Markets and Hierarchies: Analysis and Antitrust Implications* (New York: Free Press, 1975); *The Economic Institutions of Capitalism* (New York: Free Press, 1985); Benjamin Klein, Robert G. Crawford and Armen Alchian, 'Vertical integration, appropriable rents, and the competitive contracting process', *Journal of Law and Economics*, **21** (1978), 297–326. For the relevance of the idea of an 'incomplete social contract' to the choice of decision-making rules, see Philippe Aghion and Patrick Bolton, 'Incomplete social contracts', *Journal of the European Economic Association*, **1** (2003), 38–67.

9. On the notion of meta-rules in constitutional economics, see Geoffrey Brennan and James M. Buchanan, *The Reason of Rules: Constitutional Political Economy* (Cambridge: Cambridge University Press, 1985). For a thorough classification of rules and an interesting analysis of their functions in different settings, see Viktor J. Vanberg, *Rules and Choice in Economics* (London and New York: Routledge, 1994).

10. In the contributions of such distinguished scholars as Adam Bergson and Paul Samuelson it is left indeterminate how individual utilities are actually compared and weighted. See Adam Bergson, *Essays in Normative Economics* (Cambridge, MA: Harvard University Press, 1966) and Paul Samuelson, 'Bergsonian Welfare Economics' (1981) reprinted in K. Crowley (ed.), *The Collected Scientific Papers of Paul Samuelson, 1966–86*, (Volume 5, (Cambridge, MA: Harvard University Press, 1986, Chapter 293). In applied welfare economics – such as optimal taxation theory or cost–benefit analysis (on which see the classic

articles by James A. Mirrlees and the authoritative article by Jean Drèze and Nicholas Stern, respectively) – *ad hoc* assumptions are introduced, for example by assigning unequal weights to different categories of persons (perhaps on an income basis) or postulating 'isomorphic' individuals, as when deriving results from the hypothesis of a one-consumer-equivalent economy (OCEE). See James A. Mirrlees, 'An exploration in the theory of optimum income taxation', *Review of Economic Studies*, **38** (1971) and James A. Mirrlees, 'The theory of optimal taxation', in K. Arrow and M. Intriligator (eds), *Handbook of Mathematical Economics* (Amsterdam: North Holland, 1981). See also Jean Drèze and Nicholas Stein, 'Theory of cost–benefit analysis', in A. Auerbach and M. Feldstein (eds), *Handbook of Public Economics*, Volume, 2, (Amsterdam: North Holland, 1987).

11. Clear (though indirect) evidence of the differences between an approach to constitutional political economy resting on the individualistic and democratic postulates of social choice theory and a public choice perspective is provided by even a cursory glance at the table of contents of the leading journals for the two lines of research, that is *Social Choice and Welfare* and *Public Choice*. The former focuses on such issues as Pareto optimality and welfare criteria, optimal taxation and cost–benefit analysis, using the axiomatic method and refined developments from mathematical theories. In contrast, the latter is devoted to articles 'ploughing the fencerow' between politics and economics, the 'two prodigal offspring of political economy', as Buchanan and Tullock wrote in their preface to the *Calculus of Consent*. This, in an effort in which economic methods are brought to bear on issues generally pertaining to political science and the political scientist's concern. And institutional detail combines with the economist's emphasis on the 'micromotives' of individual behaviour in the political scene.

12. And actually, as Rowley and Peacock have noted, the maximization of an all-embracing social welfare function appears to be an 'imperialistic construct' in which individual free choices are improperly imprisoned. See Charles K. Rowley and Alan T. Peacock, *Welfare Economics: A Liberal Restatement* (New York: Wiley, 1975).

13. See on Bentham and the welfare state, Chapter 4 in this volume, Pedro Schwartz, 'Bentham on public choice: utility, interests and the agency problem in democracy'. Of course, Bentham, as is clear from this chapter, would not have supported a 'big' state. But he was no defender of free market *laissez-faire*, either.

14. For example, the Austrian neoclassical economists Friedrich von Wieser and Emil Sax, the Italian Giuseppe Ricca Salerno, Antonio De Viti De Marco, Ugo Mazzola, Luigi Einaudi and the Swedish Knut Wicksell and Erik Lindahl, made seminal contributions at the end of the nineteenth century and in the first half of the twentieth century. See Friedrich von Wieser, *Der Natürliche Werth* (Vienna: Hölder, 1889), translated in English as *Natural Value* (London: Macmillan, 1893); *Theorie der Gesellschaftlichen Wirtschaft* (Tübingen: Mohr-Siebeck, 1914), translated in English as *Social Economics* (New York: Greenberg, 1927; reprinted in 1967 by A.M. Kelley, New York); Emil Sax, *Grundlegung der Theoretischen Staatswirtschaft* (Vienna: Hölder, 1887); Giuseppe Ricca Salerno, *Scienza delle Finanze* (Florence: Barbera, 1888); Antonio De Viti De Marco, *Il Carattere Teorico dell'Economia Finanziaria* (Rome: Pasqualucci, 1888); *Principi di Economia Finanziaria* (Turin: Einaudi, 1934), also available in English translation as *First Principles of Public Finance* (New York: Harcourt, Brace, 1936); Ugo Mazzola, *I Dati Scientifici della Finanza Pubblica* (Rome: Loescher, 1890) (chapter IX of the book, concerning 'the formation of the prices of public goods', is translated in Richard A. Musgrave and Alan T. Peacock, eds, *Classics in the Theory of Public Finance* (New York: St. Martin's Press, 1958), pp. 37–47); Luigi Einaudi, *Miti e Paradossi della Giustizia Tributaria* (Turin: Einaudi, 1938); *Principi di Scienza della Finanza* (Turin: Einaudi, 1940); Knut Wicksell, *Finanztheoretische Untersuchungen*, (Jena: Gustav Fischer, 1896); Erik Lindahl, *Die Gerechtigkeit der Besteuerung: eine Analyse der Steuerprinzipien auf Grenznutzentheorie* (Lund: Gleerup, 1919) (extracts from the fourth chapter of the first part, entitled 'Positive Lösung' were translated as 'Just taxation – A positive solution' in Musgrave and Peacock, eds, *Classics*, pp. 168–76).

15. As observed by Alexis de Tocqueville in his analysis of American democracy. See de Tocqueville, *De la Démocratie en Amérique* (1835–40), Première édition historico-critique (first historical and critical edition) edited by E. Nolla (Paris: Librairie Philosophique J. Vrin, 1990); *Democracy in America* (Chicago: University of Chicago Press, 2000).
16. The approach based on average (or median) voters may, to some extent, be traced back to Sax's somewhat obscure reasoning. For a presentation of Sax's theory and an analysis of the similarities and differences between his theory and that of Ricca Salerno, see Francesco Forte, 'Giuseppe Ricca Salerno capostipite della scuola delle scelte economiche democratiche della finanza pubblica', *Rivista di Diritto Finanziario e Scienza delle Finanze*, **64** (1) (2005), 3–29.
17. As predicted by Maffeo Pantaleoni, who adopted such an approach as the most likely *positive* economic solution in a representative democracy. Maffeo Pantaleoni, 'Contributo alla teoria del riparto delle spese pubbliche', *Rassegna italiana*, 15 October 1883. The first formulations of the median voter theorem may be found in the works of Black and Downs: Duncan Black, 'On the rationale of group decision-making', *Journal of Political Economy*, **56** (1948), 23–34; Anthony Downs, *An Economic Theory of Democracy* (New York: Harper & Bros., 1957). For a general treatment, see James M. Enelow and Melvin J. Hinich, *The Spatial Theory of Voting* (Cambridge: Cambridge University Press, 1984).
18. Tocqueville's unidirectional exploitation trend from the well-to-do to the less well-off, under a democracy governed by the simple majority rule, is replaced by a bidirectional exploitation trend.
19. A conclusion already apparent to Antonio De Viti De Marco, who, as is well known, depicted the process of agreement in democratic fiscal choices through the model of a 'cooperative' (not yet the idea of a cooperative game); see his *Principi di economia finanziaria*.
20. See the works by De Viti De Marco cited in note 14 above.
21. See the essay 'Ein neues Prinzip der gerechten Besteuerung' in Wicksell, *Finanztheoretische Untersuchungen*, partially translated as 'A new principle of just taxation' in Musgrave and Peacock, eds, *Classics*, pp. 72–118.
22. For Wicksell redistributive choices, about which he, due to his socialist leanings, was deeply concerned, were to be made differently by simple majority.
23. See Wicksell, *A New Principle*, p. 93.
24. In their book, *Calculus of Consent*.
25. Agreement often does not seem to be a real option in the pursuit of coordination, because of insuperable information and communication difficulties. Hardin (see Russell Hardin, 'Contractarianism: wistful thinking', *Constitutional Political Economy*, **1** (1990), 35–52) considers this as an argument against contractarianism. However, it should be noted that, at the post-constitutional stage, Buchanan and Tullock assign a significant place to majority rule, because of the transaction costs consequent on supermajority decision rules.
26. Recall that in the Wicksellian approach unanimity applies only to allocative choices. Redistributive issues are decided by simple majority.
27. See James M. Buchanan, 'Social choice, democracy, and free markets', *Journal of Political Economy*, **62** (1954), 114–23; 'Individual choice in voting and the market', *Journal of Political Economy*, **62** (1954), 334–43; 'A contractarian paradigm for applying economic theory', *American Economic Review*, **65** (1975), 225–30.
28. This is a validation of De Viti De Marco's view of democracy as a process of free competition and alternation among different parties with different programmes.
29. Indeed, Hobbes, who is generally considered the most prominent early contractarian, distinguished two different ways of establishing a social order in a particular community, which he called 'Commonwealth by institution' and 'Commonwealth by acquisition'. The former is based on a covenant of everyone with everyone, while in the latter 'the sovereign power is acquired by force'. See Thomas Hobbes, *Leviathan* (Cambridge: Cambridge University Press, 1991; first edition 1651). Another reason for not being too hasty in evoking the spectre of anarchy as the only alternative to a *democratic* social order becomes immediately apparent as soon as one considers that the twentieth century experienced several authoritarian or dictatorial regimes.

30. One of the most apparent difficulties (and a major source of confusion) in the idea of a constitution resulting from a 'social contract' between individuals in a supposed state of nature lies in the implicit assumption that the only alternative to a general agreement would be a disastrous return to an anarchic condition, in which everyone stands to lose, irrespective of their relative bargaining powers. In contrast with the weaknesses of any explanatory or normative theory based on such an abstract contractarian construct, a more fruitful and relevant use of the notion of a social contract would seem to be possible in relation to the establishment or enlargement of a federation, out of already existing states or of less hierarchical international organizations. The European Union (EU) is a typical example. In the European political context the constitutional *contract* ceases to be a philosophical fiction and the exit option available to disagreeing countries would not reduce to a rollback into anarchy, but to the continuance of their autonomous relationships with residual member states and other countries outside the EU. For a preliminary treatment of these themes, see Francesco Forte, 'The theory of social contract and the EEC', in David Greenaway and Keith Shaw, eds, *Public Choice, Public Finance, and Public Policy: Essays in Honour of Alan Peacock* (Oxford: Blackwell, 1985).

31. True, Buchanan's construction is different from those of John Rawls or John Harsanyi, where one individual chooses under the veil of ignorance, in an ethical position in which s/he could be anyone else. Here, we have many different individuals and a cooperative game among them, with the (quasi) unanimity rule to reach agreement.

32. Hayek and Popper, by examining from different perspectives the process through which knowledge is created and spread, have given us enough reasons to think that it could be so. See Friedrich A. Hayek, 'The use of knowledge in society', in *Individualism and Economic Order* (Chicago: University of Chicago Press, 1948), 77–91; 'Competition as a discovery process', in *New Studies in Philosophy, Politics, Economics and the History of Ideas* (Chicago: University of Chicago Press, 1978), 179–90; Karl R. Popper, *The Poverty of Historicism* (Boston, MA: Beacon Press, 1957), (see especially the author's *Preface*); *Objective Knowledge: An Evolutionary Approach* (Oxford: Clarendon Press, 1963).

33. In this regard, De Viti De Marco's idea of a cooperative structure of the democratic polity is a seminal contribution to the economic rules of the game for such a society.

34. Harsanyi's maximization process appears to be of this kind.

35. Thus Buchanan's contract appears to be more a thought experiment than a paradigm suitable to the interpretation of real life.

36. In order for the rules of private games to emerge as stable conventions, it is necessary that they be both abstract and general, in the sense of applying impartially to anyone who could find themselves in a particular situation defined, in quite general terms, in the relevant rule. In his seminal analysis of the emergence of conventions, Hume thought of them as rules observed by two or more parties in the common expectation that everyone will obey them, since general compliance benefits all. See David Hume, *A Treatise of Human Nature* (Oxford: Oxford University Press, 2000) (first edition 1739–40); *An Enquiry Concerning the Principles of Morals* (Oxford: Clarendon Press, 1998) (first edition 1751). Such an approach has been developed in Francesco Forte, *Etica Pubblica e Regole del Gioco: I Doveri Sociali in una Società Liberale* (Naples: Liguori, 1995).

37. In testing fiscal rules one may consider their effects on economic equilibrium and growth and whether they are consistent with the mutuality principle implicit in the cooperative model. See Francesco Forte, 'Constitutions as contracts and as conventions: an economic analysis', *Contributi per la discussione* (Contribution for the discussion), **44** (1991), edited by POLITEIA, Centre for the formation in Ethics and Politics, Milan.

38. Game theorists stress that the shared belief of a common interest will not lead 'players' to a unique equilibrium.

39. And, in a more general view, in an economic constitution with the government as subsidiary to the market economy.

40. Vilfredo Pareto, *Trattato di sociologia generale* (Milan: Comunità, 1964) (first edition 1916), translated in English as *The Mind and Society: A Treatise on General Sociology*, ed.

Arthur Livingston (New York: Dover Publications, 1963). See especially chapters VI ('Residuals') and IX ('Derivations').

41. See Francesco Forte and Pasquale Catanoso, 'Disequilibrio spaziale fra offerta e domanda di beni pubblici ed evasione fiscale razionale', *Rivista di Diritto Finanziario e Scienza delle Finanze*, **64** (2) (2005), 145–87.

18. (When) do tax increases cause electoral damage? The case of local property taxes in Spain

Núria Bosch Roca and Albert Solé-Ollé

1 INTRODUCTION

Conventional wisdom among journalists and politicians is that tax increases have electoral consequences and, when races are close, they may even break an incumbent's re-election bid. The electoral costs of taxation are expected to be even higher at the local level, since the perceived unfairness and the high level of visibility of some local taxes means that voters may be really aware of the money taken from their pockets by the local council and ready to vote against a tax increase (Stults and Winters, 2002). These are indeed traits often attributed to the property tax, which is the tax analysed in this chapter. For example, it is often argued that this tax is the most unfair (Gallup Poll, 4–7 April 2005). There are two main reasons for this perceived unfairness. First, the tax is not tied to a realized stream of money but rather to paper gains, and second, its increases are usually sudden and dramatic as a result of reassessments in periods of rapidly rising housing markets. The property tax is also highly visible, since 'it is assessed on what is typically the household's biggest consumption and investment item' (Wassmer, 1993, p. 135). Given these unattractive traits it is not strange that public discontent with property taxes has led both to tax revolts and electoral defeats.

Nevertheless, there is lower consensus among the scholars regarding the electoral costs of taxation, in general, and of local property taxes, in particular. Early empirical research on the link between tax increases and elections focused on US state data. Analyses by Pomper (1968 and 1976), Turett (1971) and Hansen (1983) did not find significant effects of tax variables on the vote for the governor. Recent analysis obtained mixed results for the US, (see, for example, Kone and Winters, 1983; Niemi et al., 1995; Brooks and Prysby, 1992; Besley and Case, 1995; and Lowry et al., 1998), the UK (Gibson, 1988; Gibson and Stewart, 1992; Rallings and Thrasher,

1997; Revelli, 2002), Canada (Landon and Ryan, 1997) and Belgium (Vermeir and Heyndels, 2004). The UK and Belgian studies are especially interesting for us, since they focus on the property tax. Also here the results are mixed, with some UK studies finding significant effects (for example, Gibson and Stewart, 1992) while others offer less convincing conclusions (for example, Revelli, 2002).

There are two different answers to this puzzle. First, only some governments experience electoral losses when raising taxes and these losses depend on the specific type and timing of the tax increase. Most of the US studies cited above indicate a variable impact of tax increases on the vote depending on the specific traits of the tax raised and on the political context that surrounds a specific episode. An electoral impact is also found in Besley and Case (1995) and Lowry et al. (1998), but in both cases the impact is conditional on a variety of factors.

Second, it is clear that taxation is only one of the many motives for voting against the incumbent. This happens because voters are often ideologically attached to one of the parties. So, the utility loss needed to change the vote of many individuals may be substantial. At first sight it may seem that this behaviour should be more pronounced in national elections than in regional and local ones. However, at least in Spain, local elections are contaminated by the regional and national political environment. Since most of the candidates are aligned along national or regional party lines, a fall in the popularity of a party at this level directly translates to a loss in votes at the local level. If this is the case then the impact of tax issues on the vote results (even though they are relevant) may be statistically obscured by the ideological motive. Indeed, Revelli (2002) has shown for the UK that the conclusions about the vote effects of taxation depend on the proper control of the impact of national political factors.

The empirical analysis performed in this chapter will take into account both the mediating impact of contextual factors on the effect of taxes on the vote and the influence of national politics on the local election. With this purpose, we estimate a vote equation with a huge database of nearly 3000 Spanish municipalities and analysing three local elections (1995, 1999 and 2003). In order to obtain unbiased estimates of the effects of taxes on voting, we account for national political shocks, ideological preferences of the citizenship and government traits, and we estimate the vote equation by instrumental variables. We also allow many different traits of the government (ideology, coalition government, and first-term government) and of the tax raised (legislated versus automatic tax changes, and election cycle) to mediate the effects of taxes on voting. The results suggest that, although non-tax issues dominate the vote decision, property tax increases have a non-negligible impact on incumbent votes, specially when the government is right wing, is a coalition, and is not in its first term, and when the tax increase is legislated and is enacted in the second half of the mandate.

The chapter is organized as follows. The next section (Section 2) identifies the main factors related to the political context of the election and to the type and timing of the tax increase that mediate the effects of taxation on the vote and that will be accounted for in the empirical analysis. In Section 3, we provide some details about the local financial and political system in Spain, and describe the design of our empirical exercise, focusing on the specification of the vote equation, the econometrics and the dataset used. In this section we describe the way we deal econometrically with the influence of national politics on local elections. Section 4 presents the results and Section 5 concludes.

2 THE POLITICAL COSTS OF RAISING TAXES

The conclusion of the literature on the political costs of taxation is that tax increases entail electoral costs, but these may vary greatly by circumstance, and depend on the voter's perception of the tax increase and on his/her ability and will to assign responsibilities to local political actors. The voter's perception of the tax increase is in turn influenced by the type of tax raised and by the timing of the tax increase. The ability to discipline the incumbent for the tax increase depends on the political context of the tax increase, since some governments may be punished more severely than others for the same increase. The main hypotheses related to these issues that will be tested are discussed in the next two subsections.

2.1 Type of Tax and Timing of the Tax Increase

The voters' perception of the tax increase depends on a variety of circumstances, ranging from the particular tax raised to the ability of the politician to link the revenue with a popular expenditure programme and the timing of the tax increase (MacManus, 1999, p. 87). There are two main findings of the literature that will be taken into account here: (i) the different impact of legislated versus automatic tax increases, and (ii) the different effect of tax increases along the electoral cycle.

Type of tax increase
Different taxes may have different levels of visibility, fairness and electoral punishment associated with them. Consumers, for example, are seldom aware of sales taxes because they tend to think in terms of the net price they pay (Winters, 1996). On the one hand, the personal income tax is often seen

as the usual procedure of collection, though wage retention also reduces the visibility of this tax. On the other, the property tax is one of the most hated taxes. Its perceived regressivity and unfairness are probably the reason for this status, but also its high degree of visibility, given the huge number of taxpayers and the direct collection procedure. There are few papers analysing the electoral costs of different taxes. Most of the early US literature focused on the effect of growth of aggregate revenues, instead of particular tax rates. An exception to this rule is Stults and Winters (2002), who find that governors are more punished by sales tax increases than by income tax increases. They attribute these results to the higher perceived fairness of the income tax. Outside the US, many papers have found adverse electoral effects for the property tax: Gibson (1988), Gibson and Stewart (1992) and Rallings and Thrasher (1997) for the UK, and Vermeir and Heyndels (2004) for Belgium.

Unfortunately, in our case we only have information on the property tax rate, so we shall not be able to analyse the impact of other local taxes in Spain such as, for example, the local business and vehicle taxes. However, regarding the property tax, we shall be able to analyse the different impact of raising the effective tax rate through legislated increases in the nominal tax rate or through property tax reassessments. Some early research suggests that changes in tax rates are more likely to be perceived by taxpayers than are non-legislated increases in tax burdens (for example, Oates, 1975; Wagner, 1976). The reason for this behaviour is fiscal illusion: voters are aware of changes in legislated tax rates because these are publicized and, in any case, imply a conscious decision by the government. Tax increases derived from tax-base changes are less perceived or, at least, are not perceived as the responsibility of the government. In the case of the property tax, the tax base grows only if the government reassesses the value of the property, something that happens from time to time. It is well documented for the US that after a property value reassessment, effective property values tend to increase (see, for example, Strumpf, 2002). Some authors attribute this increase to voters' 'fiscal illusion' (see, for example, Bloom and Ladd, 1982; Ladd, 1991). This also happens in Spain, so it is natural to ask whether voters are less aware of effective property tax increases due to reassessments. If this is true, these increases should cost fewer votes than legislated nominal tax increases.

Timing of the tax increase
The 'electoral cycle' literature tells us that tax rates tend to be increased mainly during the first half of the mandate. Evidence on this kind of behaviour may be found for the US in Mikesell (1978) and for Spain in Solé-Ollé (2003). It is therefore natural to ask whether the loss in votes caused by a

tax is lower if this increase has been enacted in the first two years of the mandate than if the tax has been increased in the second half of the mandate.

2.2   The Political Context of the Tax Increase

The voters' ability to discipline the incumbent clearly depends on the political context. There are three main findings of the literature of economic voting that may help us in identifying which are the local government traits that mediate the impact of tax increases on the vote.

Ideology
The electoral cost of a tax increase may depend on the ideology of the incumbent party. Alesina and Rosenthal (1995) have argued that voters do not judge all parties equally, but rather they have different expectations regarding what is a reasonable policy depending on the ideology of the party. This means that voters should hold parties responsible for their more salient goals. Many papers in the empirical literature of economic voting have found that left-wing governments are more penalized for unemployment increases while right-wing governments are more penalized for inflation increases (see Powell and Whitten, 1993; Veiga and Veiga, 2004). The only paper testing this hypothesis in the case of taxation is the one by Lowry et al. (1998), who show that in the US, Republicans tend to be punished more severely for tax increases than Democrats, thus confirming this hypothesis. Ideological differences between left- and right-wing parties are more marked in Europe and Spain than in the US, even at the local level. Therefore, we expect that left-wing local governments will be less punished for tax increases than right-wing governments.

Coalitions
Politically divided or fragmented governments seem to be punished less for the bad results of their policies. In the economic voting literature, this is the so-called 'clarity of responsibility' hypothesis which states that the impact of economic variables on voting will be larger for governments with a greater clarity of responsibility (Powell and Whitten, 1993). That is, faced with a government that has many different members, voters encounter many difficulties in ascertaining which of the parties is actually responsible for the tax increase. Given this uncertainty, voters may decide not to punish any of the parties for the decisions taken.

There is some empirical evidence on the validity of this hypothesis. For example, Powell and Whitten (1993) and Anderson (1995) have found evidence that coalition governments are punished less than majorities for unemployment and inflation. And in the US case, Lowry et al. (1998) find that divided state governments face lower electoral costs of taxation than unified governments (that is, when the same party controls both the executive and the legislative). Despite this, some authors have questioned the validity of this hypothesis. For example, Royed et al. (2000) replicated the Powell and Whitten results and showed that they were not very robust to minor modifications in the specification of the equations. Other authors claimed for a better understanding of 'the clarity of responsibility' concept and showed that the results may depend on the definition used (see, for example, Niemi et al., 1995; Anderson, 2000). Moreover, from our point of view, there is a fundamental weakness related to this hypothesis, since there has been no attempt to explain why, given the difficulties in assigning responsibility, the voters react by not punishing any of the incumbent parties when they could have reacted by punishing all of them. However, given the huge number of coalitions among Spanish local governments (roughly 30 per cent), we shall test for the hypothesis that coalitions are punished less than majorities.

New governments

The third finding is that voters seem to be less demanding with newly elected governments (that is, governments that are in their first term) than with older governments. This could be termed a 'honeymoon effect' and can be explained by the fact that voters are willing to wait and see until the new government has developed its programme. That is, there is some confidence that the tax increases enacted by a new government are justified by the need to apply a new policy. However, once time has elapsed, this confidence erodes and the voter is less willing to tolerate additional tax increases. Although we have found no papers analysing the relationship between this honeymoon effect and the electoral costs of tax increases, there are some in the literature of economic voting that have documented its relevance (see, for example, Veiga and Veiga, 2004). We shall account for this possibility and analyse whether vote losses caused by property tax increases are indeed lower during the first term of a local government.

3   EMPIRICAL DESIGN

In this section, we describe the empirical design used here in order to test the effect of property tax increases on the votes received by local governments in the election following the tax increase. The test was performed with a large, unique database, comprising nearly 3000 Spanish municipalities with over 1000 inhabitants during three electoral periods, delimited by the elections of 1991, 1995, 1999 and 2003. This section is organized as follows. First, in order to set the scene for the analysis and to provide some information that we consider important to understand certain methodological decisions taken later, we give a brief description of the Spanish local taxation and political system. Second, we present the specifications used to test the hypotheses advanced above. Third, we describe the database and the econometric techniques used.

3.1   Local Taxes and Politics in Spain

Local taxation

Spain consists of more than 8000 municipalities, but most of these are quite small (that is, 90 per cent have less than 5000 inhabitants and represent no more than 5 per cent of the population). These municipalities are multipurpose governments, and their main expenditure categories are the traditional responsibilities assigned elsewhere to the local public sector (that is, environmental services, urban planning, transportation, welfare and so on) with the exception of education, a responsibility of the regional governments. Municipal responsibilities grow steadily with population size, something that is duly recognized by the financing system.

The municipality's own revenues account for more than 65 per cent of its current revenues, with the remaining 35 per cent being met by grants, most of which are unconditional. Two-thirds of the municipality's own revenues are derived from five taxes, with the remaining third coming from a variety of user charges. The main taxes are the property tax, the local business tax and the local motor vehicle tax, which respectively account for 50, 20 and 15 per cent of tax revenues.[1] The property tax is the only one we consider here in conducting our empirical analysis. There are two reasons for this decision. The first is that, as it is the main local tax, it is also the focus of most of the taxpayers' political discontent. Thus, not only the yearly decision concerning the nominal tax rate, but also the less frequent decision to reassess the property values of a municipality may entail significant political risks. The second reason is that we were unable to include information concerning the business and vehicle tax rates in the very large database assembled for this chapter. The main risk we run by proceeding in this way is that the effect of the property tax rate may eventually include public discontent with other taxes not included in our vote equation. However, we believe that this risk is not particularly great given that the correlation between the tax increases of these three taxes does not appear to be very high.[2]

In the early years of democracy, municipalities had no power to set property tax rates. However, at the end of the 1980s they were granted the power to set the rates of the local taxes on a completely harmonized tax base. This power, however, is limited by the fact that both minimum and maximum tax rates are imposed. In the case of the property tax, there is a minimum nominal tax rate of 0.4 per cent of the assessed property value, which is the same for all municipalities. This minimum tax rate is allowed to fall to 0.1 per cent during the five years following a reassessment. The maximum nominal tax rate increases with population size, ranging from 0.85 per cent for municipalities with less than 5000 inhabitants to 1.1 per cent for municipalities with more than 100,000 inhabitants. Additional points may be applied if a municipality complies with various other conditions, including being a regional capital (+ 0.07 per cent), having an urban transportation system (+ 0.07 per cent), and providing more services than those defined as compulsory by law (+ 0.06 per cent). As a result of this autonomy, the disparities in property tax rates among municipalities are now considerable. Furthermore, since only a few municipalities have reached the top tax rate, the use of this room to manoeuvre as regards the fixing of taxes is expected to continue in the future.

The health of the local property tax depends to a large degree on the frequency and quality of property value reassessments. In Spain, a central government agency ('Centro de Gestión Catastral y Cooperación Tributaria') is responsible for undertaking this task. The reassessment system is thus the same throughout the country. However, a lack of resources and political opposition often delay reassessment campaigns and, in practice, only a small fraction of municipalities are reassessed each year. Although the responsibility for the reassessment is a central one, in practice it is quite difficult to begin the process without the consent of the municipal government. In this sense, reassessments are not truly exogenous. The average delay between two consecutive assessments can be substantial (for example, eight years in the 1999–2003 period). Because of this delay, a reassessment leads to a considerable jump in assessed values and, although nominal tax rates are adjusted downwards, effective tax rates tend to increase considerably. This is why political opposition to a property reassessment is usually quite high. Only strong governments or governments with financial problems are willing to take such a risk.

Local politics
The local political system in Spain is similar to other systems operating in Europe (Colomer, 1995). Municipal elections are held simultaneously in all the municipalities at regular periods (every four years). Voters elect a given number of councillors, the number being determined by the population of the municipality. These councillors in turn elect the mayor and he/she allocates the various local government posts among the councillors belonging to the party (or parties) that support him/her. During the period analysed,

between 60 and 70 per cent of the municipalities in the sample analysed were governed by majorities (see Table 18.1, below), while the remaining governments can be classified either as coalitions or as minority governments. Although the power of the mayor regarding tax issues is considerable, the fact that many governments are coalitions or minorities is a clear constraint on what he/she can do in that field, since the mayor can be dismissed by an alternative coalition at any time. There has been some concern regarding the instability of local coalition governments, and the difficulties they encounter in taking decisions regarding their budgets and other issues.

In addition to the above, most of the candidates are aligned along national or regional party lines. In fact, the municipal political system is seen as the first step in the recruitment process of the regional and national political elite (Magre, 1998). There are two main national left-wing parties (the PSOE – socialists – which formed the central government during the 1983–96 period and from 2004 to date, and the IU – former communists) and one national right-wing party (the PP, which formed the central government from 1996 to 2004). There are also many parties of a regional nature, some to the left and some to the right of the political spectrum but with issues of nationalism or regionalism as their salient trait. In addition there are many local parties or candidates that run as independents, mostly in small municipalities. It is very difficult to ascertain the ideological position of these parties.

3.2   The Vote Equation

We wish to estimate the effects of taxes on the votes obtained by the local government. It is not absolutely clear how to proceed in the specification of this equation in multiparty systems with many coalition governments. Most of the previous literature on the political costs of taxation comes from the US. Because the US is a two-party system, the authors are able to use the vote share of one of the parties as a dependent variable, allowing for different responses to each of the explanatory variables if the party is the incumbent or the challenger (see, for example, Peltzman, 1992; Lowry et al., 1998). This procedure is difficult to apply in our case, given the high number of parties and the fact that in practice a party may play more than two roles.[3]

In our case, it therefore seems advisable to use the vote share of the parties in the governing council as the dependent variable. The few papers that analyse the effects of taxation in multiparty systems have followed this procedure (see, for example, Landon and Ryan, 1997; Royed et al., 2000; Vermeir and Heyndels, 2004). However, in addition to this variable, we also use the vote share of the mayor's party in the government, which is the main party in the vast majority of cases.[4]

Basic specification

With $v_{i,t}$ being the vote share of either the parties in the local government or the main party in the local government i just before election t, the equation we use in the analysis is:

$$v_{i,t} = \alpha_1.\Delta t_{i,t} + \alpha_2.\Delta y_{i,t} + \alpha_3.v_{i,t-1} + \alpha_4.z_{i,t} + \alpha_5.\bar{v}_{i,t} + f^p_{r,t} + \varepsilon_{i,t}, \quad (18.1)$$

where $\Delta t_{i,t}$ is the tax rate increase set by the municipality during the four-year period before the election date t. In this chapter, we limit our analysis to the effect of increases in the rate of the property tax, the main local tax in Spain. The term $\Delta y_{i,t}$ is a vector of variables measuring the evolution of the local economy in the municipality (for example, growth in unemployment and population) during this four-year period. It is unclear whether the voters hold local politicians accountable for the development of the economy since, given the small size of Spanish municipalities, their opportunities to improve the situation are limited. Nonetheless, it is also true that economic promotion (that is, making efforts to bring economic activity to the locality) is a prominent issue on the local political agenda.

The lagged vote share, $v_{i,t-1}$, is introduced to account for persistent shocks that may have an effect on the popularity of the government. Persistence in the vote share would suggest that once in power it becomes more difficult to lose the support gained from the public, thus giving an indication of some kind of 'incumbency advantage' (see, for example, Lowry et al., 1998). We also include a vector of political characteristics in the equation, $z_{i,t}$, which controls for the effects on the vote of having a coalition government or a government that is in its first term. The effect of these variables is unclear, but we may hypothesize, for example, that voters tend to punish coalitions for their incapacity to deal with problems quickly and efficiently. We may also expect that voters tend not to punish governments in their first term of office so severely, giving them confidence to develop their electoral programme. This honeymoon effect tends to disappear in subsequent terms of office (see, for example, Veiga and Veiga, 2004).[5]

We include two additional controls in the equation to account for other unmeasured political factors. First, we also include as a control variable the average vote share of the parties in the municipal government in the first three elections held after the establishment of democracy (that is, those of 1979, 1983 and 1987).[6] This average vote share, $\bar{v}_i$, aims to capture the long-run idiosyncratic attachment of a municipality to a given party.

Second, we include a set of regional election party effects, $f^p_{r,t}$, which measure the popularity shocks experienced at the regional level by each of the parties analysed in each election. As explained in more detail in the next section, we use both a complete list of parties and a smaller set of categories grouping the various parties according to ideology. The reason why we decided to account for these popularity differences (across elections and municipalities and for the different parties) is that ideology seems to be quite important in Spanish local elections, and the main way to identify ideological messages is by examining the national parties' platforms. This means that many voters tend to vote for the same party irrespective of the election (that is, national or local), so that a contagious effect can be said to exist across elections. Although we believe that local politics are considered important, it is also true that there is a positive connection between the popularity shocks suffered by a party at a national or regional level and its results at a local level. These shocks may be correlated with the general trends in taxation in localities governed by a given party and the results of our analysis may therefore be biased if we do not control for these influences. In fact, the results reported by Revelli (2002) for the UK reveal that any conclusions about the electoral costs of taxation may be altered when accounting for the influence of national politics.[7]

Interactions

Then we estimate whether the effects of taxes on the electoral results depend on the kind and timing of tax increase and on the political context. We take into account the type of tax increase by estimating the following interactions equation:

$$v_{i,t} = (\alpha_{10} + \alpha_{11}.REASS_{i,t}).\Delta t^{1st}_{i,t} + (\alpha_{20} + \alpha_{21}.REASS_{i,t}).\Delta t^{2nd}_{i,t}$$

$$+ \alpha_2.\Delta y_{i,t} + \alpha_3.v_{i,t-1} + \alpha_4.z_{i,t} + \alpha_5.\bar{v}_{i,t} + f^p_{r,t} + \varepsilon_{i,t}, \qquad (18.2)$$

where $REASS_{i,t} = 1$ if there has been a reassessment of property values during the mandate and 0 otherwise, Δt^{1st} = tax increase enacted during the first two years of the mandate, and Δt^{2nd} = tax increase enacted during the last two years of the mandate. Note that the parameters α_{10} and α_{20} measure the effect of increases in property tax rates for the base categories; that is, for nominal tax rate increases during the first and second parts of the mandate, respectively. The parameters α_{11} and α_{21} measure the additional electoral cost due to a tax increase caused by a reassessment. The literature reviewed in the previous section aids us in developing some predictions regarding the sign of these coefficients. Due to 'fiscal illusion', we expect that the costs of taxation will be lower for increases due to reassessments. Due to voter myopia we expect higher electoral costs when the election approaches; hence, we expect $\alpha_{11} > 0$ and $\alpha_{21} > 0$.

In order to account for the effects of the political context on the electoral costs of raising taxes we estimate the following interactions equation:

$$v_{i,t} = (\alpha_{10} + \alpha_{11}.RIGHT_{i,t} + \alpha_{12}.COA_{i,t} + \alpha_{13}.NEW_{i,t}).\Delta t_{i,t}$$

$$+ \alpha_2.\Delta y_{i,t} + \alpha_3.v_{i,t-1} + \alpha_4.z_{i,t} + \alpha_5.\bar{v}_{i,t} + f^p_{r,t} + \varepsilon_{i,t}, \qquad (18.3)$$

where $RIGHT_{i,t} = 1$ if the parties in the local government are of right-wing ideology and 0 in the case of left-wing parties, $COA_{i,t} = 1$ if there is more than one party in the local government and 0 if there is only one party, and $NEW_{i,t} = 1$ if the government is in its first mandate and 0 if not. Note that the parameter α_{10} measures the effect of increased property tax rates for the base category; that is, for taxes increased by a majority left government that is not in its first mandate. The literature reviewed in the previous section helps us to make some predictions regarding the sign of these coefficients. Due to the high voter expectations of tax increases and to honeymoon effects, the costs of taxation will be lower for left-wing governments and for governments in the first mandate, respectively. Due to the lack of clarity of responsibility, these costs will be higher for coalition governments. Hence, we expect $\alpha_{11} < 0$, $\alpha_{12} < 0$ and $\alpha_{13} > 0$.

3.3   Data

We estimated the vote equations using information from 2799 municipalities for the 1991–2003 period. We combined information on the electoral results of the municipal elections of 1991, 1995, 1999 and 2003 with property tax data and a number of socio-economic variables for all the years in this period. In order to construct the average vote share for the parties in government, we also used information from the electoral results of the 1979, 1983 and 1987 municipal elections. The property tax database includes all municipalities, but for some of the elections, electoral information was only provided for municipalities with more than 250 inhabitants, and some socio-economic data were available only for municipalities with more than 1000 inhabitants. We also discarded some municipalities with a mayor belonging to a local party, because of the difficulty of assigning an ideological label to these parties. In the end, we were restricted to the 3117 municipalities with a population of over 1000 inhabitants minus the ones with a mayor from a local party and minus a number of others for which we had data problems, leaving us with the 2799 municipalities that were eventually used. (See Table 18.1.)

The electoral database was compiled from two different files provided by the Spanish Ministry of the Interior and the Ministry of Public Administration. The first of these provides information concerning the votes received by the various parties in the local elections. The second informs us of the party of the mayor and the number of councillors from

Table 18.1 Definition of the variables, data sources and descriptive statistics

Variable	Definition	Data sources	Descriptive statistics		
			Mean (standard dev.)		
			1991–95	1995–99	1999–2003
$\Delta t^e_{i,t-4}$	Δ Effective property tax rate (Δ in % of assessed property value)	*Property tax statistics*, Centro de Gestión Catastral (Ministry of Economics)	0.155 (0.303)	0.157 (0.309)	0.152 (0.335)
$\Delta h_{i,t-4}$	% Δ Urban units per capita		7.624 (16.309)	6.362 (11.601)	3.289 (9.661)
$\Delta u_{i,t-4}$	% Δ Unemployment per capita	National Institute of Statistics (INE) & Anuario Social de España (La Caixa)	−5.81 (9.52)	−11.63 (21.51)	−14.71 (25.60)
$\Delta n_{i,t-4}$	% Δ Population	National Institute of Statistics (INE)	2.70 (6.01)	1.42 (4.63)	3.49 (10.21)
			Mean (standard dev.)		
			1991	1995	1999
$t^e_{i,t-4}$	Lagged effective property tax rate (% of assessed property value)	*Property tax statistics*, Centro de Gestión Catastral (Ministry of Economics)	0.523 (0.170)	0.678 (0.265)	0.835 (0.275)
$t^{max}_{i,t-4} - t^n_{i,t-4}$	Lagged difference between nominal and maximum property tax rate		0.391 (0.256)	0.378 (0.274)	0.365 (0.286)

			Mean (standard dev.)		
			1995 election	1999 election	2003 election
$v_{i,t}$	Vote share, all parties	Municipal Elections database, Ministry of Interior & Ministry of Public Administration	56.74 (11.41)	59.13 (12.96)	58.20 (12.16)
	Vote share, mayor's party		49.73 (13.22)	49.11 (13.11)	49.19 (14.46)
$v_{i,t-4}$	Lagged vote share, all parties		59.82 (13.51)	60.92 (15.52)	60.24 (15.00)
	Lagged vote share, mayor's party		52.00 (14.21)	50.42 (12.96)	49.88 (0.146)
$\bar{v}_i$	Average vote share, all parties		52.12 (11.65)	52.12 (11.65)	52.12 (11.65)
	Average vote share, mayor's party		46.02 (12.01)	46.02 (12.01)	46.02 (12.01)
				Mean	
			1991–95	1995–99	1999–2003
$COA_{i,t}$	1 if coalition government, 0 if majority	Municipal Elections database, Ministry of Interior & Ministry of Public Administration	0.331	0.385	0.317
$RIGHT_{i,t}$	1 if government on the right, 0 on the left		0.348	0.427	0.481
$NEW_{i,t}$	1 if government in its first term, 0 otherwise		0.398	0.289	0.269

each party. In order to compute the vote share of the local government $(v_{i,t})$ we simply added the votes of the different parties belonging to the local government during the previous four-year term of office and then divided by the number of valid votes. The lagged vote share $(v_{i,t-1})$ was computed in a similar way. Note that in any case, the parties used to compute both the vote share and the lagged vote share are the same – those belonging to the parties in the government during a given four-year term of office. The average vote share of a party or group of parties in charge during a given four-year term of office $(\bar{v}_i)$ was computed using data on the vote share of these parties in the first three local elections held after the beginning of the democratic period (that is, those of 1979, 1983 and 1987).

The local government was considered a majority (MAJ) if the mayor's party had more than 50 per cent of the councillors and otherwise as a coalition (COA). As far as ideology is concerned, there are several studies and surveys quantifying the ideological position attributed by Spaniards to the different parties (Sotillos, 1997; Molas and Bartomeus, 1998). We used these ideological indices to classify the parties into four groups: left, centre-left, centre-right and right. The regional party time dummies were devised using these four categories. For coalition governments, we computed an ideological index for the government as the summation of the ideological index of all the parties in the government weighted by the share of councillors from each of them. Using this index, we were able to classify coalition governments in the four categories described above. Finally, a local government was classified as being in its first term of office (NEW) if the party of the mayor had changed between one four-year period and the next. Table 18.1 provides information on the proportion of local governments in each category.

The property tax database comes from the Ministry of Economics and was provided by the central government agency responsible for carrying out property value assessments in all the Spanish municipalities (the 'Centro de Gestión Catastral y Cooperación Tributaria'). This database includes information about the nominal property tax rate, assessed property value, number of homes, and year of the last property value reassessment for each municipality. We used this information to compute the increase in the effective property tax rate, $\Delta t^e_{i,t-4}$, in each of the three four-year periods analysed:

$$\Delta t^e_{i,t-4} = \Delta t^n_{i,t-4} + drev_{i,t-4} \times t^n_{i,r} \times (\Delta v_{i,r}/v_{i,r-1}), \qquad (18.4)$$

where $\Delta t^n_{i,t-4}$ is the increase in the nominal property tax rate during the four-year period preceding the election, $drev_{i,t-4}$ is a dummy equal to one if there was a property value reassessment during this four-year period, $t_{i,r}^n$ is the nominal property tax rate the year before the implementation of the new assessed values, and $\Delta v_{i,r}/v_{i,r-1}$ is the increase in assessed values due to the reassessment process compared to the assessed property values just before this new reassessment.[8] If there is no reassessment during a given four-year mandate, the increase in the effective property tax rate therefore equals the increase in the nominal tax rate (that is, $\Delta t_{i,t-4}^e = \Delta t_{i,t-4}^n$) , but if there is a reassessment, it is necessary to compute the increase in the effective property tax rate in the way suggested by expression (18.3).

We included two variables as economic controls ($\Delta y_{i,t}$) in the vote equations: the growth rate of per capita unemployment in the municipality ($\Delta u_{i,t}$) and the growth rate of population ($\Delta n_{i,t}$). The first variable is frequently used in the literature of economic voting. We believe that this second variable may also measure the economic success of the municipality. Although we accept that population increases also impose costs on residents, Spanish mayors seem to feel that they tend to bring more benefits, to the citizens or to themselves.[9]

3.4 Econometrics

The main econometric problem we found – one that is widely discussed in the literature on the estimation of popularity functions (see, for example, Paldam, 1997; Revelli, 2002; Stults and Winters, 2002) – is that the tax increase in equation (18.2) cannot be assumed to be strictly exogenous. The reason for the endogeneity is that there may be shocks to the local government's popularity (included in the error term $\varepsilon_{i,t}$) that are correlated with the tax increase. For example, consider the situation of a very confident local government, a situation that has been brought about either because the citizens of this municipality have a very marked preference for the ideology of this party or because the party has suffered a huge positive popularity shock at regional or national levels. This government team can raise the local tax and still expect to be re-elected. In previous papers, Solé-Ollé (2003 and 2006) explicitly acknowledges that incumbent Spanish governments differentiate their fiscal policies according to perceived popularity, measured by the margin of victory in the previous election. In this chapter, we do not attempt to estimate a comprehensive political-economy model that includes both a vote equation and a tax-setting equation, but instead follow the procedure used by Revelli (2002) and adopt an instrumental variables approach in order to solve the tax increase endogeneity in the vote equation.

We encountered a number of difficulties in obtaining valid instruments for the tax rate increase, although this is a general problem in studies of this kind (see Stults and Winters, 2002). Note that some of the variables that may help to explain effective property tax rate increases are already included in the vote equation. For example, we could have used the margin of victory in the previous election, but this variable is very much the same (at least in our sample) as the previous vote share (included in the equation) and is, therefore, inappropriate as an instrument. It should also be noted that the financial variables that seem to be exogenous determinants of local tax rates in the Spanish case (for example, intergovernmental transfers, see Solé-Ollé, 2003) are not included in our database. Moreover, some of the variables present in our database are correlated with the residuals and are not valid instruments. This is the case of a dummy indicating whether a property value reassessment took place during the four-year term, the number of years since the last property reassessment at the beginning of the term, and the growth in assessed value per capita during the four-year term. In none of these cases did the Sargan test (Sargan, 1958) allow us to accept the validity of these variables as instruments. There are several explanations for the failure of these variables as instruments. First, these results clearly suggest that although they are carried out by a central government agency, property value reassessments are endogenous, in the sense that only when a local government feels politically safe is it able to accept this risk (which usually entails increases in tax liabilities). Second, the rise in assessed values per capita is also endogenous, as these values tend to rise because of property value reassessments. Third, the number of years since the last reassessment is a determinant of the probability of carrying out a reassessment. Although this variable seems in principle to be exogenous, if the reassessment has not been carried out previously, it is probably because the local government was especially vulnerable to popularity shocks.

The only valid instruments we have been able to find are: the increase in the number of homes per capita during the four-year term, $\Delta h_{i,t-4}$; the lagged effective property tax rate (that is, the effective tax rate in the previous election year), $t^e_{i,t-4}$; the distance between the nominal tax rate and the maximum nominal tax rate allowed by law, $(t^{max}_{i,t-4} - t^n_{i,t-4})$; and this variable squared, $(t^{max}_{i,t-4} - t^n_{i,t-4})^2$.[10] There are various arguments that may be invoked to justify the use of these variables as instruments. First, the increase in the number of homes per capita leads to an increase in the property tax base that may help to reduce the effective property tax rate. Second, the increase in the effective property tax rate may rise as its lagged value falls if local governments gradually adjust the levels of taxation to their desired levels. Third, the relationship between the effective property tax rate increase and the distance between the nominal tax rate and the maximum nominal tax rate allowed by law may be explained by two different effects. On the one hand, if property value reassessments are not carried out, local governments are forced to use the nominal tax rate in order to increase tax liabilities. However, as nominal tax rates are increased year after year, they approach the maximum nominal tax rate allowed, which reduces the margin for continuing with these increases in the future. We therefore expect that as the distance between the nominal and the maximum tax rates diminishes, the local government will pass lower nominal tax increases and, in the absence of a property value reassessment process, these will automatically lead to effective tax increases. On the other hand, the erosion of the margin for increasing the nominal tax rate may force the local government to engage in a property value reassessment process, and it is an empirical regularity that effective property tax rates tend to rise after such a process.[11] Since the two effects have different signs, the relationship between the distance between nominal and maximum tax rates and the increase in the effective tax rate may well be non-linear. We therefore chose to use both the distance and the distance squared as instruments.

The results of the estimated first-stage equation with these instruments are:

$$\Delta t^e_{i,t-4} = -0.051\ t^e_{i,t-4} - 0.893\ (t^{max}_{i,t-4} - t^n_{i,t-4})$$

$$+ 0.810\ (t^{max}_{i,t-4} - t^n_{i,t-4})^2 - 0.144\ \Delta h_{i,t-4} + \text{other}$$

t-statistics: $(-2.601)^{***}$ $(-3.379)^{***}$ $(3.286)^{***}$ $(-5.657)^{***}$

F-statistics (excluded varibles): $15{:}266^{***}$ Sargan test [*p*-value]: 7.315 [0.071]

Where 'other' simply means the instruments that are also explanatory variables in the vote equation and where *** means statistically significant at the 99 per cent level. The results suggest that the instruments meet the two conditions that should be demanded of a good instrument: correlation with the effective property tax rate increase and orthogonality with the residuals. Regarding the first condition, note that the explanatory capacity of the instruments in the first-stage regression is substantial, since the *F*-statistic on the excluded variables is higher than 10, which is the rule of thumb suggested by Staiger and Stock (1997). Regarding the second condition, note that the Sargan test of overidentifying restrictions allows us to reject the null of correlation between the instruments and the error term, so we are able to conclude that these instruments are valid.

4   RESULTS

The parameter estimates of the vote equation are shown in Tables 18.2–5. Tables 18.2 and 18.3 present the basic results (equation (18.1)) while Tables 18.4 and 18.5 present the results of the interactions specification (equations (18.2) and (18.3)). In all the cases, the explanatory capacity of the model was quite good, with an adjusted R^2 of around 0.7–0.8 when all the sets of variables were included.

4.1   Basic Results

The dependent variable is the vote share of all the parties in the local government team in Table 18.2 and the vote share of the party of the mayor in Table 18.3. The results of both specifications are fairly similar, so we shall comment in detail on the results of Table 18.2 and summarize the differences encountered when using the mayor's voter share in Table 18.3. As can be seen in the first column of Table 18.2, the coefficient of the municipality's tax increase variable was not statistically significant when the equation was estimated by ordinary least squares (OLS). Note that although the sign of the coefficient was what we expected, its value was quite low. These results suggest that the equation might need to be estimated by instrumental variables (IV).

The results of the IV estimation are shown in the second column of Table 18.2. As mentioned in the previous section, we experimented with many instruments for the municipality's tax increase, but only a subset of these could be considered exogenous. We present the results obtained when using all the appropriate instruments simultaneously (that is, growth in number of homes per capita, lagged effective tax rate, and distance between nominal and maximum tax rates, and this variable squared). The results of the first-stage regression shown above suggest that these variables do explain the changes in effective property tax rates to a certain extent. Since some of our instruments were constructed with lagged variables, it seemed wise to test for serial correlation in the residuals of the vote equation. The Arellano and Bond (1991) AR(1) test (at the bottom of the table) indicates that there was no serial correlation, which confirms the reliability of our instruments. The results of the IV estimation confirm that the municipality's tax increases have an adverse impact on the vote share. An increase of 1 point in the property tax rate (that is, an additional 1 per cent on the assessed property value) reduced the vote share of the parties in the local government by 8.4 per cent. This is not a particularly large impact, but nor is it negligible. From Table 18.1, we can see that the average tax increase during one four-year period was

Table 18.2 *Effects of property tax increases on the vote share ($v_{i,t}$) of local governments (all parties) (no. obs. = 9397, N = 2799, T = 3), 1995, 1999 and 2003 elections*

Variable	(1) OLS	(2) IV	(3) IV	(4) IV	(5) IV
			i. Property tax rates		
$\Delta t^e_{i,t-4}$	−0.031	−0.081	−0.025	−0.019	−0.083
	(−0.478)	(−4.577)***	(−0.598)	(−0.709)	(−4.653)***
			ii. Controls: economic		
$\Delta u_{i,t-4}$	−0.018	−0.015	−0.009	−0.021	–
	(−0.380)	(−0.248)	(−0.176)	(−1.321)	
$\Delta n_{i,t-4}$	0.039	0.035	0.041	0.044	–
	(1.560)	(1.500)	(0.786)	(1.120)	
			iii. Controls: political		
$v_{i,t}-4$	0.652	0.635	0.677	–	0.663
	(15.761)***	(15.901)***	(16.562)***		(15.850)***
$\bar{v}_i$	0.183	0.178	0.180	–	0.182
	(5.722)***	(5.634)***	(6.190)***		(5.635)***
$COA_{i,t}$	−0.044	−0.046	−0.045	–	−0.044
	(−7.114)**	(−7.235)**	(−7.209)***		(−7.137)***
$NEW_{i,t}$	0.031	0.045	0.040	–	0.042
	(7.209)***	(4.321)***	(3.853)***		(4.328)***
Party × Region × Time effects	Yes	Yes	No	Yes	Yes
Adjusted R^2	0.724	0.711	0.115	0.122	0.041
Breusch–Pagan (Heterosc.)	0.990	1.321	0.955	0.671	0.589
Sargan (instrument validity)	–	4.850 [0.093]	4.811 [0.097]	6.293 [0.043]	5.175 [0.068]
AR (1) (serial error corr.)	0.555	0.321	0.654	0.512	0.738
Wald (economic controls)	7.33	7.26	5.73	4.02	–
Wald (political controls)	91.23***	49.09***	43.16***	–	58.12***
Wald (Party × Region × Time)	921.15***	938.08***	–	923.54***	933.42***

Notes:
1. *t*-statistics are shown in brackets; *, ** & *** significantly different from zero at the 90%, 95% and 99% levels.
2. IV = instrumental variables estimation.
3. Breusch–Pagan test for the presence of heteroscedasticity.
4. Sargan test for instrument validity, distributed as a $\chi^2(K)$ with K = number of overidentifying restrictions (*p*-value in brackets); instruments used: increase in homes per capita, lagged effective tax rate, lagged distance to maximum allowed tax rates, and this last variable squared.
5. Arellano and Bond (1991) panel AR(1) test.
6. Wald test of the joint significance of different groups of variables.

approximately 0.15 per cent. This means that the government of the average municipality lost 1.26 per cent of its vote because of the property tax increase.

The results shown in Table 18.2 regarding the control variables also merit some comments. First, the economic controls have the expected sign (that is, increases in unemployment are punished, while increases in the population size are rewarded), although the coefficients are not generally statistically significant. Second, the coefficient of the lagged vote share is positive and significant, indicating the persistence of popularity shocks or 'incumbency advantage'. Third, the average vote share is also positive and highly significant. Moreover, the coefficient of this variable is quite high, suggesting a high degree of voter perseverance with the various ideological options. Fourth, the coalition dummy (*COA*) is statistically significant and the coefficient is negative, meaning that – other things being equal – coalitions are punished in elections, obtaining a vote share that is 4 per cent lower. This means that voters find some traits of coalition governments to be unattractive (for example, problems requiring collective action). Fifth, the first-term dummy (*NEW*) is also statistically significant and its effect is positive. This means that voters give some confidence to first-term governments, which enjoy a 3–4 per cent bonus compared to older governments. Sixth, the Party × Region × Time effects are statistically significant (see the Wald test at the bottom of the table). This should be interpreted as evidence of the influence of national politics on municipal elections. When a party suffers a popularity shock at the national or regional level, its vote share in a given municipality is also reduced. These results are consistent with those obtained by Revelli (2002) for the UK. In our case, however, the relevance of national politics does not prevent local tax increases also having some impact on the voting results. In fact, controlling for national political influences (and for other political factors) becomes essential in order to ensure that the estimated coefficients for the tax increase variables are unbiased. In columns 3, 4 and 5 of Table 18.2, we determine whether or not the significant effect of tax increases on the vote are conditioned by the inclusion in the equation of the different control variables. Column 3 excludes the Party × Region × Time effects, column 4 excludes the other political control variables, and column 5 excludes the economic controls. In our case, the statistically significant effect was guaranteed only when the political control variables were included. The results are virtually unaffected by the economic control variables.

In order to check the robustness of our results, we re-estimated the vote equation using the vote share of the party of the mayor (instead of the vote share of all the parties in the government) as our dependent variable. The basic results (presented in Table 18.3) remained qualitatively unaltered.

The municipality's own tax increases reduced the vote for the mayor's party by 4.7 per cent (it should be recalled that this number was 8.1 per cent for all the parties.

Table 18.3 *Effects of property tax increases on the vote share ($v_{i,t}$) of local governments (mayor's party) (no. obs. = 9397, N = 2799, T = 3), 1995, 1999 and 2003 elections*

Variable	(1) OLS	(2) IV	(3) IV	(4) IV	(5) IV
			i. Property tax rates		
$\Delta t^e_{i,t-4}$	−0.023	−0.047	−0.024	−0.020	−0.045
	(−1.134)	(−4.389)***	(−0.622)	(−0.765)	(−4.556)***
			ii. Controls: economic		
$\Delta u_{i,t-4}$	−0.017	−0.013	−0.011	−0.030	–
	(−0.066)	(−0.685)	(−0.152)	(−1.584)	
$\Delta n_{i,t-4}$	0.033	0.041	0.040	0.054	–
	(1.236)	(1.280)	(0.645)	(1.554)	
			iii. Controls: political		
$v_{i,t-4}$	0.687	0.676	0.682	–	0.665
	(5.002)***	(4.247)***	(16.572)***		(15.863)***
$\bar{v}_i$	0.247	0.234			0.186
	(20.432)***	(18.976)***	–	–	(5.720)***
$COA_{i,t}$	−0.016	−0.018	−0.039	–	−0.038
	(−3.456)***	(−5.761)***	(−7.215)***		(−7.100)***
$NEW_{i,t}$	0.031	0.030	0.029	–	0.035
	(11.109)***	(16.651)***	(3.966)***		(4.486)***
Party × Region × Time effects	Yes	Yes	No	Yes	Yes
Adjusted R^2	0.602	0.611	0.112	0.123	0.042
Breusch–Pagan (Heterosc.)	1.267	0.941	0.938	0.654	0.661
Sargan (instrument validity)	–	0.001	4.651	6.245	5.291
		[0.999]	[0.097]	[0.043]	[0.068]
AR (1) (serial error corr.)	0.570	0.334	0.711	0.521	0.789
Wald (economic controls)	4.78	4.22	6.01	3.76	–
Wald (political controls)	42.14***	44.87***	43.35***	–	55.12***
Wald (Party × Region × Time)	964.56***	915.27***	–	926.09***	944.22***

Note: See Table 18.2.

4.2 Interactions

The results showing the effect of the type and timing of tax increase are presented in Table 18.4. The first column shows the effect of property tax reassessments on the vote. The coefficient of the tax increase (without interaction) shows the impact for the base category: nominal tax rate increase. The interaction with the reassessment dummy (*REASS*) is positive and statistically significant, meaning that the electoral cost of a nominal tax rate increase is higher than the one derived from a reassessment: for a 1 per cent increase in the effective property tax rate, the impact in the case of a nominal tax rate increase is 8.3 per cent of the vote share, while the impact in the case of an increase in the assessed value of the property is only 3.7 per cent. In the case of the 'mayor's party' equation these impacts are 5.8 and 2.8 per cent, respectively. We interpret these results as evidence of either 'fiscal illusion' or difficulties in assigning responsibility for the tax increase. If the explanation is fiscal illusion this means that voters are more aware of the money value of nominal tax increases – which are widely publicized during the council debates and which are the same for all taxpayers – than in the case of increases in the assessed value – which differ from taxpayer to taxpayer. The lack of 'clarity of responsibility' may be due to the fact that, at least formally, calling a reassessment is not a municipal responsibility, but a central agency's one. In practice, however, it is difficult to begin a reassessment procedure without the approval of the municipal council. So, from the point of view of citizens, it is difficult to completely assign the responsibility for this decision.

The second and fifth columns of Table 18.4 analyse the difference in the impacts of tax increases issued during both halves of the mandate. The coefficient of the tax increase (without interaction) shows the result for the base category: first half. Note that this coefficient is negative and statistically significant, meaning that tax increases during the first two years of the mandate entail some electoral costs. These are, however, lower than the electoral costs caused by increasing tax rates during the last two years. For a 1 per cent increase in the property tax rate, the cost in terms of vote share is 3.4 per cent in the first half and 12.9 per cent during the second half. In the case of the 'mayor's party' equation these numbers are 2.1 and 9.3 per cent, respectively. The third and sixth columns of Table 18.4 mix the different interactions, but the main results remain unaltered.

The results showing the impact of the political context are presented in Table 18.5. The first and the fourth columns show how the effect on the vote share of 'all the parties' and of the 'mayor's party', respectively, depend on ideology. The coefficient of the tax increase variable (without interaction) shows the result for the base category (*LEFT*); to know the impact of a tax increase in the case of a right-wing government one has to add this coefficient and the

Table 18.4   Effects of property tax increases ($\Delta t_{i,t}$) on the vote share ($v_{i,t}$) of local governments (type of tax increase interactions) (no. obs. = 9397, N = 2799, T = 3), 1995, 1999 and 2003 elections

Variable	All parties				Mayor's party	
	(1) IV	(2) IV	(3) IV	(4) IV	(5) IV	(6) IV
$\Delta t_{i,t}$	−0.083 (−4.518)***	−0.034 (−2.145)***	—	−0.058 (−3.247)***	−0.021 (−2.146)**	—
$\Delta t_{i,t} \times REASS_{i,t}$	0.046 (2.457)***	—	—	0.030 (2.644)***	—	—
Δt^{1st}	—	—	−0.042 (−2.166)**	—	—	−0.033 (−2.056)**
$\Delta t^{1st} \times REASS_{i,t}$	—	—	0.030 (2.100)**	—	—	0.025 (2.314)**
Δt^{2nd}	—	−0.095 (−3.647)***	−0.122 (−4.114)***	—	−0.072 (−3.510)***	−0.095 (−3.064)***
$\Delta t^{2nd} \times REASS_{i,t}$	—	—	0.079 (3.147)***	—	—	0.064 (3.014)***
Economic controls	Yes	Yes	Yes	Yes	Yes	Yes
Political controls	Yes	Yes	Yes	Yes	Yes	Yes
Party × Region × Time effects	Yes	Yes	Yes	Yes	Yes	Yes
Adjusted R^2	0.828	0.825	0.819	0.616	0.627	0.626
Breusch–Pagan (Heterosc.)	1.026	1.169	1.054	1.637	1.201	1.304
Sargan (instrument validity)	0.004 [0.999]	0.005 [0.999]	0.006 [0.999]	0.007 [0.999]	0.003 [0.999]	0.008 [0.999]
AR (1) (serial error corr.)	0.770	0.436	0.580	0.499	0.736	0.653
Wald (economic controls)	7.09	6.01	7.00	3.45	7.09	5.67

Table 18.4 (continued)

Variable	All parties			Mayor's party		
	(1) IV	(2) IV	(3) IV	(4) IV	(5) IV	(6) IV
Wald (political controls)	100.10***	99.12***	67.12***	43.19***	46.17***	102.33***
Wald (Party × Region × Time)	876.23***	986.123***	1,198.12***	958.25***	977.12***	988.09***

Note: See Table 18.2. Same control variables as in Tables 18.2 and 18.3.

one of the tax increase interacted with the *RIGHT* dummy. The results suggest that right-wing governments are more penalized that left-wing governments. For a 1 per cent increase in the property tax rate, rightists lose 9.9 per cent of the vote share and leftists only 5 per cent; and in the case of the mayor's party these numbers are 7.3 and 3.1 per cent. These results seem to confirm our hypothesis that leftists are less punished for tax increases than rightists.

The second and fifth columns of Table 18.5 add an interaction of the tax increase with the coalition dummy (*COA*). The results show that the coefficient of this variable is negative and statistically significant, although only at the 90 per cent level in the 'mayor's party' equation. This means that the effect of a tax increase on the vote is stronger for coalitions than for majority governments. For a 1 per cent increase in the property tax rate, left majorities lose only 2.1 per cent of the vote share, right majorities lose 5.5 per cent, but left and right coalitions lose 13.9 and 17.3 per cent of the vote share, respectively. The same patterns, although less pronounced, can be found in the 'mayor's party' equation: left and right mayors lose only 2 and 4.7 per cent of the vote, respectively, while left and right mayors lose 3.9 and 5.8 per cent of the vote. These results are not consistent with the 'clarity of responsibility' hypothesis, which states that coalitions are held less accountable than majorities. There is no big surprise in checking that this hypothesis does not hold. After all, many papers analysing economic voting in an international context rejected it, at least in its basic version (see, for example, Anderson, 2000; Nadeau et al., 2002).

However, in the Spanish case, coalitions are not only held less accountable than majorities but the vote losses of a coalition are very high. It seems that voters have no big problems in assigning responsibility for taxation in the municipalities: when they encounter some uncertainty regarding which party is responsible for the tax increase they simply decide to punish all the members of the coalition. The fact that the punishment is so high may be explained by the lack of confidence of electors in the face of government coalitions that are often confronted by collective action problems that make them more profligate in approving new spending increases that benefit the different coalition partners. This lack of confidence in coalitions can be confirmed by the results of the *COA* dummy in the vote equation (see Table 18.2).[12] Note that the coefficient is always negative and statistically significant: controlling for all the other influences, a coalition always loses votes relative to a majority, and this loss is shared more or less equally between the party of the mayor and the other partners of the coalition.

The third and sixth columns of Table 18.5 add an interaction between the tax increase and the dummy, indicating that the government is in its first mandate (*NEW*). The coefficient is positive but only statistically significant at the 90 per cent level in both equations. This means that we have found

Table 18.5   *Effects of property tax increases ($\Delta t_{i,t}$) on the vote share ($v_{i,t}$) of local governments (political interactions) (no. obs. = 9397, N = 2799, T = 3), 1995, 1999 and 2003 elections*

Variable	All parties			Mayor's party		
	(1) IV	(2) IV	(3) IV	(4) IV	(5) IV	(6) IV
$\Delta t_{i,t}$	−0.050	−0.021	−0.024	−0.031	−0.020	−0.022
	(−2.248)***	(−2.115)**	(−2.041)**	(−2.495)***	(−2.934)***	(−2.740)***
$\Delta t_{i,t} \times RIGHT_{i,t}$	−0.049	−0.034	−0.030	−0.042	−0.027	−0.028
	(−3.942)***	(−3.274)***	(−2.978)***	(−2.598)***	(−2.114)**	(−1.677)*
$\Delta t_{i,t} \times COA_{i,t}$	−	−0.118	−0.092	−	−0.019	−0.015
		(−4.570)***	(−3.145)***		(−1.737)*	(−1.656)*
$\Delta t_{i,t} \times NEW_{i,t}$	−	−	0.014	−	−	0.025
			(1.689)*			(1.834)*
Economic controls	Yes	Yes	Yes	Yes	Yes	Yes
Political controls	Yes	Yes	Yes	Yes	Yes	Yes
Party × Region × Time effects	Yes	Yes	Yes	Yes	Yes	Yes
Adjusted R^2	0.830	0.832	0.831	0.625	0.630	0.617
Breusch–Pagan (Heterosc.)	1.201	1.569	1.620	1.740	1.166	1.295
Sargan (instrument validity)	0.001 (0.999)	0.002 (0.999)	0.003 (0.999)	0.001 (0.999)	0.001 (0.999)	0.002 (0.999)
AR (1) (serial error corr.)	0.667	0.442	0.702	0.786	0.672	0.703
Wald (economic controls)	6.54	8.56	7.41	2.47	3.69	5.84
Wald (political controls)	98.90***	96.25***	59.36***	39.04***	44.37***	97.36***
Wald (Party × Region × Time)	942.58***	1052.48***	1236.11***	987.33***	954.65***	935.21***

Note: See Table 18.2. Same control variables as in Tables 18.2 and 18.3.

some evidence that governments are less punished for tax increases during their first term. This may be due to the fact that first-term governments have more credibility regarding the possible uses of these additional revenues. In subsequent terms of office, this confidence has been eroded; that is, the voters no longer believe that their money will be used efficiently.

Table 18.6   Summary of results: effects of tax increases on the vote share by type of tax increase

	All parties		Mayor's party	
	REASS	*NOM*	*REASS*	*NOM*
Δt^{1st}	−1.23	−4.28	−0.83	−3.39
Δt^{2nd}	−3.25	−10.16	−2.11	−8.56

Notes:
1. Effect of an increase in one point in the property tax rate (1% of assessed value) on the vote share of the government (in %).
2. *REASS* = 1 if there has been a property value reassessment during the period analysed, *NOM* = 1 if there has not been a reassessment and thus the tax increase must come from a nominal tax rate increase.

5   CONCLUSION

We have tested whether increases in the property tax rate entail electoral costs for local governments. Results using a database of nearly 3000 municipalities and analysing three local elections (1995, 1999 and 2003) suggest that these costs are statistically significant and not negligible. But we have also found evidence that the impact on the vote of tax increases depends on a variety of factors, related both to the political context in which the tax increase decision has been taken and to the type and timing of the tax increase.

The main results regarding these interactions are summarized in Tables 18.6 and 18.7. Table 18.6 summarizes the results by type of tax increase (Table 18.4) while Table 18.7 summarizes the results by government type (Table 18.5). The main conclusions are: (i) left-wing governments tend to be punished less than right-wing governments; (ii) coalitions are punished more than majorities; (iii) governments in their first mandate are punished less than the older ones; (iv) nominal tax increases (of the same magnitude in terms of effective tax rate increases) entail higher electoral costs than tax increases caused by property value reassessments; and (v) tax increases during the second half of the mandate cost more votes than tax increases enacted during the first half.

These results should be interpreted as evidence that the political costs of raising taxes may be high in some circumstances but negligible in others. But the results are not surprising, since they may help us to understand why tax increases are enacted only in some cases (when political costs are low) but not in others (when they are high).

Table 18.7   Summary of results: effects of tax increases on the vote share
by government type

		All parties		Mayor's party	
		NEW	*OLD*	*NEW*	*OLD*
RIGHT	*MAJ*	−4.00	−7.45	−3.74	−7.81
	COA	−11.22	−12.67	−4.33	−5.62
LEFT	*MAJ*	−1.01	−2.49	−0.95	−2.29
	COA	−9.23	−12.65	−2.48	−3.70

Notes:
1. Effect of an increase in one point in the property tax rate (1% of assessed value) on the vote share of the government (in %).
2. *NEW*= 1 if first mandate of the government team, *OLD*=1−*NEW*; *RIGHT*= 1 in the case of right-wing government, *LEFT*=1−*RIGHT*; *MAJ*=1 if party of the mayor has the majority in the city council, *COA*=1−*MAJ*.

NOTES

1. The other two taxes are those on land value improvements and building activities.
2. We computed this correlation with the data available from one Spanish region (the province of Barcelona, with data from the Diputación de Barcelona for various years) and the correlation between the increase in the property tax rate and the increase in business and vehicle tax rates was only 0.08 and 0.12, respectively.

   Moreover, this problem will also be attenuated by the use of instrumental variables, since this technique corrects for any type of correlation between the instrumental variable (the property tax increase) and the error term (which includes the increases in the other taxes). This is true, obviously, if the instruments themselves are not correlated with the error term, but this will be properly tested (see Section 3 for more details).
3. For example, apart from being an incumbent or a challenger, a party may be a coalition partner or may not even stand in many municipalities.
4. Of course, these two equations are the same in the case of a majority government. However, they differ in the case of a coalition. In this case, by estimating both the vote for the government and the vote for the party of the mayor, we are able to evaluate which member of the coalition – the main party or its partners – suffers most from tax increases. See Anderson (1995 and 2000) and Wilkin et al. (1997) for analyses allowing for disaggregated government support for the party of the prime minister and its coalition partners.
5. Admittedly, Veiga and Veiga (2004) have a much shorter period than four years in mind when talking about this honeymoon effect. As they have yearly data, they are able to analyse the effects on the popularity of the government using these survey data. We are only able to measure the popularity of the local government when an election is held, so we can only attempt to differentiate between newly elected and longer-established local governments.
6. We analyse the effects of tax increases on the results of the local elections of 1995, 1999 and 2003, using the lagged vote among the explanatory variables (that is, that of the elections of 1999, 1995 and 1991, respectively) and the average vote share of the 1979, 1983 and 1987 elections. Note that the electoral results used to compute these two explanatory variables do not overlap.
7. Revelli (2002) controls for these time-invariant political preferences by including a set of municipal-party fixed effects. This procedure is not appropriate in our case since, given the

small number of elections, we cannot include such a large number of dummies in the equation. Note also that these effects could not be eliminated by first differentiation. This is due to the fact that the variable we are analysing is the vote share of the government parties, which is not necessarily the same in two consecutive elections. The municipal party effect in t and $t-1$ may therefore refer to different parties or coalitions of parties. Note that the elimination of party-specific effects would be possible if our dependent variable was the vote share of one party (the same in all the elections analysed).

8. Note that the term $t_{i,r}^n \times (\Delta v_{i,r} / v_{i,r-1})$ could be interpreted as the change in the nominal property tax rate that is required in order to neutralize the increase in assessed property values and to prevent the average tax liability from increasing.

9. As explained above, municipalities receive more responsibilities, more tax autonomy and higher transfers as their population increases. The enhanced role of larger municipalities is also usually recognized informally by the political market, by enhancing the career prospects of local politicians.

10. The lagged effective tax rate was computed by adding the increases in the effective property tax rate that occurred in the following periods to the 1990 nominal tax rate. The lagged effective tax rate and the 'distance between nominal and maximum nominal tax rates' are only slightly correlated (with a correlation coefficient of 0.256). There are two reasons for this result. First, maximum nominal tax rates are not the same for all the municipalities, but grow with population size, and second, when a reassessment is carried out, effective tax rates tend to peak and, at the same time, nominal tax rates decrease in order to avoid excessive increases in tax liabilities. These two effects compensate for the obvious increase in the effective tax rate that occurs when a municipality decides to raise the nominal tax rate.

11. There are various possible explanations for this increase. First, there is the fact that in Spain, in addition to maximum nominal tax rates, there are also minimum nominal tax rates. It is true that the minimum tax rate is allowed to fall after a property value reassessment, but it is also true that these minimum tax rates must be raised again five years after the reassessment. Second, it may be politically advantageous to increase the effective property tax rate after a property value reassessment, although it is not entirely clear whether this political advantage arises entirely from rational behaviour (as Strumpf, 2002, suggests) or is due to voters' fiscal illusion (Bloom and Ladd, 1982; Ladd, 1991).

12. Although coalitions are the reflection of a highly pluralistic system, this benefit has to be weighted against their evident decision-making difficulties. Gridlock and collective action problems are not rare in municipal coalitions, and their consequences tend to be perceived as a problem by the citizens. The increase in spending in Spanish municipalities due to lack of action, leading sometimes to more taxes and sometimes to deficit finance has been documented in different papers (see Solé-Ollé, 2003 and 2006).

REFERENCES

Alesina, A. and H. Rosenthal (1995), *Partisan Politics, Divided Government and the Economy*, Cambridge University Press, New York.

Anderson, C.J. (1995), 'The dynamics of public support for coalition governments', *Comparative Political Studies*, **28** (3), 350–83.

Anderson, C.J. (2000), 'Economic voting and political context: a comparative perspective', *Electoral Studies*, **19**, 151–70.

Arellano, M. and S. Bond (1991), 'Some tests of specification for panel data: Monte Carlo evidence and an application to employment equations', *Review of Economic Studies*, **58**, 277–97.

Besley, T. and A. Case (1995), 'Incumbent behaviour: vote-seeking, tax-setting, and yardstick competition', *American Economic Review*, **85**, 25–44.

Bloom, H. and H.F. Ladd (1982), 'Property tax revaluation and tax levy growth', *Journal of Urban Economics*, **11**, 73–84.

Brooks, J.W. and Ch.L. Prysby (1992), *Political Behavior and the Local Context*, Praeger, New York.

Colomer, J.M. (1995), 'España y Portugal', in J.M. Colomer (ed.), *La Política en Europa: Introducción a las Instituciones de Quince Países*, Ariel, Barcelona, p. 250.

Diputación de Barcelona (various years), SIEM, *Servei d'Informació Econòmica Municipal*, Barcelona.

Gibson, J. (1988), 'Rate increases and local elections: a different approach and a different conclusion', *Policy and Politics* **16**, 197–208.

Gibson, J. and J. Stewart (1992), 'Poll tax, rates and local elections', *Political Studies*, **40**, 516–31.

Hansen, S.B. (1983), *The Politics of Taxation: Revenue without Representation*, Praeger, New York.

Kone, S.L. and R.F. Winters (1983), 'Taxes and voting: electoral retribution in the American States', *Journal of Politics*, **55**, 22–39.

Ladd, H.F. (1991), 'Property tax revaluation and tax levy growth revisited', *Journal of Urban Economics*, **30**, 83–99.

Landon, S. and D.L. Ryan (1997), 'The political costs of taxes and government spending', *Canadian Journal of Economics*, **30** (1), 85–111.

Lowry, R.C., J.E. Alt and K.E. Ferree (1998), 'Fiscal policy outcomes and electoral accountability in American states', *American Political Science Review*, **92**, 759–74.

MacManus, S.A. (1999), 'Politics and taxation', in W. Bartley Hildreth and J.A. Richardson (eds), *Handbook of Taxation*, Public Administration and Public Policy 72, Marcel Dekker, New York.

Magre, J. (1998), *L'Alcalde a Catalunya*, Collecció Punt a la i, Fundació Jaume Bofill, Barcelona.

Mikesell, J.L. (1978), 'Election periods and state tax policy cycles', *Public Choice*, **33** (3), 99–106.

Molas, I. and O. Bartomeus (1998), 'Estructura de la competencia política a Catalunya', Working Paper 138, Institut de Ciències Polítiques i Socials, Barcelona.

Nadeau, R., R.G. Niemi and A. Yoshinaka (2002), 'A cross-national analysis of economic voting: taking into account the political context across time and nations', *Electoral Studies*, **21**, 403–23.

Niemi, R.G., H.W. Stanley and R.J. Vogel (1995), 'State economies and state taxes: do voters hold governors accountable?', *American Journal of Political Science*, **39**, 936–57.

Oates, W.E. (1975), 'Automatic increases in tax revenues: their effect on the size of the public budget', in W.E. Oates (ed.), *Financing the New Federalism: Revenue Sharing, Conditional Grants and Taxation*, Johns Hopkins Press, Baltimore.

Paldam, M. (1997), 'Political business cycles', in D. Mueller (ed.), *Perspectives on Public Choice: A Handbook*, Cambridge University Press, Cambridge, p. 352.

Peltzman, S. (1992), 'Voters as fiscal conservatives', *Quarterly Journal of Economics*, **107**, 327–61.

Pomper, G. (1968 and 1976), *Elections in America: Control and Influence in American Politics*, Dodd, Mead, New York.

Powell, G.B. and G. Whitten (1993), 'A cross-national analysis of economic voting: taking into account the political context', *American Journal of Political Science*,

37, 391–414.
Rallings, C. and M. Thrasher (1997), *Local Elections in Britain*, Routledge, London.
Revelli, F. (2002), 'Local taxes, national politics and spatial interactions in English district election results', *European Journal of Political Economy*, **18**, 281–99.
Royed, T.J., K.M. Leyden and S.A. Borrelli (2000), 'Is "clarity of responsibility" important for economic voting? Revisiting Powell and Whitten's Hypothesis', *British Journal of Political Science*, **30**, 669–98.
Sargan, J. (1958), 'The estimation of economic relationship using instrumental variables', *Econometrica*, **26** (3), 393–415.
Solé-Ollé, A. (2003), 'Electoral accountability and tax mimicking: the effects of electoral margins, coalition government, and ideology', *European Journal of Political Economy*, **19**, 685–713.
Solé-Ollé, A. (2006), 'The effects of party competition on budget outcomes: empirical evidence from local governments in Spain', *Public Choice*, **126** (1), 145–76.
Sotillos, I. (1997), *El Comportamiento Electoral Municipal Español, 1979–85*, Centro de Investigaciones Sociológicas, Madrid.
Staiger, D. and J.H. Stock (1997), 'Instrumental variables estimation with weak instruments', *Econometrica*, **65** (3), 393–415.
Strumpf, K. (2002), 'Infrequent assessments distort property taxes: theory and evidence', *Journal of Urban Economics*, **46**, 169–99.
Stults, B. and R.F. Winters (2002), 'The political economy of taxes and the vote', Paper presented at the 2002 Midwest Political Science Association meetings, Chicago, April.
Turett, S. (1971), 'The vulnerability of American governors: 1900–1969', *Midwest Journal of Political Science*, **15**, 108–32.
Veiga, J. and L.G. Veiga (2004), 'Popularity functions, partisan effects, and support in parliament', *Economics and Politics*, **16** (1), 101–15.
Vermeir, J. and B. Heyndels (2004), 'The electoral cost of tax policy in Flemish municipalities', Paper presented at the 2004 Public Choice Conference in Berlin, April.
Wagner, R. (1976), 'Revenue structure, fiscal illusion and budgetary choice', *Public Choice*, **25**, 45–61.
Wassmer, R.W. (1993), 'Property taxation, property base, and property value. An empirical test of the New View', *National Tax Journal*, **46** (2), 135–60.
Wilkin, S., B. Haller and H. Norpoth (1997), 'From Argentina to Zambia: a worldwide test of economic voting', *Electoral Studies*,**16**, 301–16.
Winters, R.F. (1996), 'The politics of taxing and spending', in H. Jacobs, V. Gray and R. Hansen (eds), *Politics in the American States*, Congressional Quarterly Press, Washington, DC.

Keynote Address

19. The mystery of Brazil

Gordon Tullock

On the American continents there are three very large countries, Brazil, Canada and the United States. One of them, Canada, is mostly too far north to support a dense population and hence is largely unpopulated. The other two, however, are very similar. They are roughly the same size and both have, along the Atlantic Coast, a large area which is a mix of level ground and low hills and mountains with their eastern drainage into the Atlantic. These areas were largely forested when Europeans first arrived. In both of these cases when you get through this rather large coastal area you come to the tributaries of a major river, the Amazon in one case and the Mississippi in the other.

Both areas before the Europeans arrived were inhabited by scattered Indian tribes. Mostly these Indian tribes were in the hunting and gathering stage, but agriculture was practiced by some of them. As is the custom with primitive people, the tribes were mainly at war with each other. The high civilizations of some Indians in Mexico and the Andes did not reach the area eventually occupied by either Brazil or the United States. The Maya, probably the highest of the Indian civilizations, had died out several hundred years before Columbus. The very unpleasant Aztecs had their center in Mexico and the successfully imperialistic Incas were west of the area which eventually became Brazil.

In spite of this geographic similarity, there are very great differences between the two countries. One of them is widely recognized as the world's leading power and has an extremely high living standard for its citizens. The other, Brazil, might claim to be the leading power in South America, although Argentina would contest even that claim, and it has a living standard which is in no way outstanding. The 'mystery' in the title of this chapter is why the difference is so great although the natural advantages of the two places seem very similar.

Let me begin by looking at the population distribution in the two countries. There are obvious major differences between the two. In both cases there is a reasonably dense population along the Atlantic Coast. In the United States, however, the drainage area of the monster Mississippi River is heavily populated. In Brazil the drainage area of the Amazon is almost empty. The mountains on the Pacific Coast of the United States are also well populated, but the population had to go through the Mississippi basin to get there. The Pacific coastal mountains west of Brazil are, of course, parts of other countries. Why the difference?

In talking with colleagues on the subject, I find that they begin by saying that the climate of the Amazon basin makes agriculture impossible, or at least very difficult. This indicates, of course, that the people I have asked are citizens either of the United States or of the northern part of the Eurasian continent. It is true that corn and wheat would not flourish in the Amazon basin. But the Indians (living in India), the Chinese (at least those in the southern part of China), the Japanese and the inhabitants of various islands like Java, the rest of Indonesia and the Philippines make a living very successfully with agriculture in areas which were originally tropical rainforests. Wet rice is the most productive grain crop and tropical rainforests can be converted into rice paddies if sufficient labor is available.

Another possibility is disease. The Amazon basin is certainly not a highly healthy environment for human beings. On the other hand the citizens of India live in a somewhat similar climate. The Portuguese, who were the original discoverers and settlers of Brazil, got there through a navigational error on their way to the tropics of southern Asia, equally unhealthy. They also made a number of settlements in Africa, which would seem to indicate that tropical climates were not uninhabitable to the citizens of, at least, southern Europe. In addition, the hard work on their plantations was mainly done by slaves imported from Africa. The climate of the Amazon basin is not too different from that of the Congo basin.

It should be pointed out that the southern part of the United States is also in the malaria zone, and the fact that Europeans knew this led to fewer white people going to Georgia voluntarily than to Massachusetts. Still, Georgia was populated as was Louisiana and Texas, and the South was, before the Civil War, thought to be highly prosperous. There was a period of poverty and backwardness after the war, but the South has now fully recovered.[1]

The United States began with mainly north European immigrants and has only recently received large numbers from the southern part of that continent. Since the cultures of these two European areas are somewhat different and northern Europe is more prosperous than southern, a cultural solution cannot be ruled out. Granted, however, that Argentina is, or to be more exact was, very prosperous and is largely inhabited by people from southern Europe, this solution does not seem decisive. You can, of course, argue that the Italians who make up so much of the Argentine population are, somehow, more adapted to producing a modern country than the Iberians from the same latitude and climate.

Racial explanations, of almost anything, are highly unpopular at the moment. Indeed, research on such matters is more or less taboo. Since in my opinion the racial difference between societies is not much of an explanatory variable, except possibly for the superior performance of Orientals in American higher education, I do not think that this possible explanation should be given much weight. Still it must be admitted that there is at least some racial difference because the Brazilians were much more likely to interbreed with the Indians already there and the black slaves that they brought in. Hence if we were to make a count of genes, we would find that the average Brazilian has fewer white ancestors than the average citizen of the United States. I do not, and I do not think that many of my readers will, regard this as a matter of importance.

It should perhaps be emphasized that Brazil got a big head start. There were major cities with universities in Brazil before the first English settlers set foot in Virginia. Indeed, the oldest city in the United States is Spanish St. Augustine, which also existed before the first English settlers arrived.

Having ruled out geography and race, how about culture? In the *annus mirabilis* of 1776, a Scottish instrument repairman filed a patent for a steam engine. Another Scot, a professor, published a book which would come close to controlling the development of economic policy as a theory and as a practice for the next hundred or maybe 200 years. At the same time, a document was signed far across the Atlantic in Philadelphia.

So far this chapter has dealt with the difference between Brazil and the United States, most specifically the difference between the Mississippi watershed and the Amazon watershed. If the difference is cultural, however, then we might expect different rates of development between other areas which have much the same pair of cultures. Compare, for example, the different rates of development of England and the part of the Iberian culture which is in Europe.

The first thing to note is that the Industrial Revolution occurred in England, and England developed with great rapidity throughout most of the nineteenth century. By 1890, it had the highest per capita income of any country in the world. Further, during this period, it built up the world's largest empire. Part of that empire was already densely settled, as in India, and the empire took a form of controlling the inhabitants with only a relatively few English people brought in to control it. Part of the empire, like the United States and Brazil, had little in the way of a native population. This part of the British empire was settled by Europeans from northern Europe. Canada, Australia, New Zealand and the Union of South Africa all developed very rapidly. This was certainly not true with respect to most of the Iberian world. The empire of Spain disappeared and Brazil broke off from Portugal but retained a member of the Portuguese royal family as

Emperor. Further, Portugal acquired quite a considerable empire in Africa without much fighting. All these areas were listed as rather backward, again, except for the southern cone of South America.

This does not tell us what it is about the culture about which we are hypothesizing that led to rapid growth and the exploitation of natural resources, but it surely suggests that there is something there. Before engaging in any careful effort to find the distinction, I may give the reader a little bit of Brazilian history with which most English-speaking scholars are unfamiliar.

When Napoleon moved into the Iberian Peninsula he attacked Portugal and the Portuguese abandoned most of their land in Iberia. The King of Portugal was evacuated by the British Navy to Brazil, bringing with him the bulk of the bureaucracy running the Portuguese kingdom. This was a sharp distinction between Brazil and the United States. When the US became independent it did not acquire the bureaucracy in London which had been, rather feebly, controlling the US economy before. Thus Brazil began with the Iberian-type government, retaining it when it declared independence, with the heir to the Portuguese throne proclaiming himself emperor. Thus the political difference between England and its colonies and former colonies on the one hand and Portugal and its former colony on the other remained intact.

The cultural diversity between Portugal and Spain was not great and nor was the difference between the Spanish and Portuguese colonies on the American continent. It is notable that the ex-Spanish colonies inherited from their previous imperial status a considerable amount of land in the Amazon basin. This was hard to get to from the Spanish cultural area because of the barrier of the Andes. Nevertheless, I think it is not entirely coincidental that it is just as undeveloped as is the Brazilian part of the Amazon basin. Iberian culture is Iberian culture and Anglo-Saxon culture is Anglo-Saxon. Possibly they lead to different results.

We must now turn to a brief summary of the military history of Europe. After the collapse of the Roman Empire, Europe was divided into a number of small kingdoms which were in a state of pretty much continuous war. At the time Columbus crossed the Atlantic and the Portuguese went around the southern tip of Africa, Spain was one of the major contenders. Indeed, the most warlike of the kings of Spain was also the Holy Roman Emperor and did most of his fighting in Germany. He split his empire, and succeeding kings of Spain did not control very much in Germany. Nevertheless, they continued trying to impose Catholicism on Germany.

While this was the bulk of their military effort they also obtained, almost absentmindedly, much of Latin America. Hernando Cortés and Francisco Pizarro were essentially private enterprise operators who added to the domains of Spain. A small army was actually sent out to arrest Cortés. Although the Spanish government did not try to arrest Pizarro, they gave him no support and his conquest of Peru was a private operation. The kings of Spain were not much interested in the Americas until they found gold and silver. In fact, they made efforts to prevent Spaniards from migrating to the new possessions.

England, at that time a minor power, and the Netherlands, which succeeded in becoming independent, were not major players at this time. For reasons that are not in any sense clear, both England and the Netherlands then developed as major naval powers. As a result they set up colonies along the East Coast of what is now the United States as well as trading posts throughout much of the East. Spain began to lose military power, and Portugal, which had never had very much, was for a while a possession of the King of Spain.

We must now turn to other aspects of Anglo-Saxon culture, one which it shares with its neighbors in the area from which the Anglo-Saxons came, that is, a tendency to engage in aggressive wars for the purpose of geographical conquest. This was, of course, a pretty general pattern of behavior in Europe, indeed in the world. Many modern students will regard this with grave disapproval, but it was essential for the development of the United States, Canada, Australia and New Zealand, all prosperous countries whose culture, and many of whose inhabitants, come from England or other parts of northern Europe.

Beginning some time in the eighteenth century, England began acquiring a major overseas empire, essentially by military means. Although its army and navy were mainly preoccupied with Europe and in particular France, it seized little land there. Its major conquest, of course, was India. Wellington won his first important battles in India and only then returned to beat Napoleon. But few Englishmen migrated to India and many migrated across the Atlantic so that by 1776 there was a thin chain of English-speaking settlements along the coast. Except for the language, this was rather similar to the coastal strip of Brazil.

The Netherlands and Belgium were of course much smaller places, and Belgium is at least half French. Nevertheless, the empires that they acquired were gigantic compared to their home territory. Although the Netherlands early held trading posts and some small spice islands, it was only in the nineteenth century that they conquered the bulk of their holdings in Indonesia. France also acquired a large empire but much of it was desert. It is notable that although Portugal and Spain had been major imperial powers earlier, the imperial impulse seems to have died out by the eighteenth century.

In a way we can say that the instinct for conquest drifted north from the Mediterranean to Teutonic-speaking countries. The Iberian countries not only did not expand, but they also permitted their empires to drift away or to be conquered by other countries. The fact that Brazil did not aggressively push out of the coastal area and into the Amazon basin would appear to indicate that this lack of aggressive drive was the same as in the other Iberian countries.

Empires can be divided into two general categories. First, there are those areas where the metropolitan power took political control, but did not actively settle. They developed considerable economic and political power, and in some cases significant military forces, but the personnel were primarily native. They were commanded, of course, by officers and political governors from the home country. There were also troops from the home country, but they were normally heavily outnumbered by native troops with European officers. Eventually these colonies became independent.

The second general category concerns cases in which settlers from Europe were brought in to areas which were either empty or at least thinly populated. Brazil is an example of this originally, but the expansion stopped not too far from the Atlantic Coast. Australia pushed out the Aboriginals with little fighting. There were not very many of them and their culture was very primitive. New Zealand was able to keep the Maoris from causing much difficulty and indeed the relations between the white New Zealanders who make up the overwhelming bulk of the population and the remnants of the older Polynesian population are reasonably friendly.

The United States and Canada followed another course. In both cases large numbers of immigrants came in from England or other parts of Europe and they pushed the Indians back, frequently by violent, if small, aggressive wars. The Americans became wealthy and powerful as the result of a long series of such aggressive wars.

The Iberian countries normally either tried to absorb the Indians or left them alone in backward parts of the country. The church was interested in converting the Indians, with the result that there are number of beautiful missions scattered throughout southwestern United States. There was much intermarriage and consequently Mexicans or Peruvians are apt to have Indian ancestors.

The only really large war of aggression carried out by the United States was that with Mexico. Except for a few missions the area that was taken from Mexico was not really administered by the Mexicans but by either the Indians or, in part, the Texans. In fact after the war was over, a number of Indians did not recognize the transfer of sovereignty and Geronimo was one of the most significant Indian opponents.

For some reason the US stopped annexing areas in about 1900. Cuba and the Philippines were given their independence after America took them from Spain. Puerto Rico could have independence if it wanted it (or could be a state) but its present financial situation as a dominion is very favorable and it wants this to continue.

Under the moral code of today, the Anglo-Saxon approach was clearly wicked. The Iberian approach was not exactly virtuous, but it came closer to that than the policy followed in the United States which greatly benefited the white population and provided relatively few benefits for the natives. Of course the living standard of the natives was raised, when they stayed alive, by the import of many, many artifacts and customs from the more advanced part of the world. Nevertheless, if I understand the moral code of advanced modern thought, the US method violated current views on proper behavior.

Thus to say that the US had a culture different from that of Brazil is certainly true. I believe it is also true that these cultural differences are the reasons why America fully developed its natural resources, including those in the Mississippi drainage area, while Brazil did not. The emptiness of the Amazon drainage area is merely one of many examples. In a way if we judge by what Wodehouse called 'modern advanced thought', then American behavior was wicked, or at least lacking in a highly virtuous approach. However, since America is still here, wealthy and powerful, I presume that there are few regrets.

Of course, Americans have sometimes acted as if they feel guilty. They have compensated the Indians by giving them gambling franchises. Since these actions are also suspect morally, America remains in sin. Personally, I do not mind, perhaps because I am not a proponent of the current ethical fashions. Those who are more conventional in their views may be upset by all of this. It is a case where virtue did not pay and aggression did.

But why? The United States and Brazil are really quite similar. In both cases there is a chain of minor mountains along the Atlantic Coast and then the basin of a gigantic river system. The US is wealthy and powerful and Brazil is backward and fairly weak. I shall argue that the difference is largely legal. American pioneers pushed west with only minor assistance from the central government, but with not many governmental restrictions. This did not happen in Brazil.

In order to explain what happened let me turn to a little-known part of the life of George Washington.[2] In the period before the revolutionary war the colonies in general had almost all of their population east of the Alleghenies. The existence of a vast area to the west was well known, but access was difficult. Washington became interested in opening up the Cumberland Gap for a canal or a good road. Since the present situation of this gap is quite different from then, we can say he showed good judgment, but was premature. Today there are a canal, two railroads and an interstate highway running through the gap. This was, however, beyond the engineering capacities of the late eighteenth century.

As a deviation here, I should point out that President Thomas Jefferson wasted a vast amount of government money attempting to build five canals across the Appalachians. None of them was completed; indeed none of them even got as far along as Washington's slightly earlier work in the Cumberland Gap – indeed, until the State of New York built the Erie Canal in 1825, transportation to the West was very, very difficult.[3] In spite of this difficulty, and with a well-founded belief that it would eventually be overcome, the colonies granted large tracts of land beyond the Appalachians to individuals and to companies. As a wealthy Virginia planter, Washington took fairly large holdings west of the Cumberland Gap.

Before he could develop it he found himself commanding the revolutionary armies and obviously unable to devote time to agricultural expansion. When the war ended he turned to developing this area as well as farming Mount Vernon. When he went through the gap he found that a large part of the land which he had been granted was actually occupied by squatters, all of whom had muskets and none of whom were willing to pay rent to him.

He turned to the law and after two years with a very good lawyer and at great expense, he was able to establish his ownership. However, it had taken so much time and so much investment that he apparently decided not to try to recover the rest of his grants.

What was his problem? The only legal system in the colonies and in particular in the western parts, was to summon a jury of the vicinage to try the matter. Clearly in these areas sparsely inhabited by pioneers, almost all of whom were squatting, and almost all of whom had a musket, such a jury would be unsympathetic with a wealthy man attempting to throw out some of their neighbors.

It was not only the jury that caused problems; the entire local government was democratically selected by the squatters. The sheriff and the county clerk were both local officials, locally elected. Indeed, because of continuous difficulties with the Indians, the citizens were organized into a militia and in some cases had even built private forts. Altogether, wealthy people from the east had little chance of prevailing against the immigrants.

If this was true for George Washington, the man who had commanded the army which established independence, who at the time was engaged in organizing the Constitutional Convention and shortly would be President of the United States, think of the legal prospects of a company of merchants from Philadelphia who are attempting to throw squatters off the land in order develop a sizable economic unit.

This particular bit of history is typical of what happened in the newly opened areas. State legislatures, with theoretical legal control of the areas, would attempt to organize them in larger blocks, but found that they could not prevent the squatters from taking the land. Thus the frontier settlement moved steadily west in a way which can be referred to as illegal if one considers the formal written law or as perfectly legal if one considers the traditional legal method of dealing with such situations in Anglo-Saxon areas.

Eventually, after the Civil War in 1866 the government, in essence, gave up. The Homestead Act was passed which provided that anyone who came to an empty piece of land could have 160 acres of it by merely starting a farm. In essence the squatters were made legal by the central government rather than by a jury of the vicinage.

Unfortunately this act was passed when the frontier of settlement had extended so far west, that rainfall was lighter. In general, 160 acres was not adequate, particularly since the cost of shipping things to the eastern markets would also be large. Homesteaders took their 160-acre plots, but in many cases were unable to maintain them. The opening of the West continued with large cattle ranches frequently taking up enough land for perhaps 50 homesteaders.

Thus the West was won and United States became a great power. Of course the Indians had to be driven out and they were in a series of small, even tiny, aggressive wars. The United States is the most successful of the aggressor nations. It should be pointed out, however, that the other English-speaking colonies, Canada, Australia and New Zealand, followed much the same policy with respect to the native population.

But what happened in Brazil? In essence it had a radically different legal system in which juries were not important and local officials appointed by the king were. Indeed these local officials were quite commonly noblemen who were given a large grant with the idea that they would populate the country. They took a strong hand in the event of squatters. Indeed, a small-scale conflict is now going on in southern Brazil where potential agricultural land is being plowed. This involves what amounts to a small war between large-scale landholders and peasants. Americans gained because of the disorderly and inchoate legal system, whereas Brazilians lost because they had a more efficient legal structure.

Normally economists, such as me, favor property institutions. In the United States the initial property allocation was most disorderly, but eventually these pieces of real estate became part of an orderly and efficient system. Today's Americans are beneficiaries of the illegal settlers who formed the early United States west of the Appalachians. Brazil was too legal and the government too strong and well-organized to make the same gains.

In any event that is my theory. If the reader has a better one I suggest that he/she send it to me.

NOTES

1. It might be noted that the South was important for the Industrial Revolution. The first Industrial Revolution was largely based on cotton textiles. The raw cotton was raised by slaves in the southern part of the United States.
2. The following account is mainly based on Joel Achenbach, *The Grand Idea* (New York: Simon & Schuster paperbacks, Rockefeller Center, 2005).
3. My great-grandfather moving from Scotland to Illinois took the Eire Canal.

Index